Marx's Sophistries
The Fractured Logic of *Das Kapital*

Lawrence Eubank

ISBN: 1981855769
ISBN-13: 978-1981855766

CONTENTS

INTRODUCTION

Reputation, Shakespeare has said, is a bubble, "oft got without merit." And perhaps no reputation was ever as insubstantial and unmerited as that of Karl Marx. Anyone reading *Das Kapital* for the first time, as opposed to reading secondary sources, is likely to be struck by the contrast between Marx's towering reputation as an economic genius and the chaotic muddle he actually puts on the page.

Marx's text deals with many assorted topics, but among them there can be discerned a main thread of argument which arrives at a main conclusion. The following is a preview of the outlines of that argument.

The Analysis of a Commodity

Marx's work begins with "the analysis of a commodity," a discussion of what determines a commodity's value. He broaches the topic this way:

> Let us take two commodities, e.g., corn and iron. The proportions in which they are exchangeable... can always be represented by an equation... e.g., 1 quarter corn = x cwt. iron. What does this equation tell us? It tells us that in two different things — in 1 quarter of corn and x cwt. of iron, there exists in equal quantities something common to both.
> — *Das Kapital*, Part I, Chapter 1, Section 1

By that passage we are to understand that the value of a commodity is determined by the amount of some property or attribute contained within the commodity itself, as opposed to any external consideration such as market conditions or supply and demand. Marx asserts this point without giving any substantiation in facts or logic; he adopts it whole without any supporting evidence. It must therefore be considered an arbitrary assumption -- and a rather naive one at that, having been considered, and rejected as overly simplistic, by Greek philosophers nearly three thousand years ago.

Identity of the "Common Something"

Marx asserts that the value of a commodity is determined by the amount of some property, attribute or "something common" within it. The question then is, what is the property which determines, and indeed constitutes, a commodity's value? Marx tackles the question by process of elimination:

> This common "something" cannot be either a geometrical, a
> chemical, or any other natural property of commodities. . .
> [Commodities] have only one common property left, that of
> being products of labor. . .
> We see then that that which determines the magnitude of the
> value of any article is the amount of labour socially necessary, or the
> labour time socially necessary for its production. . . As values, all
> commodities are only definite masses of congealed labor time.
> — *Das Kapital*, Part I, Chapter 1, Section 1

Thus Marx by process of elimination identifies labor as the "common something" that constitutes value. His reasoning starts by considering the whole set of those properties which can be thought of as "in" or "common to" the commodity. Then he discards everything that, for whatever reason, he deems not to fit the criteria he has established for a possible answer. (And note, Marx considers labor as being physically embodied, deposited or congealed in the actual substance of the commodity.)

That is, Marx has first begun by restricting the set of possible answers to things in, or common to, the commodity itself, with external social and economic considerations being ruled ineligible. Then he sorts through the remaining possibilities to identify his answer. The problem is that once he has reduced the investigation to his chosen boundaries, any hope of a sensible answer is lost. "Ask a foolish question, and you'll get a foolish answer."

"Formal Systems"

Marx's argument in *Das Kapital* takes much the form of a "formal system." A formal system is a framework for reasoning about a particular subject, developed using certain formalized rules and procedures.

We have all seen formal systems, though perhaps not under that name. Branches of mathematics are examples of formal systems. Each field — for instance, algebra — begins by identifying the objects it applies to, such as variables, constants, expressions, equations, etc. Next, axioms are adopted. These are statements which are assumed, not proved, and which help form the foundation of the formal system. Axioms in algebra include these:

Reflexive Axiom: A number is equal to itself. I.e., $a = a$.
Symmetric Axiom: If $a = b$ then $b = a$.
Additive Axiom: If $a=b$, then $a + c = b + c$.

After the adoption of axioms, the formal system proceeds by the deriving of theorems. These are statements proved, i.e. logically deduced, from the axioms as well as the entire body of theorems that preceded the particular theorem.

The first theorems may be only a small departure or step up from the axioms. For instance, an early theorem in algebra is the distributive theorem: $(b + c) a = ba + ca$.

Then as we progress, we derive more complicated and less obvious theorems, such as the binomial theorem, the Fundamental Theorem of Algebra, and others, with each additional theorem being based on what has already been established. We end up with a powerful tool for solving equations, simplifying algebraic expressions, and solving problems of practical significance. The final result is a formal system -- a logically consistent framework for reasoning, based on a chosen set of definitions and axioms with derived theorems.

The Formal System vs. the Real World

A formal system is not physics; that is, it is not a representation of the real, physical world. Rather, it is a logical construct telling us what conclusions can be drawn from chosen assumptions. It is not intended to be a description of physical reality. The distinction can be illustrated by the fact that in the geometry formal system, a line has only one dimension (length) and a point has no dimensions.

However, the formal system closely models the real world. The axioms of the system are chosen carefully so that, together with the theorems, they make a close parallel to the real world. As a result, when we solve a problem via the formal system — say, when we calculate the area of a triangle — we can confidently extend the theoretical result to the corresponding physical objects and their dimensions.

The deductions drawn from the theoretical system and those results in the real world are so similar that we rarely need to make a distinction between the two in our minds. The formal system is its own self-contained world, but it is a perfect mirror of the real world.

Das Kapital as a formal system

Marx's *Das Kapital* quite closely follows the structure of a formal system. His first axiom is, Value is determined by "something common to," something "in," commodities. His first theorem, which he proves by process of elimination, is that the "common something" which determines value is labor.

From the basis of those two starting points, *Das Kapital* continues as all formal systems do, adding deduced statement to deduced statement, with each new theorem being derived from all those that went before it.

Marx's system does however differ from more traditional formal systems like algebra. Their usefulness comes from the care with which the axioms are chosen, in a conscientious effort to closely model the real world.

Marx's formal system, on the other hand, is designed not to model reality, but to allow him to reach a pre-conceived conclusion – namely, that the capitalist doesn't make profit by any legitimate means, but by exploiting unpaid "surplus value" off the work of the laborers. That is the ultimate theorem which Marx derives as the peak of his theoretical formal system.

Another Important Theorem

Marx proceeds to another theorem, applying logic of a sort to declare that the capitalist does not buy labor. Rather, what the laborer sells, and what the capitalist buys, is not labor but something else:

> On the surface of bourgeois society, the wage of the labourer appears as the price of labour, a certain quantity of money that is paid for a certain quantity of labour . . .
> — *Das Kapital*, Part VI, Chapter 19

However, Marx informs us that the superficial impression is wrong. The capitalist can't buy labor, because labor doesn't exist:

> In order to be sold as a commodity in the market, labour must at all events exist before it is sold. But, could the labourer give it an independent objective existence, he would sell a commodity and not labour. . .
> — *Das Kapital*, Part VI, Chapter 19

That is, because labor does not exist in the same sense that a box of corn flakes exists, Marx concludes that it is not a commodity, not something that can be bought or sold. Having established that point, he announces that what the laborer really sells is his *ability* to labor:

> What the [labourer] sells is his labour-power. . .
> By labor-power or capacity for labor is to be understood the aggregate of those mental and physical capabilities existing in a human being, which he exercises whenever he produces a use-value of any description...
> — *Das Kapital*, Part II, Chapter 6

The purchased commodity is then "consumed" by its purchaser:

> The purchaser of labor-power consumes it by setting the seller of
> it to work.
> — *Das Kapital*, Part III, Chapter 7, Section 1

(That is, the laborer's efforts are equivalent to the capitalist's consuming
of a commodity – a novel viewpoint.)

It only remains to add that labor-power, like all other commodities, has
a value. Marx will later show, by logic too convoluted to go into here, that the
value of a day's *labor-power* is half a day's *labor*. The capitalist pays the laborer
the money equivalent of half a day's labor, in return for the use (or
consumption) of a day's labor-power.

Denouement

These beginning theorems are followed by others, in the standard
manner of formal systems. Marx develops theorems about the value of
commodities, the purchasing of labor-power, and the value of labor-power.
Those serve as stepping stones to his ultimate theorem, which states that the
value of the finished commodity is exactly the same as the total values
expended in producing the commodity.

Marx illustrates this apex theorem via a hypothetical example involving
the production of ten pounds of yarn by the spinning of ten pounds of cotton
(and built on numbers chosen arbitrarily by Marx). In his example, the
capitalist's expenditures for production include 1) ten pounds of cotton (the
raw material); 2) wear and tear on the capital equipment (the spindle); and 3) a
day's-worth of labor-power (not labor). To repeat, the value of a day's labor-
power is half a day's labor, i.e., six hours of labor.

The total of those "labors" is 2 1/2 days of labor. That is the production
cost, or what we may call the "value in."

Next we can pick up Marx's exposition of the "value out," i.e., the value
of the finished product:

> Let us now consider the total value of the product, the 10 lbs. of
> yarn. Two and a half days' labour has been embodied in it, of which
> two days were contained in the cotton and in the substance of the
> spindle worn away, and half a day was absorbed during the process
> of spinning. . .
> — *Das Kapital*, Part III, Chapter 7, Section 2

I.e., two and a half days' labor was expended and is therefore embodied
or congealed in the commodity. That is the commodity's value:

Introduction

> Our capitalist stares in astonishment. The value of the product is exactly equal to the value of the capital advanced. . . The price of the yarn is fifteen shillings, and fifteen shillings were spent in the open market upon the constituent elements of the product. . .
> — *Das Kapital*, Part III, Chapter 7, Section 2

The implications of this point are major. If "value in" equals "value out," if the cost of production equals the value of the finished product, then profit as normally conceived of is impossible. I.e., profit as an excess of selling price over production costs is impossible.

This impossibility means that the capitalist gains wealth not by profit as conventionally considered, but by some more devious and underhanded method. (Marx will show later that the underhanded method is one of robbing the laborer of unpaid labor or "surplus value.")

"Stares in astonishment"

> "I have a theory about television. . . I don't believe it is possible!"
> -- "The Return of Edwin Carp," an episode of "The Dick Van Dyke Show"

Our hypothetical capitalist "stares in astonishment," and well he might. Marx has demonstrated that profit, something the capitalist sees every day and indeed participates in, is impossible. There must be a flaw in that line of logic.

But this conundrum is easily explained. Marx is not writing about the real world and real markets. Rather, he is developing his formal system, expounding on theorems that have been logically derived from chosen premises.

In other words. Marx's text sounds like a description of the real-world economy, because the terms he uses are the same -- labor, capital, commodity, etc. But Marx's book is something of a bait-and-switch. He is proving a point in an artificially-constructed logical system, or theoretical construct, which readers assume to be a point about the real world. But "here in the real world," Marx's conclusions are irrelevant.

An Alternative, Science-Fiction World

Formal systems can be an essential tool when their founding axioms are intelligent and faithful to the subject matter. But if the founding axioms are not intelligently and honestly chosen, the resulting system is fraudulent, and any conclusions derived from it are inevitably specious.

Marx's theoretical system has no bearing or influence on real-world economies. Those economies continue to function in accordance with their own rules, ignoring any contrived, abstruse theories that purport to prescribe how they must work. "The dogs bark, but the caravan moves on."

1. SETTING THE STAGE

> The wealth of those societies in which the capitalist mode of production prevails, presents itself as "an immense accumulation of commodities," its unit being a single commodity. Our investigation must therefore begin with the analysis of a commodity.

Thus does Marx begin *Capital – A Critique of Political Economy*, his monumental work devoted to detailing the crimes and inequities of capitalist societies and market economies. It is a surprisingly innocuous beginning, considering the history of conflict, bloodshed, and political oppression which resulted from attempts to put his ideas into effect. A newcomer to Marx's work may be forgiven for expecting to find more thunderous pronouncements in a theory that has accumulated such a record.

Yet this beginning passage serves Marx well as a point of departure, from which, adding argument to argument and deduction to deduction, he eventually proceeds to the thesis which is his destination: that capitalism is corrupt in its essential nature, and that capitalists gain wealth not by any legitimate means, but by appropriating unpaid labor from the working masses.

Despite the utter collapse of Communism, that is still a widely-believed doctrine, even in countries that never were subjected to Communist rule. That doctrine, and the course of argumentation by which Marx arrives at it, together form the subject of this work.

Certain unspoken assumptions

Marx identifies his subject: "the capitalist mode of production" and societies employing that mode; and he announces that he will approach his subject by way of an analysis of commodities. But there are assumptions even in his use of the word "capitalist" which don't readily appear.

On one level of course the term "capitalism" (coined by early socialists) is simply another term for "free-market economics." But on another level, the term carries with it a considerable baggage of ideological assumptions; and these assumptions need to be challenged.

One of those ideological assumptions has been explored by Thomas Sowell. He objects to Marx's use of the term "capitalism" on the grounds that it identifies free-market economics too exclusively with one group of people and one factor in the economy. As Sowell says,

> Marx's ringing use of the term "capitalism" was something of a verbal coup. It implied a system for the benefit of a small class of people with a unique monopoly of capital assets. But capitalists as thus defined receive only a small fraction of the total income received by labor; yet no one thinks of calling the economic system "labor-ism," even though that is where three-quarters or more of the income goes. [1]

Not only did the term "capitalism" imply a system that benefited only a small class of people; it also tended to diminish or constrain the scope of "capitalism." That is, it suggested that capitalism was an "ism," just one form or variety of economics, on a level with and comparable to other equally valid forms of economics. In other words, much as "mercantilism" was one form of state economic policy to be compared and contrasted to other forms, so also "capitalism" presumably was one form of economic life, comparable to other equally valid economic alternatives.

Besides implying the above by his term "capitalism," Marx said as much explicitly; that is, he predicted that capitalism would eventually be replaced by socialism, just as it itself had replaced feudalism. Kenneth Minogue referred to this type of argument as "the central ideological technique of revealing that what we imagine to be universal is actually a particular in masquerade."[2]

We might apply the term "particularism" to this view of Marx's, meaning that it sees "capitalism" as a phenomenon of a particular time, place and set of circumstances.

The contrary view, which might be called "universalism," is that capitalism is a universal phenomenon. That is, "capitalism" is nearly synonymous with economics; it is just another word for the economics of free choice and free enterprise, and as such it stands alone in deserving the name of a fully-functioning economic system. Other "forms" are not economies at all, but stifled or stilted versions of economies; they are characterized by the hindering of economic activity, not by economic activity itself.

In this view, non- "capitalist" societies are those in which economic activity is inhibited, either by a lack of freedom on the one hand or by a lack of sufficient security for trade on the other. Such societies are not alternatives to "capitalist" economic activity, but stiflings of it. Thus "forms" such as feudal manors and modern communist states aren't really full-fledged alternatives to market economies, but rather situations in which economic activity has been systematically impeded or hindered in some manner. They are not viable systems on the same level as "capitalism." These supposed alternatives are mere crippled versions of the real thing.

Thus, rather than "capitalism," the phenomenon under consideration could have simply been called "market economics" or even "economic freedom," and in that case it would have been more apparent that there are few if any substitutes for it.

The merits of these two contrasting views, the particularist and the universalist, cannot be fully debated here. They are brought up only to point out the theoretical baggage certain terms bring with them in Marx's prose, and to say that we must always identify Marx's assumptions, even if we are reluctant to agree with them.

Commodities – Marx's first topic

Let us now move from Marx's implicit assumptions to the particulars of what he says. Capitalist wealth, he informs us, "presents itself as 'an immense accumulation of commodities'. . ." The question is. as opposed to what? Don't all economic "modes" have as their aim the production of economic goods (and services) – that is, the making or growing or building of the necessities of life? So how does this fact differentiate capitalism from any other "mode"?

The question may be answered by recognizing that Marx is using a rather narrow definition of the word "commodity." In his lexicon, commodities are goods produced only for sale on the market, i.e., for ultimate consumption by the buyer, as opposed to being produced for home use, for consumption by the producer. Nikolai Bukharin discusses this issue in his book, *The ABC of Communism*. As he explains it:

> If we study how economic life is carried on under the capitalist regime, we see that its primary characteristic is the production of commodities.
>
> "Well, what is there remarkable about that?" the reader may ask. The remarkable point is that a commodity is not simply a product, but something produced for the market.
>
> A product made for the producer himself, made for his own use, is not a commodity. When a peasant sows rye, gathers in the harvest, threshes it, mills the grain, and bakes bread for himself, this bread is certainly not a commodity; it is simply bread. It only becomes a commodity when it is bought and sold; when, that is to say, it is produced for a buyer, for the market. . .
>
> Under the capitalist system, all products are produced for the market, they all become commodities. [3]

To put it another way, commodities are produced for their exchange value, rather than for their "use-value." Or in more colloquial terms, commodities are "store-bought" (and store-sold) goods, as opposed to "homemade."

This distinction between homemade and produced-for-sale goods looms large in Marx's theories, because for him the profit motive and market mechanisms taint everything associated with them. Goods produced for the producer's own use are, so to speak, morally pure, untinged by oppression and social injustice; whereas market goods are tainted and corrupted by the profit motive of the capitalists who produce them.

This moral superiority of the one type over the other is reflected in the Marxist catch-phrase, "For use-value, not for exchange-value" (or in its pidgin-Marxist modern version, "For people, not for profit").

At any rate, it is doubtful whether there ever was a society in which goods were produced for home use and yet never produced for sale. Thus there probably was never a society that wasn't in some degree a "commodity" society. While Marx lists the production of commodities, or market goods, as one of the defining characteristics of capitalist societies. Whether this actually differentiates "capitalist" societies from any others is debatable, but at least we must understand Marx's terminology and his somewhat eccentric definition of the word "commodities." *

The analysis of a commodity

So far we have the statement that capitalist societies are characterized by goods produced for the market, which goods constitute the wealth of such societies. All of this is more or less reasonable, give or take a quirky definition or two.

Marx has advanced the premise that, "Our investigation must therefore begin with the analysis of a commodity." Actually, "the analysis of a commodity" is a somewhat illogical place to begin. Commodities are, after all, mere static things (or to use Marx's term, "metaphysical" things), and they appear at the end of the production process, as the end product. It might have been more useful to begin the investigation by looking at the process by which goods are produced (the "dialectical" process, again using Marx's term), and all the processes whereby capitalism functions.

To put it another way, the production system in capitalist societies consists of productive machinery and physical facilities; systems of distribution and exchange; the institution of employing labor; transportation and distribution systems; credit and finance systems; and a variety of other systems and institutions which make possible the production and sale of goods on the free market. To attempt to analyze such societies by dissecting a commodity – by, as it were, putting a static object under the microscope – is not only contrary to the true nature of the phenomena being studied, it is also contrary to Marx's stated principle of always viewing things dynamically, "dialectically," and in terms of processes, rather than in terms of dead, static objects.

A unit of one

A minor quibble with Marx's opening statement could be made. He says, capitalist wealth consists in "'an immense accumulation of commodities,' its unit being a single commodity." What does that last phrase mean? It is a truism; one could just as easily say "a forest is an immense accumulation of trees, its unit being a single tree." There's no extra information conveyed by that final phrase.

But Marx, first of all, was a writer who habitually explained his subject matter to the nth degree and to the uttermost detail; he left nothing unexplained, nothing taken for granted – possibly because he trusted only himself to give the actual truth of any matter. Thus in the present case, as usual, he approaches his subject as one that must be explained from the ground up.

Then, too, Marx purports to write "scientific socialism," and lays claims for his work of being scientific. Possibly for that reason, the beginning of his book is patterned somewhat after science textbooks. Such books most often begin with definitions of terms, identification of elementary concepts and entities to be dealt with, and descriptions of units of measure. Marx's book, at its start, is much in the same pattern, at least superficially; it follows the form of such works, but without the meaningful content. Marx's present comments about commodities and their unit are in that vein.

Marx's analysis of a commodity

Let us now move to the specifics of Marx's "analysis of a commodity." He says:

> A commodity is, in the first place, an object outside us, a thing
> that by its properties satisfies human wants of some kind or another.
> The nature of such wants, whether, for instance, they spring from the
> stomach or from fancy, makes no difference. Neither are we here
> concerned to know how the object satisfies these wants, whether

directly as means of subsistence, or indirectly as means of production.

No one explains things in such minute detail as Marx does when he really gets started, as we see here: commodities are first of all objects "outside us," external objects, not body parts or any other properties or characteristics of ourselves. We can accept his assertion; we might even say it goes without saying: we ourselves, and the goods we buy on the market, are in most cases distinguishable.

The next remark Marx makes about commodities is equally unexceptionable: commodities are useful items, items that by their properties satisfy human wants or needs. That is in fact one possible definition of the term "commodity," conveying a good deal of what is meant by the term in common usage. And even if it is not a definition, if instead commodities are defined as goods produced strictly for sale on the market, even in that case commodities are such because of their usefulness. That is, goods (and services) bought and sold must be items in demand. They must be desired by people, so that people are willing to spend money for them; and thus they must be capable of satisfying some human need or want.

These terms "need" or "want" can be quite loosely interpreted, of course. As Marx indicates, it is hard to identify any objective need satisfied by some goods. Items like pet rocks, and other novelty and fad items, don't satisfy an objectively discernible need; they don't satisfy hunger, or keep out the cold, or perform any other objective service. But what matters is that, for whatever reason, there is a demand for such things when they're offered for sale. People are willing to buy them; there is an observable market demand at a given price. And from that, we may take it for granted that the goods serve some purpose or meet some human need or desire.

The demand, as measured by actual sales at a given price, is the defining characteristic here; it is what makes goods marketable, i.e., makes them commodities. A commodity, in other words, does not have to have an objectively demonstrated use. People may buy it for no better reason than that "everyone else has one"; i.e., it may be a senseless fad. The item is a commodity for all that, being an article of trade, for whatever ill-defined purposes, sold on the market.

If, as Marx acknowledges, the source of the demand or the nature of the wants is not pertinent to our current discussion, neither is the distinction between consumer goods and production equipment, or capital goods. Both types of commodities are similarly produced and sold; both types obey similar economic laws, although the intended market or potential purchasers of the two types are different sets of people. Commodities are commodities, whether they serve as means of subsistence or means of production. There will come a point in Marx's text where that difference will become significant, but at this point, where Marx is explaining the elementary characteristics of all commodities, he can legitimately treat both types as one.

How good, and how much of it

At this point Marx, perhaps still trying to sound as scientific as possible, gives us further but puzzling data on commodities: "Every useful thing, as iron, paper, etc., may be looked at from the two points of view of quality and quantity."

It must be admitted that what Marx mentions is one way of categorizing or characterizing commodities – by "how good it is and how much of it."

Other means of characterizing commodities, might be in terms of cost of production versus selling price; weight versus volume; durability as opposed to quality; and so on. At any rate, commodities can be looked at from many points of view; these include the characteristics of quality and quantity – Marx is right about that. Whether his two criteria of categorization are any more valid or significant than any other two, is open to question.

He continues:

> It [every useful thing] is an assemblage of many properties, and may therefore be of use in various ways.

That is true. Different properties may give rise to different uses, in a sort of one-to-one correspondence. For example, iron is strong and thus is useful for all types of structural objects, like wrought-iron fences. It also has magnetic properties, and is useful for making magnets, such as those used in loudspeakers. These two properties of iron lend themselves to two different "applications," or products.

Moreover, different uses don't necessarily come from different properties; an object, with its whole assemblage of properties, can simply be used for assorted purposes. Wood is used for house frames as well as for baseball bats; steel is used for auto bodies and for watch cases – not necessarily because of a one-to-one correspondence between properties and products, but simply because some materials are versatile and suited for a variety of purposes or products.

For this reason we might make a somewhat subtle distinction: the usefulness per se of a given substance is not a physical property of the substance. Rather, it is in a sense a function of what use people make of it; and that in turn is dependent on the physical properties of the substance. For example, steel is strong, malleable and ductile. For this reason it is useful both for sheet-metal applications and for guitar strings. The strength, malleability and ductility are physical properties of steel, but its usefulness is not. The usefulness is in a sense derived, a result of those properties and of the uses people put the steel to. Usefulness requires the interaction between people and steel – the actual putting of the steel to various uses – in order to appear as a phenomenon at all. (This point may be philosophically debatable, but it seems valid to this author.) All this is said in anticipation of remarks later in Marx's text, implying the contrary, that "use-value" per se is an actual property of commodities.

Uses and measures

The Smoot as a unit of measure was invented in 1958 at the Massachusetts Institute of Technology when fraternity pledges were ordered to measure the length of Harvard Bridge using only chalk and the body of one of their peers.
"Out of the 14 pledges, I had the distinction of being the shortest," said 5-foot-7 inch Oliver Reed Smoot, Jr.
– Los Angeles Times, June 06, 1989

Marx continues:

> To discover the various uses of things is the work of history. So also is the establishment of socially recognized standards of measure for the quantities of these useful objects. The diversity of these measures has its origin partly in the diverse nature of the objects to be measured, partly in convention.

It is hard to know what Marx means by "the work of history." He may mean it is the work of historians; that is, to discover what uses things have been put to in the past is the work of historians.

Whatever he meant by it, the statement is murky enough; and that extends to his next sentence about "the establishment of socially recognized standards of measure." This too is "the work of history," presumably meaning in this case that "it was done in the past" or "it is the work of people in society."

The work continues in modern times, as scientific advances require new types of measurements. For example, angstrom units and nano-seconds are units of measure that either were not defined prior to modern times or else were not useful measures of anything. But both are useful today, and we may say their creation was "the work of history."

In the last sentence of the passage under consideration, Marx offers us more Physics 101. Various units of measure, he informs us, arise because of first, the different characteristics of the things to be measured. For instance, if apples and wheat are measured by the bushel, and cloth is measured by the square yard, it is so partly because it would be difficult to do the reverse and measure apples by the square yard and cloth by the bushel. That is, it is so because of the different natures of the things being measured. Area is more significant than volume in measuring cloth, because for one thing, a particular piece of clothing requires a certain number of square yards of fabric. Thus it makes sense to sell cloth by the square yard. Moreover, cloth does not lend itself to measure by volume – it is compressible and doesn't have a fixed volume. So it is sold by the square yard, i.e., by lengths of cloth a yard wide.

Wheat and apples do, for practical purposes, have a fixed volume. While they could be and sometimes are measured by weight, both their physical properties and the purpose they are used for make measurement (and sale) by volume more practicable.

On the other hand, not "the diverse nature of the objects" but conventions and circumstances account for specific units of measure. The English-speaking world has traditionally adhered to the "foot/pound/ second" system, relying on those units of length, weight and time, respectively. The rest of the world has mainly adopted the metric system, using meters, kilograms (a unit of mass, not weight) and seconds. Either system manages to measure the same things; the choice of one or the other is a matter of custom and usage, not the inherent characteristics of the things measured.

There can even be fanciful, totally impractical units of measure that are never adopted by society at large. For example, one author suggested "furlongs per fortnight-squared" as a unit of acceleration (in *The Official Rules*, by Paul Dickson, Dell Publishing Co., 1981). And then there is the Smoot, as described above.

Use-value

We now arrive at Marx's introduction of two essential properties of commodities, twin characteristics that will be of pivotal importance throughout the remainder of his text. He states:

> The utility of a thing makes it a use-value. But this utility is not a thing of air. Being limited by the physical properties of the commod-ity, it has no existence apart from that commodity. A commodity, such as iron, corn, or a diamond, is therefore, so far as it is a material thing, a use-value, something useful.

In other words, there is no such thing as a sort of disembodied usefulness, floating around unattached to any physical commodity. There is no such thing as an independent, self-existing "usefulness" apart from the physical object of which it is a property. It follows that a commodity is useful "so far as it is a material thing," or we might say, because, or inasmuch as it is a material thing. (For example, the useful properties of hardness and ductility are properties of iron; there is no such thing as an abstract "hardness" free-floating around us, unconnected to any object.) That seems to be what Marx is saying – as if there were anyone who needed to have the point elucidated.

A semantic issue: at this point in his text Marx is still wavering between two meanings of the term "use-value." He still at times refers to "use-value" in the normal sense of the word, as a property of objects. (Indeed, that is the whole point of the above passage.) But he is also beginning to use the term as a synonym for "commodity," saying that a commodity *is* a use-value, it doesn't *have* use-value.

The distinction is not really a crucial one, except that it illustrates Marx's penchant for creating his own vocabulary, a jargon that has to be almost decoded rather than simply read. Perhaps this manner of, in effect, creating his own language helped to render his text incomprehensible, mysterious, and intellectual-sounding, and thus helped force the reader to accept Marx's theory on his own authority, rather than understanding it.

More about use-value

> This property of a commodity is independent of the amount of labor required to appropriate its useful qualities. When treating of use-value, we always assume to be dealing with definite quantities such as dozens of watches, yards of linen, or tons of iron.
>
> The use-values of commodities furnish the material for a special study, that of the commercial knowledge of commodities. Use-values become a reality only by use or consumption: they also constitute the substance of all wealth, whatever may be the social form of that wealth.

First of all, we are informed that the use-value of a commodity "is independent of the amount of labour required to appropriate its useful qualities." The latter is a bit of Marxian jargon; Marx says "to appropriate its useful qualities" rather than "to produce it," though the latter is what he means. Marx always prefers to divert the reader's attention from the fact that it is the entrepreneur or capitalist who produces the commodity and bears the expense of doing so. Rather, he prefers to imply that the capitalist seizes the commodity wrongfully, that he "expropriates" or "appropriates" it – ignoring the fact that the commodity didn't exist prior to the capitalist's efforts, and that it wouldn't exist for anyone to appropriate without him.

The main significance of the remark, however, is probably by contrast to exchange value, which *is* dependent on the amount of labor required to produce the commodity (as Marx will show later on). Thus this point is one significant distinction between the two types of "value."

A quibble might be made here: depending on how we consider the term "use-value," it is not always completely independent of the amount of labor required to produce the commodity. Theoretically, the two are unrelated, though in practice it is not always so.

Some commodities are like apples, diamonds and so on – they are almost purely products of nature, and their usefulness is pretty completely defined by their inherent nature. Their useful properties, such as an apple's being good to eat, are inherent. Or, if we construe "use-value" to mean "the amount of usefulness" of the commodity, then in that case too the amount of usefulness or goodness of an apple is fairly well fixed by its inherent nature – by what variety of apple tree it is, conditions of soil and climate, and so on. The amount of labor applied to it can only affect the "amount of usefulness" to a limited degree. Whether we prune a lot or a little, or fertilize a lot or a little, the use-value of the resulting apples will only be affected (we will assume) to a certain small degree.

Similarly, the size and purity of a diamond are pretty well fixed by nature. The diamond can be cut in various ways, but the amount of influence our labor can have on its "use-value" is constrained within certain limited bounds.

Other commodities are less clear-cut cases. Consider the "use-value" of a piano: one could argue that a hand-made concert grand, with a large amount of labor invested in it, is more useful, and useful for more purposes, than a mass-produced spinet made by less labor-intensive methods. In this case the amount of use-value is not independent of the labor required to "appropriate," i.e., produce, the piano. (On the other hand, if Marx is using "use-value" to mean "what it's used for," then in that sense use-value is independent of the labor: a piano is to play. Such ambiguities come from having a variety of definitions, some of them crude and imprecise, to choose from at will.)

Puzzling remarks

We are now presented with a couple of puzzling remarks. When discussing use-value, Marx tells us, "We always assume to be dealing with definite quantities, such as dozens of watches, yards of linen, or tons of iron."

Well, maybe. We can always assume we're dealing with definite quantities – unless we're not. This point is so basic, it is hard to know how to state it. In some circumstances we deal with definite quantities, as on an invoice, where we're making a record of a certain number of items to be shipped. At other times, we talk of commodities or "use-values" in general, not quantitatively. Even when Marx himself uses expressions like "treating of use-values," or when he refers to "watches," or even "dozens of watches," he doesn't give specific numbers.

In short, some discussions are quantitative; some are not. Perhaps Marx, a one-time student of philosophy, abstruse metaphysics, and such matters, was so fixated on elementary distinctions, that he thought such comments necessary. Or perhaps his comments are included for the purpose of sounding scientific, in order to evoke the quantitative nature of science and to mimic the thorough definition of terms, units of measure, etc. common in scientific works. If the latter, he gives us form without content.

Marx's next sentence is likewise somewhat elusive in meaning: "The use-values of commodities furnish the material for a special study, that of the commercial knowledge of commodities" – a murky formulation if ever there was one. Marx tells us that the "use-values of commodities," or we might say their useful properties in a broad, general sense, are studied under the name of "the commercial knowledge of commodities." Or we might say, those who deal in goods on the market must be familiar with their properties – their method of manufacture, the characteristics of various brands and types of goods, and so on. If there is any intelligible meaning in that sentence of Marx's, perhaps that is as good a guess as any.

He also says, use-values "also constitute the substance of all wealth, whatever may be the social form of that wealth." The phrase "the social form of that wealth" is perhaps open to various interpretations, but the most direct interpretation is probably this: use-values or useful goods are present in all epochs and all "modes of production," but they are not always commodities. That is, useful goods have not always been produced for sale on the market; not all economies have been "commodity economies." But regardless of whether goods are produced on a feudal estate for consumption by the inhabitants of the estate, or produced in the modern capitalist era for sale on the market – whatever the circumstances, use-values are the substance of all wealth. And regardless of whether a society is nominally based on money and the "cash nexus," or on self-sustaining feudal estates, goods are the real and ultimate form of wealth. This is perhaps a difficult idea to get used to in a money economy, but it is hard to deny.

Exchange-value deposited in use-values

Marx now makes a final remark on the subject of goods, or use-values:

> In the form of society we are about to consider, they are, in
> addition, the material depositories of exchange value.

From a more down-to-earth viewpoint, we could paraphrase Marx's statement like this: "In the form of society we are about to consider, use-values or goods are articles of trade; they are bought and sold on the market." Such a formulation would avoid the more metaphysical overtones of Marx's statement. His version perhaps displays his metaphysical orientation – his tendency to over-philosophize straightforward matters. He seems to imply that exchange value is an intangible, ethereal entity that is incarnated or deposited within the physical bodies of commodities – sort of on the order of ectoplasm. He portrays it as an intangible entity, which enters into the commodity and takes up residence.

Whichever interpretation is appropriate, it is clear that Marx considers exchange value a property of commodities, i.e., of use-values, which by its very presence we may say turns them into commodities. Exchange value is something contained within commodities; goods are imbued, suffused, inhabited, haunted by exchange value, and exchange value is to be studied as such – as a property, or internal ingredient of goods. By contrast, a more traditional view would say, people produce goods for sale, and exchange value is a result of that fact and a product of the market nexus.

Smith's description of the value of commodities

For purposes of comparison, we might look at Adam Smith's approach to the same topic (from *Wealth of Nations*, Book 1, Chapter 4):

> The word VALUE, it is to be observed, has two different meanings, and sometimes expresses the utility of some particular object, and sometimes the power of purchasing other goods which the possession of that object conveys. The one may be called "value in use"; the other, "value in exchange." The things which have the greatest value in use have frequently little or no value in exchange; and, on the contrary, those which have the greatest value in exchange have frequently little or no value in use. Nothing is more useful than water, but it will purchase scarce anything; scarce any thing can be had in exchange for it. A diamond, on the contrary, has scarce any value in use; but a very great quantity of other goods may frequently be had in exchange for it.

(The difference between the two types of "value" might be illustrated by rephrasing the famous remark of Oscar Wilde to read, "A cynic is one who knows the exchange value of everything, and the use-value of nothing." That is, price or exchange value is a prosaic economic quantity, one knowable and openly observable at the marketplace. Use-value, or intrinsic, human-related value, by whatever standards it is judged, is less of a concrete, market phenomenon; it is a result of judgment and thought. Compared to exchange value, it is more subjective and aesthetic.)

Smith doesn't formally define the word "commodity," apparently taking it for granted as a term in common usage. Moreover, he uses the term in its common, ordinary sense, not any specially-invented sense.

He identifies the goods or articles his economic treatise deals with no more explicitly than to say this:

> Every man is rich or poor according to the degree in which he can afford to enjoy the necessaries, conveniencies, and amusements of human life.

Thus he identifies commodities or economic goods only in passing, as the necessities, "conveniencies" (or we might say, luxuries), and amusements of life. We all buy such goods, and we all recognize economic commodities or goods when we see them.

(By including "amusements" Smith also might be seen to include non-tangible items, such as admission to performances of plays and such things. These too are articles of trade, though they don't fit either the "goods" or "services" category exactly.)

All in all, Smith's analysis seems more natural and less contrived, more in accord with the normal way of thinking about goods and their value, and more in accord with normal human experience.

On the other hand, Marx's view offers the benefit (for him) of making commodities entirely self-contained; that is, commodities can be completely analyzed or dissected in isolation, as mere physical objects, without reference to society, trade, human actions, or the economic activities taking place outside of and around commodities.

More particularly, his analysis offers the benefit of removing people from economics. There is no direct reference to human beings in Marx's statement that, "they are. . .the material depositories of exchange value." That becomes a continuing characteristic of his text. The removal of human beings, so far as is possible, from economics will become a continuing feature of Marx's approach to his subject, and it will facilitate his treatment of commodities (and economics) as a study of material objects rather than of human activity. He treats economics as a quasi-physics, rather than as a social study or an examination of human behavior in the economic realm. This is a serious misapprehension of the nature of the subject under consideration.

NOTES – Chapter 1

1 Sowell, Thomas, *Marxism*, New York, Morrow, 1985, p. 195.

2 Minogue, Kenneth R., *Alien powers: The Pure Theory of Ideology*, New York, St. Martin's Press, 1985.

3 Bukharin, Nikolai Ivanovich, and Preobrazhensky, E., *The ABC of Communism*, Baltimore, Penguin Books, 1969, p.26.

2. THE LABOR THEORY OF VALUE

With the appearance of exchange value in his text, Marx is ready to introduce the "labor theory of value," a fundamental component of his work, critical to the development of almost everything that follows it in *Capital*. Thus it merits thorough consideration.

Marx's exposition of this theory begins as follows:

> Exchange value, at first sight, presents itself as a quantitative relation, as the proportion in which values in use of one sort are exchanged for those of another sort, a relation constantly changing with time and place. Hence exchange value appears to be something accidental and purely relative, and consequently an intrinsic value, i.e., an exchange value that is inseparably connected with, inherent in commodities, seems a contradiction in terms. Let us consider the matter a little more closely.

> A given commodity, e.g., a quarter of wheat is exchanged for x blacking, y silk, or z gold, &c. – in short, for other commodities in the most different proportions. Instead of one exchange value, the wheat has, therefore, a great many. But since x blacking, y silk, or z gold, &c. each represent the exchange value of one quarter of wheat, x blacking, y silk, z gold, &c., must as exchange values be replaceable by each other, or equal to each other. Therefore, first: the valid exchange values of a given commodity express something equal; secondly, exchange value, generally, is only the mode of expression, the phenomenal form, of something contained in it, yet distinguishable from it.

> Let us take two commodities, e.g., corn and iron. The proportions in which they are exchangeable, whatever these proportions may be, can always be represented by an equation in which a given quantity of corn is equated to some quantity of iron: e.g., 1 quarter corn = x cwt iron. What does this equation tell us? It tells us that in two different things – in 1 quarter of corn and x cwt of iron, there exists in equal quantities something common to both. The two things must therefore be equal to a third, which in itself is neither the one nor the other. Each of them, so far as it is exchange value, must therefore be reducible to this third.

The passage begins with a fairly unexceptionable statement about exchange value: "Exchange value, at first sight, presents itself as a quantitative relation, as the proportion in which values in use [yet another of Marx's terms for "use-values"] of one sort are exchanged for those of another sort."

That is entirely accurate; in fact it is the definition of exchange value (and thus exchange value "presents itself" as such at first sight, last sight, and every other sight). The exchange value of a particular good is by definition the amount of any of various other goods for which it can be exchanged – meaning, for which it actually *is* exchanged, at the current time, on the market. (Or as Adam Smith puts it, an object's exchange value is "the power of purchasing other goods which the possession of that object conveys," this power being measured by the amount of those goods.) That is the entire extent of the meaning of the term; and it is important to note, for future reference, that there are no metaphysical subtleties involved in it. The concept is a matter of observed fact: we can observe that two goods are exchanged on the open market in a certain proportion; or that they are sold at money prices from which such a proportion can be derived. This proportion, or an aggregate of such proportions, constitutes, by definition, a particular commodity's exchange value.

The meaning of the term "exchange value" is entirely transparent, and the method for determining, i.e. measuring, a commodity's exchange value is straightforward. Goods are exchanged, and in this exchange a definite proportion is attained; this proportion is the exchange value.

(This is of course an over-simplification. While exchange value can be conceived of in terms of goods of various kinds being directly exchanged for one another, of course it usually doesn't happen that way. Most things are bought and sold for money; but this money, serving as a medium of exchange, can be treated as a mere intermediary. The various money prices of goods, by a brief calculation, give us the respective amounts of various goods which are equivalent to each other. If a bushel of corn sells for $3.20 and a bushel of soybeans sells for $2.80, the proportion is 7/8 bushel of corn exchangeable for 1 bushel of soybeans. This comparison of goods to goods, rather than to money prices, is considered the more basic meaning of exchange value.)

Of course, all of this says nothing about how that proportion was arrived at, or *why* it is 7/8 to 1. That is another topic, the one of *what determines exchange value*; it is a much more complicated subject than the simple definition of the term. But as for the definition of exchange value and our method of knowing or measuring its magnitude, that is more straightforward: exchange value is simply what you can get, or what you must give, for an item on the market. It will be well to keep these simple guidelines in mind in the face of future rhetorical subtleties of Marx's.

What all this indeed means is that exchange value is a "quantitative relation," in a literal, mathematical sense. This being the case, some characteristics of mathematical relations bear discussing, as pertinent to the subject of exchange values in a general way.

Mathematical relations

A mathematical relation can be defined as a set of corresponding pairs of values (i.e., numbers), with each pair having a number of the first kind (an x-value) associated with a number of the second kind (a y-value).

These paired or corresponding values can be specified by an algebraic equation such as $y=x^2$; such an expression defines a relation. Another method of describing a particular relation is a graphical representation, on Cartesian coordinates, with the pairs of values plotted as (x, y) points along x and y axes.

An example of a relation pertinent to economics is the "demand curve" for a product. This curve graphs the amount of a product which can be sold, or which one would expect to sell, at a given price for the product. For example, if the asking price is $3.00, one may sell 5000 units per week; whereas if the price is $3.50 one may sell 4500, and so on. All these points or ordered pairs – ($3.00, 5000), ($3.50, 4500) and so on – together form the mathematical relation which is the demand curve.

Exchange value as a philosophical concept

It should be kept in mind that exchange value is just one type of a mathematical relation, and it has no magical properties different from any other relation.

Notice then: the way we find out the pairs of corresponding values or quantities in the exchange-value relation is simply by observing the respective prices at which goods actually are being exchanged, i.e. sold, on the market. It is a matter of open observation, not of metaphysics or logical deduction.

This is important to note because various authors, and not only Marx, have at times been inclined to approach exchange value from the wrong end, as it were – as if it were an *a priori* philosophical category which it is up to us (i.e., to economists) to determine by logical deduction.

For example, in *The Capitalist Manifesto*, Mortimer Adler and Louis Kelso write about exchange value in these terms:

> [Exchange value is] the problem of finding an objective measure
> of the economic value of goods and services, so that a just exchange

of commodities is possible.

Marx accepts Aristotle's principle of justice in exchange as requiring that the things exchanged be of equal value. . . Aristotle raises the question of how we can equate the value of beds and houses so that a certain number of beds can be justly exchanged for a certain number of houses. [1]

The problem of finding an objective standard for the just exchange of commodities is not ours. That is, the question is not how *we* can equate the value of beds and houses; they are already equated or commensurated on the market. People already deal in beds and houses, and the proportionate worth of the two commodities is already determined daily on the market. Our problem is finding out, after the fact, how it was accomplished; it is finding out what market factors come into play in the spontaneous determination of prices.

(The process is spontaneous not in the sense that people are not involved in the it, but because price determination is not governed from above, by economic or philosophical theorists. Prices arises spontaneously, amid the economic dealings of people involved in trade. Perhaps this is part of the concept of the "invisible hand" – meaning not that no one's decisions and choices are involved, but that the theorists and economists are not in control.)

If we consider exchange value from the above viewpoint, it is similar to various aspects of natural science. The phenomena being studied exist already, independent of the scientist, having their own pre-established nature and behavior. It is not up to the scientist or the economist to deduce a set of rules which we then assign to the phenomena; rather it is up to us to discover what rules already govern their behavior, independently of our observations and theories.

In other words, the market functions, and has always functioned, in such a manner as to enable goods to be exchanged or traded at various rates or proportions. The market does not wait for us as theorists to determine by logical reasoning what a certain thing *should* exchange for. Exchange value is not a deductive or logical category which we define or establish by a system of argumentation.

(All of this is not to say there may not be a question as to whether the actual exchange value, as arrived at by market forces, is in some philosophical sense a "just" or fair exchange. For example, in time of famine the price which food can command on the open market may be exorbitant and indeed unjust, even though it is the actual economic exchange value. Similarly, in a time of a greatly depressed real-estate market, someone selling a house in which he has invested a lot of money and labor, may believe he is forced to sell at an unfair price. Yet as a strictly economic matter these prices are determined by economic factors, and our primary task is to determine those factors. They will tell us what determines exchange value. In times of "normal" market conditions, the question of whether the actual market price is the "just rate of exchange" is far less problematical.)

In this light, if our subject is purely economic, i.e., if the subject is simply the economic aspects of exchange value and not historical or other aspects, then it is reverse logic to say that commensurability or "justice in exchange" requires "that the things exchanged be of equal value." The fact that they are exchanged as being equal on the market already, *by definition*, makes them of equal value. What a thing is exchangeable for, what you must give for it on the market, *is* its exchange value.

One final observation should be made about the example of exchange value as a relation: all the amounts of various goods for which, say, one bushel of corn may be exchanged, are equivalent and may be exchanged for one another. That is, if one bushel of corn is exchanged for 1.15 bushels of soybeans, or for $3.20 in cash, or for a quarter-ton of iron, then in turn we would expect the 1.15 bushels of soybeans to be exchanged for $3.20, and the quarter-ton of iron to be exchanged for 1.15 bushel of soybeans, and so on. "Two things equivalent to a third thing are equivalent to each other," is the rule we naturally expect to find at work in this relation.

(Of course the real world is less than ideal. For various reasons, including lack of perfect knowledge and varying local conditions, disparities sometimes exist. Disparity of price depending on location is always a reality; arbitrage, or trade in the currencies of various nations, is a good concrete example of this.)

In short, exchange value, and mathematical relations in general, are fairly transparent concepts. Both the meaning of the term "exchange value" and the method of discovering or measuring it for any given commodity are simple and straightforward propositions. Any attempt to endow the term with metaphysical subtleties, or to convert the method of determination of exchange value into a philosophical exercise, must be resisted.

The problem, then, will be in finding the operative generalization governing the magnitude of exchange value. It is always good to have the object of an investigation explicitly stated beforehand. This helps us ignore a lot of tricky maneuvering performed on the meaning of the concept under consideration.

Characteristics of exchange value

To recapitulate what has been said about exchange value so far: exchange value has at least this in common with physical quantities from the natural sciences, that it is an empirical phenomenon. It is objectively discernible; we can see the exchange of goods and services, and we can observe the relative proportions attained in these exchanges.

Moreover, exchange value exists independently of the observer, i.e. the economist. Like quantities studied in the physical sciences, it has an independent nature of its own, not subject to arbitrary definition or manipulation at will by the observer. It is the economist's job to discover its nature; it is not his task to invent a nature for it from scratch, or to approach it as an arbitrary logical category, subject to whatever rules and definitions one might like to prescribe for it. Exchange value must be approached scientifically, which means empirically.

Besides being an empirical phenomenon, exchange value is a *market* phenomenon. It derives from the fact of exchange, i.e. from economic activity as such, and is an offshoot or ancillary property of exchange: two goods are exchanged in definite amounts or a definite proportion, and that proportion is then termed the exchange value.

Exchange value must not be divorced from the notion of exchange; it always means "what you can get (or must give)" for a thing. Exchange value is the empirical notion of what a thing sells for on the market. We must not lose sight of that reality.

And, exchange value is a human or social phenomenon: again, it derives from the fact of exchange, i.e. from the economic activities of people. In this aspect exchange value diverges from the purely physical quantities studied in the physical sciences. While it is empirically observed and measured, like physical quantities, unlike them it is governed or determined by human behavior. Exchange value thus has a little of the nature of both natural phenomena and human or social phenomena.

Exchange value doesn't exist in nature; it is not a physical property or natural phenomenon. For economics itself does not exist in nature; economics is "something people do." For this reason we must be on guard against all purely mechanical or natural-science type explanations of exchange value. The factors that govern exchange value must always be, ultimately, human factors, human constraints. Any purely mechanistic, impersonal explanation of it *must* be specious.

All this must be said at the outset, so that we can first understand the nature of the phenomenon we will be discussing, before deciding what questions are pertinent to it and judging the plausibility of Marx's answers to any such questions.

Determination of the magnitude of exchange value

Now, moving from the definition and characteristics of exchange value, we can proceed to the subject of how its magnitude is determined. Marx notes that exchange value is "a quantitative relation"; it is the proportion in which various goods are exchanged for one another – "a relation constantly changing with time and place." (More pertinently, it is constantly changing with conditions of supply and demand; but that is not the point here, nor would Marx accept that view.)

"Hence," he continues, "exchange value appears to be something accidental and purely relative, and consequently an intrinsic value, i.e., an exchange value that is inseparably connected with, inherent in commodities, seems a contradiction in terms."

Marx's reasoning is not immediately obvious here. It is not easy to say in what sense exchange value is "accidental"; nor is it easy to judge exactly what Marx is ruling out in stating that exchange value cannot be "inseparably connected with, inherent in" commodities. (This kind of vague, ambiguous terminology is one of the things that make Marx's text hard to analyze with any degree of certainty.) And, it is not self-evident how his conclusion follows from what preceded it, as Marx indicates it does by his use of the word "hence."

First of all, we may perhaps accept the terms "accidental" and "purely relative," applied to exchange value, as somewhat hyperbolic expressions of the proposition that exchange value is not a fixed and constant property of the commodity itself. It must be hyperbolic, for exchange value is not literally *accidental*; it is not a purely random phenomenon.

On the other hand, it is indeed relative (but relative to what, Marx does not say); by its very nature it is an expression of the relative amounts of goods that are exchanged for each other. We can only speculate, and try to infer from the context, what Marx might mean, beyond that, by his comments.

Turning from what exchange value is to what it is not, we might say that indeed, a fixed and intrinsic exchange value for goods does seem a contradiction in terms. If Marx's point is that exchange value is not a fixed constant, and not an intrinsic physical property of the commodity itself, his statement is a truism. No one has ever thought otherwise, and Marx's point is then simply a statement of the obvious.

The notion of exchange value as an intrinsic, built-in property of commodities is strange, just on the basis of general common-sense principles, quite apart from questions of the validity of Marx's deductive argument. In fact it is strange that of all the possible views or explanations of exchange value Marx could have chosen to refute, he chose one never held by anyone, one so patently false as to be beneath serious consideration. A likelier candidate for his attention, if he had wanted to refute contradictory views, would have been the classical explanation of value: the theory that it is governed by the "dialectical" interaction of the forces of supply and demand. It would have been more to the point to show the reader how that viewpoint is wrong, rather than to dispel ideas no one ever held.

But Marx ignores classical theory entirely and occupies himself with defeating a straw man, before going on to issue his own explanation of value more or less as a bald pronouncement. He really gives no supporting data or arguments other than the implied one, "The first possibility (value as an intrinsic property) was incorrect, so my answer must be correct." This may be considered one form of what Marx termed "dialectical" reasoning: it evades issues of substance while presenting a semblance of consideration of contradictory points of view. It is a stage-managed presentation that says "It's not A, so it must be B" – and that is the sum total of the support advanced for the conclusion.

Further discussion of exchange value

The passage in question can bear more detailed consideration. Marx writes in a rather elliptical, circuitous style at most times, and it may not be out of place to attempt to extrapolate from his text, to infer a precise interpretation of what he means by his vague terminology.

Marx says exchange value is a quantity "constantly changing with time and place," and "Hence," exchange value is a relative, and not intrinsic, quantity. In what sense does he mean this?

Let us consider the term "inseparably connected with." We cannot know how a particular value could conceivably be "inseparably connected with" a particular commodity, attached to a commodity so that the commodity would always have the same value. On the other hand, we can readily agree with Marx that such a situation indeed does not exist. We accept his logic that if exchange value is constantly changing, then indeed, a commodity cannot have a fixed value attached to it. If exchange value fluctuates, then there cannot be a fixed exchange value physically attached to the commodity, for such an unvarying physical arrangement would not be capable of fluctuating.

So while not understanding perfectly what situation he envisions, we are in agreement that the situation he speaks of can be ruled out. As for how this fixed value could conceivably be attached to the commodity, or what was the exact situation that Marx intended to dismiss, the possibilities are limited. The obvious way an exchange value could be a fixed quantity "connected with" the commodity and "inherent in" it, would be if exchange value itself were to be a physical property of the commodity, or if exchange value were directly related to such a physical characteristic. Either of these two possibilities could be construed as an exchange value "inseparably connected with, inherent in" commodities; either of them may have been what Marx meant to rule out by observing that exchange value fluctuates.

Besides the fact that exchange value fluctuates, we know that the physical properties of goods do *not* fluctuate – specifically, the physical properties which contribute to the usefulness or "use-value" of the goods do not fluctuate. Corn continues to be an edible grain, iron remains a hard, malleable metal, cloth remains a good material for making clothing, and so on. For all practical purposes, the physical nature of commodities, their intrinsic useful physical properties, remain constant.

(Arguably, there is *some* fluctuation. In some growing seasons corn may for instance contain more calories, or more protein or minerals, per kernel than in others. But such variations are slight and obviously do not account for variations in exchange value.)

And this is probably what Marx is pointing out by his argument. Exchange value is something "accidental and purely relative" in that it is, first of all, not a physical property of the commodities, not a fixed part of their physical makeup; and second, it is not a direct expression or *function* of such properties. In short: exchange value is not a direct function of use-value; to that extent exchange value is "accidental and purely relative."

Marx's chain of reasoning may be considered to proceed thus: exchange value fluctuates, but the physical properties of goods remain constant; and not only the physical properties, but the usefulness which they possess on *account* of their useful properties, remains constant. That is, their "use-value," in the general sense of their degree of usefulness, * remains constant.

Therefore exchange value and physical properties, or exchange value and use-value, must be entirely unrelated.

It is a common characteristic of Marx's "dialectical" reasoning that he is able to see only two possibilities, two contradictory extremes: the choice is heads or tails, all or nothing, with no option in between. Either exchange value is a physical phenomenon, fixed once and for all by the inescapable physical makeup of commodities, or else it is random, capricious, "accidental and purely relative."

Since it isn't A, it must be B; since it isn't at one end of the spectrum, it must be all the way to the other, and there's no middle ground. Such is the crude and artificial form of Marx's "dialectical" reasoning.

---

* "Use-value" itself is a Protean term, as Marx uses it. It means usefulness per se, but it also means the *amount* of usefulness (evaluated somehow). Confusingly, it can also mean what a commodity is used for (to eat, to wear, etc.); that is, it means usefulness in the sense of identifying the particular *use* it is put to. From this meaning Marx extends the term to be synonymous with "what a product is," since goods with different uses are, presumably, different commodities. Marx uses each of these meanings at various and random points in his text.

He is able to construct and destroy a straw man without fearing that any theory actually dangerous to his own will be considered. As will become more and more apparent as we proceed, this gives his text a portentous, lofty-sounding character, but makes it actually like a soufflé – overblown, but hollow in the middle.

The "common something"

At any rate, Marx has made the point that exchange value fluctuates while use-value remains constant (and thus the two are entirely unrelated).

Since use-value is not the answer to what determines exchange value, he must look further. He continues:

> Let us consider the argument a little more closely.
> A given commodity, e.g., a quarter [-ton] of wheat is exchanged for x blacking, y silk, or z gold, &c. – in short, for other commodities in the most different proportions. Instead of one exchange value, the wheat has therefore a great many.

It would be more accurate to say that it is the entire collection of these respective amounts of various commodities which, all together, constitute the wheat's exchange value. They all together establish the "quantitative relation" which is its exchange value; the entire collection of pairs of values forms the relation. Marx is creating a rather eccentric definition of the term "exchange value."

But to continue with his text:

> But since x blacking, y silk, or z gold, &c., each represent the exchange value of one quarter of wheat, x blacking, y silk, z gold, &c., must as exchange values be replaceable by each other, or equal to each other.

As has been stated before, this means simply that the relation, exchange value, is a transitive and symmetric relation. That is, the relation of exchange value is a social phenomenon which most closely resembles, in the realm of pure mathematics, the relation of mathematical equality. The axiom holds that, "If $a = c$ and $b = c$, then $a = b$."

Similarly, if x blacking equals a quarter-ton of wheat, and x blacking equals y silk, then a quarter-ton of wheat must equal y silk; if the blacking and wheat are directly exchangeable, and the blacking and silk likewise, then the wheat and silk must be exchangeable.

One lesson to be drawn from all this is that there is nothing special about exchange value as concerns various equal exchange values. "Two things, each equal to a third thing, are equal to each other" – that rule applies to all equivalence relations, i.e. all real-world situations that behave like the mathematical relation of equality. This property of exchange value comes from no special peculiarity of exchange value, but is true by the inherent mathematics of all such situations.

Marx proceeds, drawing a conclusion from this equivalence of the various exchange values of a commodity:

> Therefore, first: the valid exchange values of a given commodity express something equal; secondly, exchange value, generally, is only the mode of expression, the phenomenal form, of something contained in it, yet distinguishable from it.

That sentence is a very model of equivocal language, but giving it our best attempt at interpretation, Marx seems to be reading more into the facts than is warranted. The various valid exchange values express "something equal," no doubt; they express equal exchange value. They express *equality*: the fact that the wheat, blacking, silk, etc., are all deemed commensurate, that they are all of equal market value or purchasing power.

That is, someone with wheat to exchange considers a quarter-ton of it to be equivalent to, or a fair exchange for, x amount of blacking; and conversely for the owner of the blacking. Or more realistically, the sellers of each receive amounts of money such that the comparative values of x amount of blacking and one quarter of wheat are equal. (This ratio applies to all sellers of wheat and blacking generally, or in the aggregate.)

That is all there is to the matter; no conclusion about why such bargains are struck, i.e. why the two goods are exchanged at that particular rate, can be drawn from the mere surface facts as given.

What Marx means by saying exchange values express "something equal," is not just the obvious equality expressed in the exchange value. He means that the equality of the exchange values is an expression of something *else* equal about the goods, something besides exchange value and logically prior to it. His stance will be, that there is some other equality besides equal exchange value at work: there is some other factor or property whose presence in the wheat, blacking, etc., in various proportions determines what amounts of them will have equal exchange values.

In this vein he continues, "exchange value, generally, is only the mode of expression, the phenomenal form, of something contained in it, yet distinguishable from it."

Marx does not put his case very explicitly here, but the minimum he is saying seems to be, "Exchange values were caused by something; they were made to assume the magnitudes they did by some causative factor, and not spontaneously." This is an elementary notion; scientific thinking does not normally assume a given phenomenon is uncaused. The usual point of entry is to ask, "What are the factors that determine such and such a quantity or outcome?" Classical theory would respond with assertions about supply and demand, cost of production, and such economic considerations. Marx's statements so far imply something similar; but he answers on a much more abstract level.

It is hard to discern an exact meaning for his remarks, but he apparently means that the "quantitative relation" which is exchange value is a superficial or "phenomenal" refection of something deeper. That something deeper is a prior and more fundamental "something," which we can tentatively assume is another, "quantitative relation." To put it crudely, the exchange value of 1 quarter wheat equals the exchange value of x blacking because something else was first equal. Something else about the quarter of wheat equaled something about the x blacking. It was this first, prior, unseen "something equal" which manifested itself in visible, "phenomenal form" as equal exchange.

In any case, this is not a cause-and-effect explanation, but metaphysical rhetoric. For one thing, there is no evidence to support his claim that that is how equality of exchange value is determined. Despite his implication that it is a matter of logical deduction, there is no "therefore" to it. He simply makes an unsupported assertion.

That is, there is no observable evidence of any other equal "common something." His formulation is not the language of science, but the language of metaphysics or mystic gnosticism.

At any rate, the picture of reality Marx now conjures up is that of a "something" within the commodity, the magnitude of which determines the commodity's exchange value; so that if goods are of equal exchange value, these equal exchange values express the presence of equal amounts of this "something" within them. In this sense exchange value is an outward expression or "phenomenal form" of the inner something or inner equality-relation.

The presence, within goods, of various amounts of this common something constitutes an inner "quantitative relation," of which exchange value is a subordinate or secondary relation – a reflection in "phenomenal form." Goods are equal in exchange value because they were first equal in the amount of this "something" which they contain.

Marx's line of reasoning

Assuming that the above is an accurate characterization of Marx's theory, we need to study next how he arrived at it. Marx's conclusion was, "Therefore, first: the valid exchange values. . . express something equal"; and, "exchange value. . . is only the mode of expression, the phenomenal form, of something contained in it. . ."

One of the above deductions is vapid and pointless, and the other is incomprehensible. But from what line of reasoning did Marx derive his "Therefore, first. . ."? That is the question.

He deduced his conclusion apparently from nothing more than the fact that one thing, for example a quarter of wheat, is exchangeable for a variety of different things in different amounts, which different amounts he terms different "exchange values" and all of which are equivalent. From these facts alone, he would have it, "therefore" the existence of a third substance can be deduced.

Actually, there is no "therefore" to his discussion. There is no logical or factual connection between the starting point of his argument and the conclusion. Retracing the argument: the wheat is exchangeable for a great variety of commodities in various amounts; or at least, its worth is expressible in terms of any other commodity. And therefore – nothing. There is no conclusion to be drawn from this fact, nor from the fact that all the various "exchange value" are equivalent; that is in the nature of *any* equality relation.

In actuality, what Marx is entitled to give us, from the facts presented in his text up to this point, is not a definitive explanation of exchange value, but only a statement of the problem. The question before us is how commensurability is established or determined – how such diverse and non-uniform objects as houses, wheat, silk, harmonicas and so on can all be assigned exchange values and thus by inference by exchanged on an equal or commensurate basis.

Or rather, the question is not how it *can* be done (as if we were free to devise a system ourselves), but how it *is* done, every day on the market. Taking the price of a house and the price of a harmonica (a particular house and a particular type of harmonica), it is possible to compute that, for example, "The exchange value of the house is 8,000 harmonicas."*

How can relative worth for such diverse items be determined? How, in fact, is it done? Those are empirical questions, and they must be answered in empirical, real-world terms – not with specious arguments trumped up from whole cloth, mere "dialectics" or verbal gymnastics.

To get a perspective on the question, it may help to turn to another author for a more thorough and explicit statement than Marx's of the basic problem of exchange value.

---

* These figures are chosen assuming a price of $8 for the harmonica and $64,000 for the house.

Mortimer Adler writes in *The Capitalist Manifesto*:

> So far as we know, Marx and Aristotle offer the only recorded solutions to the problem of how to commensurate the value of heterogeneous things in order to determine equivalents for the purpose of. . . exchange. [2]

Adler goes on to explain that for heterogeneous goods there is no obvious standard, no one characteristic which in the case of all commodities can serve as a measure of their exchange value. We can't say for instance, "Equal weights of all commodities should be of equal value." The useful properties of different commodities are different; and commodities are measured in different ways.

Edible things like wheat are measured by weight, and even so a pound of apples is not self-evidently equivalent to a pound of wheat. Moreover, houses aren't weighed and sold by the pound. There is no one property which can serve as a universal standard.

While there seems to be no one physical, objective standard, nevertheless heterogeneous goods are traded; their exchange values are determined. How is it done?

"Aristotle recognized," Adler continues, "that we cannot equate qualitatively different commodities, unless they can somehow be made commensurable; but lacking any objective and common measure of their exchange value, he found that there was no way to commensurate qualitatively different things." That is a succinct statement of the problem.

Now let us switch for a time to Marx's voice. He has his own perspective on Aristotle's inquiry into this subject (*Capital*, Part I, Chapter I, Section 3):

> He [Aristotle] further sees that the value relation which gives rise to this expression ["5 beds = 1 house"] makes it necessary that the house should qualitatively be made the equal of the bed, and that, "without such an equalization, these two clearly different things could not be compared with each other as commensurable quantities." "Exchange," he says, "cannot take place without equality, and equality not without commensurability." . . . Here, however, he comes to a stop, and gives up the further analysis of the form of value ["form of value" being a jargon term of Marx's]. "It is, however, in reality, impossible. . ., that such unlike things can be commensurable" – i.e., qualitatively equal. Such an equalization can only be something foreign to their real nature, consequently only "a make-shift for practical purposes."
>
> Aristotle therefore, himself, tells us, what barred the way to his

further analysis; it was the absence of any concept of value. What is that equal something, that common substance, which admits of the value of the beds being expressed by a house? Such a thing, in truth, cannot exist, says Aristotle.

Marx, however, believes in the existence of this "common substance," and will reveal its identity to us. He says Aristotle lacked "any concept of value" because he could not find a common thing or substance which was every commodity's value. Marx can find such a common substance, we are to understand, and he will present it as the physically incarnated "value" of commodities. Marx proposes to "dissect out" the exchange value from within the actual physical confines of the commodity itself.

From this we can see how Marx's view of exchange value and Aristotle's can be characterized by Adler as the only two views of exchange value, the only two explanations of how "the value of heterogeneous things" is compared. Marx's view is what we may call the organic, or internal, viewpoint: that there is something within the commodities themselves which serves to establish their value – some physical property or "common substance" whose existence in particular amounts in various commodities is the more basic reality, of which exchange value is only "the mode of expression, the phenomenal form." This unseen, inner property actually serves to commensurate various amounts of different commodities. It is logically primary; exchange value is secondary and dependent on it, and is an outward, observable expression of it, a "phenomenal form" of it which is observable in the real world.

To the "organic" or "internal" theory of exchange value, we may oppose Aristotle's view, which indeed became the view of almost everyone else who considered the question until Marx. Aristotle considered what the common inner substance could be, and concluded that there in fact could be none, and that the key to the determination of exchange value lay *outside* the commodity.

As Adler sums this viewpoint up,

> [A] just exchange of qualitatively different things requires that they be of equivalent value. "All goods," Aristotle declares, "must therefore be measured by some one thing," and "this unit. . . is in truth demand, which holds all things together; for if men did not need one another's goods at all, or did not need them equally, there would be either no exchange or not an equal exchange." Aristotle admits, as Marx says, that it is impossible for the qualitatively heterogeneous to be made perfectly commensurate; "but. . . with reference to demand they may become so sufficiently."[3]

Aristotle's view thus was contrary to Marx's later one. He saw exchange value as externally-determined, not as a property or characteristic of the commodity itself. His conclusions were remarkably insightful for the time, and despite all that has been added to economic theory over the centuries, his basic explanation of exchange value as located outside the commodity retains its validity.

To Marx's organic or interior theory, then, we can contrast Aristotle's external or social theory. Exchange value is not a purely physical or material phenomenon, reducible to the physical properties of goods. Exchange value after all is a result of human activity; it doesn't exist in nature. Exchange value is not a physical phenomenon, but a social one, determined by human interactions, i.e., markets; and it cannot be analyzed in purely physical, material terms like mass, energy, velocity, and so on. Exchange value is external and social, not internal and physical.

Aristotle gives us no exact quantitative formula governing value; for nothing social, or human-determined, can be entirely reduced to mathematically rigorous and exact terms. It is impossible to assign exact, objective exchange values to heterogeneous goods, making them perfectly commensurated; "but . . . with reference to demand they may become so sufficiently." Or, as Adam Smith would put it, within the bounds of the "higgling and bargaining" of the marketplace, commensurability could be established.

In sum, then, Aristotle resolved on an external or social determination of exchange value, while Marx gave an "internal" view, one which was mechanistic or deterministic, based on the perceived or deduced amounts of a "common substance." It will perhaps not be giving anything away to reveal at this point what Marx will come to identify as the "common substance." He says, "What is that equal something, that common substance, which admits of the value of the beds being expressed by a house? Such a thing, in truth, cannot exist, says Aristotle. And why not? Compared with the beds, the house does represent something equal to them, in so far as it represents what is really equal, both in the beds and in the house. And that is – human labor."

Thus Marx not only sets out hunting the snark, he finds it. He equates his inquiry into the determination of exchange value to the search for a "common substance," and he identifies the substance: labor. (The reader may as well begin getting used to the notion of labor as a substance; it will be a central theme of Marx's text.)

To apply a bit of *a posteriori* reasoning, the fact that in all the centuries between Aristotle and Marx no one had ever attempted to return to the internal, "common-something" view of exchange value, could plausibly be attributed to the fact that Aristotle was right – indeed compellingly, obviously right. The contrary view, Marx's view or what we might for convenience call the "pre-Aristotelian" view, has been, at least since the time Aristotle wrote, untenable.

(The term "pre-Aristotelian" is used, not to imply that anyone actually *held* that view before Aristotle wrote, but simply to indicate that such a view could never have been respectable *after* he wrote. The term "pre-Aristotelian" is used to denote a view Aristotle considered and rejected before going on to state his own view. An equally accurate characterization, in this day and age, would be the "Neanderthal" view.)

Marx however gives a different explanation of where Aristotle went astray:

> There was, however, an important fact which prevented Aristotle from seeing that, to attribute value to commodities, is merely a mode of expressing all labor as equal human labor, and consequently as labor of equal quality. Greek society was founded upon slavery, and had, therefore, for its natural basis, the inequality of men and of their labor powers. The secret of the expression of value, namely, that all kinds of labor are equal and equivalent, because, and so far as they are human labor in general, cannot be deciphered, until the notion of human equality has already acquired the fixity of a popular prejudice. This, however, is possible only in a society in which the great mass of the produce of labor takes the form of commodities. . . The peculiar conditions of the society in which he lived, alone prevented him from discovering what, "in truth," was at the bottom of this equality.

Thus Marx's patronizing and superstitious explanation of what prevented Aristotle from finding the truth. This is an example of a common trope of Marx's, a particular type of mystical sophistry to which he frequently resorts. Marx's underlying assumption is that material things, i.e., physical externalities, somehow control or influence what goes on in the intellectual realm, in men's thoughts. Marx adopts this anti-scientific attitude on no basis at all except that it fits the system of thought he wants to establish. He assumes it from whole cloth and clings to it adamantly, as if it were proven fact.

It is actually a view much like astrology; it asserts that the conditions of external, material objects somehow have a controlling effect on the internal realm of human thoughts and behavior. For Marx, economic externalities have "a mysterious power to cloud men's minds."

And thus we are shown Aristotle, unable to discover what was at the bottom of exchange value because Greek society had slaves! That is very convenient for Marx; by directing his remarks to the nature of Greek society and thus the supposed limitations it placed on Aristotle's thought-processes, Marx is able to issue a patronizing *ad hominem* dismissal, without having to respond to the specifics of what Aristotle said. It is a shallow rhetorical maneuver. (This is especially so when we consider, as noted, that in the first place Aristotle gave the right answer to the question of exchange value; Marx's theory is crude and atavistic.)

To sum up then, Marx's theory of a "common something" displays his materialistic or naturalistic view of exchange value, which treats value as a result of some physical characteristic of the commodity. For him, the fact that particular goods have equal exchange value is due to their possessing equal amounts of this common internal property or substance. The respective amounts of this hidden common something form a relation "contained in" exchange value, on which relation exchange value depends and of which it is an external, visible, "phenomenal" reflection.

Thus goes Marx's theory; it is a denial not only of classical economics but of modern science and the principles of causation. In contrast, there is the Aristotelian view of exchange value as being determined externally and economically, by factors impinging on the people involved in trade – not mechanistically in a kind of quasi-physics of value.

1 quarter corn = x cwt. iron

Let us pick up Marx's argument again. He elaborates on his view of exchange value:

> Let us take two commodities, e.g., corn and iron. The proportions in which they are exchangeable . . . can always be represented by an equation in which a given quantity of corn is equated to some quantity of iron: e.g., 1 quarter corn = x cwt iron. What does this equation tell us? It tells us that in two different things – in 1 quarter of corn and x cwt of iron, there exists in equal quantities something common to both.

That is precisely what it does not tell us. That assertion is produced from whole cloth; it is an assumption chosen by Marx with no basis in fact or logic. And in addition, it is an incorrect, wrong-headed and primitive view.

At any rate, Marx does not immediately identify the "common something"; but his text will address that topic in due time.

The two things must therefore be equal to a third

Now from the fact that the common factor or property exists in equal quantities in the two different commodities, Marx deduces a third "something."

> What does this equation tell us? It tells us that in two different
> things – in 1 quarter of corn and x cwt of iron, there exists in equal
> quantities something common to both. The two things must there-
> fore be equal to a third, which in itself is neither the one nor the
> other. Each of them, so far as it is exchange value, must therefore be
> reducible to this third.

That is, "the two things must therefore be equal to a third," whose existence is thus proven.

To recapitulate: the point of Marx's proof seems to be that, since each of the two commodities contains something (presumably exchange value) in equal amounts, these "two things" must be equal to a third. This third thing is the ultimate source of value. That is, each of the first two "common somethings" (or perhaps each of the first two commodities) is "reducible to," or caused by, this third – the unidentified "common something."

The law which Marx is implicitly propounding is, *Whenever two things are equal to each other in exchange value, they were first each equal to some prior third quantity; and they are therefore "reducible" to it.* By invoking this law, Marx deduces the existence of the third quantity or "substance," and states that this third quantity is what caused the equality of the first two quantities, the exchange values.

Fractured algebra

The provenance of Marx's logic is fairly easy to see; it is derived from algebra. In fact, his argument is a corruption of one of the axioms (basic assumptions) of algebra.

In essence, his proof of the existence of a third thing could be expressed like this: two commodities contain equal amounts of some property or "common substance" (perhaps exchange value). That is, we have two equal quantities, A = B. These two quantities "must therefore be equal to a third" – that is, for some C, A = C and B = C.

According to Marx, it was this third quantity, C, which actually caused the equal exchange values all along: "Each of [the first two quantities], so far as it is exchange value, must . . . be reducible to this third." That is, A equals B because in the first place A equaled C and B equaled C. Thus C is the original, ultimate substance which is the source of exchange value.

Regardless of what the various substances or letters stand for, the logic of this proof is mangled algebra. Marx's axiom, if we may label it such, is "If A = B, then there is some C such that A = C and B = C." That is a corruption or misstatement of a genuine axiom: "If A = C and B = C, then

A = B." Marx has it just backwards.

The real axiom, to repeat, is "Two quantities, each equal to a third quantity, are equal to each other." Marx renders that as, "If two things are equal, it is because there was first some third thing to which they both were equal." That is a puerile misstatement – a mistake on an elementary level. Not only is it *not* an axiom, it is nonsense.

The real algebraic axiom is easy to understand, and is generally covered in beginning arithmetic or algebra courses. For example, if a+2b = 17, and 3a+b = 17, we have two different algebraic expressions which are both equal to 17. We are then justified in saying a+2b = 3a+b. "Two quantities, each equal to a third quantity, are equal to each other." That is an axiom, a truism, of mathematics.

By contrast, what conclusion can we draw from the bare fact that, say, x+2y = 5? Or from the fact that A = B? Nothing – at least, not Marx's conclusion that A = C and B = C.

For what he is really saying is that whenever A = B, *there is* some C such that A = C and B = C. That is an unwarranted assumption. If we know that $x^2 = y+3$, for instance, what is the third quantity to which both x^2 and y+3 are equal? There isn't any third quantity; you have to pull it out of your hat. Marx's implicit axiom is a fallacy, and a mathematically illiterate one at that.

The genuine axiom

In economic terms, we can see the validity of the genuine axiom. If one quarter corn is exchangeable for z gold, i.e. if 1 quarter corn = z gold (whatever the amount z is); and if 1 quarter corn = x cwt. iron; then z gold should = x cwt. iron. There's no great mystery in that.

Or, again: if 1 quarter corn sells for $180, and z gold sells for $180, then we say the gold and the corn have an equal monetary exchange value, and we would expect them to be directly exchangeable, should anyone want to do so.

But try to illustrate Marx's inverted form of the axiom; if 1 quarter corn = z gold, then what? The only inference that can be drawn from this fact is the fact itself: that for whatever economic reasons, the present exchange value of 1 quarter corn is equal to z gold. That is *all* that can be deduced from the simple fact of exchange at the given relative amounts.

If 1 quarter corn = z gold, what is the c, the third quantity such that 1 quarter corn = c and z gold = c? There might be such a quantity, but simply from the facts as given, we don't know it. One has to invent it, conjure it up from thin air; or else look at the market to find another quantity by observation (not by deduction from the given premise).

A geometrical "example"

Not content with butchering algebra, Marx goes on to mutilate geometry with this "illustration":

> A simple geometrical illustration will make this clear. In order to calculate and compare the areas of rectilinear figures, we decompose them into triangles. But the area of the triangle itself is expressed by something totally different from its visible figure, namely, by half the product of the base into the altitude. In the same way the exchange values of commodities must be capable of being expressed in terms of something common to them all, of which thing they represent a greater or less quantity.

It is hard to make coherent sense out of this, but perhaps we can discern the general contours of Marx's meaning. His overall point, again, is something like, "When two quantities are equal, there is a third quantity to which both were first equal." Or, "If A = B, then A = C and B = C."

In broad terms, Marx first introduces two quantities: one, the polygon as a whole, and two, the triangles carved from it. We want to calculate the area of a rectilinear figure, or polygon – that is presumably the first quantity.

We will assume then that the first quantity is the area of the single polygon, and the second is the areas of the triangles – that is, the sum of the individual areas of the triangles. These two quantities are equal. The reasoning then proceeds, Since the first quantity equals the second quantity, there must be a third quantity which each of them equals and to which they are "reducible." And in this role Marx places 1/2bh, that is, half the product of the base times the height (of each triangle in turn – the "1/2bh's" would also be summed). Thus we have illustration or proof that whenever there are two equal quantities, they are "reducible to" or due to a third quantity, in this case 1/2bh.

In reality, there are not two separate quantities here, each putatively caused by the amount of the third "something." The area of a triangle and 1/2bh are the same quantity, the same "substance"; 1/2bh is just one way (among several) of calculating the area of the triangle; it is a formula for deriving the area. It is neither a third quantity nor a substance.

The main problem with Marx's geometrical illustration is (and here it is necessary to speak in general terms) that it is arrant nonsense. The whole illustration is completely malapropos, inapt and preposterous, and in no way illustrates what he thinks it does.

Ultimately, what Marx means to show in his illustration is, "If two quantities are equal, there must be a third quantity to which they were first equal." His geometrical example fails to show that. What his example really shows, if anything, is, *The whole is equal to the sum of its parts.* Other than that, no coherent point is made by it. It doesn't rise to a sufficient level of coherency so as to be subject to criticism. As one author remarked,

> According to Bertrand Russell, some propositions lack even the capacity to be false, by which he meant that they are too shapeless to be refuted. . . Karl Popper argues along the same lines: only a statement that has a minimum degree of coherence can be proved false.[4]

Marx's fractured geometrical "example" is just such sub-coherent prose.

Review

In his elaboration of his labor theory so far, Marx has made two main points: first, that use-value is not what determines the magnitude of exchange value; and second, that what does determine exchange value is some "common substance" or property within the commodities themselves. His reasoning proceeds this way: first, exchange value is "accidental" and "purely relative," in that it is not a constant magnitude "inseparably connected with" a commodity. To put it another way, exchange value is not a physical attribute of the commodity, and not a direct result of such an attribute.

Next, exchange value is nevertheless due to "something equal" about commodities, some "common substance" contained in all commodities in definite amounts; exchange value is determined by the amount of this "common substance" and is in fact a "phenomenal form" of the magnitude of this internal substance. Having established all this, Marx can proceed to identify this unknown inner substance.

That is the point his text has reached so far; we will now form a broad view of that much of the argument before proceeding further.

One striking fact is that Marx's argument has almost nothing in common with the modern scientific method of investigation. There is almost no analysis of factual data, no reference to experiment or observation designed to verify or refute a hypothesis. In particular, it is not an attempt to discover empirically what objectively-discernible factors govern the magnitude of exchange value.

Rather, what Marx gives us is a deductive argument, applied to a starting set of selected facts and arbitrarily-chosen axioms.

Broadly speaking then, Marx's text is a path of logical deduction within the context of an arbitrarily-constructed theoretical system. In this sense it is a throwback to the methods of previous ages – methods of purely mental investigation in an "ivory tower" or armchair environment. These methods (as one author expressed it) "subordinated sensory observation and promoted the abstract at the expense of the practical." [5]

The same author stated that the method of armchair theorizing, which was adopted by the Schoolmen or the Scholastics, is what results when "science is regarded merely as cerebration or introspective thought-process." [6]

In fact, we can express the mentality of the "dark ages," as compared to modern scientific inquiry, as a matter of the deductive as opposed to the inductive method of investigation.

According to *Man and the Cosmos* (a general, survey work), science, in the sense of factual investigation, was not unknown to the ancient Greeks:

> [W]hat we are so often disposed to call "modern scientific method" existed in its essentials 2,500 years ago. It went astray because of the Platonic enthronement of the intellect that subordinated sensory observation and promoted the abstract at the expense of the practical. (Experiment was popularly held to be for rude mechanics and not for the intellectual aristocracy.) This carried over into the age of the Churchmen and the Schoolmen, many of whom sought to discourage inquisitiveness as a threat to belief and dogma.[8]

That describes Marx's method perfectly – a series of deductions from self-evident (at least to Marx) premises. It is useful to ask ourselves how such a method as his, reverting to the practice of the centuries before the arrival of modern science, ever came to be deemed "progressive." That was unfortunate, because:

> Science depends on the power of observation, and observation means contact with external events or natural phenomena through the senses. When (as happened with the Schoolmen) science is regarded merely as cerebration or introspective thought-process, it becomes stagnant...

Like the Schoolmen, Marx reasons deductively, from chosen premises, within his created, closed system; not inductively, from a mass of pertinent objective data – i.e., not scientifically.

We have seen the general outline of Marx's argument. The facts on which he builds his theory of exchange value are first, that exchange value fluctuates; and second, that use-value, or the useful physical properties of goods, does not. Beginning from this slim basis in facts, he embarks on a series of deductions, some based on those "facts" and some (like his adoption of the "pre-Aristotelian" view of value) assumed out of thin air. Deduction builds on deduction, with each successive theorem being based on those which preceded it. In this sense Marx's approach is like mathematics, with a set of initial axioms, and each successive theorem being deduced from preceding theorems and axioms. But Marx claims his theorems are binding on the real world.

One author, Eugen von Böhm-Bawerk, has commented on the nature of Marx's work, in *Karl Marx and the Close of His System*. He said,

> The fundamental proposition which Marx puts before his readers is that the exchange value of commodities. . . finds its origin and its measure in the quantity of labor incorporated in the commodities.
>
> Now it is certain that the exchange values, that is to say the prices of the commodities as well as the quantities of labor which are necessary for their reproduction, are real, external quantities, which on the whole it is quite possible to determine empirically. Obviously, therefore, Marx ought to have turned to experience for the proof of a proposition the correctness or incorrectness of which must be manifested in the facts of experience; or in other words, he should have given a purely empirical proof in support of a proposition adapted to a purely empirical proof. . .
>
> Now Marx, instead of proving his thesis from experience or from its operant motives. . . prefers another, and for such a subject somewhat singular line of evidence – the method of a purely logical proof, a dialectical deduction from the very nature of exchange. [7]

Thus it is that one of the first striking aspects of Marx's exposition of his labor theory of value is not what he says, but what he does not say – his failure to present factual data, and his whole approach to his subject as a matter for logical and "dialectical" reasoning, not factual inquiry.

This "dialectical" method, or this method of deductive logic, has been shown to be totally inadequate for discovering objective, scientific facts. Since the development of the modern scientific method, it is a great wonder that anyone would have had the effrontery, or perhaps ignorance, to revert to it again. Even when used honestly, and not accompanied by specious logic and deceptive rhetorical maneuvers, it is inadequate for investigating factual matters.

Elements of Marx's method

Marx has one fundamental assumption, passed off as logical deduction: that exchange value can only be caused or determined by "something in" the commodities, a common property or substance.

At the same time, Marx's "pre-Aristotelian" viewpoint excludes from consideration such unwelcome views about exchange value as that it is controlled or determined from outside the commodity (by such factors as market conditions, or as Aristotle concluded, by demand). In short, his chosen assumption saves him from considering the entire, widely-held body of thought known as classical theory, a system of thought worked out over centuries, intuitively credible because of its treatment of the nature of economics and human economic behavior, and firmly supported by the enormous mass of facts available. Marx simply writes as if this entire theory or viewpoint did not exist; or at least, he offers no rebuttal of it in its own terms.

In other words, rather than considering and dismissing the factors of supply and demand in determining exchange value or price, Marx goes for a soft target, a straw man – use-value. He easily sets this up and then knocks it down again. Presumably he felt justified in this approach because classical theory, with its appeal to the factors of supply and demand as determining exchange value, did not fit within his closed system. It lay outside his assumption of a "common internal substance" and therefore could not be correct. Therefore it required no discussion at all.

The advantage of Marx's approach is at least as much in what he is able to keep out of the discussion as in what he introduces into it. The ability or willingness to stage-manage the discussion and hem it in within certain restricted channels is a great advantage for pre-determining the results; and it is made possible by his purely rhetorical, "dialectical" method: he turns the whole investigation into "a thing of words," not a matter of substance. It is a reductionist, as well as a deductive method: it reduces what should be a thorough inquiry into all the facts and every possible explanation, to a circumscribed, closed system of chosen assumptions, axioms and definitions. From an investigation of the real world, it becomes a pointless exercise within the context of an artificial theoretical model.

Scientific laws

If Marx had been interested in an empirical investigation, in finding an *actual* correlation of factors in the real world, he would have been forced to resort to classical theory; for such cause-and-effect relationships can be established. One can identify the pertinent factors, such things as the market environment; economic considerations like cost of manufacture and conditions of supply and demand; human economic behavior and the factors motivating and impinging on each agent involved in the market; and so on. One can find a direct correlation among supply, demand, and exchange value. On a cause-and-effect, empirical level, classical economics gives the answer.

Instead of working on that level, Marx embarks on a dissection of the commodity, a microscopic "analysis of a commodity" in metaphysical terms. Using philosophical speculation and sham logic, he can produce the answer he wants.

Marx disdains merely "phenomenal" things, which have as their only merit the fact that they actually exist in the real world. He clings to the inner, unseen reality which can only be inferred or deduced through his sophistical rhetoric, and he endows that rhetoric with a higher order of validity and authority. This is Gnostic mysticism, not science.

Dialectical form of reasoning

It remains to be said that Marx's "dialectical" form of reasoning is in this instance hopelessly inadequate. Judging from the present argument, what that reasoning consists of is the mere outward form of Socratic dialogue. That is, Marx first asks himself a question, and then answers it; this presumably constitutes proof.

His "dialectic" with himself is: "What does this equation tell us? It tells us. . ." and so on. Now, there may be points to be made in favor of the Socratic method. (As a teaching method, a means of getting students to think, it is excellent. However, as a method for deriving factual matters – as science – it is inadequate; it is nothing like the modern scientific method.)

But surely no Socratic dialogue was ever as thin, substanceless, and meretricious as Marx's imitation of it. Arm-chair philosophizing or the use of "thought experiments" is in general an unscientific method; but surely before Marx it had never sunk so low. In his case it reduces to simple unsupported assertion. It should be apparent to anyone with even a modicum of scientific understanding that it is not proof.

Recapitulation of Marx's Method

> *"You'll have to think of a fresh theory now, Doctor."*
> *"It is not necessary. My theory was a perfectly good one. The facts were misleading."*
>   – "The Lady Vanishes," directed by Alfred Hitchcock, 1938

We have already seen how Marx demonstrates the existence of a "common something," first algebraically from the fact that two quantities equal to each other "must therefore be equal to a third," and then by mathematical illustrations. Nothing more needs to be said about those proofs, but perhaps a perspective of his overall argument can be added.

The question, as it has emerged from Marx's text, is, "What is the common property existing in all goods, whose magnitude in any given item determines its exchange value?" The field of inquiry has been restricted to the "internal contents" of the commodity itself, to those properties or phenomena which can be considered (whether plausibly or implausibly) to be properties *of* the commodity, contained in it. That the question could devolve into this state is a consequence of a whole series of assumptions made by Marx about exchange value.

Exchange value is treated, first of all, much like any other physical property of objects. A dynamic quantity which arises as a result of human activities is treated like an objective aspect of nature. This is an abuse of the nature of exchange value. Human behavior, markets, economic exigency — these do not make an appearance in Marx's analysis. Marx's theory is a misrepresentation of the very nature of the subject.

Let us examine some of the specific characteristics of Marx's text which deviate from genuine science. First of all, Marx's system is *deductive*, in contrast to the scientific method, which could be called *inductive*. Marx's reasoning proceeds very much in the manner of say, a geometry textbook. There is a setting forth of certain axioms and definitions (with one or two objective facts being allowed into the discussion); and from this basis all further results are deduced, with each further "theorem" being based on what has gone before it (adding whatever further definitions and axioms are necessary). The entire theoretical system that emerges thus depends entirely on the axioms and definitions chosen; the system is arbitrary and purely theoretical. Marx's theory is a "formal system," in the sense that it is a system of formal logic, produced "for argument" only. It is theoretical and conceptual, as opposed to empirical and actual.

As opposed to this let us say, "top-down" approach, genuine science is a "bottom-up" approach. Typically, it proceeds by the accumulation of a body of facts through observation or experiment; the scientist attempts to discern the regularity or underlying law at work in the facts: the reasoning is inductive.

And while in modern science the actual work of forming a hypothesis does not proceed in a clear-cut inductive manner, the process of verification of a hypothesis is inductive; experimentation or observation is done exhaustively until one can say with some degree of confidence, "It has happened this way in every case we have observed; let us conclude that it always happens this way."

The distinguishing feature, then, is that science is above all a report of the facts, often taking the form of the discovery of order implicit in the facts, or of valid generalizations which can be drawn from the facts.

Marx's method is one of abstract logical deductions from chosen assumptions. And there are three main problems with his use of this method:

first, his assumptions are bad; second, his logic is bad: third, the method itself is bad – it is not science and says nothing accurate about the real world.

Besides being deductive, Marx's system is *prescriptive* (as opposed to descriptive). He adopts a general approach of bullying or browbeating reality. Marx creates a theoretical system, which he then grants presumptive authenticity as a representation of the real world; he imposes his theory by fiat, brute force and overbearing rhetoric. His attitude seems to be, "My theory is correct; it is the facts that are mistaken."

Marx's text proceeds not so much by a seeking out of the facts as by excluding the facts so that he can proceed with creating his hypothetical world. But rather than admit that his result is a formal, not actual, system, and that it in no way describes the facts of the real world, Marx blithely assumes that his theory is authoritative. His theory overrules any objections of the real world.

Marx turns his attention from the real world to the constructing of a fantasy, and seeks to enthrone that fantasy as reality (or, if not as the real or "phenomenal" world, then as an "inner" reality, of a higher order of validity than the real world). In fact, from this point on in Marx's text, his subject will not actually be the real world, which is now discarded as irrelevant, but rather the hypothetical system he has produced from his own imagining. He will base his logic and reasoning on the already-deduced "theorems" of that fictive system.

Marx produces his answers from nothing, by working up rhetoric and specious logic into the consistency of an argument. It is the height of superstition to take the resulting product as a true picture of the real world.

The mystery factor

What we have so far, then, is this: exchange value is determined by some "common substance" or mystery factor within goods. Marx's viewpoint is that "the exchange values of commodities must be capable of being expressed in terms of something common to them all, of which things they represent a greater or lesser quantity."

Marx now turns to the task of discovering the identity of the common something, the value-determining factor within commodities. He continues:

> This common something cannot be either a geometrical, a
> chemical, or any other natural property of commodities.

That is an unexceptionable, even obvious, statement. No one would ever suppose exchange value was determined by the shape, or geometric configuration, of commodities. ("Square goods are more valuable than round goods," etc.?) Nor could the answer be chemical. ("Acidic compounds are worth more than basic; organic more than inorganic," etc.?) The suggestion is childishly simple-minded.

Its function is apparently not to supply information, but to supply a semblance of an argument, a straw man to knock down. This is the more evident in that Marx does not feel compelled to discuss any other, more normal, possible explanations of exchange value, like supply and demand. He discusses only a possibility ridiculously easy to dismiss.

Marx explains the reason physical properties cannot be the "common something": "Such properties claim our attention only in so far as they affect the utility of those commodities, make them use-values. But the exchange of commodities is evidently an act characterized by a total abstraction from use-value."

That is, physical properties do only one thing – or as Marx puts it, they "claim our attention" for only one thing; they create or cause the commodities' use-value. And use-value, as we presumably already know, is entirely unrelated to exchange value, or "is . . . characterized by a total abstraction from exchange value." Thus, since the only thing physical properties do is cause use-value, they can't determine exchange value; that is, natural properties don't determine the magnitude of exchange value.

That is a perfect bit of circular logic. Physical properties cannot be the cause of exchange value, because they only cause use-value. And the reason he knows they only cause use-value is that they don't determine anything else, including exchange value.

Marx *appears* to be giving a reasoned argument; but the result of his argument is actually implicit in his original premise or assumption; and he had adopted that assumption without supporting evidence of any kind.

Let us also consider for a moment the statement, "the exchange of commodities is . . . characterized by a total abstraction from use-value." Marx has proved this statement, to his own satisfaction at least. But how does it compare to the real world?

(It is useful, every once in a while, to lift our eyes from Marx's abstractions and consider the real world. "Paper will accept anything," as the Russian proverb has it. It is important not to be lulled by the hypnotic droning effect of words alone, but to mentally cross-check even the most seductive line of reasoning against our own experience of the world around us.)

Is the actual act of exchange, or let us call it the actual purchase of an item of merchandise, totally "abstracted from" considerations of use-value? Does the useful nature of the goods never enter the mind of the buyer? Are we to believe the buyer wants bread or apples, but that the thought never crosses his mind that these commodities are useful as food? Such an assertion is far-fetched. It is more realistic to say that, far from being totally unconnected to exchange, use-value is the ultimate reason for all exchange – that it is for their useful properties that goods are purchased, and that use-value is the source of all demand and thus of all exchange as such.

To be fair, we might assume generously that in saying use-value is totally abstracted from exchange, he means in a quantitative sense: use-value does not determine the magnitude of exchange value. That is after all what his whole argument is pointed at – use-value remains constant in magnitude, while exchange value varies, and so on. Marx's prose puts the case a little too definitively, but we can overlook that.

The fact remains that first, it is not obvious that use-value remains a constant; it is not precisely quantifiable. And as previously stated, use-value, even though constant, may be one factor among several that determine exchange value; it may set a base magnitude for exchange value, over which other factors superimpose a modulating influence. Though not the complete answer, use-value itself may still be related to exchange value. (In any case, use-value is not, as Marx conceives it, a natural property contained in the commodity. Usefulness is defined in relation to human *use* of the product; it does not exist in isolation as an actual physical entity. It is not a phenomenon on the same level with exchange value.)

Whatever determines the magnitude of exchange value, it is use-value which is the ultimate reason for trade, for demand, for exchange, and for exchange value. The two are not entirely unrelated. And anyway, Marx's ultimate subject is exchange itself; and even if use-value can be entirely divorced from exchange value, it must yet be seen as the motivating factor for exchange as such.

There is of course the question of the *magnitude* of exchange value, i.e., of what factors determine it. But we may discern or distinguish another question, namely, that of the *source* of exchange value. This latter is not necessarily subsumed in the former.

To be explicit: the reason for all exchange, the source of all exchange value, is (arguably) demand for products, which in turn may be seen as due to the usefulness of the products. It is for their useful properties that people buy goods (that is, useful either in the strict, utilitarian sense of being good to eat or wear, or in the broader sense of being good to look at or listen to, like art or music).

This question of the *source* of exchange value can be distinguished from that of what determines the magnitude of exchange value. This is not a difficult concept.

In the same way, use-value is an ever-present consideration in human minds, in the matter of exchange; it cannot be considered to be entirely unrelated to exchange value, for it is the source of demand, and ultimately, exchange; and without exchange there is no "quantitative relation obtained in exchange," no exchange value.

The magnitude of the exchange value is another matter. Here market conditions are determinative. While use-value in an abstract sense may be constant, the amount a person will be willing to pay for the useful product will depend on conditions that vary; and so will the amount the seller will be willing to accept.

(For example, the usefulness of bread, let us say, is constant, at least in the sense that it is edible; its physical characteristics are constant. But the *amount* someone will pay for a loaf of it will be much greater in conditions of greatly-decreased supply, as during a war or famine. We see again how exchange value is determined by more objective, quantifiable factors than use-value. Usefulness, "use-value," is less definitive and less quantifiable.)

Marx goes on to further document his case that use-value is "totally abstracted from" exchange value, and that thus by inference physical properties are also unrelated to exchange value, since their only function is to produce use-value:

> Then one use-value is just as good as another, provided only it be present in sufficient quantity. Or, as old Barbon says, "One sort of wares are as good as another, if the [exchange] values be equal. There is no difference or distinction in things of equal value. . . An hundred pounds' worth of lead or iron, is of as great value as one hundred pounds' worth of silver or gold." As use-value, commodities are, above all, of different qualities, but as exchange values they are merely different quantities, and consequently do not contain an atom of use-value.

The significance of this passage is mostly lost on us today (much as is that of "Old Barbon"). It seems to concern a point which, if it ever had economic significance, is by now settled and moot, so much so as to be a truism.

The passage, remember, is an amplification of the statement, "the exchange of commodities is evidently an act characterized by a total abstraction from use-value." The point Marx is making here is apparently this: all commodities have different use-values, different uses (that is, they are different *commodities*); yet they may have the same exchange value. Therefore it follows that use-value must be unrelated to exchange value. Marx says then, use-value is irrelevant to exchange value: "one use-value is just as good as another, provided only it be present in sufficient quantity."

That is, one *commodity* is just as good as another, provided you have enough of it to equal the other's exchange value. (Marx now uses the term "use-value" to denote the identity of the good itself.)

Marx's statement then becomes, "the exchange of commodities is. . . characterized by a total abstraction from what the commodities are." That is, exchange value functions the same for all commodities; what the commodity is makes no difference. And similarly, Marx's statement means "one commodity is just as good as another," provided its exchange value is great enough.

Barbon says, "One sort of wares are as good as another, if the values be equal." That is, one kind of wares are as valuable as another if their values are equal. Or, "There is no difference or distinction in [the exchange value of] things of equal [exchange] value" – not exactly an earthshaking revelation. We are told that a hundred pounds-sterling's worth of lead or iron is worth as much as a hundred pounds' worth of silver or gold – to be specific, a hundred pounds. But the fact remains, this doesn't prove use-value is unrelated to exchange value.

In any case, Marx has made the point that exchange value is not dependent on "use-value" in the sense of what the product is. One use-value is just as good as another if the exchange value is sufficient. This sentiment is seconded by old Barbon, and in regard to this line of argument it can only be said that Marx has an inexhaustible affinity for banality. He finds marvelous depths of significance, great intricacies of meaning, in the most pedestrian observations.

Identifying the "common something"

> If then we leave out of consideration the use-value of commodities, they have only one common property left, that of being products of labor.

Marx makes a quick finish to his argument. Here we see the glib finale of Marx's chain of deductions: exchange value implies the existence of a "common substance," which cannot be use-value and which therefore must be, by process of elimination, the only remaining common property of all commodities: labor. It is a suspiciously facile argument, and suspiciously definitive.

What is absent from the argument is first, any indication that Marx's logical deductions are honestly arrived at. Is he actually considering all the reasonable candidates for the role of "common something"? Is his text a serious and sincere logical exercise, or a glib excuse for advancing his chosen candidate for the key role, labor?

Let us consider the minimal landmarks of his argument. To his chosen assumption of the "pre-Aristotelian" point of view with regard to exchange value, he adds only two further ingredients, use-value and labor. (Those are the only two possible candidates he considers for the role of "common something.") He adds these ingredients and grinds his logic mill; use-value falls out and is rejected; only labor remains, and it is therefore by default the missing "common something."

One objection to this course of reasoning was cogently expressed by von Böhm-Bawerk: "It strikes one as strange that instead of submitting the supposed characteristic property to a positive test . . . Marx tries to convince us that he has found the sought-for property, by a purely negative proof, by showing that it is not any of the other properties."

That is, Marx uses abstract logic, rather than a factual investigation, to determine the facts. Let us turn now to his logic.

Actually, we could do no better than to continue quoting von Böhm-Bawerk's "cross-examination" of the theory. He first quotes Marx's deduction:

> "If the use value of commodities be disregarded. . . there remains in them *only one other property, that of being products of labor.*" Is it so? I ask today. . . is there only one other property? Is not the property of being scarce in proportion to demand also common to all exchange-able goods? Or that they are the subjects of demand and supply? Or that they are appropriated? Or that they are natural products? For that they are products of nature, just as they are products of labor, no one asserts more plainly than Marx himself when he declares. . . that "commodities are combinations of two elements, natural material and labor." Or is not the property that they cause expense to their producers – a property to which Marx draws attention in the third volume – common to exchangeable goods?
>
> Why then. . . may not the principle of value reside in any one of these common properties as well as in the property of being products of labor? * [12]

These are pertinent questions, and difficult to answer convincingly. (They weren't answered convincingly when posed, either. It seems that in his time, von Böhm-Bawerk was not so much responded to as howled down and vilified.)

The answer, realistically, is that two possibilities were all Marx needed to reach his pre-conceived conclusion, any others being superfluous. The impression is very strong that Marx didn't desire to consider other possibilities besides labor, even supposing he thought of them; but it is doubtful that he was very diligent in thinking of them.

---

* This is a different translation of Marx's words; the italics are von Böhm-Bawerk's.

What he needed was just two possibilities to consider: his chosen one, pre-ordained for the role, and one alternative to consider and dismiss, just for the sake of presenting the appearance of "dialectical" argumentation. Such a perfunctory argument, advanced for appearances' sake only, allowed Marx to avoid the blatant and obvious method of simply issuing a pronouncement, "Exchange value is hereby decreed to be due solely to contained labor."

The real answer

If Marx had considered all the properties of commodities enumerated above by von Böhm-Bawerk, he might have encountered more difficulty in selecting labor alone. A couple of those properties are especially plausible: the fact that goods are the subjects of supply and demand, and the fact that they are produced at some expense to the producer (both in labor and in money, or "capital"). Indeed, a brief look at the real world, as opposed to Marx's abstract system, will tell us that those are precisely the factors that actually govern exchange value. Each of them is pertinent from a different perspective.

There are two ways of looking at exchange value; one is that the interaction of supply and demand mainly determines the actual market price of a good.

Another way to look at it is to say that, for a *successful* product, one produced and sold on a continuing, profitable basis, the price obtained may be divided into three factors which the price goes to pay. These three factors are labor, rents, and profit. Thus from the entrepreneur's perspective, the price he receives for his product must cover his labor costs, any rents or costs for the physical plant, and a certain percentage left over for his own profit. *

In terms of the entrepreneur's own calculations, the expense of producing the product is the starting point for determining how much to ask as a price for his product. That is not to say he will invariably get his asking price; he will not invariably make a profit. The response of buyers, the actions of other producers of similar goods, or in short, all the vagaries of supply and demand, will affect how much he will receive for his product.

---

* He also has such expenses as capital equipment to pay off; these costs can similarly be divided into labor, rents and profits - the three "basic particles" of exchange value. This analysis of Smith's is however some-what outmoded in modern economic theory.

Thus these two "common properties" of goods – the fact that they are produced at a certain expense, and the fact that they are subjects of demand and exist in an economic environment of varying conditions of supply and demand – are influential in the determination of the exchange value of goods. They are and were just as good candidates for being the "common something" as the two things Marx actually considers – better, in fact, for they actually do determine exchange value. That is, they actually determine the market value of goods in the real world.

However, all this is an attempt to fit classical theory to Marx's theoretical framework. It is more realistic to discard his framework entirely, and not to express classical theory of exchange value in terms of the search for a "common something." It would be better simply to say that as a matter of empirical fact, the above-named considerations are the pertinent factors determining exchange value. *That is how the world really works*, and we don't derive it from any arbitrarily-constructed theoretical system, but from direct observation and empirical correlations among the named factors (together with a generous amount of insight enabling us, or rather Smith, to discern the quantitative relation implicit in the raw data).

Each of us can actually verify classical theory from our own daily experience and from our knowledge of human economic nature as experienced in ourselves.

We know human economic behavior because we know how *we* act; when buying, we wish to "buy low," and when selling we wish to "sell high." If producing a product, we want to get more for it than it cost to produce. This is perhaps a minimal expression of human economic nature, but as far as it goes it is surely accurate.

Is it too much to think that the interaction of these contrary impulses (of buyer and seller), this "dialectical clash," might somehow help to determine what a good sells for? And as to broader economic factors, more impersonal and abstract ones expressed in such terms as "demand" – is it too much to think they are ultimately founded on human economic behavior?

Each of us is a source of real-life, common-sense data about economics, and these data support classical theory, not Marx's fantasy world.

What kind of "property"?

There is however one possible justification that might support Marx in eliminating all but the two possibilities he permits for the "common something." His viewpoint might be that not all properties are properties in the same sense. In other words, some properties can more reasonably be considered as actual physical properties *of* the commodity than others can.

The question then becomes, In what sense does Marx mean that labor is a property of commodities, or a common substance in them?

Of the commodities

> *Antiphanes said merrily, that in a certain city the cold was so intense that words were congealed as soon as spoken, but that after some time they thawed and became audible; so that the words spoken in winter were articulated next summer.*
> – Plutarch, *Of Man's Progress in Virtue*

In looking for the identity of the "common substance," what Marx is looking for is a property which can truly be said to be a physical property *of* the commodity, a part of the physical makeup of the commodity itself. It is not, like the property or characteristic of being "the subjects of demand," something added on or imputed from outside. Demand for goods is something only loosely describable as a property of the commodity, and more accurately characterized as a property of people or society, or of people's economic behavior. As such it would not fit Marx's category; what he apparently envisions is a literal, physical property of the commodity.

Marx's language describing the mystery factor indicates that this is so. He says exchange values are equal because there are equal amounts of the common factor "*in* two different things." He says of goods that "they *have* a common property," meaning, if we take him literally, that it is a property of the goods themselves, not of external conditions. His entire analysis revolves around a minute examination, almost a dissection, of the commodity; the answer is to be found within the physical confines of the commodity, not in the institutions, economic arrangements, and external conditions of society at large.

Moreover his subject or method is "the analysis of a commodity," not the analysis of market forces or human economic behavior. It is plain that he considers the commodities as having all the answers within themselves; and he slices into the commodity for the answers which it contains.

Later on in his text he will speak of labor as "embodied or materialised" in the commodity, and of commodities as being "definite masses of congealed labor-time." (As the Antiphanes quote above shows, it is amazing what sorts of things can congeal.) That is in fact the whole thrust of his "pre-Aristotelian" point of view – that some physical property of the goods, and not any external or social circumstance, determines exchange value. He can even go so far as to say, "the bodies of commodities are combinations of two elements – matter and labor."

Marx will even give us the testimony of the commodities themselves: "Could commodities themselves speak, they would say: Our use-value may be a thing that interests men. It is no part of us as objects. What, however, does belong to us as objects, is our value." (Note in passing that he too describes usefulness or use-value as something imputed to commodities from outside, a result of people finding them to be useful.)

The "common something" Marx is looking for, then, is a property *of* the commodity in a strict, literal sense. It is a characteristic of the goods in and of themselves, and not a property in a loose or figurative sense, as for instance the "property" a certain commodity may have of being a subject of demand. The fact that goods are scarce in proportion to demand, that they are the subjects of supply and demand, that their production entails a monetary cost – these are loosely speaking "characteristics" of goods, but they are really characteristics of our own behavior toward goods. Thus the fact that the category of "somethings" Marx considers is a very narrow one – two properties only – may possibly be justified: the rest of the "properties" of goods do not really fit the category.

Nature of the common something

As described by the natural sciences, physical or natural properties are objective characteristics which things possess in and of themselves – properties of an object *per se*. They are well-defined, objectively observable, and measurable.

For example, objects have mass and volume; these are characteristics of objects in and of themselves – no one has to do anything to give objects their mass or volume. They are not characteristics imputed or supplied from outside (though they may be *measured* from outside). Whether anyone observes the object or not, its mass and volume are present as characteristics of it. This is different from a property like demand, or "the fact that goods are subjects of demand." Goods have physical properties in and of themselves, as a part of their physical nature or existence.

Moreover, physical properties are usually quantifiable, at least in principle – it is not always easy to do so in practice. Most natural properties, like mass, volume, specific heat, and so on, exist in definite, measurable amounts. If a characteristic is not quantifiable, it may fail to be a physical property just because it is not sufficiently precise as to be of any use in physical sciences.

For example, wavelengths of light are measurable; one can say what wavelength of light is reflected from an object when the full spectrum of sunlight shines on it. Wavelengths are precisely quantifiable. On the other hand, one could ask what color the object is. Color is too loosely-defined and subjective to be quantifiable. Colors like "blue," and even more specific terms like "cyan," are not standardized; each person may choose his own particular shade and call it cyan. Colors *per se* don't lend themselves to precise measurement.

The above characteristics define the physical properties, as has been determined by the natural sciences. And if we speak of properties *of* objects, characteristics found in them, then we can only mean physical properties. If a characteristic is not a physical property it is not a property "of" the object, but something external like beauty or "the fact that they are subjects of demand." These are the only two real alternatives.

The "common something" as a physical property

The cumulative picture presented by Marx's description of the "common something" is that of a natural property. Everything he says about it adds up to that.

That is, each individual aspect of the "common something" which Marx describes adds up to that. On the other hand, Marx himself says that the common something is *not* a physical property. This should not disturb us, however. Marx says the common something cannot be "intrinsic," "inseparably connected with, inherent in commodities." It "cannot be. . . [any] natural property of commodities." That is his *explicit* position; yet by implication, by the accumulation of the details of his description, a picture of the "common something" emerges which is that of a physical property.

At one point or another, Marx attributes all the characteristics of physical properties to his "common something." Thus while on the one hand he says flatly that the missing "something" cannot be a physical property, on the other he says that it has every *characteristic* of the physical properties. Let us examine these two sides of the issue in more detail.

As we have seen, the description he gives of something "in" and "of" commodities, something "embodied in" commodities, a "common property" of goods, and so on, adds up to a complete and detailed profile of a physical property. Therefore despite what he tells us out of one side of his mouth, he tells us out of the other side that the "common something" we are looking for is indistinguishable from a physical property in any respect. Just in the same way, a naturalist might say, "An animal just flew by, but it was not a duck. However, it was a heavy-bodied migratory waterfowl with a bill and webbed feet, of family *anatidae*, subfamily *anatinae*, and it was quacking," and so on listing all the identifying characteristics of ducks. We would then have to choose either the explicit denial or the implicit, cumulative sum of the descriptive detail; both couldn't be correct. The bird could not be both "not a duck" and at the same time a bird with all the distinguishing characteristics *of* a duck. There is a contradiction in terms, a logical fallacy, a canard in such descriptions.

(It is not, by the way, at all unusual for Marx to take both sides of an issue, one in his explicit remarks and another in the cumulative gist of what he says.)

In the current instance, Marx's use of Orwellian language may represent simple willfulness or obstinacy – Marx simply didn't want to accept that he was describing a physical property. Or, it may represent scientific ignorance.

Possible extenuating arguments

Another possible explanation of Marx's dual stance above is that what he means to rule out, in saying his missing "something" is not a physical property, is only the possibility that it might be one of the recognized, traditionally-identified physical properties, like mass, volume, chemical composition, etc. The common "substance" in other words, is not one of the previously-known physical properties; but once Marx identifies it, it will be a new physical property; or at least it will be like a physical property in every respect. Perhaps that is one way to make sense of what Marx says.

More likely, Marx simply had no clear idea of what constitutes a physical property. Thus he ruled out physical properties, meaning the recognized, known ones, and didn't recognize the implications of what he was saying when he portrayed his missing factor as in every respect like a physical property. It was a simple case of scientific illiteracy.

Let's continue with the idea of labor as an actual, physical property of commodities: in actuality, labor doesn't become a physical property of commodities; it doesn't embed or embody itself as a physical entity within them. It is not "in" the commodity, and it can't be dissected out. It doesn't congeal, crystallize, or otherwise embody itself in physically-incarnated form within the commodity. Labor is rather something done to the commodity, a part of its history; it shapes the commodity, and its effects can be seen. In the sense that a certain amount of labor was expended in producing a commodity, in that sense the commodity represents or "embodies" a given amount of labor. But to take this subtle point and distort it in an idiotically reductionist manner, saying that labor is *physically* embodied in material form, is to display reasoning of great crudity.

Labor is effort, an activity, the expenditure of energy; it doesn't congeal or metamorphose into matter, or attach itself to matter as a physical property of that matter. Marx's eagerness to reduce the discussion to a simple-minded schema has led him out of the realm of science into fantasy and ignorance.

All the characteristics of commodities which Marx refused to consider, like their being "subjects of demand," their being produced at some financial expense, and so on, are properties *of* goods to the exact extent that labor is – no more and no less. Any of these properties is just as good a candidate for the "common substance" as any other. Marx's glib pronouncement that labor is the only remaining choice, then, is meretricious.

Marx's identification of two and only two properties as fitting into his category is typical of much of his of work: it is a "non-reproducible result." That is, it is not based on any explicitly-stated principles and criteria which would enable a reader to judge for himself whether Marx's theory is valid, or enable him to retrace and reformulate each successive step. There is, so to speak, no way of "checking Marx's math," of verifying that each step along the way is justified within the terms of the discussion; for there aren't any explicit terms of the discussion. Everything in Marx's exposition of his theory is given on an *ad hoc* basis, and develops as it does for no better reason than Marx's idiosyncratic decision: it is so because he says it is so.

In the present instance, he makes no explicit statement about what kind of property he is looking for, or what criteria a characteristic must meet in order to be considered. He simply issues the decree that only two properties, use-value and labor, fit the category. He gives no justification of this in general terms, nor any strictly objective, *procedural* method of following his path of investigation to see if it actually leads where he says. Rather, he leads his readers by the nose and demands that they accept his personal assurances on everything. This is not science; it is "cult of personality."

This method has the advantage, for Marx, of allowing him to reach whatever conclusions he wants. But it means his text is not science, or even honestly-reasoned philosophy, but arbitrary pronouncements. There is no general or objective rule for guiding us through the discussion, no means of forming an objective judgment for ourselves as to which points and inferences are correct. At every fork in the road the reader must wait blindly until Marx tells him which way to go and what conclusions to draw. There is no objective method for predicting what Marx will say next; we can only wait for his arbitrary fiat.

No one could say why labor, but not the necessity of expenditure, should be considered as a common property of goods and a candidate for the role of "common something." We must await Marx's instructions. This very character of Marx's text, of being a non-reproducible result or non-verifiable theory, marks it as not science but a series of arbitrary pronouncements, or as the description of a fantasy world. Marx requires that his readers, or his followers, simply *abandon themselves* and their critical powers to him. To anyone the least bit literate in genuine scientific method, that is an unacceptable sacrifice.

Criticism of Marx's method should not make us lose sight of the larger point: his entire discussion, his very definition of the question in terms of such a common property, is bizarre and misleading. Once his investigation of exchange value reduces itself to the search for a "common property" inherent in all commodities, any hope of a sensible answer is lost. "Ask a foolish question, and you get a foolish answer." Thus, even more fundamental than the incorrect answers that Marx gets is the fact that his question itself is inappropriate.

What kind of labor?

Marx now embarks on a strange journey, a side excursion in his analysis, whose purpose is hard to discern. The subject of the excursion seems to be, "identifying the particular kind of labor that constitutes the 'common something'." But let's look at his text. He has said that the only remaining common property of commodities

> [is] that of being products of labor. But even the product of labor itself has undergone a change in our hands. [*Let's hope so, or else the labor was ineffectual.*] If we make abstraction from its use-value, we make abstraction at the same time from the material elements and shapes that make the product a use-value; we see in it no longer a table, a house, yarn, or any other useful thing. Neither can it any longer be regarded as the product of the joiner, the mason, the spinner, or of any other definite kind of productive labor. Along with the useful qualities of the products themselves, we put out of sight both the useful character of the various kinds of labor embodied in them, and the concrete forms of that labor; there is nothing left but what is common to them all; all are reduced to one and the same sort of labor, human labor in the abstract.

It is hard to know exactly what to make of this passage, or of Marx's concept of "human labor in the abstract" (which he apparently regards as a concrete thing). Nor is it easy to see why Marx thought the explanation was necessary. While Marx devotes a large part of his works to reducing complicated and subtle topics to idiotic simplicities, here he adopts an alternate mode, the hyper-inflation and mystification of what is straightforward and simple. (He does have a third mode of analysis which may be said to occupy the middle ground between these two: the detailed belaboring of the painfully obvious.) *

---

* Kathleen Nott, in "Pavlov and his Bad Dog," *Encounter*, London, 1964, has neatly summed up the rhetorical patterns of academic jargon under categories like "(1) Grandiose-inflationary… (2) Disguise by obvious-ness… and (3) pejorative reference to unacceptable concepts…" Marx uses all three modes.

At any rate the present passage presents something of a puzzle. In general terms Marx seems to be saying that what he meant by the statement that commodities are "products of labor," was that they are products of "human labor in the abstract."

That is the kind of labor goods are the products of. The question remains, how does that differ from ordinary labor?

First, however, let us look at the path of argumentation by which Marx developed the concept. We might term this path Marx's process of "abstraction" or "abstracting from" – a process he applies to what he started with, just plain labor.

What Marx apparently means by "make abstraction from" is, "ignore or disregard as irrelevant." We "make abstraction from its use-value" because, as Marx has shown, use-value is irrelevant to exchange value. He continues to enumerate and discard other properties which are irrelevant. Thus he "makes abstraction from" the identity of the particular commodity, i.e., whether it is a table, a house, or what have you; and he "makes abstraction from" the particular type of labor that produced it – that of a mason, joiner, etc. He continues to strip off all the irrelevant considerations in this manner until he arrives at the remaining core of essentials, from which we cannot "make abstraction," i.e., which are relevant and cannot be discarded. Then we see the true, essential nature both of the commodity and of the labor that produced it.

Marx's process of "making abstraction from," or mentally stripping away, is thus like the process cited by the sculptor who was asked how he could make a life-like statue of, say, a horse. He answered, "It's easy. I just start with a big block of stone and chip away everything that doesn't look like a horse." That is Marx's method here – he starts with the commodity and "chips away" everything that doesn't look like the true, essential nature of the commodity and its value.

In this case, Marx is dealing with the commodity as "the product of labor." What he really wants to do is "chip away" all the inessentials from that labor, to reveal its true nature. But to do this he must first apply his eccentric logic to the commodity itself.

We already know that we can "make abstraction from" the use-value of the commodity, for all the voluminous reasons Marx has given us so far. And if we chip away use-value, "we make abstraction at the same time from the material elements and shapes," etc., that is, we can ignore what the particular commodity is; "we see in it no longer a table, a house, yarn," or whatever. This follows because Marx is now using definition number two for "use-value," namely, "the use the commodity is put to." If we ignore use-value (in the sense of what the commodity is useful for), we ignore at the same time what the identity of the commodity is; if we don't care about its use in the present instance, we don't care about what it is.

At any rate, if it doesn't matter to us whether the commodity is good to set things on, or to live in, or to wear, then we can also chip away the question of whether it is a table, a house, or yarn. And if we don't care what the commodity *is*, that is, what *use-value* we're dealing with, then we don't care what particular kind of labor produced the commodity – whether that of a carpenter, mason or spinner; we chip that away too. And if we chip away the particular kind of labor that produced the commodity, all that is left, all we know and care about as relevant, is general labor, labor without specifying any one particular type of labor, or "human labor in the abstract."

The entire argument follows from the fact that we first discarded use-value, as irrelevant to exchange value. Commodities with different use-values (different uses) are different commodities: in Marx's jargon, their "material shapes and elements" are different. Different commodities are produced by different kinds of labor. Thus if one of these factors is irrelevant, all are.

In sum, after all the chipping away has been done, we are left with "human labor in the abstract."

"Labor," or "human labor in the abstract"?

The question then becomes, How is that any different from what we started with, namely, commodities as "products of *labor*"? The word "labor" doesn't specify any particular kind of labor. It doesn't connote whether the labor is that of "the joiner, the mason, the spinner." The term "labor," in fact, is already general, or "abstract." It is not a name for any one particular labor. So what is the point of Marx's excursion?

It may be that the concept, "human labor in the abstract" is the same as "labor," but with pretensions; it is set up by Marx as a formalized category, being put on a more rigorous and (presumably) scientific basis: it is labor with a social pedigree.

Or we might say that "labor" is just plain old, everyday labor, which is itself unspecified or "abstract." Marx seems to have been afflicted with a persistent inability to distinguish between the abstract and the concrete, and at times attributed to each the characteristics of the other. *

When we disregard or "abstract from" the particular kind of labor, we don't actually "reduce" all labor to "one and the same sort of labor" (as if "human labor in the abstract" were a particular form of labor).

---

* One good example is his concept of the individual human being. He labeled the individual "the ensemble of the social relations," as if society were the primary entity and the individual were merely derived from it, as a product of the aggregate of social institutions He takes that viewpoint, rather than recognizing individual humans as the primary entity, and society's being an abstraction derived from them.

Rather, we conceptualize from all kinds of labor; we rise above the particulars or subsume all particular kinds of labor in one conceptualized category of just plain "labor" – "human labor in the abstract." It is not a matter of reducing all kinds of labor to one concrete form of labor, but of conceptualizing from the concrete forms of labor to derive an abstract or conceptual category.

Marx reverses the roles of the concrete particulars and the abstract concept. It should first be observed that as between the abstract and the concrete, the concrete is primary and prior. In other words, what exists first, and arguably *all* that actually exists, is the numerous concrete instances or individuals. These are real; any generalizations or abstract concepts drawn from them are not real in the same sense of having concrete or physical existence. And the existence of the conceptual notion is secondary to and dependent on the prior existence of the physical individuals.

In the present instance Marx says, "[C]oncrete labor becomes the form under which its opposite, abstract human labor, manifests itself." Here we see the skewing of the relationship between the abstract and the concrete; it is as if "abstract human labor" were primary, and expressed or manifested itself as the secondary, concrete labor. Max Eastman said of that sentence, "It would be difficult in the whole history of science to find a more mystical and unreal construction." [13]

To repeat: what actually exists, what is actually done, is labor of a great variety of different kinds, i.e. manifold instances of particular kinds of labor, performed by particular individuals. A process of abstraction or of forming conceptual notions is applied to the various particular instances of labor. This produces the abstract, generalized notion of just plain labor – labor "considered apart from any particular instances." But the *concept* is secondary, and is derived from the concrete instances.

So in the end we are left just where we started out; we began with "labor" and end up with "human labor in the abstract." Probably only Marx himself could tell just how these two are different. Without more information his point is unfathomable.

"Value"

Marx continues:

> Let us now consider the residue of these products; it consists of the same unsubstantial reality in each, a mere congelation of homogeneous human labor, of labor-power expended without regard to the mode of its expenditure. All that these things now tell us is,

that human labor is embodied in them. When looked at as crystals of this social substance, common to them all, they are – Values.

We have seen that when commodities are exchanged, their exchange value manifests itself as something totally independent of their use-value. But if we abstract from their use-value, there remains their Value as defined above. Therefore, the common substance that manifests itself in the exchange value of commodities, whenever they are exchanged, is their value. The progress of our investigation will show that exchange value is the only form in which the value of commodities can manifest itself or be expressed. For the present, however, we have to consider the nature of value independently of this, its form.

Looking at the first sentence, we see that we are now to examine the "residue of these products" – i.e., the remainder after we have finished the chipping-away or "abstracting" process. This residue "consists of the same unsubstantial [i.e., non-material] reality in each" – that is, in each product or commodity. This same "reality" in each commodity is "a mere congelation of homogeneous human labor, of labor-power expended without regard to the mode of its expenditure." (Marx doesn't mean that last part quite as it sounds; it's not that the labor is *expended* without regard to the mode of its expenditure, but that we do not need to take into account the "mode of expenditure" of labor, that is, the particular kind of labor which it is. All types are equivalent.)

In this statement we see more clearly Marx's concept of the process of "abstracting," or the forming of abstract concepts. He does not see it as beginning with a lot of individual kinds of labor, from which we "abstract" a concept or generalized notion of general human labor. He sees labor as beginning with one transcendent essence, "human labor in the abstract," which is then expressed or expended in a variety of "forms." The process of abstracting means peeling away nonessentials to find this inner essence.

He speaks of this inner essence almost as if it exists as an independent concrete entity in its own right, not just as an abstract notion formed from the many instances of actual, concrete labor. It seems to exist prior to the individual modes of labor – it is sort of a raw clay, perhaps like ectoplasm, which is molded into a variety of actual modes of work. Thus, to repeat, for Marx "human labor in the abstract" is a concrete thing.

Values

To continue: we see in the commodities only the single reality, homogeneous human labor. "All that these things now tell us is, that human labor is embodied in them."

All they tell us now is all they told us at the start. That is, after the "abstracting from" process, their only remaining common property is that they are products of labor – plain, ordinary labor, the same as abstract or "homogeneous" labor. When everything else has been chipped away, that is the last remaining "residue," and thus it is the only factor that can account for their exchange value.

Marx continues, rephrasing the same point: "When looked at as crystals of this social substance, common to them all, they are – Values."

The above sentence is nearly incomprehensible, and almost entirely devoid of meaning. "Crystals of this social substance" is more poetic than scientific, or even meaningful. True, labor by some standard could be termed "social"; but is it a substance, and does it form crystals? (We had been led to believe it congealed, like chicken fat.)

Marx sums up, "We have seen that when commodities are exchanged, their exchange value manifests itself as something totally independent of their use-value. But if we abstract from their use-value, there remains their Value as defined above."

This is a recapitulation of his proof: use-value is eliminated as the explanation of exchange value, because it is constant while exchange value varies. Therefore use-value and exchange value are completely unrelated. Once having discarded use-value, Marx is left with only one factor which can be the determiner of exchange value: labor.

Marx goes on to assert that "Value" is, identically, the embodied labor. "Therefore, the common substance that manifests itself in the exchange value of commodities, whenever they are exchanged, is their value."

In making the above statements, Marx makes a distinction between "value" and exchange value; or to put it another way, he adds a definition to the word "value." The real value of commodities is not their exchange value or their use-value, he implies, but the "common substance" congealed in them. Exchange value is a manifestation or "phenomenal form" of this inward property.

In fact, it is the only phenomenal form; for Marx continues, "The progress of our investigation will show that exchange value is the only form in which the value of commodities can manifest itself or be expressed." Exchange value is not real value, but is only crude market value, a mere "phenomenal form." That is, its only merit is that it is an empirical entity: it actually exists and can be observed in the real world. In other words, there is exchange value, or just plain market price; but behind this visible phenomenon there is an unseen, underlying phenomenon which actually controls things. This unseen "value" is true value; that is what Marx intends to study, not the superficial, merely "phenomenal" exchange value.

(A preliminary objection to this part of Marx's theory is that exchange value is the only *visible* form or manifestation of value; it is the only form which we can examine and investigate directly. Marx's "Value" is unseen, hidden within the commodity; we can never know anything about it except through its outward form or manifestation, exchange value. Thus we can only infer things about "Value," and never really know anything for certain about it – not even that it actually exists.)

Value declared equivalent to labor

This segment of Marx's text, with the introduction of the entity "value," as distinct from use-value and exchange value, contains a number of curious features. Primarily, there is the fact that "value" is a ringer, a specious entity brought into the discussion in place of the legitimate one.

Marx has begun his inquiry aiming to discover what factors determine exchange value. That is in principle a matter of finding a cause-and-effect relationship, or to put it another way, it is a matter of more or less scientific inquiry. Marx presumably set out to discover something on the order of a scientific law: a quantitative correlation between phenomena, one that always holds true, verified by empirical observation.

It might be useful to backtrack and compare what Marx has really shown (by his thought experiment in "abstracting") to what he represents himself as having shown. Marx has sought to discover what determines exchange value. He never really articulates the task, of course; he expresses it no more specifically than, "Let us consider the matter a little more closely."

But what the "answer" to exchange value means, if anything, is a quantitative correlation between entities; if Marx is genuinely a scientist, he sought some objective evidence that a cause-and-effect relationship exists between (say) labor and exchange value. That is, he means to say that a correlation is observed between these two objective entities. This correlation, if it is actual science, is then part of the natural order of the universe – it is Marx's discovered law of exchange value, $V = kL$, exchange value equals labor times a constant factor.

But now that Marx has identified his "common factor," he represents his discovery not as part of a cause-and-effect statement, but as a statement of equivalence or identity; value is not *caused* by factor X or dependent on factor X; it is *identical* with factor X. This is much less respectable, scientifically speaking.

Marx has changed the discussion from a scientific one wherein factor A causes phenomenon B, to one consisting of metaphysical gibberish concerning factor A being a "phenomenal form" of factor B. He reduces it to a search for alter egos or "manifestations" of unseen, mystical entities. The terms of discussion have been diverted from the scientific to the mystical and metaphysical.

And at the same time the very identity of the subject under discussion has changed. Marx had originally set out to investigate value, meaning market value – "the proportion in which goods of one sort or exchanged for those of another sort." But now he has invented a new "value" meaning not exchange value or use-value but only the amount of an inner, congealed "common substance." He now discards exchange value, which in the economic sense *is* value, and substitutes his own impostor, value meaning identically "congealed labor." This is the entity he will concern himself with in the rest of his analysis, rather than the real economic entity we were originally concerned with.

Marx was unjustified in equating value with the congealed labor. To say that "A causes B" does not justify saying "A is identical with B." If labor (a "social substance" in Marx's witless jargon) determines the magnitude of exchange value, that is not the same as saying that labor is identical with value. Marx apparently just didn't grasp the distinction between the two. Marx's approach turns the discussion into a kind of "black hole" – anything that gets near it is sucked in and merged in one leaden mass. All subtlety or differentiation among various aspects of the question disappears; no entity, no question, can retain a distinct identity.

The logic of equating value and labor

Marx goes on to say, if we eliminate or "abstract from" use-value, "there remains their Value as defined above. Therefore the common substance that manifests itself in the exchange value of commodities, whenever they are exchanged, is their value."

How "therefore"? What is the chain of logic in Marx's conclusion? Assuming that he has shown A *causes* B, how does that prove that "therefore" A is *identical* with B, i.e., that "the common substance. . . is their value"? There is no "therefore" to it, but just bald assertion.

Again, to make the analogy to scientific laws: if we show that the electrical current flowing over a given wire (with a given resistance) is determined by the voltage applied to it (that is, $E = IR$), we do not then go further and say, "Therefore, the voltage that manifests itself in the flow of current, is their current." Voltage *produces* a current, in a corresponding magnitude; it is not the same as the current.

Marx's "therefore" is mere handwaving – a flourish of rhetoric to distract the reader's attention from the fact that no justification for his conclusion has been advanced. Abraham Lincoln once characterized an argument of Stephen Douglas's as "a specious and fantastic arrangement of words, by which a man may prove that a horse chestnut is a chestnut horse." We will see many instances in Marx's text of "specious and fantastic arrangements of words"; the present non-argument is one such.

Having once identified his "common substance," Marx tells us that it does not *determine* exchange value; rather it "manifests itself in their exchange value." Marx thus changes the metaphysics and the entire set of assumptions of the discussion.

Marx's process of reasoning

So now let us see what Marx *considers* he has shown. He says: "Let us now consider the residue of each of these products*; it consists of the same unsubstantial reality in each, a mere congelation of homogeneous human labor, of labor-power expended without regard to the mode of its expenditure."

Nevertheless, he wants to discuss the "residue" left over after the chipping or "abstracting" process, so let us indeed consider this "residue," the remnants of the chipped-away commodity. It consists of the "unsubstantial reality" of congealed "homogeneous human labor." The labor can't be seen, it's not a physical object, and in fact the normal mind might consider that it's not "embodied" in the commodity in any such sense as Marx means it. Nevertheless, Marx assures us that it is there, it is reality.

Actually, the only sense in which labor can be "embodied" in the commodity is that labor is *invested* in the commodity; a certain amount of labor is exerted in the production of the commodity; the commodity represents or "embodies" the exertion of a certain number of hours of labor. But labor is an action, it is the expenditure of energy – it doesn't in any actual, realistic sense congeal or crystallize in the physical commodity.

Marx couldn't really discern it in any "residue." That is just his way of saying that labor is the only conceivable common factor of all commodities that could account for their exchange value.

So even though no one can see labor embodied in the commodity, we'll pretend it is there, as Marx says; and we'll conclude that this "unsubstantial reality," based on no more solid evidence than Marx's unsupported word, is the "common factor" which governs exchange value.

By rhetoric and sophistry Marx can focus on this one remaining "residue" or "common something." As Marx puts it, "All that these things now tell us is that human labor-power has been expended," etc. Let's just say the only common characteristic of goods, besides use-value, is the property of being products of labor.

----

* Or maybe, "Let us now sift the ashes of our imagination."

Value as a definition

Marx goes beyond this, blurring the conclusion he is entitled to make. He says, "When looked at as crystals of this social substance, common to them all, they are – Values. . . But if we abstract from their use-value, there remains their Value as defined above." Marx then refers to this, or to his entire line of reasoning, as a "definition" – value "as defined above" being equivalent to the "homogeneous human labor" contained in the commodity.

Marx has given us a proof or (if you prefer) a line of logical reasoning showing value to be identical with labor; it seems superfluous now to *define* value as labor.

First of all, we are not looking for a definition of value; we already know what value is – it is, in the economic sense, practically identical to exchange value. In the plebeian, cut-and-dried, dollars-and-cents realm of economics, "value" is synonymous with "exchange value." Exchange value is what interests us, and that is all we are competent to discuss. (Other senses of value such as "worth" or aesthetic "merit" or even "use-value" are not concrete and quantifiable enough for us to write scientifically and definitively about them.)

We don't need another definition of value; we have one already – value is exchange value, the only value that can concern us scientifically. Exchange value is what Marx set out to investigate. But what Marx now attempts to do is to pull a bait-and-switch operation – to yank exchange value out of sight and put "Value" in its place; that is, to define Value as labor.

It is not easy to see this immediately in Marx's typically sloppy prose: "When looked at as crystals of this social substance, they are – Values." That is, again, almost a senseless juxtaposition of words, very nearly gibberish. It is not how we look at them that makes them values or not values. They were in fact already "values" – that is, they had exchange value – before we began analyzing them. They have exchange value in that they are exchanged; there is a market in them.

The word "value" is not open for redefinition; it has a very definite meaning already, and it is because of that meaning that we are interested in it. Moreover, in looking for the explanation of value, we are looking for a scientifically respectable relation of cause and effect, wherein one quantity (say, labor) determines the magnitude of another quantity (say, exchange value). We are not looking for alternate guises or "forms" of the same entity, on the model of ancient Greek philosophy or mythology. "Value," for our purposes, means exchange value. That is what the discussion is about; it is what Marx originally set out to explore, and it is the economic entity that really exists in the real world. *Hic Rhoda, hic Salta!*

A special meaning for "value"

The end result of Marx's redefinition of "Value" is this: throughout the remainder of his text he will refer to the subject of value, and the naive reader will assume he's talking about value in the ordinary sense of the word – exchange value. However, that will not be the case; he will be talking about his own pet, personal term "value" – value meaning the "embodied labor," crystals of a "social substance." Marx's entire theoretical framework from now on will concern this specious concept, not value as normal users of language think of it but a very particular, peculiar, jargon sense of the term. Marx no doubt profits by this confusion. If Marx had chosen a clearer, non-conflicting term for embodied labor, like "friblitz," his text would have been recognized at once as the kind of driveling fantasy it is. As it is, his whole text, revolving as it does around discussions of the "value" of various entities, ends up as a nonsense discussion, because it is based on a fantasy concept.

What Marx actually needs, it should be noted, is for both definitions of value to be held in the reader's mind at the same time. Value is supposed to mean "embodied labor" so that Marx can prove the things he wants to prove about it. He will construct a complete system, a set of categories defining or deducing what the "value" of any given entity is, using the definition of value as embodied labor. All of his determinations of the magnitude of value for different commodities will be calculated from the amount of this "social substance" contained in them (which Marx will derive by further sophistries).

At the same time, "value" has to mean value in the normal sense of the word; that is, it is supposed to mean "exchange value" as well, because exchange value was Marx's initial topic and it is what concerns us. If we are not discussing exchange value, the discussion holds no interest for us and has no economic pertinence.

The two definitions cannot merge or coexist; that should be plain. The exchange value of a commodity is not manipulable; that is, it doesn't produce the results Marx wants. It is an objective entity, whose magnitude can only be known by seeing what a commodity actually does bring on the market. It cannot be guaranteed beforehand to conform to any of Marx's *a priori* definitions of what the value of a commodity must necessarily be. Marx derives his laws of value using his specious definition, and expects the reader to believe they hold true for exchange value.

That is, if we look at both conflicting meanings of "value," we see at least one contradiction. The laws Marx derives using deductive logic relying on value as embodied labor, can't be guaranteed to hold true for value as exchange value. In a sense, what Marx thinks he can do is stipulate a real-world quantity by sheer force of definition. He has developed the theoretical underpinnings to his own satisfaction – value is proven to equal a certain thing, and *defined* to equal a certain thing; and, thus ideologically bound, it has no choice but to equal that. By Marx's definition of value as embodied labor, he apparently considers that exchange value can be logically compelled to correspond to this analytically proven determination of the category "value."

Thus by sheer force of definition, exchange value (this remains part of the meaning of the term "value") is compelled, or deemed logically, to correspond to the amount of embodied labor. This superstitious attitude that "definition can compel the facts," is exactly opposite to the scientific view. Marx derives his conclusions from logic and from willful definition, and assumes that the facts must correspond. This attitude of "My theory (or definition) is correct – it is the facts that are mistaken" should not be dignified with the term science.

When Marx's casuistic theory mandates what value must equal, it tells us at the same time what exchange value must equal. But exchange value is a real-world, objective entity, measured by inspecting the market. To think it can be defined by an *a priori* category or a series of specious deductions is fatalistic and superstitious, not scientific.

You cannot define objective quantities by force. One can't for example define the distance to the sun as 50,000 miles; it is a certain distance in its own right. It is a quantity not subject to definition – it can only be measured. (It is reported, in a similar vein, that an Indiana legislator once introduced a bill to round pi off to 3, so as to make life easier for students. Even the most unscientific reader will see the fallacy in such attempts: objective quantities cannot be capriciously redefined.)

Marx has no conception of the meaning of science or the task before him, and therefore he speaks all the more authoritatively.

Scholastics' Reasoning

For the remainder of his text, then, Marx will deal with the "value" of various entities; but this "value" will be an impostor, a "ringer" substituting for exchange value. His "value" always means embodied labor – and that is a fantasy concept, irrelevant to real-world economics. Not that labor itself is irrelevant; the labor *costs* of producing a commodity are one of the main factors which determine its price. But labor as a crystallized "substance," which automatically and spontaneously determines the exchange value of a commodity by first depositing itself within the commodity and then manifesting itself externally in the stated guise of "exchange value" (the "phenomenal form" of embodied labor), is a fiction. Exchange value, or value itself, as an *a priori* category pre-determined by the simple circumstance of how much labor an article "contains," and with no reference to people or the market, is a misperception of the nature of economics itself.

Marx's text purports to be an investigation of exchange value, which is initially defined as the "quantitative relation ... the proportion in which values in use of one sort are exchanged for those of another sort." For discussing this issue, his chosen method is. . .to change the subject. Exchange value is too observable, too concrete, too open to investigation to serve Marx's purposes. Marx prefers to deal with a tamed concept of his own creation, "Value." This entity is invisible (indeed nonexistent), transcendent, unobservable, subject to no method of verification or refutation, and subject only to the rules, laws, and definitions Marx wishes to invent for it. It is an entirely malleable, subservient little concept, just suited for Marx's purposes, helping him prove whatever he wants to about "value." Its only drawbacks are that it doesn't exist and that it is not exchange value (and thus has no bearing whatsoever on what actually happens in the economics of the real world). No one is interested in Marx's fictitious entity, "value," any more than one can really be interested in economic affairs on other planets as they might be described in some science fiction novel. These things aren't real. To understand economics, to understand *value*, is to understand market value and markets; that is the ground of investigation, and the manufacturing of fantasy concepts will supply no insights into it.

Marx's malleable world

Marx has come a long way from his initial statement of the problem of exchange value and what determines it; and he has come a long way from science. His view of the problem in terms of "forms" and "manifestations," with one entity manifesting itself in alternate guises, is a reversion to mythical concepts, philosophical methods and generally a pre-scientific manner of approaching the whole issue.

One could say the principle of Occam's Razor applies to value. * The observable facts of the matter, involving market value as an observed phenomenon, supply and demand, and so on, are sufficient in themselves to supply a rational explanation of exchange value; therefore no reference to spooks or unseen entities is necessary. Exchange value isn't a "form" or "manifestation" of any unseen, embodied, invisible "common substance" in commodities.

---

* One version of Occam's Razor goes, "Entities ought not to be multiplied except from necessity." A more modern form is, "The explanation requiring the fewest assumptions is the most likely to be correct."

There is no ectoplasmic entity inside commodities, taking on corporeal form as price tags. Exchange value is determined by a variety of economic factors, ultimately hinging on decisions and actions of human beings. It is not a spontaneous or automatistic "manifestation" of some "common substance."

This is not to say there can be no inquiry into what determines exchange value; but it must be a rational inquiry. If it identifies causative factors, they must be real and observable factors; and the manner in which those factors are supposed to influence exchange value must be described rationally and explicitly, in terms which can be verified or refuted by observation of real-world events and entities. In other words, the explanation must fit in with how the world really works; and we can have no more of "manifestations" in "phenomenal form" of unseen "common substances" such as "congealed labor," defined by brute force to be identical with "Value."

Most of all we must respect language, and not presume to redefine terms like "value" to fit our personal agenda.

This is, again, not to say that labor doesn't exist. It does exist, that is, it is performed. But it doesn't "congeal" into a substance, it is not a bodily presence inside the commodity, it is not "value," and it does not determine or "manifest itself as" exchange value in a direct, automatistic manner.

In short, we must have science, a description of how the world really works, and not mystical assertions, specious rhetoric, and sophistical logic, all rolled up in a ball of speculative philosophy and verbal trickery. That is what Marx offers us. And when he tells us that "we have to consider . . . value independently of this, its form," he tells us that he will henceforth be dealing *first* with his fantasy concept, with unseen, Gnostic "Value," which exists only in his mind and in his unsupported assertions, rather than with actually-observable exchange value, "its form."

To Marx, the real is only a "form" or "manifestation" of the imaginary. Marx prefers his trumped-up fantasy world to the real events and things of the "merely phenomenal" real world.

The nature of "value"

Marx's redefinition of the term "value" carries with it a variety of implications. His transformation of the meaning of the word carries with it a transformation of the fundamental character of the concept referred to. This transformation might be briefly summed up by saying that value now becomes a static, rather than a dynamic, entity; it becomes an *a priori*, logical category, rather than an empirical, *a posteriori* quantity; and it becomes, in Marx's jargon, a "metaphysical" rather than "dialectical" entity.

Consider first exchange value, or value in the normal sense of the word.

It is, we know, the proportion in which goods of various kinds are exchanged, that being a mathematical relation. Alternatively (and speaking practically), exchange value is market price. Now this quantitative relation or this market price is governed by no logical imperatives or *a priori* philosophical rules. It is determined dynamically by people who have things for sale and people desiring to buy them, as they together strike their bargains. (All these people are however influenced by other objective factors like cost of production.)

But there is no pre-established formula for knowing beforehand, to a logical certainty, what exchange value must of necessity be; it is determined *in the event*, by the dynamics of the market, i.e. by supply and demand. In this view, exchange value is volatile, fluctuating, human-determined and *a posteriori*; it is not pre-determined by logical necessity. It is an aspect of trade and not a fixed physical property of goods themselves. Thus it is not pre-determined by an *a priori* rule or logical imperative: it has no existence "before the fact."

By contrast to this, Marx portrays "value" as a physical property of the commodity. He presents value, or embodied labor, as a reified or concretized thing, or at least as a physical attribute of a thing. Rather than being determined dynamically, in the act of exchange; it exists statically, "within" the commodity, as a pre-existing property in a certain magnitude, waiting to manifest itself. Once the labor has been performed, once the commodity is a finished product, value is a fixed, static, intrinsic property of the commodity.

This "value" is an *a priori* phenomenon: Marx's rule is, measure the amount of labor that was embodied in the commodity, and by logical necessity, or by definition, we know that this is precisely the value of the commodity. Marx's law serves as a logical category for determining, without ever having to follow the commodity to the marketplace, what its value is and must be.

Marx's "value" thus is static, pre-determined, *a priori*, and "ready-made." It has all the characteristics he condemns in "metaphysical" science. In fact, while Marx purports to supersede "metaphysical" science by making all things dynamic, interactive and interrelated, he takes the opposite tack with exchange value; he reduces it to a static, concrete thing.

Such an approach should be anathema to Marx; to give just one quote, Engels described the "metaphysical" approach of the ordinary scientist this way (in *Socialism: Utopian and Scientific,* Chapter II),

> [H]is method of work has. . . left us as legacy the habit of observing natural objects and processes in isolation. . . in repose, not in motion, as constants, not as essentially variables. . .
>
> Dialectics, on the other hand, [he brags] comprehends things. . . in their essential connection, concatenation, motion, origin, and ending. . .

> The old method. . . preferred to investigate *things* as given, as fixed
> and stable. . .

Marx deplores this approach and this view of "things as finished objects," and applauds the dialectical view "that the world is not to be comprehended as a complex of ready-made *things*, but as a complex of processes. . . ."

Yet value, which actually is the end result of a complex of processes, he portrays as a static, ready-made thing. His purported examination of physical entities in "dialectical" manner is mostly rhetoric and obfuscation, and his treatment of a genuinely dynamic principle – exchange value – is likewise exactly the reverse of the appropriate method. Marx is at least consistent in that everything he says is in all cases the reverse of the truth.

The difference between the classical view of exchange value and Marx's view of "value" may be described as follows. In the classical view, commodities can be known to have a certain exchange value because they sell at that price. In Marx's view, things sell at a certain price because that is their value.

More exactly, the classical view is that, to say a commodity has a certain exchange value is the *same* as saying it sells at a certain price. That is how we know what its exchange value is – we see what it exchanges for on the market. Exchange value emerges only in the act of exchange; there is no pre-determined formula for it and no pre-conceived determination of it. All that exists is what we see – the dynamics of the market, the "dialectical clash" of supply and demand producing a resultant price. Exchange value itself is not a thing, but the result of a process; it is not so much "value" (a thing) as *valuing* (a process): it is the judgment of the market on a product. A commodity thus has a certain value, i.e. a certain exchange value, by virtue of the fact that it sells at a certain price.

For Marx, the logic is just the reverse. Value exists beforehand, i.e. before an object is put up for sale in the marketplace. The magnitude of value is logically determined in Marx's analysis as an *a priori* category – it is knowable beforehand by application of a formula. The whole concept of exchange is separated from that of value; value as "commensurability in exchange" is abandoned. Now we have value as a sort of transmutation of labor into solid form as "Value," and exchange value as a manifestation of this congealed, physically-contained labor. Exchange value is mystically determined by the guiding influence of the physical quantity of labor deposited inside the commodity.

For all these reasons it is accurate to say that in Marx's schema, a commodity first of all possesses within itself a definite value; and it then achieves a certain exchange value because of that pre-determined "value."

We can see this more clearly by looking at some statements Marx makes further on in his text. He says for instance, "It becomes plain that it is not the exchange of commodities which regulates the magnitude of their value; but, on the contrary, that it is the magnitude of their value which controls their exchange properties." That is, value exists *a priori*, in isolation from the market; and it controls or determines exchange value. Goods have a certain *exchange* value because they first possess a certain transcendent or mystical inner "Value."

We see another indication of this when Marx also states his "assumption, that all commodities . . . are bought and sold at their full value." That implies that there is an independent standard, *apart from exchange value*, for determining "value." Exchange value is assumed by Marx to correspond in magnitude to this prior, independent standard of value.

By contrast, in the classical view, value is for all intents and purposes synonymous with market price. Whatever the commodity sells for, that is ipso facto its value; there is no ulterior value such as Marx conceives of. Value is determined in exchange, not as an *a priori* category.

For Marx, "The price, then, is merely the money-name of the quantity of social labor realised in his commodity." Value is absolutely static, pre-determined, "ready-made" and "metaphysical." Exchange value is represented as a mere offshoot of this basic concept: it follows after and is a subordinate, "phenomenal form" of this fixed, pre-determined value of Marx's.

Marx says, of any given commodity, "Its value, like that of every other commodity, is already fixed before it goes into circulation, since a definite quantity of social labor has been spent upon it. . ." Value is fixed and determined beforehand, and accompanies the commodity to market like an invisible price sticker. Marx's skill in twisting logic and making "value" appear to mean "embodied labor," now pays off. He has this personal, pet concept he can discuss, a "value" which is totally imaginary and has nothing whatsoever to do with genuine economic value, but which advances his purposes. His text is simply a matter of "dialectics," of verbal gymnastics, sophistical logic, and "specious and fantastic arrangements of words." Marx can make this fictitious entity appear to be anything he wants it to be, and the real world cannot intrude to refute him.

As between the two views of value, the reader can judge for himself, from his own experience, which is the accurate view. This author will venture his opinion, that Marx is seeing ghosts and goblins in positing an invisible "Value" exercising its influence over real-world, market value. The visible, apparent facts are explanation enough in themselves, and do not require any such *deus ex machina* to make sense of them. By the principle of Occam's Razor, and by common experience and common sense, Marx's view of value seems untenable.

Further comments on value

Marx states, "A use-value, or useful article, therefore, has value only because human labor in the abstract has been embodied or materialised in it."

That is true by definition, that is, by Marx's personal definition. If value is *defined* as crystallized labor, then obviously the commodity has value only because human labor has been embodied in it.

That is then a trivial statement; but Marx apparently means it to carry along part of the connotations of the normal, or classical, sense of the word "value." That is, value is supposed to mean simultaneously his new, personal concept and at the same time value in the original sense of market value, everyday value, exchange value.

The compounding together of these two meanings of the word, so that the reader keeps two entirely different definitions in his mind at the same time, makes the statement above seem meaningful. The statement appears non-trivial, but actually it is only a restatement of the fact that Marx defined, by force as it were, value as simply "embodied labor."

Marx can't, by sheer force of logic or definition, make exchange value always be quantitatively in direct proportion to the "Value" – the embodied labor. The massive, overwhelming preponderance of factual evidence shows clearly that exchange value does not form such a simple, or simple-minded, relationship. It depends on more factors than labor – rents and profits, for instance. And ultimately, it is actually determined by supply and demand. Marx's specious syllogisms and definitions can't compel exchange value, by sheer force of logic and mystical power of words, to comply with his system. Logic can't compel the facts.

Recapitulation of the proof

Marx's proof, to recap, was something like this: first, exchange value, a mathematical relation, exists only because all goods contain a "common substance" whose amount determines (or constitutes) their exchange value. By process of elimination, Marx reduces the possibilities for the "common substance" to one: the property of being products of labor. Since labor is the substance that determines the exchange value of all commodities, or "manifests itself in the exchange value of commodities," it follows that labor, the common substance, is their "Value." (Thus labor is now *identical* with value, not merely its determiner.) For good measure Marx defines labor, or "crystals of this social substance," as Value; so labor is value both by definition and by proof.

This fundamental illogic of Marx's entire argument is mingled with a weird metaphysics of transmuting entities, of alter egos, of one thing "manifesting" itself in various "forms" or guises. This substitutes superstitious metaphysics for the more prosaic scientific understanding of what it means to say that one quantity is determined by another. The accurate model is cause and effect, or a quantitative correlation between two separate and distinct entities; it is not various "forms" and mutations and manifestations of an unseen "Ideal" or transcendent phenomenon.

More about the proof

The question of whether value is determined by the amount of labor invested (let us not say "embodied") in the commodity is a factual one. We should be able to say, by empirical investigation, whether exchange value is always in direct proportion to the total amount of expended labor. It should in principle be possible to measure the productivity of some set of industries, that is, to find the ratio of labor to output, and to compare that to prices. Conceptually it should not be a difficult study to set up.

However, Marx did not proceed that way. He proceeded in several directions at once, one of them being to redefine the subject. "Value" ceases to mean what the normal user of language thinks it means, and is redefined as embodied labor. By this method a biology student could prove that the tiger is native to North America: "Let us define the tiger as a large, tawny-colored predator of the cat family, often found in mountainous and desert regions, and native to North America." Thus the desired point is easily proved, if one's attitude towards words is Humpty Dumpty's: "The question is . . . which is to be master – that's all." By this process however the investigation ceases to be an inquiry about the real world or about a substantive issue, and becomes an exercise in verbal manipulation.

The amazing fact is that Marx has trumped up his entire labor theory from nothing, from thin air. Literally the only fact he has adduced is that exchange value fluctuates while use-value presumably remains the same. All else is arbitrary assumption, specious logic, blatant redefinition of words, and *ex cathedra* pronouncements.

That Marx dealt with the subject thus was not due to its being closed to empirical investigation. To refer again to von Böhm-Bawerk's comments,

> [E]xchange values, that is to say the prices of the commodities as well as the quantities of labor which are necessary for their [production], are real, external quantities . . . Marx ought to have turned to experience. . .he should have given a purely empirical proof. . . [However,] instead of submitting the supposed characteristic property to a positive test. . . Marx tries to convince us

that he has found the sought-for property, by a purely negative proof, by showing that it is not any of the other properties.[14]

That is, he does it by a sophistry, by logic with a stacked deck. Specifically, he does it by a process of elimination that excludes from the start any embarrassing entities. His entire argument is based on a system of abstract syllogistic deductions constructed *ad hoc*, rather than by scientific investigation – a process that shows Marx knew nothing of the nature of economics or of science. The contents of his own head were much more malleable than the facts of the real world, but much less reliable.

As von Böhm-Bawerk succinctly sums up, "He knew that the prices of commodities were not in proportion to the amount of incorporated labor, but to the total cost of production, which comprises other elements besides" – those elements being profits and rents.

Marx's metaphysics simply invents a world from whole cloth; he constructs a schema of interlocking logical categories whose nature and behavior are arbitrarily chosen by him. His new category "Value" is not real-world, everyday value, but a category invented to fit into his hypothetical schema. Many other entities, categories, rules, assumptions, theorems and definitions are also adopted, much as a science-fiction writer invents descriptions of life on some distant planet. In very real fact, Marx invents a fantasy world, and the remainder of his text will concern itself almost exclusively with that fantasy world.

The magnitude of value

Marx continues: "How, then, is the magnitude of this value to be measured?"

By looking at the market price, perhaps? That is how one would measure real value. But let's continue with Marx's version:

"Plainly, by the quantity of the value-creating substance, the labor, contained in the article. The quantity of labor, however, is measured by its duration, and labor-time finds its standard in weeks, days, and hours." (Marx amazingly refrains from adding that these units in turn have their origins "partly in the nature of the physical universe, partly in convention.")

As to how one measures amounts of labor, Marx's comments are unexceptionable. They do show in succinct form the "bait-and-switch" operation Marx has accomplished: the measuring of labor is now synonymous with the measuring of value. The term "value" has been totally divorced from any connection with exchange value; in fact it has ceased to have any recognizable economic relevance. It means purely and simply "embodied labor" – a synthetic, not to say fictitious, entity.

We see too how value is now an *a priori*, logical category. One measures it simply by measuring the labor: the two are logically equivalent. And the amount of value is fixed by the logic of Marx's philosophical system, before the market ever passes judgment on the commodity. His economics becomes a closed logical system, deriving its validity from the definitions, rules and theorems he invents for it, and not on anything the market, i.e. the real world, may do.

From this fact too it appears that Marx is not describing how economics actually works in the real world; rather he is conceiving a hypothetical or "formal" (as opposed to "actual") system. It is a system of logic applied to chosen axioms, much like a field of mathematics.

In the real world we have to wait to see how the market passes judgment on our product, i.e., we have to await the event to know what a good actually sells for. (We may make predictions based on our production costs or on estimates of demand and supply; but the market has the definitive say as to what the exchange value is.) In Marx's system, value is pre-defined by the internal logic of the system. Goods go to market with an invisible price sticker already on them; their "value" has already been determined by the amount of labor embodied in them. (However, Marx never actually measures the amount of labor in any commodity; he established his theory entirely on shifty metaphysics and fancy footwork, without ever needing to measure labor at any time.)

Marx sets out, in his labor theory, to find out what establishes the "quantitative relations" which is exchange value: what determines the magnitude of value. He turns his answer, labor, into the be-all and end-all, the omnipresent explanation of value. In fact, labor becomes actually synonymous with value, and exchange value becomes a neglected poor cousin, a "phenomenal manifestation" or real-world instance of this dual entity, embodied labor or value. The actually significant phenomenon goes unstudied, and Marx directs his readers' gaze toward a fictitious concept. And all subtlety and all distinguishing of various aspects of the nature of value is lost.

NOTES – Chapter 2

1 Adler, Mortimer J. and Kelso, Louis O., *The Capitalist Manifesto,* Westport, Conn., Greenwood Press, 1958, p.56.

2 ibid., p.58.

3 ibid., p.57.

4 Revel, Jean-Francois, *The Totalitarian Temptation,* translated by David Hapgood, New York, Penguin Books, 1978, p.16-17.

5 Calder, Ritchie, *Man and the Cosmos; the Nature of Science Today,* New York, New American Library (Mentor Books), 1969.

6 Calder, Ritchie op cit., p.11.

7 Böhm-Bawerk, Eugen von, *Karl Marx and the Close of His System,* Clifton N.J., A. M. Kelley, 1973, p.68.

8 Duruy, Victor, *A Condensed History of the Middle Ages,* New York, T. Y. Crowell & company, 1900.

9 Postman, Neil, *Amusing Ourselves To Death,* New York, Viking Penguin, 1985, p. 23.

10 Calder, Ritchie, op. cit., p. 11-12.

11 Calder, Ritchie, op. cit., p. 21.

12 Böhm-Bawerk, Eugen von, op. cit., p.75.

13 Eastman, Max, *Is Marxism Scientific?,* New York, W. W. Norton & Co., 1940, *p.*122.

14 Böhm-Bawerk, Eugen von, op. cit., p.69.

3. QUALIFICATIONS AND CLARIFICATIONS (OF LABOR THEORY)

With the portion of Marx's text we have examined so far, the exposition of his labor theory is for the most part complete. Some additional qualifications do however remain to be added to it.

Marx introduces the first qualification (at the end of Chapter I, Section 1) like this:

> [N]othing can have value, without being an object of utility. If the thing is useless, so is the labor contained in it; the labor does not count as labor, and therefore creates no value.

The point made here seems to be a valid one: useless things have no market value. But if we examine the course of reasoning by which Marx arrives at the conclusion, we may observe some interesting anomalies.

The first question to be asked in this matter is, *Why* do things without utility have no value? Is Marx's qualification a statement of something that happens in the real world, some characteristic of people, or goods, or markets, that prevents useless goods from having market value? Or is it an arbitrary statement, introduced to maintain the logical self-consistency of his theoretical system?

The classical view is this: useless goods have no value, and the reason they have no value is that people do not desire them and will not knowingly part with money for them. That is, the demand for useless products is nil. *

This is an observable phenomenon, and a line of cause and effect can be established connecting the particular phenomenon (the fact that useless goods have no value) to basic realities or axioms of human economic nature. One of the most basic facts we can know about people in general, starting with ourselves, is that we want to get as much as we can for our money, preferably at least a commensurate exchange. We don't want to get absolutely nothing

---

* Some quibbles might be made, about fads like "pet rocks." Perhaps there is simply no analyzing such fads, or perhaps the "utility" of those was for a jokebook packaged with the rock.

for it; and a useless product is as close to absolutely nothing as we come. (That is: ultimately, *utility* is the source of exchange value or demand.)

And all this can be established by normal observation and inquiry, and without the necessity of trick definitions of words like "value" and without first constructing an interlocking theoretical system of axioms, definitions and phony proofs. In other words, we learn it from the real world, not from convoluted sophistries.

That is, the fact that useless goods have no (market) value is obvious and almost axiomatic; yet it does present a problem to Marx's theory. The problem, and the factor compelling Marx to devise the qualification in question, is that in its original form Marx's theory would *not* lead to the conclusion that useless goods have no value. Within the context of his theory in its original, unaltered form, useless goods should have value; it is not their utility or lack of it that creates value, after all, but the labor that has been expended on them and thus congealed in them; labor in congealed form is Value.

In Marx's theory as originally stated, there is no basis for making any distinction between goods in which "human labor in the abstract" has been embodied and which have utility, and those in which human labor has been embodied and which have no utility. The whole thrust of his argument centers around one thing only, labor; goods have value because they contain some amount of this common substance.

We cannot allow him to retract his proof. To refer to usefulness or use-value as a prior necessity of value, is to bring the judgment of the marketplace into his theory, which means bringing in the wishes of buyers, supply and demand, and all such considerations. Such a move would destroy Marx's closed, theoretical system. So we are stuck with this result: all goods in which labor has been invested have value; this is a direct logical consequence of Marx's labor theory.

Thus, for example, if someone thinks it is a good idea to chip large boulders into smaller boulders, and to bring these small boulders to market as patio furniture, Marx's system says that they have value equal to the labor embodied in them. Someone will presumably pay the price for them, as logically pre-determined.

But we know this is, factually speaking, nonsense, and that it is contrary to the workings of the real world. To avoid such contradictions between the real world and his system. Marx had to adjust and modify his system; the current qualification thus had to be added.

The questions we then must address are, Is Marx's qualification logically consistent with the rest of his theory as stated up to the point? And could the explanation he gives really be the reason why useless goods have no value? Some considerable discussion must be devoted to these questions.

One thing that could be said is that the question of what goods are useless is not a clear-cut one, and it may even represent circular logic on Marx's part. Of course, the example of chipped boulders would seem clear-cut, but we don't often see such offerings of patently useless goods on the market. Most capitalists produce goods which they consider to be useful, and they offer them on the market in that belief and in the hope that the public will agree, and will pay enough for them to recompense production costs and return a profit. The question is not so much whether the goods are useful, but whether they are useful and desirable enough to command a full, profitable price level on the market.

For example, at the time of this writing there are in a local department store some miniature staplers, marked down from $3.99 to $2.00 (half-price). Their package bills them as "The smallest stapler made using #10 [standard] staples." They're tiny, and of some novel interest; but apparently few people feel the need for a miniature stapler – there is quite a stock of them on sale.

So this stapler has utility – it staples. And the manufacturer produced it with the expectation that his estimation of the stapler's utility would be matched by the public's. But that has not happened. Now, in Marx's system, these staplers have utility, and thus value, and that value should be the full complement of the embodied homogeneous human labor. For him it is either yes or no, the goods have value or they do not. (For this reason too his reductionist and simple-minded theoretical system cannot account for the real world.) His theory is not borne out in practice.

In sum, it is not a simple yes-or-no question of whether the goods have utility, but whether the degree of that utility is perceived by buyers as sufficient to justify a full, profitable exchange value. And in fact, the method of telling which goods are useless is not a straightforward one. It is not always a matter of goods that absolutely don't work. Using Marx's system, the way to identify "useless" goods (like the stapler above) would be to identify those that don't sell: these have no market value, and thus we know they are useless. Thus what we are really doing is allowing the market to first have its say. We know which goods are "useless" because they don't sell, not the other way around, as Marx asserts. It isn't that they have no value because they are first (logically) identified as useless. We identify them as useless because they have no value, or not enough to sell at full price. In any but the simplest cases, like cars with no motors and machines that don't work, that is all Marx's qualification amounts to – a case of circular reasoning, in which he represents the line of cause and effect as going one way when it is actually going the other way.

But all this is more or less incidental; it says only that the category of "useless" goods may not be as clear-cut or as objectively identifiable as Marx seems to assume. Taking the term at face value, however, and considering it as identifying absolutely non-functional goods like cars that don't run, machines that don't work, etc., let us examine the logic of Marx's qualification concerning useless goods.

Why can nothing have value, without having utility? Because "If the thing is useless, so is the labor contained in it; the labor does not count as labor, and therefore creates no value."

This rationale has two basic parts: first, there is the statement that if an object is useless, the labor expended in making it is useless; second, the proviso that useless labor creates no value. Here again we may reflect on what *kind* of statements these are; neither could be said to be exactly a matter of objective fact.

The first assertion, that labor exerted in creating a useless object is useless labor, might be seen as a logical deduction with a certain amount of validity to it. If labor doesn't produce a useful product, it's useless labor – that might be a definition we could accept under certain circumstances. But it is essentially an arbitrary statement, a matter of personal choice on Marx's part; certainly it is not a self-evident or irrefutable statement of fact.

For example, work is often considered useful for therapeutic value, even if no good product is produced. Some people clear weeds or cut wood even if there is no need to do so. It could be said that hard work is intrinsically virtuous, or that it helps one lose weight or sleep better. In times of economic depression people sometimes get jobs doing things which produce little of objective utility, just so they can get a paycheck and help "prime the pump" of economic activity. Convicts have at times, or so the popular image has it, been set to work breaking rocks for little reason but the rehabilitative effects of hard labor. For all these reasons labor might be considered useful, even if the product produced is not. The connection is not as direct and self-evident as Marx presumes.

The second part of the rationale, that "useless" labor creates no value, is an entirely new thesis which makes its first appearance here. There is no basis for it in Marx's labor theory as derived; no reason to suppose that "useless" labor does not congeal as readily as useful labor, and no reason to suppose that congealed "useless" labor cannot, equally with congealed "useful" labor, constitute the "common something" which lies hidden in all commodities and accounts for their exchange values. The entire logic or rationale of Marx's labor theory has nothing which would justify any distinction between "useless" labor and "useful" labor in creating congealed value. This, despite the apparent bland assumption of Marx that the point has already been discussed and made before he ever got to his qualification. He writes as if this new stipulation he is adding were already a foregone conclusion. "[T]he labor does not count as labor, and therefore creates no value." The word "therefore" indicates that he is not adding a new, arbitrary stipulation to his labor theory, but making a logical inference from some already-established premise.

Marx's qualification, or his rationale explaining why useless goods have no value, is by no means the real reason for that phenomenon. His qualification is an *ad hoc* rationalization added to his theory after the fact, in an attempt to bring his theory into accord with certain inescapable facts of the real world. The real reason useless goods have no value is that there is no demand for them, i.e., people won't buy them. On the principle of Occam's Razor, these simple and adequately explanatory facts should have been given some credence by Marx.

Marx, however, has a weird theory of value in which value is mechanistically created as a static, physical substance, by the congealing or precipitation of labor. And according to this weird theory useless things should have value; thus Marx was compelled to come up with yet more arbitrary stipulations in order to bar useless goods from having value, and thus to bring his theory back into some semblance of accord with reality. Thus we have, "Useless goods imply there was useless labor, and useless labor has no value."

But again let us look at Marx's rationale: Why does useless labor not create value? "[T]he labor does not count as labor, and therefore creates no value." This is surely not a statement of any objective fact of nature; there is no such category or relationship in objective reality as "A *counts* as A." Marx is creating arbitrary categories which are completely subject to his authority and can be created at his whim. He is not describing an independently existing reality, but constructing the rules for an arbitrary, purely theoretical system. In short, Marx is writing like someone making up the rules for a new game: "If the ball goes outside the blue line, it doesn't count."

That brings us to the fundamental distinction between what Marx is writing and genuine science or genuine economics. Marx is not describing the real world and the forces, entities and phenomena that occur in it. Rather, Marx has an imaginary world which he has created from arbitrary assumptions, questionable deductions, and various other elements. He has a theoretical system built up from axioms, elementary defined entities, and deduced interrelationships; but it is a completely fictive or imaginary system. (More precisely, it is what we might call a "formal system" – formal as opposed to actual; it exists "for the sake of argument" and is built of theoretical, or formal components, much as a field of mathematics is built up from axioms, definitions and added theorems.)

This theoretical system has no objective existence; it is something Marx has partly defined and partly "proved" (by fractured logic) into existence. Yet Marx takes it to be the real world, and deals with it as if it were the real world. His entire text, in fact, will be based on it and will refer to it, explaining every new phenomenon in terms of it. It is the fictional world composed of Marx's collection of definitions, axioms, theorems, and so on; it is a logical entity referring only to itself, not by any means an accurate picture of the real world.

Most of the time Marx can simply work within the context of his fictive world, without ever referring to the real one. He puts a question or input into his fictional system, and he derives the appropriate answer or output (freely inventing as he goes along). The real world doesn't intrude into his reasonings.

But there are difficulties at times, when the real world cannot be ignored. At some points his theory may be said to touch the ground, where certain actual real-world results are to be anticipated. In these cases Marx must try to make his theory square with the facts and indeed seem to be the valid explanation for those facts. In such cases his theory must be adjusted and brought into line with reality, so that events do not patently refute it. But Marx's theory is never the real explanation for those facts; he brings it seemingly in line with the facts, but it remains a fictional theory and an imaginary world, and the adjustments to his theory are always *ad hoc* rationalizations, sophistries added on after the fact to preserve his theory. The theory itself is never the true picture.

Thus in the present instance: in the matter of useless goods, the facts are too well-known to be distorted, and Marx's theory cannot remain purely indifferent to them. The results predicted by his theory must be the facts as they actually obtain (namely, useless goods have no value, rather than the contrary, as his theory would naturally predict).

Thus to twist his theory just enough to make it seem to be in accord with the real world, Marx has to introduce his qualification – consisting of new stipulations and added sophistries to achieve the desired outcome. While this makes the results of his theory consistent with the real world – in that useless goods have no value – the picture, the rationale he presents, is added on after the facts, not based on them. It is not the real *explanation* of the phenomenon – not the real reason why useless goods have no value.

As an overview of the sophistry Marx devises for this qualification, we might say that Marx displaces the uselessness of the product onto the labor. That is, the real reason useless goods have no value is that the *goods* are useless; that's why people won't buy them. But to find a loophole to make this fit his system, Marx says that useless goods imply useless labor, and "useless labor is hereby declared to create no value." Thus he shifts the responsibility for the lack of value from the shoulders of the useless product onto that of the (now-declared) useless labor.

This makes his system work, but it is not the real explanation. No one thinks, "I don't want to buy useless labor, so that useless product with its useless labor is not for me." The real reason is simpler and more direct: people will not buy useless goods, simply because they *are* useless. People won't spend money for useless goods; there is no demand for them. The facts cannot be redefined to fit Marx's theory.

In displacing the uselessness from the product to the labor, Marx is compelled by a previous part of his text. He has already dismissed use-value (utility) from being a pertinent consideration in determining exchange value. Exchange is characterized by "a total abstraction from use-value," he has informed us. Thus when Marx comes up against a case where quite plainly utility *is* related to exchange value, Marx is unable to accept that simple, unadulterated fact. He cannot simply report that useless goods give rise to no demand, cannot be sold, and have no value. Yet useless goods as treated by his theory must be shown to have no value for *some* reason; his theory must be brought into accord with the real world in some manner.

Thus use-value or utility reappears, but in a sublimated or repressed form as the usefulness of the *labor*, not as what it really is, the usefulness (or lack thereof) of the commodity itself. But if we pay a little attention to his theory in detail, we see that it is in no way a description of the real world; that the real world doesn't work like that; and in fact that Marx's whole theoretical model is a hypothetical, and entirely non-existent abstract system, not a picture of the real world.

Further qualifications

A few more qualifications remain to be added to Marx's labor theory of value. We have already seen one, namely, that the commodity produced must be a useful one, in order for the labor to "count" as labor and thus to create value. Marx now introduces another qualification, as follows:

> Some people might think that if the value of a commodity is determined by the quantity of labor spent on it, the more idle and unskillful the labor, the more valuable would the commodity be, because more time would be required in its production.

Exactly so; that would follow from Marx's labor theory. The labor performed on the commodity, measured by its duration, that is, in units of time, constitutes the congealed "common something" which Marx has proven to be identical with value. We have been given no basis for supposing anything except that all labor congeals alike; or to put it another way, one man's labor of half an hour should congeal just like another's. There seems to be no basis for saying that less "congealed labor-time" would result from a half-hour of one laborer's efforts than from another's.

There is a kind of inverted or anti-economic logic at the core of Marx's system: the slower laborer should add more value to the product, because it takes him longer to produce it. He is paid the same per hour, thus costing the entrepreneur more per unit of production. But the only relevant factor in the value of his product is the time he spends working (not what he accomplishes).

Of course no economic system could really function for long in the real world on the basis of Marx's kind of inverted logic. Certainly real "capitalist" economics do not function that way; we don't see goods with a higher price, i.e. a higher market value (corresponding to a higher internal, transcendent "Value") selling successfully alongside identical goods produced at lower cost by a more efficient workforce.

People don't pay more for goods produced by "idle and unskillful" laborers just because the internal logic of a theoretical system somehow requires it. They don't pay more as a reward to the laborers for their efforts, or for the satisfaction of owning a certain number of hours of embodied labor, idle and unskillful as it may be. Rather, they try to pay less. If there are cheaper goods of the same quality for sale, people will buy the cheaper goods. The manufacturer whose labor force is idle and unskillful, or hampered by antiquated machinery or some other difficulty, cannot automatically expect to recover the full "embodied labor-time" in his selling price; not if there is any competition at all in the market for that product. He will have to produce the good at a competitive price, or go broke.

That is, he would have to do so in a real-world market environment. Once again the logic of Marx's labor theory, in its original form, is at odds with the nature of real "capitalist" economies. Therefore, if the inference we draw from his theory, as it applies to the case of "idle and unskillful" labor, stands, his theory is not borne out by market events. However, if there is some convincing reason why that is not a necessary conclusion from his theory, his theory may be defensible. Marx is thus at some pains to dispel that notion. He continues,

> The labor, however, that forms the substance of value is homo-geneous human labor, expenditure of one uniform labor-power. The total labor-power of society, which is embodied in the sum total of the values* of all commodities produced by that society, counts here as one homogeneous mass of human labor power, composed though it be of innumerable individual units. Each of these units is the same as any other, so far as it has the character of the average labor-power of society, and takes effect as such; that is, so far as it requires for producing a commodity, no more time than is needed on an average, no more time than is socially necessary.

---

* Here it appears Marx uses the term "value" in its normal sense; that is, he refers to the value *of* a commodity, rather than using "value" to mean the commodity itself. This is a rare occurrence.

Thus we have a new distinction to deal with: not just any old labor "counts" as value, or congeals as value; but only a particular, pre-eminent kind of labor, "homogeneous human labor." "Idle and unskillful" labor, falling short as it does of the standard of this "homogeneous" labor, does not create value, or at least not as much value as it should create based on the duration of the labor.

One obvious question that arises is, on what authority does Marx make this qualification? Is there some objective characteristic that justifies him in making this modification of his theory, or is he just adding an arbitrary stipulation aimed at preserving his system? The answers to these questions will tell us whether the qualification is warranted.

Preliminary investigation

Paraphrasing Marx's current qualification, we could say this: to determine the value of a commodity, we don't simply measure in a straightforward way what might be called the *actual* labor embodied in it. That is, we don't simply observe the production process, time the labor actually performed on a particular article, and declare this actual amount of embodied labor to be the value of the product. Rather, we must by some means (it turns out to be a mathematical means) determine the amount of a *special* kind of labor embodied in the commodity. We must evaluate the commodity's content of "homogeneous human labor," parenthetically identified by Marx as "expenditure of one uniform labor-power," rather than measuring its content of actual, ordinary labor.

This process is an abrupt reversal of what we had been led to believe about value. If there is one conclusion we could have drawn from Marx's exposition of his labor theory to this point, it is that "labor is labor," that it is not differentiated into different kinds and degrees and types.

The entire gist of Marx's text so far draws a picture of labor as a straightforward mechanistic entity, embodying itself or "congealing" within the body of the commodity, with no differentiation on the basis of what kind of labor it is. We would no more expect there to be differences and distinctions to be made as to particular *types* of labor, than to find out that some kinds of steam don't yield the proper amount of water when they condense. Straightforward physical processes don't behave so capriciously.

Marx's proven equivalence of embodied labor (the "common something") and value gives no basis for supposing anything other than that all labor is equal in its power to constitute value. We don't expect to see some kinds of labor more "valuable" or more value-creating than others. So we can conditionally say, at this point we can see no justification for making distinctions between one worker's labor and another's.

For further insight into this question, let us turn to the question of how to calculate a commodity's content of "homogeneous" labor. This can perhaps best be approached by paraphrasing Marx's exposition, and then extrapolating from it somewhat.

The passage in which Marx derives his concept of "homogeneous labor" is not very explicit (even less so than his usual prose). But it appears that his concept of "homogeneous human labor" means the following: to find the value of a commodity, first find the *average* amount of labor (i.e., the average amount of *actual* labor) embodied in the commodity, taking into account all units of the commodity produced in the entire society.

That is, find the nation-wide average (which Marx calls the "social average," the average across the entire society). That is value.

That simple instruction is not given explicitly in Marx's text, but it is implied. He says, first, the "total labour of society," which produces "the sum total" of all the commodities produced, is considered, or "counts," as "one homogeneous mass of human labor-power." (We will restrict ourselves here to dealing with one commodity at a time, not to the "total labour of society.")

That is, as Marx says, we consider all the labor and all the commodities (or the total amount of one commodity, in our case) in the society. And to consider all the labor performed on a commodity as a "homogeneous mass," what we have to do is add it all into one lump sum; that is, we add all the "man-hours" together, without differentiating or making distinctions among any of them, and arrive at a sum representing the total number of labor-hours embodied in the production of the commodity throughout the entire country. This is then a "social," or society-wide, figure.

Then, we consider this lump sum or "homogeneous mass" of labor-hours as composed of "innumerable individual units," that is, we divide it back into parts again.

However, this time we want each of the "innumerable individual units" to be "the same as any other," meaning that we divide the lump sum of man-hours into equal parts. Each part or unit must have the characteristic that "it requires for producing a commodity, no more time than is needed on an average."

This calculation produces a quotient which represents a certain amount of labor, namely, a period of labor of that duration which produces one unit of output in the average time. Each of these quantities of labor produces a commodity in "no more time than is needed on an average."

In short, this mathematical process yields a quotient which is the average amount of labor-time needed to produce a certain standard quantity of the commodity. It is the average labor-time embodied in the commodity; and it is this figure which Marx now wants us to take as the value of the commodity.

This quotient, notice, is a result of dividing the total mass of labor (for one product) into "innumerable" identical pieces, each piece sufficient to produce one unit of the commodity. The size of these pieces is the average amount of time, or the amount of time "socially necessary." If we divide the entire quantity of labor into segments, each of which produces one unit of the commodity in the average time, that is the same as saying each of these segments is equal to the average amount of labor per unit. And "homogeneous labor" then means labor in terms of these homogeneous units, or average units. *

And in Marx's terminology, "homogeneous human labor" probably means labor of average productivity – that is, it is "expenditure of one uniform labor-power." It is this labor, he tells us, that constitutes value.

Let us examine this more closely: when Marx divides the two sums (of labor and the produced commodity), each of the "innumerable individual units" is supposed to be the same as all the others in that "it has the character of the average labor-power of society." Average labor-power, or productivity, is labor that produces a commodity in "no more time than is needed on an average." The value of a commodity is now defined as the amount of this *average* labor contained in the product; we must somehow calculate it, and then we will know the product's value.

Of course, the average amount of embodied labor *time* is the reciprocal of average *productivity*, or average labor-power. Thus "expenditure of one uniform labor-power" may mean work performed at the rate of average productivity; and "homogeneous human labor" is then such an expenditure, i.e., the expenditure of labor at the average rate of productivity, or at the rate of "uniform labor power."

Thus it may be that what we first need to do is to find the average rate of labor-power for the commodity, that is, to calculate the average productivity: the average number of units produced per man-hour. This is "expenditure of one uniform labor-power," or "average labor-power." The amount of this labor, embodied in this commodity is the value.

But the amount of "labor of average productivity," is identical to the average amount of labor. Average productivity is the reciprocal of the average labor per unit of commodity. As Marx correctly points out, labor of average productivity, or "average labor-power," is precisely identical to that labor that produces a unit of the commodity in "no more time than is needed on an average" or in the average labor-time. Regardless of which figure one calculates first (that is, which way one divides first), the result is the same.

---

* We can see from this example why in actual calculations it would be
necessary to restrict ourselves to one commodity. It would be impossible
to deal with the total number of units of wheat, bicycles, and everything
else at once, and get a meaningful figure.

It becomes apparent that there is nothing in Marx's notion of "homogeneous" labor which is not contained in the concept of the average. That is, there is nothing peculiar to the subject of economics, or value, or labor in what he has to say about homogeneous labor, uniform labor-power, and the rest. Marx is just saying, We'll find the average and consider that to be the value.

Averages as a conceptual entity

There is however, this difference: Marx speaks of the average, a merely conceptual or statistical entity, as if it were an actual or concrete thing; he writes as if using the average were not an arbitrary choice but an acknowledgment of something inherent in the phenomena themselves – as if in some manner the average labor were found in nature. He says the total labor of society "counts" as a homogeneous mass – that is, not that he simply *chooses* to count it as such, but rather that for some implied substantive reason in the nature of things, it necessarily "counts" as such. He speaks of the innumerable divided units as if they were actual, concrete entities; each of them *"is* the same as any other," that is, each is the same as the result of an automatic or spontaneous process – he doesn't speak of *making* them all the same.

For that matter, he seems to assume that the mass of labor is *automatically* divided into innumerable units. He says the total labor counts as a homogeneous mass, "composed though it be" of many equal units. He neglects to say that we ourselves must do the dividing in order to see it as composed of equal units, i.e., in order to obtain an average.

Thus Marx speaks of a conceptual, statistical process as if it were concrete and actual and occurring in nature. An average doesn't exist at all until somebody calculates it – only the actual, individual values concretely exist. But Marx speaks of the average as if nature itself supplied it, as if it were a concrete phenomenon.

The result then is this: value is the amount of "homogeneous human labor" embodied in the commodity. That is, value is the amount of *average* labor, meaning labor of the average rate of productivity ("expenditure of one uniform labor-power"). To the extent or proportion that a laborer's efforts are not "homogeneous" labor, are not equal to the average rate, to that same extent the amount of labor-time he invests in a product must be adjusted. For instance, if his rate of productivity is only half the "uniform" rate of productivity, then each minute of his labor "takes effect" only "as such," or only to that extent – i.e., only to the extent of one-half. Since his rate of productivity is only half what it "should be," since it is only half of "uniform labor-power," it follows that his labor is only half of "homogeneous labor," and each minute of his labor correspondingly "counts" as only half a minute. It "takes effect as such."

That is, if his rate of productivity is half the "uniform" rate, each unit of his *actual* labor only amounts to half a minute of "homogeneous" labor; it "counts" as only half a minute. In this sense "homogeneous" or average labor is the standard for measuring value; the standard is not the duration of the labor actually performed on the commodity.

This line of argument, relating "uniform labor-power" to "homogeneous labor" and so on, (to use a phrase of Marx's) "turns all around in a circle and never leaves the spot." Labor at the "uniform" rate of labor-power is "homogeneous" labor; the amount of labor of the average rate of productivity is the same as the average amount of labor. The entire meaning of the qualification is simply this: For value, take the average amount of labor (-time*) invested in the commodity.

The rate of productivity and the time invested per unit of commodity are reciprocals. Thus to start by calculating the rate of productivity (called "uniform" labor-power) and then to "discount" the labor-time by the ratio between this particular rate and the homogeneous rate, is mathematically identical in every case to just using the average figure for the amount of embodied labor. All Marx's qualification means is this: For the value of a commodity, don't use the actual labor-time; use the average.

To say that the value of a commodity is the amount of "homogeneous human labor" embodied in it, where "homogeneous" labor is defined as labor which "requires for producing a commodity, no more time than is needed on an average," is just to say that the value is the average amount of labor.

Marx's argument is founded on this average; it works its way out from it in a broad rhetorical circle and then returns to it. This qualification means simply, "For value, take the average." The rest is just detritus.

What's the difference?

The question naturally arises, if Marx's qualification means no more than, "For value, take the average amount of labor," why didn't he just say so plainly? What is the difference between saying value is the "amount of average labor," and saying value is the "average amount of labor"?

---

* Since labor is, as we already know, measured in units of duration, the term "labor-time" is redundant.

The difference between the two alternative formulations, and the apparent reason Marx didn't simply say "Value is the average amount of labor," once again involves the issue of the source of authority for Marx's qualification, or the kind of statement Marx supposes the qualification to be.

The reason for Marx's formulation, briefly put, is this: Marx purports to write as a scientist, and he has presented his labor theory as more or less a statement of scientific fact. His theory is purportedly a naturalistic description of the behavior of certain material phenomena; not a matter of arbitrary definition or speculative theorizing. Marx's labor theory is based (we are to understand) on the observed objective fact that labor congeals or condenses physically in a commodity, where it constitutes "Value" (as proven logically by Marx; Marx allows logical proofs into his "science").

Given this scientific nature of Marx's labor theory, in which its status is that of a factual report of the generalized "laws" of behavior of objective phenomena, Marx could not qualify his theory with arbitrary stipulations or definitions. But an average is something arbitrary (and even worse, it's statistical). It is an entirely man-made phenomenon: it doesn't even exist until someone calculates it. Any qualification based on an average would thus have an arbitrary nature and would inextricably be a matter of human choice or definition. This arbitrary nature would conflict with the supposedly factual and scientific nature of the theory as a whole; the two parts would be logically inconsistent.

Thus Marx presents his qualification not in bold and arbitrary terms, but as if it were also a matter of objective fact, a matter of the substantive, physical nature of the phenomena in and of themselves.

Thus we see that Marx's authority for making his qualification, the purported basis for its validity, is that it is a statement of objective fact about the behavior of physical entities; it is part of the natural and spontaneously-occurring behavior of the phenomena themselves. Marx purports to find a naturalistic imperative, something in the real world itself that causes only the average labor to constitute itself as value. The value, i.e. the embodied labor in the commodity, *on its own* turns out to equal the amount of "homogeneous" labor, for reasons in the nature of the physical universe itself, and not just because Marx stipulates it to be so. Such is the light in which Marx presents the qualification; or at least, that is the most plausible inference concerning Marx's source of justification or authority.

"Homogeneous" as qualitatively different

Marx's theory cannot be modified by the arbitrary stipulations he introduces. The entire thrust of Marx's text is to portray the average, which is a conceptual entity, as a phenomenon found in the objective nature of the entities under discussion – as something observable in nature, rather than as an arbitrarily-chosen point on a continuum of equally valid quantities. The word "homogeneous," used in this manner, allows Marx to avoid use of the plainly conceptual term, "average." Marx implies that labor *actually* is homogeneous, not that he himself arbitrarily adds all labor together in a homogeneous mass; he writes as if describing spontaneously-occurring phenomena, rather than as if calculating a purely statistical quantity. He uses the deceptive term "uniform labor-power," falsely implying the existence of actual uniformity rather than the process of calculating average productivity.

Marx writes of homogeneous labor as "the labor" that counts as value; this seems to imply a type of labor, with a difference in kind, a qualitative difference from other "labors." In other words, it is a type or kind of labor, not a mere quantitative difference in the amount of labor contained.

Similarly, Marx writes that each individual unit "is" the same as any other – i.e., spontaneously, actually the same. He doesn't state clearly that we divide and find the average, and thus we *make* each unit the same as any other.

He says the labor-power "*counts* as one homogeneous mass"; and this may be seen as a partial admission that the assertion is somewhat arbitrary. (He doesn't simply say it "is" a homogeneous mass, after all.) But he seems to imply there is some substantive reason why it counts as a homogeneous mass – not that he just chooses to count it so in order to derive the average.

Everything Marx says in converting the concept of "average" to "homogeneous" seems aimed at presenting the arbitrary use of a statistical entity as instead the description of a substantive phenomenon, something found in the objective nature of the things themselves. This face which he puts on the "homogeneous" labor thus makes his qualification seem to be in accord with the objective, scientific nature of his labor theory itself.

The difference between value as "the amount of average (or homogeneous) labor," and value as "the average amount of labor" is this: in the former guise the average is dressed up as a substantive, objective phenomenon, whereas the latter formulation clearly speaks of a statistical entity. Marx implies a qualitative distinction which makes only "homogeneous" labor fit or capable of becoming value (for some unnamed reason). Thus in this scheme there is an objective justification for discounting the labor performed in an "idle and unskillful" manner, and accepting only a certain percentage of it, according to how well it measures up to "homogeneous" labor. Without such a justification, the whole amount of unskillful labor would have to "count" (we infer from Marx's theory) as value; and that would be contrary to the evidence of our own senses, or that is, our experience of economic realities. The fallacy of Marx's "homogeneous labor" is that in actuality there is a mere quantitative difference between average labor and labor at any other rate of productivity. Thus the use of homogeneous labor is a matter of mere arbitrary decree on Marx's part.

The difference between "value as the amount of average labor" and "value as the average amount of labor," is the difference between a supposed actual or concrete phenomenon called "homogeneous labor," and a conceptual, statistical entity called an average. Marx does literally mean to invoke "homogeneous" labor as an objective phenomenon. "Homogeneous" labor is for him labor of a particular kind; there is a qualitative difference, not just a quantitative one. Labor is composed of units which must "have the character of" average labor. It is a matter of what kind of labor "counts," for some substantive reason in the nature of the different kinds of labor. It is not just a matter of stipulating an average or of making quantitative adjustments in what is defined as value; or at least it presents that appearance. Thus Marx's qualification, stating that only homogeneous labor constitutes value, has more scientific and objective-sounding overtones than the prosaic command, "For value, take the average."

Labor theory as science

The reason Marx's qualification is presented in quasi-naturalistic guise is that only in such a form can it possibly merge with the basic core of Marx's labor theory in order to form a coherent whole. Marx has initially presented value itself as a physical property of commodities, and has presented his value theory as a naturalistic analysis, the discovery of an objective relationship between physical or naturalistic entities: as, actually, scientific law. This objective law cannot be qualified by the addition of arbitrary stipulations such as "Value is the average amount of labor." Arbitrary, statistical concepts cannot be parts of any scientific law purporting to describe objective reality. The respective natures of the two are inconsistent; they proceed from entirely different assumptions about the nature of the phenomena under consideration; they will not merge. Thus Marx had to present his qualification as objective fact, just like the initial theory.

In order to make this disparity plain, the supposed scientific nature of Marx's labor theory can be further elaborated on.

Value as a natural property

The first point to be made is that value, as Marx presents it, comes quite close to meeting the requirements for being a physical property of the commodity.

Physical properties, or natural properties, like weight (or mass*), volume, specific gravity and so on, are the subjects of concern in the natural sciences. Such properties have as their distinguishing characteristic the fact that they are precisely definable, objectively discernible, measurable properties of an object in and of itself. Only properties which meet these requirements are subject to treatment by the natural sciences.

Natural properties are *precisely definable*; that is, one can tell exactly what does and does not fit into the category of a particular property. For example, color is a property of objects, but it is perhaps not definable precisely enough to be treatment by sciences; there are many shades of red, and it is hard to say at times whether a color is green, or blue, or blue-green, or what have you.

On the other hand, frequency, meaning the frequency of the light reflected from the object (which is perceived as color), is a more scientifically-rigorous property than color, and it is treated by science as being closely related to color but more precise.

Physical properties must be *objective*, not subjective or perceptual. To repeat, color is somewhat in this category: an object reflects light of certain wavelengths, true; but color itself is a matter of perception. The subjective image or perception a person experiences from a particular wavelength is not open to investigation.

Another example is beauty: the shape or form or appearance of an object such as a painting is perhaps objective and describable, but the *beauty* of the object is more a matter of subjective opinion. The beauty may plausibly be said to be not a property of the object itself, but a function of people's perception of it. That is, the property "beauty," unlike the objective physical arrangement of the object, is not a part of the object, but is in the beholder's perception of it as aesthetically pleasing.

Physical properties are, above all, *quantifiable*, at least, in principle. The properties in which science is interested, and which it is equipped to deal with, are quantities of objective magnitude.

Other characteristics may be as real and as important, but science is unable to discuss them — they do not adapt themselves to treatment by the scientific method. Thus properties like mass, volume, density, and so on can be discussed quantitatively. The taste of an apple, or the niceness of a person, or the moral worth of a society, cannot be quantified. They must be discussed and debated by other methods, using standards more humanistic than scientific.

---

* Mass is an actual physical property of the object itself; weight depends on the pull of gravity at a particular place, and thus might be considered a property of the object and its environment. It is determined by the mass of the object and other factors like the mass of the attracting body (the earth). An object weighs less on a high mountain, or on the moon, for example.

(Actually, not every physical property is measurable at all times. Sub-atomic particles may be said to be something of a special case, since according to the Heisenberg "uncertainty principle," it is impossible to determine both the position and the velocity of a particle at the same time. One or the other can be determined, but the act of determining one disturbs the other, so only one at a time can be measured.)

By the terms of almost all of these criteria, value as described in Marx's labor theory is a physical property of goods. Value is represented as a common *substance*, found "in" all commodities – this indicating that Marx considers it a property *of* the commodity, something found in the commodity, and not a matter of externalities like how the market treats the commodity.

Value consists in the fact that in commodities "there exists in equal quantities something common" to all commodities. That is, it is quantifiable; it exists in certain fixed amounts (determined directly by the amount of labor invested in the commodity).

Marx says that "the magnitude of the value of a commodity represents only the quantity of labor embodied in it," or "congealed" or "crystallised" in it – a sure indication he is referring to an internally-contained property. Moreover, he says "the bodies of commodities are combinations of two elements – matter and labor." That is clear indication that he means congealed labor is physically contained in the commodity.

In every way Marx portrays value as a physical property: it is a characteristic of the commodity in and of itself, a part of its physical makeup; it is definable and objectively quantifiable.

(It should be emphasized that Marx's view of value is diametrically opposed to the classical view in this respect, since he regards value as a physical property possessed by the commodity itself in a fixed amount, and not a matter of human market interactions with respect to the commodity.)

If there is one respect in which Marx's portrayal of value is not a picture of a physical property, it is this alone: value is not *directly* discernible in the commodity. That is, it can't be directly observed or measured within the object, as physical properties like mass, volume, and so on can. Value can only be measured beforehand, that is, while it is being embodied in the commodity. The labor exerted to produce the commodity is measured, i.e. timed, to determine the resulting value of the commodity.

That is, value is congealed labor, but it can't be perceived or measured in the commodity itself; the labor itself must be measured before it "congeals," i.e. while it is being performed. Only thus can one know how much value the object contains. In all other respects value as Marx describes it has exactly the nature of a physical property.

This type of self-contradictory rhetoric may be illustrated by a recent newspaper article. Reporting on a statement made during a recent election campaign, the news story says,

> Gov. Buddy Roemer said Thursday. . . that he cannot endorse longtime political foe Edwin Edwards.
>
> But in an emotional speech, Roemer said he'll vote for Edwards in the Nov. 16 runoff – and urged his supporters to do the same.[1]

The joke is this: the politician quoted said expressly that he couldn't endorse a certain candidate; but he seems to have done, implicitly, everything required by the definition of "endorse." Under the terms of the definition of the word, he did endorse the candidate. He only *professed* not to endorse the candidate; he succeeded only in rejecting the word "endorse."

Similarly, in Marx's exposition of his theory, he says value is not a physical property; yet he attributes to it all the characteristics of a physical property.

Labor theory as natural law

If value is a physical property, Marx's law of the determination of value is likewise an account of an objectively-existing quantitative relationship between value and other physical entities. In essence, his law is, "Exchange value is directly proportional to the amount of invested labor." (Actually, his law is that value is equal to the labor, but presumably labor and exchange value would be measured in different units; thus "is proportional to" may be a fairer statement.)

In fact, to go even further, his law is that value and the embodied labor are identical. That is, they are not only quantitatively equal; the value *is* the labor. Marx describes the physical process by which this occurs: labor "congeals" into value (much as steam condenses into water). Value is labor in a congealed or solidified or embodied state, so value must necessarily equal the labor: the two are identical.

This statement of identity, with the description of the physical "condensation" process, is a statement of an objective nature (whether true or false is another matter). It has the character of stating a uniform regularity, a relationship between physical phenomena which always holds true. It asserts an unfailing generalization about physical entities. In sum, it purports to be natural law.

Marx's labor theory then – "Value equals labor" – is scientific law, as Marx portrays it. The process of creation of value, by the condensation or congelation of labor, has the same nature as other physical processes, for example literal condensation. To elaborate:

Labor becomes value *automatically*. It requires no choice or decision by human agents. Nor is it a mere matter of definition, of saying "Let us consider value to be equal to labor." Value and labor are physical, or at least objective, quantities. Labor transmutes into value as part of the natural order of things, simply because labor congeals into value, and not by any human or social decision or intervention. Thus it is like condensation of steam into water – it occurs by itself and requires no human input or intervention to occur. (The creation of value does of course require human labor. But the *decision*, as it were, of whether this labor will constitute value, is out of human hands.)

The process also occurs *invariably*, in all cases. Like all natural processes, there is a natural regularity in it. Whenever the appropriate starting conditions are met, the process occurs. Scientific law is an expression of the regularity of the physical universe, a statement that an event, under the same conditions, occurs the same way each time. When the temperature of steam drops below a certain point, it condenses, without fail. When labor is performed, it embeds or embodies itself as value, presumably also without fail. Such is the nature of physical processes.

Moreover, this process occurs in a predictable and predetermined manner. Just as the amount of water you get when steam condenses depends on the starting amount (i.e., mass) of steam, so the amount of value embodied in a commodity depends on the amount of labor exerted in producing it. The result depends on objective, mechanistic and knowable factors, and is not human-defined or human-controlled: a certain amount of water comes from a given amount of steam, and a certain amount of value congeals from a given amount of labor.

(A side effect of this, mentioned before, is that value is for Marx something of an *a priori* category – when goods go to market, they have a certain fixed, pre-ordained value already contained within them. Value is not a dynamic entity; it is not the result of bargaining in the marketplace, the clash of opposing interests in the bargaining process. Value is an *a priori* property, a substance contained by the commodity itself in a fixed magnitude. Once the production process is finished, the magnitude is fixed. Human factors do however determine the amount of labor required to produce a commodity.)

Homogeneous, not average

Given this naturalistic foundation behind Marx's labor theory, and given its supposed status as science, value as "average" labor could never have fit in as a consistent part of the theory. Averages are human-derived, not natural. They are statistical descriptions of the natural events themselves; they could never serve as natural factors determining those events. Thus, the average appears in Marx's text in a sublimated or disguised form, as "homogeneous" labor. Homogeneous labor is presented as somehow objective, found in nature, as a category brought into being by the substantive nature of the phenomena themselves. Marx does not show it to be, like an average, arbitrary, human-defined and a matter of human decision or choice.

We will, however, consider "homogeneous" labor not for what Marx claims it to be, but for its actual nature as revealed by his text as a whole: as an average. The problem for Marx is that a quantity cannot simultaneously be an average and at the same time have the character of an objective physical property – it cannot have the dual nature Marx seeks to impute to his homogeneous labor. Labor embodies itself in goods in a physical process of congelation or condensation; well and good. But how then can the resulting value be not the labor actually invested in that particular object, but some social average? How can a physical process at the same time be an arbitrarily-defined category?

Physical processes work on the physical objects actually present. If steam condenses into water, it is the steam *actually present* which condenses; and the amount of water which results is entirely determined by the starting amount of the actual steam. The steam doesn't condense into a "socially average" amount of water.

Or to put it another way, if a dog buries a bone in a hole, then digs it back up, the bone he retrieves is the same one he buried, not some "socially average" bone. (In this respect, dogs could be said to have a better instinctive grasp of physics than Marx did.) When you churn cream, the amount of butter you get depends on the amount of cream and its particular composition; it would be senseless to expect the amount of butter yielded to be determined by a "social average" of the amount of butter yielded using the best kinds, the most state-of-the-art kinds, of cream generally available. You can't say, "The average household uses only a half-pound of butter per week; therefore it is 'socially necessary' to produce only that amount, therefore the yield from what you just churned equals half a pound of butter." Physical processes of this sort simply obey certain commonsense rules (so elementary that they don't often need to be stated), such as that a thing is itself and not something else.

Marx's idea that labor embodies itself as value, but as a "social average" of the amount of labor, is scientifically incoherent; it envisions an Alice-in-Wonderland world, chaotic and lacking in a basic natural order.

To repeat: if labor embodies itself in commodities, then what is embodied must be the actual labor exerted, and not some other arbitrarily-chosen amount of labor. There is no rational basis for supposing that the average amount of labor invested in a commodity could play a part in Marx's quasi-physical system. There is no objective, real-world means by which an average could embody itself as value.

This is not because averages are intrinsically an illegitimate concept in natural sciences. For example, if we had some sort of law saying, "The amount of growth a plant undergoes depends on the amount of rainfall it gets," we might be justified in saying that by amount, we mean the *average* rainfall received over a period of time – that that is what matters. However, this example is different from what Marx is doing. What really makes Marx's "social average" an invalid category is that it is an average of quantities entirely unconnected to the entity under consideration.

That is, in the case of plant growth, the "average rainfall" means the average falling on the plant we're concerned with; the average amount of rain falling on *this* plant determines *this* plant's growth.

By contrast, a social average of labor is, as Marx describes it, an average of all the labor done on items similar to the one under consideration, even though they may be physically removed from it in every way. In Marx's theory, the labor required to produce the commodity, both at this particular factory and at all others, is averaged to determine the value of the output of *this* factory (and all others). But this kind of social averaging cannot apply to a process like "condensation." Marx is positing a physical process whose outcome is affected by events and objects totally unconnected to it and never directly impinging on it in a physical manner. There is no naturalistic or scientific relationship which functions like that; there is no way a "social average" of some property could embody itself physically within a commodity.

It's like saying, "$E=mc^2$, except on Thursdays." "Thursday" is a man-made, human-defined concept; Thursdays don't exist in nature. The day of the week could never actually serve a function in any genuine law of physics; it is too arbitrary, too much a matter of definition, too non-naturalistic. And Marx's qualification contains the same kind of self-contradiction. It attempts to interrelate two principles which inhabit different realms, which are on different levels of existence, and which have no way of impinging on or affecting each other. The two can never combine to make a coherent whole.

What this means is that there is no way a "social average" of the amount of labor can embody itself in a particular commodity. If the creation of value is, as Marx portrays it, a naturalistic, mechanistic, self-governing process like other purely physical processes, then it is incoherent to suggest that a "social average" is the determining quantity. The average is a figure not present, not known, not a factor accessible to the labor and the commodity in a particular workplace. If the process is of a mechanistic nature, as Marx describes it, then what embodies itself in the commodity must be the labor which is actually "there" to be embodied, namely the labor actually performed on the commodity. The rule must be, "From the laborer's hand, to the commodity – and that is value." Measure the amount of labor actually performed, with no intermediary and no conversion factor between the worker and the commodity, and you will know how much labor has "congealed."

As for the concept of the labor socially "necessary," this too is an Aesopian* term, merely restating the qualification as Marx has already outlined it – value is a "social average," and whatever that average is, is the "necessary" amount. It is tautological or vacant term, not a basis for the qualification it renames.

The real basis and justification for Marx's qualification, then, is this: Marx needs it to save his theory from blatant refutation by market events. His theory in its original form would attribute a higher value, a higher congealed labor, to goods produced by "idle and unskillful" (that is, slow) labor, than to goods produced in a smaller amount of labor-time. But the market obviously does not validate this conclusion, and thus, Marx's hypothesis is disproved by direct observation of the behavior of phenomena under discussion.

To forestall this refutation of his theory Marx had to resort to an added "fudge factor"** to save his theory, namely the qualification under consideration. He needed the qualification in order to make his theory work – that is its only justification.

The net result is that Marx's theory in its original form cannot be merged coherently with the qualification proposed for it. The two are mutually inconsistent in their assumptions about the nature of value. A law or hypothesis about the workings of the natural universe cannot be arbitrarily adjusted with artificial, man-made stipulations. There are no such laws as "$E = mc^2$, except on Thursdays." To quote Marx, "Such a self-destructive contradiction cannot be in any way even enunciated or formulated as a law."

Two alternatives

The basic law and the qualification are mutually inconsistent, and one or the other must be discarded. If the theory is to be considered what Marx says

---

* "Aesopian" is a term used by Lenin and others, referring to code language: as in a fable, a thing is simply given another name. Another term for this is "Orwellian" language.

** A "fudge factor," sometimes also called the "finagling factor," is a facetious entity present in laboratory sciences; it is defined as "that quantity which must be added to, subtracted from, multiplied by, or divided into the result you actually got, in order to yield the result you should have gotten."

it is, a scientific statement about the objective nature of things, then the qualification, an arbitrary stipulation, must be dropped. The theory must remain alone in its original form; labor constitutes value by a direct and immediate physical process, with no modification of it on the basis of distant events, as the qualification envisions. The value must be the labor actually performed on the commodity, as indeed Marx has already "proved" it to be in his entire dissertation about the "common something."

If on the other hand Marx wants to retain his qualification along with his theory, he can do it. However, there must be a revision in our view of the basis of the theory. That is, the theory can be adapted and qualified, but in that case we must cease to consider it a statement of natural law. It cannot be a scientific description of objective fact, an impersonal rendering of the way physical nature works in and of itself. If the theory can be modified by arbitrary stipulation, then the theory must have been arbitrary to begin with, and not a representation of physical reality. The supposed basis and justification on which Marx advances the theory must be discarded, including his proof and his description of value-creation as a physical process of "congelation." Marx's results can be adopted whole, but as an arbitrary definition, or as a tentative hypothesis (or guess), or perhaps as a dogmatic decree *ex cathedra*. But if Marx's theory is the kind of thing subject to arbitrary modification, the justification originally presented, one of scientific basis in objective fact, must be dismissed as groundless.

The Classical View

We have looked at Marx's qualification explaining why the value of goods is not a straightforward function of actual labor-time. We may now look at the classical view and what it says about things like the exchange value of goods produced by excessive amounts of labor, i.e. by "idle and unskillful" workers.

In the first place, in classical theory there is no naturalistic law of value, and exchange value and labor are not conceived of as physical quantities related by an impersonal mechanism. Economics is not reduced to pseudo-physics, in other words. Thus classical theory is not in the position of having to explain the shortcomings of an iron "law of determination of value."

Having said that, we can consider what classical theory does say. It agrees with Marx's labor theory this far: the amount of labor invested in the production of an item does affect production costs. Workers are usually paid by the hour, and thus the higher the total hours of labor exerted, the higher the total labor costs. If the rate of productivity is low, the labor costs per unit will be correspondingly higher, in which case the price must also be higher. At this point however classical theory diverges from Marx's labor theory. Labor does not automatistically and by a physical process of condensation transform itself directly into the commodity's quantum of value, with no required further input or intermediation by people, i.e. by market forces. It is not a physical transformation that determines the amount of value; it is the whole complex of economic considerations and human decisions.

For the capitalist the key constraint is labor *costs*. He must recover his production expenses in the sale of the finished product, and for that reason labor is one factor determining value. It can be seen that there is a rational and coherent line of cause and effect in this explanation. The line of cause and effect connecting labor to value proceeds via the mechanism of labor *costs* (rather than, as in Marx, labor's spontaneously constituting value in its own right). It is the economic constraints on the entrepreneur, rather than a spontaneous process of transmutation, which explains why labor affects exchange value. The capitalist's concern (again, understandable to anyone who has ever dealt in the economic realm) is to make income exceed outgo. The amount of labor-time per unit is significant, but it is so because each unit of time is paid for at a certain price, adding up to certain labor *costs*. That makes the labor time (partly) determine value, or at least the price asked.

This rational line of cause and effect is in marked contrast to Marx's convoluted labor theory, which offers only a proof and never an explanation in real-world terms. He never shows why his labor theory is what is at work in the real world, and how labor itself, as a concretized or reified entity, can exert direct control over market value. He doesn't supply any explanation leading to an intuitive understanding of the real world or a description which we can conceive of as plausibly occurring in reality. He offers a proof, to compel us to believe his theory, not an explanation to enable us to understand it. The picture he does supply, his elaborate line of hocus-pocus about "congelation" and so forth, acts in quite the contrary manner to giving an understanding – it is nothing that could actually occur in the real world, and it thus tends to discredit his theory, rather than to illustrate it.

In short, Marx's labor theory lacks any coherent line of cause and effect and is a work of sophistry. Thus for a rational explanation we turn to classical theory, with a cause-and-effect explanation couched in terms of human economic behavior; because after all it is people who are the source of economic actions – "Economics is something people do."

In this context, let us consider the capitalist who has an aging facility or a work force "idle and unskillful" for some other reason. The capitalist is trying to recoup his labor costs in the sale price of the product. But while the labor costs help determine what he must ask for the product, they don't automatically guarantee that he'll get it. For one thing, besides himself there are likely to be other producers of the same product. If these producers' workforces are not "idle and unskillful," they are likely to be offering the product at lower prices than his. Thus there are numerous varied factors impinging on him (and not just one factor, as in the reductionist situation Marx envisions, where labor alone "condenses" into value). It is not always possible to sell a product at a higher price just because the workforce is "idle and unskillful" and the amount of time embodied in producing the commodity is high. In such a situation the capitalist may resort to expedients to cut costs; he may resign himself to a much smaller profit, if he can make any at all; he may try to replace his workforce; or he may be driven out of business. But there is not the fatalistic assumption which is implicit in Marx, that value as pre-determined by some mechanistic law or formula can automatically, by presumption, be paid for the commodity as its price or exchange value. There is not the assumption that the buyer is forced by fate of by force or logic to pay the amount determined by an *a priori* formula.

The real reason excessive amounts of labor do not show up in correspondingly high selling prices, then, is that economic exigencies are at work, rather than the automatistic theory Marx envisions. Market forces, or human economic behavior, have a say; and these forces work to prohibit inordinately high prices. Competition usually makes it impossible to sell goods at a higher price when essentially identical goods are available at a lower price. That is the human-oriented or real-world answer to the problem (if any) posed by Marx in discussing this qualification.

The question of small variations in value due to small, moment-to-moment fluctuations in the time spent on each item by the worker, does not even arise in classical economics, that is to say, in the real world. *Of course* the capitalist prices all the units alike. He has no basis or motivation for pricing them differently, and since they are all essentially identical, the buyers would resist paying different prices. It is only Marx's mechanistic theory of labor and its metamorphosis into value that would suggest otherwise. Classical theory has no resemblance to his theory, and hence no need to explain away his theory's more peculiar logical implications. Common sense and a down-to-earth understanding of how the economic marketplace behaves are much more applicable, and are sufficient to eliminate such situations as the one referred to in the qualification.

Another Alternative

When we compare Marx's proposed law, "Value is in direct proportion to the nation-wide (or *social*) average amount of labor invested," to real market phenomena, we see that his law fails. His hypothesis is not borne out by reality; it is in fact refuted by reality: market prices show that labor alone doesn't determine value.

It is not true that the exchange value of a commodity is always directly proportional to the average amount of labor expended in producing it. (Exchange value, not Marx's transcendent or internal "Value" will be considered here, because that is the real-world meaning of the term. Exchange value, or price, is what we must look at; Marx's hidden, private entity, "Value," does not actually exist.)

That's *close*, of course: labor costs are a major factor in determining what price must be asked for a commodity; they make up a large component of production costs. Another component of production costs would be rents, that is, the cost of renting, leasing or otherwise acquiring the land for the productive facility. These two, along with a desired amount of profit, are the component elements of price. The price received goes to recompense all three of these factors; it goes to pay off all three contributors to the production process, not just one. Labor is not the only factor in the production process, and labor costs alone do not determine the asking price. (Note: the supply-and-demand view is now out of date; using modern analysis, the "marginal utility" of an item is considered a more fundamental determiner of price, or of what a buyer will pay for an item.)

The market refutes Marx's theory, in that for one thing, some products fail. That is, the three factors, labor plus rents plus a desired profit, may be added together by the capitalist to arrive at an asking price; but that is no guarantee the price will be met. The mere existence of a formula or deduced law does not (as Marx assumes) fatalistically guarantee that the market price will meet that formula. Potential customers too have a say in the entire process. Marx assumes that "Logic can compel the facts," that his deductive arguments and derived laws are conclusive: they say what value must be, and the real world – meaning market prices – necessarily fall in line. That is superstition, and market results aren't in keeping with it.

To return to the classical view, labor, rents and profits are the three factors covered by price – that is, covered assuming a successful product. But the formula itself is not to be conceived of as somehow compelling the market. "Consumer resistance" to the product may prevent the capitalist from receiving his desired price. What really controls prices is not some formula or even the conceptual division of price into its component factors. What really controls it is the customers' acquiescence in paying a certain amount, together with the sellers' willingness and ability to produce the product (profitably) at that price. That means it is supply and demand, the intersection or "dialectical" interaction of the will of buyers and sellers, that establishes market price. Marx's proposed law of value, in any form, is wrong in its entire conception and set of assumptions; it is a gross misappreciation of the workings of economics at their most basic level; and quantitatively it is inaccurate. His law is wrong, as the real world shows; and only mysticism, wishful thinking, obstinacy and extreme scientific ignorance enabled him so self-confidently to maintain his assertions. In this he fit in with the facetious maxim, "If you can keep your head while all around you others are losing theirs, you probably just don't understand the seriousness of the situation."

The determination of value is never over until the public – the entire population of potential buyers – has had its say. That is how economics works in the real world, as opposed to Marx's closed system of metaphysics.

It might be worthwhile to refer again to the previously-cited example of the production of the 1903 Model A Ford:

> James Couzens had worked out the sums precisely. The basic machinery from the Dodge brothers would cost $250. Body, wheels, and other parts came to an additional $134. Labor costs totaled $20, and he set aside $150 for selling costs, to include advertising, salaries, and commissions. This added up to a total expenditure of $554, and the car would be offered for sale at $750, leaving a margin of $196 per unit. Deduct $46 for contingencies, and that left a clear profit of $150 per car. [2]

The author also records the result: "By the end of March 1904, the Ford Motor Company had sold 658 automobiles with a margin over expenses of $98,851 – a profit per car of $150, as James Couzens had calculated."

The point of the above, for our purposes, is that it shows how the final selling price goes to recompense the costs of production, including profit. But market value is not set in a deterministic manner; it depends ultimately on being able to sell the product at the required, profitable price.

The example, again, shows how economics really works. There is no direct transmutation of labor into a mechanically-set value, tying the producers' and the buyers' hands and inexorably fixing value by an impersonal, immutable process. Human and economic factors determine value.

Of course, it should be added, for Marx there was not $98,851 of "profit" in the Ford automobile. Rather, that amount of "surplus value" was squeezed out of the laborers who produced the cars. Profit, as an excess of selling price over the sum of production costs, is impossible – that is the import of his Yahoo economics. Let us address that supposition here, preliminarily, by saying that it was not from the non-existent wealth of its laborers that the Ford company squeezed $98,851, but rather from the purchasers of the cars.

Third qualification

Marx introduces another qualification to his labor theory, as follows:

> The labor-time socially necessary is that required to produce an article under the normal conditions of production, and with the average degree of skill and intensity prevalent at the time. The introduction of power looms into England probably reduced by one half the labor required to weave a given quantity of yarn into cloth. The hand-loom weavers, as a matter of fact continued to require the same time as before; but for all that, the product of one hour of their labor represented after the change only half an hour's social labor, and consequently fell to one-half its former value.

What Marx is now saying is that the value of commodities is "the labor-time socially necessary" for their production. And the labor-time socially necessary is the "normal" time, that is, the time necessary under normal conditions of production, meaning the normal or average conditions of "skill and intensity" prevalent at the time. We might say value is the labor necessary using state-of-the art technology and methods, understanding that by "state-of-the-art" we mean the state of the art prevalent or generally available at the time (not necessarily the most advanced equipment in existence). Thus Marx stipulates that value is equal to the labor-time "socially" necessary, using up-to-date, rather than obsolescent, equipment. How this is different from Marx's previous formula for value, and why the qualification was necessary, will be discussed in due time.

Preliminary examination

The first question raised by this qualification is, What objective justification does Marx have for making the qualification? On a fundamental level, we need to ask, What kind of statement is it? Is it a report of an observed pattern of cause and effect concerning objectively-identifiable phenomena, or is it an arbitrary stipulation or decree, based on nothing but the need to preserve Marx's theory against the destructive evidence of reality?

We may also ask ourselves once again how the criterion for establishing value became, not the labor directly embodied in the commodity and "congealed" or "crystallised" into value, but rather "the labor-time socially necessary." (How, that is, did the model change from a quasi-physical or quasi-"physics" model to a quasi-sociological model?) All these questions will have to be addressed in discussing this qualification.

Fundamental self-contradictoriness

First, looking just at the results of this qualification and not its basis, we can say about it, as with the first: if value is said to be identical with the "embodied" labor contained by a commodity, then what is contained must be the labor actually, physically performed on the commodity itself. This is the only labor the commodity "has access to," the only labor that touches it and can be incorporated within it as value. If Marx's physical model is accepted, then there is no basis for social, or sociological, qualifications like the present one. The physics of material objects is not subject to such qualifications.

So if the view of value posited by Marx's labor theory in its basic form is accepted, any question of how much labor is "socially necessary" is irrelevant. On the other hand, if we reject that original basis and picture of Marx's labor theory in order to admit considerations of what is "socially necessary," then the original proof and support for Marx's labor theory must likewise be abandoned; we might as well throw out the whole theory. Thus, even prior to the issue of whether we can find any factual support for this qualification, the attempt to make such a hybrid theory – part physically based and governed by the laws of physics and part sociologically-determined – is incoherent. There is no basis for such hybrid constructs in any even minimally literate scientific method.

Basis for the qualification

As concerns any evidence supporting the qualification, here again we see that Marx is imposing a stipulation on events with no justification but his own decree. He is fitting the world to his theory, and not vice versa.

To support the qualification, which is essentially a redefinition of value, Marx offers, apart from mere assertion, the illustrative example quoted above.

The example itself is accurate enough – when machine-woven cloth came onto the market, hand-woven cloth could no longer be sold at its higher price. The question, however, is whether Marx's theory gives the reason for the phenomenon, or whether the mechanism at work was actually something quite different. As was done with the previous qualification, Marx appends this qualification to his theory to make its predicted outcome or end result align with actual results; but that does not necessarily mean his theory is the real *explanation* for those results. It has been said that for every event there is someone who thinks it happened in accordance with his own pet theory; the task is to find the actual line of causation somewhere in the mass of contending theoretical explanations.

We may anticipate somewhat and say, classical theory gives the obviously valid explanation for the events Marx describes. The reason the value of the hand-woven cloth falls to the price of the machine-woven cloth is this: people will not pay more for a product when they can get essentially the same thing for less. The classical explanation for the situation described in Marx's example is that when a product from one source comes onto the market in sufficient supply at a cheaper price, demand for the same product at the original, higher price drops to zero. If all consumers can find all of the product they want at a cheaper price, no one will buy at the higher price.

This explanation illustrates again that classical theory, or genuine economics, deals in terms of human behavior, conceiving of economics as predicated on the basic elements of universal human economic behavior. Value is not an abstract, philosophical category, nor is it a physical automaton. A fall in a product's value is not explained by *ad hoc* modifications of Marx's definition of an abstract category, that is by a redefinition of the entity as "the labor-time socially necessary," having already redefined it in terms of "normal conditions" or the "average degree of skill and intensity." To deal in such speculative abstractions is simply to conjure up an imaginary world, a conceptual world made of invented categories, abstractions and relationships, with, to be sure, rules and "theorems" of its own, but with no relation to reality.

Marx is thus writing not scientifically, as one who must construct a theory in accord with all the facts, but as one conveying revealed truth, or as one possessing an *ex cathedra* authority to say what the truth is. (Nevertheless, if there by chance should be any objective support for the qualification, we must find out what it is or what evidence Marx offers.)

The need for the qualification

Let us examine the qualification in its particulars. The situation Marx describes in his example is one he must address, of course. One of the most striking characteristics of the Industrial Revolution, and a defining characteristic of technological progress in general, has been the continual lowering of the amount of labor required for producing a product. This lowering has generally been accompanied by a lowering of the item's price. Goods became cheaper with the advent of each new piece of machinery, and the standard of living of the "common people" rose significantly, for the first time in centuries.

And of course if the price of goods made with the new machinery declined, the price of similar goods made in the old way, using the former production methods, could not be maintained. The question is then, why does the price of *both* sets of goods — those made the old way and those made the new — fall to the level of the price of goods made with the new equipment? Which explanation is valid — Marx's or the classical one?

There is hardly a problem here at all for those who take the classical viewpoint. The working principle might be called supply and demand, or it might be placed more broadly under the category of the desire of the buyer to buy as cheaply as possible. (That is an even more elementary article of economic explanation than laws of supply and demand, and is in fact the basis for them.) However one terms it, the fact is that people will not pay more for goods, when they can get what are (for practical purposes) the same thing for less. If the supply of machine-woven cloth is adequate to meet demand, buyers will buy it rather than pay the price for hand-woven cloth. This means that the hand-woven cloth becomes "distressed merchandise," merchandise which can only be sold by cutting the price to make it competitive with machine-woven cloth. * People – that is, human economic behavior in the aggregate – determine the price; the process is *economic* in nature. It is not determined by a set of abstract, philosophical definitions and categories. And it is not governed by the laws of a system of quasi-physics.

For Marx's theory, however, the situation is more problematical. His theory, in its original form, states that value is embodied labor. The more labor "congeals" in a commodity, the higher its value. Therefore the hand-woven cloth, with a high internal content of labor, should continue to have a high value, meaning that it should also have a high price; and machine-woven cloth should have its own appropriate, lower price. By the terms of his theory, there should then be a "two-tiered" pricing level.

This of course is not what happens in the real world, and Marx must explain why; he must show why a price dichotomy is not really called for or predicted by his theory. That is, he must adjust his theory so that it seems to fit the real-world situation and even to be the cause of it – so that, at this one point where his theory impinges on the real world, the results as predicted by it are like those which do obtain in the real world. To this end, he must modify his theory in order to salvage it.

He accomplishes this mainly by leaning more heavily on the definition of value as "the labor-time socially necessary." Note that this all-purpose phrase, this formula for determining or defining value, has been insinuated into Marx's text without any direct argument in support of it. It simply makes its appearances and is assigned its role as the proper determiner of the amount of labor which is value.

Value up to this point was the amount of "homogeneous" labor contained by a commodity. Now Marx tells us that the "labor-time socially necessary" is such and such, by which we are to understand that "value" is such and such. He doesn't tell us why, all of a sudden, "socially necessary" is the standard for determining the labor contained by the commodity.

---

* It may not be necessary to lower the cost all the way to that of machine-woven cloth, however. Presumably the quality of hand-woven cloth is better and, even though not sufficient to induce people to pay the full price for it, this fact would support a slight price differential or premium above that of everyday goods.

Marx inserts the phrase as if that had been the definition of value all along; and proceeding upon this definition, he explains that "the labor-time socially necessary" is the labor-time using the most efficient method of production generally available, etc.

The sleight-of-hand in this qualification is in making "labor-time socially necessary" the accepted definition of value. Value was supposed to be the labor embodied in a commodity, the amount actually performed on it. Now Marx has introduced social criteria and semi-articulated entities like "social necessity" into the picture. That was his real conjuring trick.

His exposition of what is contained in the "labor-time socially necessary" is in turn unsupported by any empirical explanation or theoretical justification. Marx simply chooses to define "labor-time socially necessary" the way he does, because he needs it to mean that; that is, he makes it serve his own purposes. It is a definition "pulled out of his hat," assumed from nothing.

That should be qualified in one respect. Taken simply at face value, there might be a certain amount of sense in Marx's statement that the "labor-time socially necessary," for producing a commodity, is the amount required using the most advanced equipment generally available. That amount is the minimum time needed using readily available means. Literally speaking, that is indeed the amount of labor *necessary*; we need not invest more labor in the commodity than that, because equipment is available that will enable us to produce it with just that given amount of labor. For instance, when power looms are available, no more labor is "socially necessary" than is expended in producing cloth with them; with power looms generally available within the society, it is not "socially" necessary to spend any more labor in producing cloth than is needed using them. So in this sense the labor "socially necessary" could perhaps be defined or viewed as meaning the minimum amount necessary given readily-available means within the country, or society.

Thus an argument could be made that this definition of "the labor-time socially necessary" makes a certain amount of sense, if not good syntax. What cannot be shown is that this category of "socially-necessary labor" has direct equivalence with the price, or value, of a commodity in the real world; nor that it has any valid or logical connection with Marx's theory of value as originally expounded. In other words, the connection cannot be made coherently between Marx's original theory and this qualifying redefinition; nor can any connection be made from his abstract categories to events in the real world such as the determination of prices. He needs to show some line of cause and effect, not simply to define a category and then assume that, through sheer force of rhetoric, his category is the defining one and his argumentation must be authoritative. If his "labor theory of value" is now to be seen as a "socially-necessary-labor theory of value," he must make the connection and justification for this change explicit, and not merely insinuate it into the discussion.

Again, we see with this qualification Marx completely changing the ground of the discussion, along with the imputed character of value. His labor-as-value starts out as a physical entity, its magnitude determined through an impersonal, physical process. However, this qualification, like the previous ones, introduces social criteria and concepts like the amount of labor "socially necessary." The question again is how such social matters can affect an automatistic physical process, or to put it another way, how the two directly contradictory natures attributed to value can merge coherently in a unified theory. We will consider this in detail as we go along.

Detailed analysis

Let us now examine the qualification in its particulars. Goods became cheaper with every new development in productive methods. And the situation at such times, of course, has always been that the price of the particular goods has fallen to a single, more or less uniform, lower price; there wasn't such a thing as machine-made goods' becoming cheaper while hand-made goods retained their former high value (i.e., price). *All* goods of the same description have been governed by the lowest price such goods could be made and sold for, namely, the price as made with the most advanced productive equipment. The prevailing price is determined by the cheapest one.

The above are the facts; the question is how Marx makes them appear to fit in with his theory and indeed to be caused by his theory's mechanism.

It should first be noted, there are actually two slightly different situations which could be envisioned under this qualification. One is the case Marx discusses, where goods are produced, at the same time, by the two different methods, old and new. These two sets of goods, produced simultaneously, have different amounts of labor actually embodied in them, and the question is, How do their prices come out the same?

The other case is that of goods previously produced by the older method, i.e. already embodying a certain amount of labor, but as yet unsold when the new method of production comes in. The question is, What happens to the value of these goods?

Let us consider first what Marx's law of value, in its original, unembellished form, would say about these situations. We can extrapolate from his basic law, "Labor congeals into a corresponding amount of value."

It is entirely appropriate, then, to ask what Marx's law of value predicts for the particular situations given. And the answer is plain enough: labor congeals into value; that is, the labor invested in the production of an item congeals into its value; and the value of goods, including hand-made goods, is always the amount of labor invested in their production. Regardless of what someone else may be doing somewhere else, the labor actually performed on this particular commodity must congeal into its value – any other suggestion would be nonsensical and capricious.

Steam condenses into water; that is, the steam *right here* condenses into the water resulting from *it* – not some other amount of steam somewhere else, or a "social average" of steam. And since we are unaware of any process of deterioration or evaporation of value, labor must work the same way. Barring some unknown process of radioactive decay of value, the amount of labor initially embodied in a product remains its value "for life," regardless of what may occur later or what other methods of production may later come into use.

Thus in both situations – in that of already-produced, pre-existing goods, and in that of goods which continue to be made by the older method even while other goods are made by the new method – in both cases the value of hand-made goods remains at its full, "statutory" level as specified by Marx's formula.

If labor congeals into value, if it is an impersonal, quasi-physical process, and if the entire basis of value is as Marx describes, the above conclusion is the only one possible. A particular commodity's value is, identically and by definition, the self-same labor actually performed on it in the course of its production. If that is not the commodity's value, and if a set of social criteria and arbitrary stipulations is to be added, then we have been misled in believing Marx's labor theory; the whole basis for it is thereby destroyed. The situation must be one way or the other.

The result then, as predicted by Marx's core theory, should be this: machine-made cloth comes on the market and sells for, let us say, half the price of hand-made cloth. At the same time, hand-made cloth continues to be made and sells for its old, higher price. Each has its own appropriate value, and there is no interconnection between them.

(It might be said however that hand-made cloth continues to have the same value as before but that it just can't be *sold* at that value. That is, it accumulates on the shelves of warehouses, but its value continues to be the same. Since in Marx's schema the word "value" has no connotation of "what a thing can be sold for," this contention could be made.

But while Marx claims to mean by value *only* "the contained labor," in practice he is forced to consider value as normal people do, that is, as market price. That is why he even discusses the given examples in the first place. In practice it makes no sense to speak of a commodity as having a certain value when it cannot be sold for that amount – as if value were an abstract entity existing apart from market considerations. Whether he wants to or not, Marx from time to time is forced to speak of value as normal humans do, as an aspect of market economic conditions and not as an abstract philosophical entity.

Thus we can safely discard the above possible interpretation of his theory and its predicted results as, at the least, irrelevant to real-world economics. Besides, it sounds too much like supply and demand to be what Marx meant.)

The facts as they obtain in the real world, then, are at variance with Marx's theory, at least in its initial form. Thus a qualification or further stipulation had to be added, to bring the results as predicted by his theory more or less into line with actuality. In the present instance, as with his first qualification, Marx shifts his ground by saying, in effect, that the labor which constitutes value is not the actual labor performed on the particular commodity, but theoretical labor, labor as a theoretical category defined in a manner stipulated by him. It is not actual labor, but "homogeneous" and, now, "socially necessary" (or just "social") labor. That is, it is the amount of labor embodied in the commodity using "normal" or "average" or "prevalent" productive methods. We would say, the value is the smallest amount of labor needed using the best equipment generally available – "state-of-the-art" equipment, if you will.

This arbitrarily-defined quantity is now given by Marx as the new definition of the value of a commodity. But again, in arbitrarily redefining value, Marx loses all the explanatory power presumably provided for his labor theory by his picture of labor's being a physical entity which congeals into value. He also loses the partly logical, partly "quasi-physics" proof he provided for the theory. We are left with a theory backed only by arbitrary decrees and pronouncements, by Marx speaking *ex cathedra.*

At any rate, value is now to be considered, not the actual labor, but the amount of labor "socially necessary." And the socially-necessary labor is the smallest amount of labor, or the lowest price, for which goods can be produced using "state-of-the-art" equipment; that is, using the best equipment generally available or "prevalent."

One question of interest which now arises is whether this redefinition of labor produces the desired solution, i.e., whether it makes "value-as-labor" correspond to market prices and real-world events. It appears that Marx has brought his theory quite well into line with actuality. When a new, more efficient, method of production cuts the "average" or "normal" amount of labor "prevalent" in producing goods, the value of all goods falls. Both the hand-made and the machine-made goods get cheaper: they both sell for the same lower price. Thus Marx's theory has escaped a possible contradiction from the real world. Of course we aren't given a quantitative example showing that the price corresponds to the new amount of labor; but we are shown that the price of hand-woven cloth must fall to the level of machine-woven cloth – for his purposes that's evidence enough.

The next subject of concern is the validity of Marx's redefinition. Do the real-world events described occur for the reason Marx's theory advances? Is his theory, and its accompanying qualifications, the *explanation* of events, or is it simply an *ad hoc* rationalization or sophistry added after the fact in order to bring his theory into a semblance of conformity with the real world? He seems to have dodged the bullet in this his second qualification, but has he really?

The question is no sooner asked than answered. The real reason the price of all goods, both hand-made and machine-made, falls to the same low price, is that people will not pay more for goods when essentially the same items are available for less. The demand for goods at twice the price, when the same, or for all practical purposes the same, goods are available at half the price, is nil.

That is, the real reason is a matter of economics, and this comes down to a matter of human economic behavior. The reader may ask himself what he would do if faced with the situation described, of similar goods at two different prices. The response is universal – everybody prefers to "buy low."

The real explanation is an economic one, a matter of real-world exigencies and behaviors; it is not a matter of philosophical abstractions or arbitrarily-defined theoretical entities. The value of the goods doesn't fall to a uniform lower price because Marx has defined a theoretical entity called "Value" in a certain way. Logic does not compel the facts.

In essence, Marx's "explanation" of events is not an explanation at all. It is an arbitrary stipulation or decree, which *seems* to bring his theory into accord with the facts as they occur. But it is a rationalization, not the real reason for events.

Mechanistic Assumptions

This points up another problem with Marx's theory: its mechanistic assumptions. His elimination of human action, with his belief that labor itself can be a basis for determining value, without recourse to the intermediary of a money equivalent of that labor, is a large factor in the mystical, anti-rational character of his labor theory. Marx expresses his theory as a kind of quasi-physics. Physical quantities interrelate, yielding determinate conclusions in a kind of mechanical automatism, independent of any human action.

In physics, for example, we see that when a rock falls off a cliff, its rate of descent depends on nothing but the laws of the physical universe. That is, it depends on the workings of the physical universe, given generalized expression – the laws of physics. In the same mold, Marx is creating a theoretical system in which one quantity (of labor) automatically, or automatistically, produces a determinate result – a definite quantity of value.

This too is portrayed as part of the natural order of things and not a matter of any human-derived consideration such as market supply and demand, and so on.

This mechanistic assumption, applied to a realm self-evidently human, is nonsense. The world of markets, of production, sales, labor, supply and demand, and so on, is not on the same level with the world of inanimate objects, of falling rocks and orbiting planets. It is scientifically incoherent to suppose one can produce an automatistic system of economics, leaving out human inputs: to suppose that labor can directly, automatically, constitute value, as if labor and value were purely material phenomena like rocks, water, steam and so on. In sum, it is scientifically illiterate to write a "physics of economics."

Thus it is more rational and coherent to speak of value in terms of labor costs, rents, and profits, than to speak of a certain amount of labor (even a "socially necessary" amount of labor) constituting the value, or automatically equaling the value, by some metaphysical process, without any intermediary in human, economic terms.

One further unfortunate product of this mechanistic view is what might be called the fatalistic assumption. For Marx, the contained labor (once it has been properly defined and modified) constitutes the commodity's value: the commodity itself contains a certain value in and of itself. The forces of supply and demand, the vagaries of the marketplace as envisioned by classical theory, are irrelevant.

Presumably, since the embodied labor is the commodity's "value," the commodity can be sold for that; and people have no choice but to pay the value, i.e., buy the product for the full "statutory" price. That is, the question of whether a commodity can find a *buyer* at Marx's theoretically-established value is waived. No matter how shoddy, tasteless, and undesirable a commodity may be, still it has a theoretically or categorically ordained value, and presumably, someone will pay it. (For Marx has not dropped the sense of "what a thing sells for" from his redefined concept of value.)

But suppose the consumers reject a product? Suppose a new soft drink has a vile taste. It still has calories, so it still has "use-value"; and it contains a certain magnitude of "average socially-necessary labor," that is, it has a fixed value. How can people be assumed, or made fatalistically, to pay this philosophically pre-ordained value? Do economic commodities have the power of mass hypnosis, to cause people to pay the contained values regardless of whether anyone can stand the product or not?

In classical theory, the price is ultimately said to be determined by supply and demand. This is just a mathematical generalization of behavior — if people do not like the product, the demand for it at a "normal" price is low; it cannot be sold. "Supply and demand" as abstractions don't set the price; supply and demand are (supposedly) mathematical representations of what people do at various magnitudes of price, supply, and purchases (depending on which ones are considered fixed and which variable).

The price of a successful product is sufficient to recompense the components of labor costs, rents, and profits. If a product is not accepted by the public – despite having certain "use-value" in an abstract sense – the full price cannot be received for the whole produced output. The price may be lowered to get rid of these "distressed goods"; but by this expedient the third factor of price, the profit, disappears.

Thus there is always the possibility, in classical theory and in the real world, that a product will fail. In this there is not the fatalistic assumption that a product, once manufactured, already contains a definite value and hence presumably can always be sold for it. This aspect of Marxist theory is a concomitant of the *a priori* nature of his view of value, which sees it as a pre-contained substance, a part of the commodity itself even before the commodity goes to market.

The mechanistic assumption, along with its corresponding fatalistic assumption, is at variance with the real world. Examples may be given. For example, one newspaper article described daily life in the U.S.S.R. as follows:

> Russian retailers feature four product lines: plentiful and awful; awful and scarce; scarce and good; good and nonexistent.
>
> People have to eat. If they can't eat good sausage, they'll eat awful sausage. Russians eat awful sausage by the ton. But they have their limits. Anybody can buy a radio that gets only one station; hardly anybody does. A man with two atrocious suits doesn't buy a third. Truckloads of this unbought junk get carted to small towns, where wholesalers try to dump everything at a ruble apiece.
>
> "They might just as well burn it," says Vasily Selyunin, an economist who picked up a coat that way. "The factory will go on making those coats for years – and thinking they're profitable."[3]

And under the heading "A Lesson In Capitalism," *U.S.A. Today* gives this example:

> The Soviets have learned something about the laws of supply and demand – and pricing. At the international media center, commemorative summit T-shirts that sold for $20 were marked down 10 percent as the 3,000 reporters prepared to leave Moscow.[4]

All those hours of congealed, "average socially necessary labor" – and 10 per cent of it suddenly evaporated? No, rather, Marx's entire view or paradigm of the nature of value and the manner of its determination is wrong.

Value is established not by any internal, automatic mechanism, but by human actions and economic exigencies, the workings of "the marketplace," that is, of human economic behavior in the aggregate. Marx's entire method of attempting to turn the social science of economics into a kind of impersonal self-regulating quasi-physics, is a gross misrepresentation of the essential nature of economics itself. Any theory attempting to reduce economics to a system of purely physical laws, eliminating the human factor, is scientistic and specious on the face of it. Such a theory demonstrates complete ignorance not only of economics but of science itself as a realm of endeavor.

Overview of Qualifications

Let us now turn from the specifics of Marx's qualifications, and get an overview or perspective on his overall method and on what he accomplishes in making the qualifications.

First of all, what he accomplishes with his qualifications is to bring his theory into general accord with events in the real world; he brings the results as predicted by his theory into line with the results actually obtaining under the given circumstances. (That is, he accomplishes this, if we accept his qualifications as valid.)

Once value has been defined as not the labor actually, physically invested in the commodity, but the amount of "homogeneous labor" "socially necessary," his results appear to fall roughly in line with the actual behavior of prices as observed in the marketplace. We may further translate Marx's final definition of value by saying, value is the average amount of labor, smoothing out any unavoidable variations in labor-time invested from one unit to the next; and it is calculated only on a basis of those workplaces using the most efficient (least "labor-intensive") means of production generally or "socially" available. Value is "socially necessary, homogeneous labor."

By these qualifications Marx thus escapes two great difficulties which were caused to his theory of value's being tied inexorably to the actual, physical production of a particular article. Value escapes the quasi-physical paradigm in terms of which he originally defined it, and acquires a "social" definition, based on general and abstract social categories and less rigorously tied to concrete, physical fact. The capricious, self-contradictory change in the fundamental character of Marx's "Value," at least makes his definition of value plausible in its results.

In its finished form, then, Marx's definition of value has eliminated a couple of the more glaring fallacies apparent in the original definition. His theory no longer logically predicts continual minor fluctuations of value from item to item and workplace to workplace, corresponding to the minor fluctuations of labor embodied in the individual units of a commodity. And, value is no longer the amount of labor embodied in a commodity by whatever method of production is used, regardless of any more efficient means of production which may have come into existence. These two obvious difficulties have been removed; and his theory ends up seeming roughly in accord with reality.

His theory says: Value is labor; but not just any old labor, or rather, not actual labor. Value is the average, "smoothed-out" labor, and only the minimum labor necessary, the amount using state-of-the-art methods. You can't expect to get the full, "statutory" price (statutory as defined by his original theory) for hand-woven cloth in an age of machine-woven cloth. And you can't expect to see minute variations in price from one piece of cloth to the next. And in general, anything that lowers (or raises) the amount of labor required to produce an item will lower (or raise) its price.

All these statements are true. If we thus view Marx's labor theory as a "black box," looking only at what goes into it and what comes out of it, and not concerning ourselves at all with the interior workings of the box, the theory appears valid. Results in the real world are more or less as predicted by the theory: when labor costs go down, prices go down, and the reverse when labor costs go up. And since Marx gives no quantitative examples with actual amounts of labor and actual prices (this would in any case be impossible in practice), a rough correlation is all we can have to judge by. His theory then would seem hard to deny.

The real issue at this point becomes whether his theory is the *explanation* for the events it describes – that is, whether it is the actual reason for the events, and whether his law or definition of value is what governs and determines value; or whether his law is an *a posteriori* rationalization, something added on after the fact, being actually irrelevant in the determination of any of the quantities it deals in.

Of course the latter is true. The two qualifications are mere "fudge factors," pasted onto his theory to redeem it from the shattering effects of reality, having no compatibility with the original view of value which they purport to modify. They amount to a new and entirely different theory of value, adopted out of "dialectical" necessity, or expediency. As scientific method they are atrocious, even illiterate.

Marx's theory as modified is not the explanation for the phenomena it describes. The reason there are no minor variations in price from item to item is that capitalists use common sense – it would be senseless to charge different prices for identical articles, and besides, the capitalist doesn't calculate his required price on the basis Marx envisions.

In sum, Marx's theory-with-qualifications is not the reason prices (or "Value") are what they are; his theory is a rationalization added on after the fact, attempting to co-opt the facts and make them seem to be a result of the law or definition he provides. Marx tries to show how all events are governed by his theory; to show how phenomena in the real world fit into the schema provided by his theories, and how his theories are the ultimate explanation of the whole of reality. In the one realm where actual events are available for inspection to verify or refute his theory, his qualifications adjust his theory just enough to make those results appear to be the ones his theory would predict. But events are not actually governed by his law of value – they are determined by entirely different factors, and his theory is a separate, irrelevant matter which, thanks to the aid of "fudge factors," runs parallel to the facts.

Marx's modified law of value may appear to give the right answer, or at least to show value and price moving in the right direction under certain circumstances. Still, it is not scientific and not an explanation. It is specious; it cannot by its very nature be correct; and it is mere sophistry, a case of modifying Marx's theory after the fact in order to preserve a semblance of reality. Marx's theory is pure invention, and the qualifications added onto it deserve no serious consideration as science.

Unverifiability

Marx's theory is non-verifiable, since it deals in non-scientific entities. The terms and entities in which his theory deals are not sufficiently concrete or "real-world" to enable us to measure or observe them. They are speculative, and they do not lend themselves to definitive measurement.

Marx's "value," after all, is invisible. The labor that creates it, or condenses into it, is of course visible and, in principle, measurable. But value, while it lies internally within the commodity, is invisible, unmeasurable, unobservable. Unlike such physical properties as mass, color, and volume, it cannot be seen or measured. And we cannot calculate its magnitude by simply timing the labor that produces the product, for that is just what Marx is telling us – the actual labor creating the product may not be what is embodied in it. Some of the labor, by some unknown mechanism, may fail to embed itself within the commodity, and its value may turn out to be less than we would have expected. Or in other circumstances the commodity may attract to itself labor floating free in the atmosphere, perhaps released from other commodities where it previously failed to embed, and thus an article may end up with more than the strictly "local" labor or value to which it seems to be entitled.

So we can't tell what the value is by measuring anything directly observable about the commodity. We can't see "value" in Marx's sense of "congealed labor"; we can only take his word for its existence and magnitude.

And by the same token we can only take his word that value is as described by his qualifications. He decrees that only "homogeneous" value, or an average amount, congeals in the commodity. He decrees that value is the minimum amount practicable – that only the amount of labor needed using state-of-the-art equipment congeals: that is, only the smallest price is acceptable. We have no way of determining any of this ourselves. We can only accept Marx's word for it, and grant credence to his Byzantine line of argumentation. We have no way of measuring value – that is, internal "congealed labor" – for ourselves.

On one hand labor exists and can be measured. And on the other, price can be known. But "congealed labor" is invisible and unknowable, not to mention scientifically incoherent. We can know nothing about it except what Marx tells us (assuming we take his word for it). Not only is the notion of "congealed labor" a scientifically incoherent one; the concept of some such relationship as one entity's being a "phenomenal form" of another is scientifically illiterate – a nonsense phrase. It is thus not just that Marx's labor-only theory is wrong in fact, as to the magnitude of value it would predict; the very nature of the theory, its foundation in the entities and relationships he describes, is profoundly unscientific. It owes more to mysticism, verbal gymnastics, and metaphysical speculation than to science.

It is not only not the right answer; it is not capable of being the right answer, by its very nature at the most basic level. Unless we are willing simply to abandon ourselves to Marx, and to discard all the methods and discipline of modern science, reverting to the superstitions and ignorance of past eras, we must reject Marx's theory and qualifications as much for their form as for their content.

The mechanism

It is difficult to see how these various entities could be related in a cause-and-effect manner. By what mechanism does market price come to equal, in every case, the magnitude of the internally-contained "value" – an entity which no one can see or measure, and which no one had ever heard of until Marx wrote?

Karl Popper addresses this issue, as follows:

> The fundamental law of the theory of value is the law that the
> prices of practically all commodities, including wages, are determined
> by their values, or more precisely, that they are. . .proportional to the
> labor hours necessary for their production. Now this "law of
> value". . .at once raises a problem. Why does it hold? Obviously,
> neither the buyer nor the seller of the commodity can see, at a glance,
> how many hours are necessary for its production; and even if they
> could, it would not explain the law of value. For it is clear that the
> buyer simply buys as cheaply as he can, and that the seller does

exactly the opposite. . . In order to explain the law of value, it would be our task to show why the buyer is unlikely to succeed in buying below, and the seller in selling above, the "value" of a commodity. This problem was seen more or less clearly by those who believed in the labor theory of value. . . [5]

Popper then goes on to discuss their response. Indeed, Marx himself supplied an answer to this problem (which will be treated later in this text).

The point is, real economies don't work like that; they work as Popper describes above; and these real-world facts, rather than a theoretical picture drawn up from whole cloth, should be the starting point of our analysis.

Our question, again, is what mechanism, what real-world line of cause and effect, causes price to correspond to internal "value"? Is it the sheer magical effect of the phrase "phenomenal form" that acts as a powerful incantation or magical charm?

"Forms"

The phrase "phenomenal form" is a mere nonsense phrase; it has no explanatory content at all. The mere waving around of the phrase, price as a "phenomenal form" of value, cannot cause prices to conform to the internal value of commodities. What then is the mechanism?

Prices are governed by people. Someone decides what to write on the price sticker – what to ask. Someone decides whether or not to pay that price – how much he will give. How does the price thus arrived at – which would seem to be arrived at partly by the action of free will of men, or at least by the interaction and "conflict" of their free wills – how does that price come always, in every case, to equal internal unseen "value"? What is the mechanism?

Of course, Marx himself doesn't give us one. He has proved his theory to be true, by various twists and turns of "dialectic." If the theory is proven, it needs no other elucidation – logic can compel the facts.

Thus price, which is set at least partly by the interaction of human decisions, somehow corresponds fatalistically, without the exertion of any conscious effort by anyone, directly to the congealed, internal value.

For the remarkable thing is, no one pricing a commodity ever sets out to calculate the internal "Value." No one says, "I have to calculate the one, true value for this commodity, namely its internally-contained congealed labor; I have to put that price on the commodity, otherwise I will be violating the laws of the universe." No one has to take thought to keep from violating the genuine laws of the universe! For the laws of the universe – natural laws of physics, chemistry, etc. – apply to purely material phenomena. They apply spontaneously – they enforce themselves, as it were. And they are not concerned with matters where human will and choice enter into consideration. That is Marx's scientistic fallacy, one common to this day – though few people have been as abjectly under its sway as he was.

So if no one calculates the internal "Value," or indeed the embodied labor, if no one consciously tries to peg price to this internal "value," how then does price come to equal, in every case, the internal value? Again, what is the mechanism?

One possible answer is that perhaps someone *does* calculate the embodied labor. While true "value" lies unseen within the commodity, it equals the labor, and labor is recognizably a significant economic factor. Perhaps for purely economic reasons, because of some complex of real-life economic constraints and considerations (unelucidated by Marx), price is forced to equal labor, and thus value. Could there be a line of cause and effect like that?

Perhaps there is. Labor, after all, is probably the main factor in production costs, so it would seem plausible that prices might end up corresponding to labor. This could be so even though no one consciously calculates the number of hours of labor and says, "This product took X hours of labor to produce, so the one correct price corresponding to its true value is" – whatever the amount may be. It may result simply from the production costs, i.e., the amount of the payroll.

Price may indeed correlate somehow to labor, but the above-described process is more like the classical view; it depends on economic entities, not metaphysical ones; and it is certainly not what Marx posits. His explanation is that labor congeals directly into value, which is a substance within the commodity. He rules out conscious calculation of any kind, including the pegging of price to payroll costs. (Any such conscious calculation would bring in human will and the possibility that such calculations and considerations might be ignored or overruled or changed, thus flouting Marx's law of value.)

Marx's explanation is that by sheer force of logic, or by a physical transformation, labor becomes value. And price, for its part, equals value because it's a "form" of it, in the mystical or philosophic sense; it is an alternate guise of it, a manifestation of it, a different incarnation. Thus price equals value, essentially, by philosophical mumbo-jumbo, by dogmatic pronouncement, or by the effects of "a specious and fantastic arrangement of words." Marx tells us that it is by a chain of metaphysical necessity that price equals value – not from pedestrian economic considerations.

In short, the whole paradigm Marx envisions, and the entire basis of his argument, is not a matter of real-world economic constraints. To admit market forces into the argument would be to break the spell of his entire veil of shimmering, abstract pronouncements by admitting grubby, pedestrian economic facts. We might devise or suggest some argument or line of cause and effect such as we've suggested; but it would be foreign to the nature of

Marx's text.

To admit market forces into the picture would be to dismiss the whole self-contained, philosophical system of proofs and mechanical inter-relationships Marx has set up. It would be to abandon his purely self-referring, materialistic quasi-physics. Once we are on the firm ground of market forces and human choices, there is no reason to stop with labor alone. We would go all the way and say price is a complex of three factors, not one: labor costs, land costs or rents, and profits. If real-world considerations and actual facts are to be admitted, then the classical explanation will easily overwhelm Marx's theory.

Thus, once Marx has proven, to his own satisfaction, that price is a "phenomenal form" of value and that value equals labor, it is senseless to ask by what mechanism in the real world such an equivalence could come about. He saw no need for any explanation or elaboration of any working mechanism.

Marx's theory is not based on the facts, and not designed to explain the facts. His logic proceeds in the other direction: first he designs his theory, then he attempts to make the facts appear to result from his theory: he co-opts the facts. Rather than seriously and honestly – scientifically – allowing any theory he devises to be subject to the facts, he would subjugate the facts to his theory. If to do so requires sudden and illogical revisions of his theory, transforming its entire basis and theoretical framework, then such changes of course will be made; anything to preserve his "labor-only" theory.

Evaluation

To sum up, we may say that Marx adjusts his theory to make its results correspond superficially to facts. However, while the results predicted by his theory seem to tally loosely with actual results, that is just a result of sophistry and rationalization.

Marx's theory is not science. It doesn't actually give the right results – it only seems to because it is vaguely formulated and not quantitatively investigable.

Not to put too fine a point on it, his explanation is incorrect because the classical explanation is correct, and is known to be correct from massive amounts of observation. Second, the very nature of his theory, purporting to reveal deterministic laws governing a realm subject to human control, is anti-scientific and superstitious. And thirdly, the justification or reasoning he advances for the qualifications is specious. There are "internal contradictions" in his theory, a lack of logical coherence between the basic theory and its added modifications.

The first qualification is justified mainly by declamation and decree, by simply declaring that only "homogeneous" labor "counts" or creates value. It is supported with hand-waving arguments. That is, Marx devotes himself to describing how labor can be divided up into "homogeneous" units, but fails to give any coherent reason why only these "homogeneous" units create value. He shows that the invested labor can be averaged; but this is not a revelation. He doesn't really say why the average should be taken as the value.

For his qualifications, Marx announces a new standard, pulled from thin air: "socially necessary" labor, as opposed to plain old actual labor. And he arbitrarily defines what is socially necessary.

None of these "social" redefinitions of value can merge coherently with Marx's initial picture, which has labor directly, materially embodying itself in the commodity.

Marx's next qualification leans even more heavily on the arbitrary standard of "socially necessary" labor. Marx defines that term as meaning only the minimum amount of labor, that is, the smallest practicable amount (or, to speak plainly, the cheapest price). This minimum amount of labor is the only valid value. Again, this new definition cannot merge into a coherent whole with Marx's picture of labor congealing directly within a commodity. It is mere arbitrary re-definition.

Thus the basis of Marx's qualifications, the source of their justification, is just "dialectics" – glib rhetoric and specious manipulation of words. There is no solid foundation for them in any event or fact, and his theory contains no attempt to describe or codify real-world events. It is not science, but the creation of an imaginary world from words, assumptions and argumentation. It is, at best, science on the Scholastics' model.

The net result is this: Marx's labor theory of value as originally stated, together with the added qualifications, is an attempt by sheer force of words to make that which is untrue seem true. There is no effort on Marx's part to find out how the world really works and to describe it. He does not exert himself to fit his theory to the facts; rather he would co-opt the facts for his theory and make only such modifications to his theory as will keep it more or less in line with the facts, at those few points of reference where his theory can be factually checked. He fits the following description, written by Medvedev (but about Stalin, not Marx):

> His approach to theory was wrong in essence. He did not derive theoretical positions from concrete reality; he forced theory to fit his wishes, subordinated it to transient situations – in a word, he politicized theory.[6]

To take a patent falsehood and attempt to make it seem true by sheer force of logic, voluminous flow of words, and convoluted argumentation – that is just the kind of thing Marx does in his "labor theory of value."

Final appreciation

Marx's treatise bears very few of the earmarks of an empirical investigation. It is not an analysis based on the facts, a search for the underlying order and regularities behind observed phenomena. Rather it is a statement of the convictions of Marx's own mind, an elaboration of the picture of the world which Marx had constructed in his own internal thought-processes. This structure of preconceived notions about the nature of capitalism, with various added assumptions and deductions, is what Marx advances as a scientific account. He offers it with great conviction and vehemence, mostly in the form of dogmatic utterances supported by nothing but his own inner convictions.

Marx's method, then, is simply to elaborate the picture of the way the world works which he has formed in his mind. He sometimes condescends to adduce deductive proofs of what he says; at other times he just issues his decrees *ex cathedra*. But in whichever way he attempts to convince the reader of what he says, he is always inventing a world out of his own mind, not describing the real one as it might appear from any serious investigation or observation. His method is "dialectical" in the sense that it is based on argumentation, on armchair theorizing and syllogistic deductions. It is a reversion to Scholastic methods, with no investigation of facts. Direct observations, experimentation, and objective verification of his theories are not employed. His main concern and interest is in constructing a self-consistent schema; each feature he adds to his theory must be logically consistent with what has gone before it, and make a unified whole. His picture of the world, like the worlds of science-fiction writers, may be fanciful and imagined, but it should hang together as a unified piece.

Another concern is this: there are certain points where his imagined world does touch the ground, so to speak: where it concerns observable phenomena and where the results as the theory would predict them can be compared to the results that actually obtain in the real world. These touch-points are few, and Marx's theory generally is able to present a semblance of accord with reality at these points.

The correlation between reality and Marx's theory at these widely-scattered touch-points adds credibility to his theories. But while the end results may correspond, the actual explanation of what caused those results is not found in Marx's theory. Moreover, the points of comparison are so widely scattered, and the correspondence is so vague and inexact, that these comparisons constitute no proof at all.

Marx's conception of science is "whatever I put down on the page." But we should be suspicious of his glib efforts to give his theory credit for real-world events.

NOTES – Chapter 3

1 "Roemer: Duke 'Suicide' for Louisiana," *USA Today*, November 1-3 (weekend edition), 1991.

2 Lacey, Robert, *Ford, the Men and the Machine,* Boston, Little Brown, 1986.

3 From the *Wall Street Journal*

4 *USA Today, June 2, 1988.*

5 Popper, Karl, *The Open Society And Its Enemies*, Princeton, N.J., Princeton University Press, 1963, p. 361-362.

6 Roy Aleksandrovich Medvedev, *Let History Judge: the Origins and consequences of Stalinism,* edited by David Joravsky and Georges Haupt, New York, Vintage Books, c1971.

4. EXAMPLES

Marx now gives a few examples of the workings of his labor theory. As we have seen, according to his theory, the value of a commodity is determined by the amount of labor invested in its production. It follows then that changes in the amount of this invested labor will bring about changes in value. Or, to put it another way, changes in value which one observes on the market may be assumed to be the results of prior changes in the amount of labor required to produce the item. Marx gives examples as follows (beginning by quoting himself):

> "As values, all commodities are only definite masses of congealed labor-time."
>
> The value of a commodity would therefore remain constant, if the labor-time required for its construction also remained constant. But the latter changes with every variation in the productiveness of labor. This productiveness is determined by various circumstances, amongst others, by the average amount of skill of the workmen, the state of science, and the degree of its practical application, the social organization of production, the extent and capabilities of the means of production, and by physical conditions. For example, the same amount of labor in favorable seasons is embodied in eight bushels of corn, and in unfavorable, only in four. The same labor extracts from rich mines more metal than from poor mines. Diamonds are of very rare occurrence on the earth's surface, and hence their discovery costs, on an average, a great deal of labor-time. Consequently much labor is represented in a small compass. Jacob doubts whether gold has ever been paid for at its full value. This applies still more to diamonds. According to Eschwege, the total produce of the Brazilian diamond mines for the eighty years, ending in 1823, had not realized the price of one-and-a-half years' average produce of the sugar and coffee plantations of the same country, although the diamonds cost much more labor, and therefore represented more value. With richer mines, the same quantity of labor would embody itself in more diamonds and their value would fall. If we could succeed at a small expenditure of labor, in converting carbon into diamonds, their value might fall

below that of bricks. In general, the greater the productiveness of labor, the less is the labor-time required for the production of an article, the less is the amount of labor crystallised in that article, and the less is its value; and *vise versâ*, the less the productiveness of labor, the greater is the labor-time required for the production of an article, and the greater is its value. The value of a commodity, therefore, varies directly as the quantity, and inversely as the productiveness, of the labor incorporated in it.

Marx thus implicitly defines a seemingly scientific law for the determination of value: value is directly proportional to the quantity of labor or inversely proportional to the productivity (to use the modern form of the word) of labor: $V \propto Q$ or $V \propto 1/P$.

It should be noted that Marx's first examples, and indeed all his examples, are relative ones. They concern relative changes in value, fluctuations up and down, rather than dealing in absolute numbers. They only tend to correlate changes, rather than demonstrating a precise numeric relationship.

Having said that, let us look at Marx's first, agricultural, example. We see that Marx finds fluctuations in the productivity of labor, in agricultural matters, in the form of changes of productivity from growing season to growing season. That is, from one year to another there are changes in the amount of harvested output, which correspond to changes in the ratio of the amount of goods produced to the labor invested (this ratio being the productivity).

Let us look then at his first, agricultural example. He says "the same amount of labor in favorable seasons is embodied in 8 bushels of corn and in unfavorable only in four." That is, the same total amount of labor is exerted by a farmer in a good year as in a bad year; but for extraneous reasons beyond the farmer's control, the harvested output in one year is only half what it is in another.

Marx cites the figures eight or four bushels: the total amount of labor is conceived of as being divided up into "innumerable individual units" of a certain size. Each of these labor units of a certain size has produced, or has "embodied" itself in, its corresponding fraction of the total output, that being in either of the two years respectively eight or four bushels.

It is obvious that if the same amount of labor accounts for either eight or four bushels of corn, the ratio of labor-hours per amount of output is twice as high in the case of four bushels as in the case of eight. According to Marx's theory, this difference in "productivity" accounts for the fact that prices of foodstuffs are higher in years of bad harvests; this example shows how the prices were determined, and demonstrates that Marx's labor theory is what is at work in exchange value or market prices.

In sum, any time the ratio, "labor-hours/output of goods," changes, the exchange value correspondingly changes, just as Marx's theory predicted. Thus the example demonstrates the working of his law of value.

Rebuttal

On a certain superficial level of understanding, the cited example might seem to bear out Marx's theory. His definition seems to give the right answer: value is the amount of embodied labor per unit, and when crops are bad the usual amount of labor is divided up among fewer units of output, so the resulting value is larger. Thus his theory is in accord with reality as represented by the example.

If we consider Marx's formula or theory only as a "black box," looking only at the inputs and outputs without worrying about the internal mechanism, the example may be convincing. Given the right amounts of labor and commodities as input, it yields the right value (presumably) as output.

But if we concern ourselves with his explanation *as* an explanation, if we concern ourselves with the internal mechanism of his theory and how it functions in the real world, the example is less convincing. Then the question tends to arise: His formula gives the "right" answer for value, but how does anyone know the formula or the answer? How do the people involved in determining value – the capitalist who sets an asking price, the buyer who agrees to pay it – how did these people know how to adapt their actions and decisions to fit Marx's formula when determining prices? In short, what is the working mechanism?

That is to say, Marx's formula or law of value apparently works well as an *a posteriori* description of what goes on. But it is difficult to see how it could work in an *a priori* manner, in a forward-moving direction so as to determine the value in a cause-and-effect fashion. It is difficult to see Marx's "explanation" as an explanation, in other words. We have a price going up on one side of the black box, and either an amount of goods going down or an amount of labor going up, on the other side. The two seem to be in accord, but there is no rational connection that can be made between the two. Marx doesn't really give us a picture of how the varying factors like the weather produce the given result in the human milieu which is the marketplace. He gives no mechanism whereby his abstract theory or numerical formula might exert its effect on real-world economies.

The fact that Marx's formula for value seems to give the right result under certain carefully chosen circumstances does not prove that his theory is what actually is at work in those circumstances. Perhaps, on the contrary, his theory is just an *a posteriori* rationalization, an invented schema which somehow closely approximates or mimics the actual working dynamic.

That is what must be decided. Marx's entire labor theory in its finished version adheres so closely to supply and demand that it is hard to find a demarcation line between the two. Marx has so thoroughly modified, propped up, and adjusted his theory that its workings are almost indistinguishable from those of supply and demand; the predicted results of labor theory are the same in most cases as those of supply and demand. Thus it is difficult to think of a test situation or a set of circumstances which could be used to distinguish the results of the one from the other. His theory in effect "piggybacks" along with supply and demand – it sneaks in on the merits of classical theory, by molding itself to supply and demand so closely that the results of one can be mistaken for the workings of the other. Our task will be to determine which of the two is actually at work in determining prices.

Consider the first, agricultural example. Marx presents the higher prices of food in years of bad weather as a matter of "the productiveness of labor": a given amount of labor is embodied in, or divided up among, fewer bushels of grain in bad years than in good. He is in effect saying that prices are higher in bad years "by division," i.e., by the terms of a calculation based on his formula, "Value = total labor/total output." When output is low, and the labor remains the same, value is high. This is presumably a complete explanation because he has already proved his formula to be correct; and thus when he can show the results of its application in varying circumstances, he has given us the entire truth about why prices fluctuate. It is mechanistically and logically determined.

But suppose the producers and sellers haven't read his proof. How, in the real world, do prices arrive at Marx's prescribed level? What mechanism in real-world terms, apart from Marx's abstractions on a page, ensures that prices will correspond to embodied labor? Do producers actually calculate the embodied labor and then peg prices to that figure?

No, if conscious calculation is what is envisioned, the calculations are much more in terms of starting with production costs (including, to be sure, labor costs) and adding on a profit. What Marx proposes is that prices automatically, by either a mystical or a naturalistic mechanism, correspond to the embodied labor, apart from any human calculation; value is a condensation of labor, a physical equivalence. Because value *must* equal embodied labor, market prices somehow, mystically, must conform themselves to the required figure. No other mechanism beyond that is offered by Marx. Human will and calculation don't enter into the process.

Thus Marx does not offer any mechanism or chain of cause and effect whereby prices adjust themselves to the levels of labor (apart from his illiterate notion that value can be simply the substance, labor, in another state). Apart from such fractured physics, and apart from the presumptive authority of his deductive proofs, Marx gives no mechanism or explanation at all. There is no logical or coherent connection made between amounts of labor and resulting prices, or between bad harvests and prices. His "correlations" between the two are as irrational as the "correlations" of astrology.

As an example of the difficulties with his view, we might ask this: how do people even know how much labor is embodied in the grain? If the value is directly determined by that labor, still a money price must be set, and it is set by people; how do these people know where to set the price?

There might be a quasi-explanation for this: perhaps they base their reasonings on money, i.e., on the expenses incurred in producing the crop; and these expenses are (let us suppose) proportional to the labor. Thus, while the producers reason in terms of money, it is actually labor which determines the value of goods.

That is, we might say that the producers have paid just as much as in previous years, and that the expended labor is the same. Moreover, they want to get the same net return as always; and since their output is lower, they must charge more per bushel for it. Thus labor indirectly determines the value of the goods.

But that is simply the classical view with added, extraneous complications. It's an explanation based on supply and demand, or expenses, profit margins, and such; it's too much an explanation in human terms to be in accord with Marx's theory.

A formula is not an explanation; what we need to see is a mechanism, some factor which can operate in the real world to determine events. A formula may on an abstract level appear to give the right numbers under certain circumstances, but the people involved in the marketplace, the buyers and sellers, don't govern their behavior by such formulae. If Marx's theory cannot show a mechanism whereby the forces active in the marketplace can result in the formula, then it is not an explanation at all. Rather, it is an assertion that there is a "correspondence" between two quantities, with no evidence given as to how there can be — much as it is asserted that the movements of the planets astrologically "correspond" to events on earth. The amount of scientific credibility is the same in both cases. Formulae derived by exercises in abstract logic don't govern the marketplace, any more than abstract theories about celestial constellations can control human behavior.

Counter-explanation

To Marx's "example" we may oppose the classical explanation. That explanation is that prices are high because, in years of bad harvests, demand is as high as ever, while supply is sharply lower. As Smith put it (*Wealth of Nations*, Book I, Chapter VII),

> When the quantity of any commodity which is brought to market falls short of the effectual demand, all those who are willing to pay the whole value of the rent, wages, and profit, which must be paid in order to bring it thither, cannot be supplied with the quantity which they want. Rather than want [lack] it altogether, some of them will be willing to give more. A competition will immediately begin among them, and the market price will rise more or less above the natural price according as either the greatness of the deficiency, or the wealth and wanton luxury of the competitors, happen to animate more or less the eagerness of the competition...Hence the exorbitant price of the necessaries of life during the blockade of a town or in a famine.

Comparing these two contrasting explanations of the price fluctuations in agricultural commodities, we see that Marx gives us a deduced formula through which value is determined, purely by the quotient, labor/output. The authority for this formula is sheer force of logic. On the other hand the classical view gives not so much a formula as a picture. It illustrates the determination of value within a context of human economic nature and the decisions and actions taken in certain circumstances. The reader may judge for himself which of these two explanations is more credible. The point to be kept in mind, though, is that we are looking for a cause-and-effect explanation of the determination of price. The question is not whether a rote formula can be devised which will more or less coincide, after the fact, with real-world movements of prices. The question is what determines prices; what are the motive factors; what causes price movements and what factors can function, in a cause-and-effect manner, to control prices.

Being a labor theory, Marx's theory is quite close to classical theory. To a great degree, in classical theory (that is, in real life), labor does determine price. Labor costs are one of the three components of price; when labor costs go up, prices have to rise, and similarly when labor costs go down. For the most part, in giving his examples Marx is not so much demonstrating the validity of his theory as saying again what classical theory also says: leaving aside other factors, where the amount of labor needed to produce an item changes, price will change in the same direction.

What classical theory has that Marx does not, is a coherent, cause-and-effect explanation of why this is so. The capitalist desires to cover his production costs and also make a profit. Therefore, if labor costs go up, his tendency is to raise prices. If labor costs go down, he might attempt to keep prices the same and thus increase his profit; but if there is competition from other producers, he will probably be unable to do this, and prices will fall. Thus there is in classical theory a chain of cause and effect, in terms of human economic behavior, showing how the end result derives from the initial factors. Moreover, this explanation is of great intuitive force for anyone who has ever had any economic dealings whatsoever.

By contrast, Marx's theory is devoid of any intuitive explanation or any demonstration of a working mechanism. It is simply a formula, putatively proven to be valid, whose results are therefore deemed conclusive, without the need of any elucidation as to its inner workings. Prices of food products rise in bad years "by division," because the quotient labor/output is (presumably) higher when output is lower; and because, as Marx has proved to his own satisfaction, value is identical with embodied or transmuted labor, and price is the "phenomenal form" of value. Thus his point is proven.

As one author said,

> During a famine a sack of potatoes does not represent any more work-hours than it does in a time of plenty, but it has, nevertheless, a much higher value. . . Marx's "labor theory of value" was just such an artfully-constructed piece of logical subtlety as one might expect from him. But it was obviously built up on an over-simplified foundation: from among a variety of possible causes only one was taken into consideration – *pars pro toto*. The result was in direct contradiction to the most palpable facts of everyday existence. [1]

And how did prices set themselves before Marx even wrote his theory? When no one knew prices were supposed to correlate exactly to embodied labor, certainly no one made any such calculations; yet prices presumably corresponded exactly to labor. There is no conscious mechanism whereby this could have occurred, and he offers us no credible *automatic* mechanism. The whole theory is simply not tenable.

A complicating factor

There is some problem with even saying that the same amount of labor is embodied in four bushels of corn in bad years as in eight bushels in good years. Marx's view of value, remember, is a very mechanistic, literalistic one – labor congeals or physically embodies itself within a commodity.

It is hard to form a coherent picture of how this works in his agricultural example; it would seem on the contrary that, in bad years, some of the labor is simply wasted; or it is embodied in the corn that "doesn't grow," as it were.

What Marx probably envisions in his agricultural example is a situation where every producer's crops are down 50%, and where the entire amount of expended labor must be counted as "embodied" in the decreased output. The growth of the plants is stunted everywhere in the same proportion, let us say.

But suppose on the contrary the situation is this: some regions of the country have normal weather and normal harvests, while others have drought and total failure of the crops, producing nothing; thus there is the net result that, adding both regions, total output is half the usual harvest. We see then that the amount of labor directly, physically exerted on the grain which grows is the same as ever. That is to say, the labor embodied in the grain brought to market is the normal amount. The labor in the drought region has produced nothing.

In this case how does the price of the grain produced, which has only the usual or normal amount of labor actually embodied in it, become double the normal price? (That is, we know from experience and almost instinctively that the price would be high. We are interested, to repeat, in distinguishing the results as predicted by classical theory or real-life experience, from those predicted by Marx's theory.) How does the labor invested, in the bad area, in the production of no crops, "know" that it has to go over and embody itself in crops from the good area? Why isn't that just lost, with the actual harvest, containing the normal amount of labor, bringing in the same price as ever?

This raises again the issue of Marx's qualification concerning "homogeneous" labor, and his rationale for averaging the embodied labor in a commodity, society-wide. Labor as value should be the labor actually performed in producing a particular item – we have seen that. There is really no basis for saying that labor can average itself out. If labor physically embodies or congeals itself in the commodity, how can the resulting quantity be an average or "homogeneous" quantity? In the present example, the labor embodied in the grain produced in a particular field, let us say, should be the labor actually performed in that field. There is no basis for averaging it out over a region, or over a country, or over the entire world for that matter.

There are other considerations that could be brought into the equation. We might accept Marx's estimation that in certain circumstances an output of half the grain means twice the price. But some questions need to be asked about certain other situations.

Would it make a difference, for instance, whether granaries and silos all over the country were still filled with grain from previous years, or whether they were empty? If they were full, common sense might tell us that any price rise would be moderated (but this is common sense from the viewpoint of classical economics, and not necessarily Marx's view). On the other hand, if the only grain available was the current year's harvest, and if that harvest was down by half, then prices would probably rise sharply to reflect the shortage (leaving aside considerations of the world market).

That is, again, the classical viewpoint. By contrast, it is questionable whether Marx's theory would make the above distinction; if this year's grain has a labor content twice the normal level, then its value and price should be twice the usual, and this presumably holds true regardless of whether there is any stored grain or not. It is the current "prevalent" state of "productiveness" that determines the price. This result from his theory, however, seems to be contrary to what we know of actual market prices.

Counter-arguments

Presumably this objection could be countered by an added-on stipulation similar to Marx's previous two qualifications, perhaps by saying that value must be calculated on a basis of all the grain present. That is, if the labor content of the stored grain is the normal amount, and the labor content of the current harvest is double that amount, then the average for all the grain would be somewhat less than double the normal price. Thus his theory could explain why the price rise is moderated in such a case, bringing it once again into accord with reality.

That is, if the labor "socially necessary" is the amount required under "normal conditions of production," using the "average degree of skill and intensity prevalent," then maybe agriculturally speaking it would make sense to average the harvests over a period of years. That should be the standard of what is average or prevalent. This is especially the case if there is a large grain reserve in storage, buffering the market from the effects of one bad year.

This issue has several facets and several answers. First, we can say that classical, market economics might work like that, but it is not what Marx's theory says. Within his theory, what the harvest might have been the previous year, and how much grain is being held in storage, is irrelevant to the current price. The average degree of skill and intensity, the prevalent conditions, are those which obtain *now*, at the present moment, at the time the value is being calculated. You don't average the past price of hand-woven cloth together with machine-woven cloth, and you don't average past harvests together with the current one. The value has to be as Marx's theory stipulates: the ratio of labor to output in the current growing season.

We might ask ourselves what the situation would be if no grain were produced in the current year, but grain previously stored in warehouses or silos were put on the market to help make up for the shortfall: what should the price of that previously-produced grain be, according to Marx's theory?

Such a case would probably fall under the heading of the second qualification of Marx's labor theory. The value of a product, or the "labor-time socially necessary," is the amount under "normal conditions of production," those "prevalent at the time." In other words, the situation is analogous to the one where a new method of weaving cloth comes into use: the price of hand-woven cloth, previously produced, falls to the level of machine-woven cloth, the machine method being now considered the "prevalent" or "normal" condition of production.

In the same way, in a bad harvest the higher amount of embodied labor is the current, prevalent, now-normal value of grain; previously-produced grain would also assume the current, normal value. To take this reasoning farther, whether previously-stored grain is put on the market or not, the price of grain remains the same, being determined by the prevalent condition as to the amount of embodied labor contained by the grain. (That quantity is its value, and price is the phenomenal or observable form of it.)

The conclusion then is that the value of stored grain brought onto the market in times of bad harvests, would be the same as newly-produced grain; and whether stored grain is sold or not, the price of grain would be the same.

This result, which Marx's theory predicts, is contrary to all common sense and experience. It seems intuitively obvious that if grain is brought out of storage to help meet the shortfall, the price rise will be moderated. (Or perhaps it is not intuitive sense that tells us that, but our general observations of actual events in the real or "phenomenal" marketplace.)

It may seem glib to say that real-world events verify classical theory and refute Marxism; it seems too easy just to say, "The real world bears out classical theory." But such is the case; it is only that Marx has disdain for the real world. The results of his conceptualized or theorized deductions carry more weight for him than mere "phenomenal" facts. His concept of science was not the modern one of experimental, observational verification of hypotheses; but rather, he reverted to the Scholastics' method of accepting the results of his deduced theories as authoritative. Thus there is a misconception, or actually sheer ignorance, at the root of Marx's very concept of the nature of science itself, causing appeals to the real world and its facts and events to be of little weight in Marx's theory.

A complicating question

The interesting issue is whether Marx *could* have, consistently with the rest of his theory, stipulated that agricultural value should be averaged over a period of several years; and also, on what basis we can decide that question. Whether the stipulation would have been satisfactory to Marx is hard to say; we have little basis for answering that question. He generally proceeds by *ad hoc* logic and bald pronouncements, and it is thus hard to develop a method for knowing what he would have permitted. As was previously stated, Marx gives us no procedural rules for making our own inferences; he gives his own ready-made pronouncements, and we have to take them or leave them.

Ultimately, however, we can come to the same conclusion about our hypothetical qualification as we came to about Marx's actual qualifications. It is untenable for the same reasons that Marx's "qualifications" are untenable; there is a contradiction between his picture of value as a physical component of the commodity, and the notion of labor's or value's shifting itself around from grain to grain and averaging itself out. It cannot be averaged from year to year or from grain field to grain field. Marx's theory is again too inflexible and simple-minded to cover the variety of real-world considerations involved.

Non-weather example

So far our agricultural examples have been concerned with bad weather as the cause of a decline in output. Another situation we could envision is when a decline in both the labor performed and the food harvested occurs as a result of the simple abandonment of productive effort, where for some reason a great number of farmers simply cease to grow anything.

During the time of the "collectivization" of agriculture in the Soviet Union (two periods, really, roughly 1918-19 and 1928-33), many peasants simply refused to grow more food than they and their own families could consume. At the same time, large numbers of the marginally more prosperous peasants ("kulaks") were rounded up and shipped off into concentration camps of the Gulag. As a result of all this, there was little farm output. And there was famine in the U.S.S.R., famine, as Solzhenitsyn points out, "without war or drought," of sufficient severity to starve millions. (Adding to the severity was the fact that the Soviet Union continued to export food; moreover there was actual destruction of grain and livestock by some peasants.)

The issue that concerns us here, though, is what value Marx's theory would predict for foodstuffs at the time. The amount of grain produced was small, but the amount of labor expended was also small; in fact it would be reasonable to say labor was small in proportion to the decline in output (ignoring the wasted labor "embodied" in the destroyed livestock, that is).

Thus we could say that if the amount of grain produced was half that of normal years, the amount of labor invested was scarcely more than half the normal amount. So by the terms of Marx's formula, the labor content per unit of output of grain must have been the same as in normal years; the value should have been unchanged. That predicted result is of course preposterous.

During the time of collectivization of agriculture in the U.S.S.R., prices of food soared — as they have in every similar instance in history, whether in besieged towns, or in times of famine, or *whenever* the supply of food has been gravely inadequate. Prices of food were described by people who lived through the two main periods as "disastrous" and "atrocious."[2]

One author describes the period this way:

> Crowds of starving wretches could be seen scattered all over the
> potato fields. They were looking for potatoes left over from last

year's harvest. No matter what shape the potatoes were in, whether frozen or rotten, they were still edible. . .

There were some villagers who saw their salvation in the cities' marketplaces. There they brought for sale their best clothes, from prerevolutionary times, their family heirlooms, handicrafts, women's jewelry which had been passed on from generation to generation, homemade shirts, towels, tablecloths – all embroidered with traditional Ukrainian designs – handwoven Ukrainian rugs, and other valuables. These they sold for next to nothing, or bartered them for something edible.[3]

Another author adds:

Only in the bazaars, the independent market-places, were there no waiting lines. But here prices were fabulous. . . here cheese cost 3 roubles a pound; meat, 2 to 3 roubles; butter, 7 and 8 roubles. . . a wilted winter radish, 50 copecks; beets and carrots, also 50 copecks each.[4]

These are prices on the uncontrolled or "black" market. Rationed food, of course, was cheaper, but it was not subject to economic laws – it was doled out via centralized governmental control. But on the black market, and in what free markets were allowed, food brought phenomenal prices.

At the height of the famine, the situation in the Ukraine was this:

The wives of officials, who had large rations, would attend the Kiev bazaars and market their surplus food for the peasants' valuables, at bargain prices. A richly embroidered tablecloth would go for a 4 pound loaf of bread, a good carpet for a few such loaves. Or beautifully embroidered shirts of wool or linen. . .were exchanged for one or two loaves of bread. . .

At Torgsins, golden crosses or earrings would go for a few kilogrammes of flour or fat. A teacher got "50 grammes of sugar, or a cake of soap, and 200 grammes of rice" for a silver dollar.[5]

(And consider the amount of "labor-time" embodied in such works of embroidery! The shirts and other items should normally have been quite valuable, and worth a lot of food.)

A more quantified general statement of the situation is given by another author, in these words:

> The earlier deliveries of grain requisitioned by the state had com-
> pletely disrupted the kolkhozi [collective farms]. The granaries of the
> Ukraine were empty of all the grain required for the subsistence of
> the peasants and their livestock. The peasants were exhausted and
> refused to do any work, made no effort to gather their harvests, left
> the wheat to rot in the fields. . .
>
> A dreadful famine overran the countryside. . . This crisis was
> accompanied by gigantic inflation. The wholesale price index, on the
> basis of 100 in 1913, rose from 156.9 in 1927-1928 to 197.5 in 1931.
> In the same period the purchasing power of the ruble fell in consid-
> erable proportion. [6]

There was a rationing system at the time, of course, with food being doled out to all those with the proper papers. But where the market could be observed, where the workings of "capitalist" economics occurred (and that is what Marx's labor theory attempts to describe), supply and demand determined price as always. Mechanistic formulae as expounded by Marx held no sway.

The situation has always been the same, in times of severe shortage brought about by war, famine, or other catastrophe. After the Russian Revolution, during the resulting civil war, conditions were much the same:

> Subjected to constant requisitions that were organized by
> [Communist-] party commandos in the rural areas, the peasant limit-
> ed his efforts to what was required for his own subsistence. At once
> famine set in in the cities, which were abandoned by the workers. . .
>
> The heart of Moscow, the real center of its activity, was now the
> "Sukharevka," the citadel of the black market. A mass of many
> thousands of persons swarmed over it, proletarians and former
> aristocrats jostling one another in the struggle for survival. Here the
> most miserable object had a price. Here everything was barter: butter
> was traded for silk handkerchiefs, six eggs for one jacket, a tool for
> slippers. Sometimes in this market one would stumble on an old
> woman offering two lumps of sugar on a saucer – her total assets. [7]

And similarly during the Second World War; one author describes the situation thus:

We found, alas, that the prices, already inflated, had skyrocketed in the few months of war. The cheapest tobacco cost forty rubles a glass, which is the peasant measure; a pint of milk cost fifty rubles; a chicken, 1200 rubles or almost the equivalent of two months' pay for an officer. The ordinary private, whose pay ranged from eight to twelve rubles a month, would have to serve nine years to pay for one chicken at open prices in November, 1941.[8]

The same author reports:

I visited the free city market [in Vladivostok], where food and clothes were on sale, at fantastic black-market prices, in greater profusion than I had seen anywhere in the U.S.S.R. Much of this merchandise was clearly American, no doubt stolen from lend-lease consignments or brought in by Russian sailors. I saw a simple pair of women's shoes fetch three thousand rubles in this market. I saw a kilo of bacon sold for 1200 rubles. [9]

Perhaps the most suggestive illustration of the inflation of prices in times of war and famine, is this eye-witness report, from right after the War:

There was an invasion of rats. All the cats had disappeared during the siege of Leningrad, when people would pay two hundred rubles for a cat. [10]

How much "labor-time" is normally invested in raising a cat, and how much is a cat generally worth as a food item?

Still more counter-examples

We could pose other, even more prosaic, agricultural counter-examples. In the United States during the winter months, vegetables can be grown only in some southern and western states. During these months they are grown there and are shipped throughout the country. Now, what should the value of these winter vegetables be, according to Marx's theory?

The average amount of labor required to grow them is, let us say, about the same as in the warm months anywhere in the country. Shipping costs add to the price somewhat, since on the average the produce must be shipped farther during the winter than food grown during the summer. Or rather, properly speaking Marxian-wise, we should say it is the *labor* embodied in shipping the vegetables to market which adds to their value.

At any rate, apart from the added transportation costs, according to Marx's theory the value of winter vegetables should be about the same as that of summer vegetables. In fact, this is not the case. In the winter the price of fresh produce can be two or three times the summer price. This is because in the winter, when the supply is lower, there is little competitive pressure to keep prices low. Supply and demand determine the price, and the real world does not conform to Marx's theory.

It is possible to conceive of some responses Marx's theory might make to this example. It might be said that value, in the sense of inner, labor-determined "Value," is just what Marx's theory says it is, but that capitalist tactics make for a higher "phenomenal form" or market price. That is, the capitalists take advantage of the short supply of vegetables in the winter to exploit the consumer and charge more than the inner, transcendently valid "Value."

This response however is just a mystification of the subject. Inner "Value" is an unseen, unknowable entity; it can't be measured or its existence verified. We have only Marx's word for its existence. Thus to say that "phenomenal" price deviates from the pure theoretical value is just to say that Marx's theory is not in accord with the facts; his theory is not what determines price and is fit only to be discarded. Everything in the real world not in accord with Marx's theories cannot be dismissed as an aberration or special circumstance. If Marx's "Value" is overruled and displaced by market price, then of what use or pertinence is it? It becomes just a mystification, a theory of unseen entities with no real-world significance, like such past theoretical entities as phlogiston. We must adopt as our theory that which in actual practice determines price, i.e. the classical theory of supply and demand. Applying the principle of Occam's Razor, we must discard useless, irrelevant (and invisible) entities.

One important technique in Marx's work is his use of various sophistries to explain away conflicting facts, the application of various ad hoc rationalizations after the fact as a way of saying, "My theory is correct; it is the facts that are mistaken." When actual market price does not fall into accord with Marx's theory, he produces rationalizations explaining how his theory of inner, transcendent Value is actually valid, but that because of this or that peculiar circumstance present in the case, it appears not to be so, or it must be calculated in a different way, or other ad hoc considerations must be factored in.

It has been said that any theory can be proved if the theorist is allowed to add as many assumptions as he wants at any time he wants. That is how Marx's theory is preserved, and how its apologists continue to cling to it. "Value" – inner, invisible, and transcendent – remains inviolate and always just what Marx's theory says it is. But whenever market price threatens to upset the theory, added assumptions and sophistries are produced to modify the theory and account for discrepancies. Thus Marx's theory becomes rebuttal-proof, unfalsifiable, buttressed by an endless succession of tacked-on assumptions and sophistries. It ends up as a faith or creed, adhered to with a ferocious tenacity, about something unexaminable which is expounded in an unfalsifiable theory. This theory may be the ameliorist "vision of a better world" Marx so disparaged, but it is certainly not the science he professed it to be.

Another complicating factor

> *We live in a planned society, which means we don't know what is going to happen tomorrow.*
> – Gerasimov, a Soviet citizen

Another question could be asked about Marx's theory: would it make any difference to the value of a harvest if, say, the wheat crop was drastically down, but harvests of corn, oats, and barley were good? Wouldn't that added factor moderate the price rise for wheat, more so than if harvests of other crops were bad too?

An issue not addressed by Marx's theory is the existence of alternative foodstuffs. So far we have been speaking of one product or a generic category, "grain"; but we have been speaking of it as an indivisible category and as if it were essential to the diet. We haven't addressed the possibility that one crop might suffer but that there might be other things to eat; we have spoken as if a shortage in the product under consideration meant a shortage of food in general, and thus a high demand in proportion to supply.

It is possible, however, for one crop to suffer while other foodstuffs are in normal supply. In such a case there might be a shortage of a particular food, but a sufficient supply of other foods so that people are not really in danger of going hungry. Even though it might mean switching from a preferred food to one less desirable, there could be a change of diet in response to the shortages.

Surely this would be a pertinent consideration. Wouldn't it be reasonable to suppose that it would make a difference in the final market price of a commodity whether there were other foods to take up the slack, or whether all foods were in short supply simultaneously?

In Marx's theory, of course, it would make no difference. The value of a commodity is the labor invested per unit of output; what other competing or complementary products are available makes no difference.

Here we encounter a side issue not discussed by Marx. What constitutes a single commodity? Is a single type of grain, say wheat, a commodity to itself, its value to be calculated as a separate thing apart from other grain crops? Or should all cereal grains be lumped together as constituting one commodity? Marx apparently did so (speaking of "corn" in the sense of grain, not in the sense of maize).

Or on the other hand, it might be asserted that individual varieties of a grain, like durum wheat, red wheat, and so on, constitute separate commodities because they are marketed and priced separately. How do we know where the divisions can be made, and how does Marx's theory make the distinction?

Actually, there is no objective way of knowing, and Marx does not issue any general rule for making any such distinction credibly. We make divisions only where he tells us there are divisions, and we know only because he tells us. His theory is based on his authority only, and not on any objective, distinguishable characteristics of different produced goods.

At any rate, it seems clear that if a wheat harvest is bad, the price rise will be less if other crops are good than if all crops fail together. Economists have long noted that the existence or lack of alternative products affects the price of a given commodity; under certain conditions of supply, at various price levels, a proportion of the demand for one product can be satisfied by a switch to another product. Thus the price rise is moderated.

That is, again we make the appeal to self-evident facts. Marx's theory attributes to the grain in question one statutory price only: labor divided by the amount produced. However, we can see that other considerations enter into the determination of market price. Marx's theory is inadequate to account for the facts – if the facts are what we are interested in.

Also, it makes a difference what the crop is, or how important a part of the diet it is. If the wheat crop were bad and other crops good, there still might be a quite large rise in wheat prices, because in this country people would be reluctant to switch to other grains. If the rice crop only were bad, the price rise would be moderated, because rice is not a staple of the diet here, as wheat is. In oriental countries, the situation might be just the reverse.

The leads to another homely agricultural example. At the time of this writing, rutabagas are for sale in a local market for 19 cents a pound, and tomatoes are 59 cents a pound. What this means, according to Marx's theory, is that the amount of labor required for producing rutabagas is pound for pound approximately one-third that for growing tomatoes.

This ratio of respective amounts of labor may indeed be correct, or close to it, because labor is no doubt the largest single factor in the costs of these agricultural products. However, Marx's theory willfully excludes the other pertinent factors of price, profits and rents.

To continue with the example, however: let us take as valid Marx's representations about the relative amounts of labor in the two products. Then let us suppose that in the next growing season, three-fourths of all the tomato growers in the country somehow decided *en masse* to switch to growing rutabagas instead.

Under such circumstances, we have to assume that the respective amounts of labor needed to grow tomatoes and rutabagas will be unchanged; there is nothing different about the new situation that should make them change (other than perhaps a slight increase in efficiency due to the nature of production on a more massive scale). And according to Marx's theory, the sudden change in the amounts of the two vegetables brought to market, that is, the difference in supply, should make no difference: the congealed labor determines price, and that is unchanged. The net result should therefore be simply a highly increased quantity of rutabagas selling at the same 19 cents a pound, and a greatly curtailed supply of tomatoes at 59 cents a pound. The reader may estimate for himself the plausibility of such a result.

The key difference here is in the quantity of the two products normally sold. The price of rutabagas is 19 cents a pound for a crop which is only a minute fraction of the size of the tomato crop. The demand for rutabagas is small in relation to the demand for tomatoes; tomatoes are an inestimably more popular vegetable. These earthy realities, which form no part of Marx's theory, make it very unlikely that a price of 19 cents a pound could be maintained for a massive harvest of rutabagas.

If there were a sudden flood of rutabagas on the market, producers would find it difficult to sell their rutabagas at any price. The price would plummet, perhaps to whatever minuscule amount the crop could bring for use as pig fodder. Or the crop might be good for nothing but to be plowed under, to enrich the soil.

Smith aptly characterized this situation (*Wealth of Nations*, Book I, Chapter VII):

> When the quantity [of a commodity] brought to market exceeds the effectual demand, it cannot be all sold to those who are willing to pay the whole value of the rent, wages and profit, which must be paid in order to bring it thither. Some part must be sold to those who are willing to pay less, and the low price which they give for it must reduce the price of the whole. The market price will sink more or less below the natural price, according as the greatness of the excess increases more or less the competition of the sellers. . .

He also adds an interesting side issue:

> The same excess in the importation of perishable, will occasion a much greater competition than in that of durable commodities; in the importation of oranges, for example, than in that of old iron.

At the same time the price of rutabagas fell, the price of tomatoes would do as it always does when the supply is low in relation to demand; it would rise to just that level that could be supported by the current conditions of supply and demand. This would mean a large price increase, as it has throughout history whenever a desirable commodity has been scarce. Price does not conform itself to Marx's reductive formula.

(It should be pointed out that later on in his text Marx does attempt to account for situations such as the one just described. A full treatment of his explanation is out of place here. Suffice it to say that his argument turns around the phrase "socially necessary," which is part of his definition of value. A condition of excess supply means that more of a product than is "socially necessary" is produced, and that therefore more labor than is "socially necessary" is performed. Thus only the "socially necessary" labor contributes to value; the rest must be discarded, not figured in with the value. His explanation, another qualification of his theory, is again an *ex post facto* rationalization or fudge factor.)

To sum up this example, then: rutabagas can be sold for 19 cents a pound when a normal amount of the crop is raised; but a crop of three or four times the normal size cannot be sold at that price. (And this is not because rutabagas lack "use-value." Rutabagas, objectively speaking, do serve a function; they do have calories.) The equilibrium of the market is disturbed; the point at which effectual demand just about meets effectual supply, at what Smith calls the "natural price," is displaced. The price falls.

Market conditions, and the entire complex of real-world economic consideration, actually determine price. The amount of "embodied labor" is not determinative; Marx's abstractions and prescriptive formulae are irrelevant to the real world.

Incidentally, the type of occurrence referred to above, where there is a sudden flood of one commodity onto the market, is most typical of communist centrally-controlled economies, not free-market economies. For example, consider this incident, reported in the *Wall Street Journal*:

> As communism falters nearly everywhere else, dedicated advocates of China's planned economy are having trouble defending Beijing's cabbage crisis. . .
>
> For several weeks every November, thousands of oversized trucks rumble into the city center, carrying hundreds of thousands of tons of *baicai*, or long-stemmed Chinese cabbage. The trucks dump the cabbage in deep piles on street corners, where they are tended by workers. . .known to some locals as the "cabbage doctors."
>
> Normally, the vegetable sells out in days. . . But things have gone badly awry this year. At the root of the crisis was last year's disappointing cabbage harvest, which prompted Beijing officials to take action. First, they ordered peasants in Beijing's suburbs to increase the farmland devoted to cabbage by 24%. Then they raised

the price the state pays for cabbage, to encourage farmers to grow more. . .

[T]he trucks kept coming, and the city was soon awash with cabbages. Some makeshift cabbage depots resembled five-foot-high green snowdrifts, with narrow passageways shoveled out to let people pass. . .

So the planners. . . introduced regulations aimed at coercing citizens buy [sic] at least 110 pounds of cabbage apiece, for the good of the nation. . .

A worker says he and his wife had to buy 110 pounds of cabbage apiece. "We'll probably have to move out of our apartment just to store the stuff," he says.[11]

Note that the order to increase the amount of farmland devoted to cabbage, and the ordered rise in its price, both were decreed by central authority. Perhaps such difficulties of command economies, and the myriad unintended side-effects of economic decrees, explain the comment quoted above, "We live in a planned society, which means we don't know what is going to happen tomorrow." [12]

It is true however that some accretions similar to the above example are also found in the "farm policies" and agricultural marketing orders of capitalist or democratic societies.

Another example

Another hypothetical situation, similar to the preceding one but non-agricultural, could be devised. Suppose the Rolls-Royce carmakers suddenly decided to expand production, to an output more on a level with that of Ford or Toyota. Let us also assume quality were to remain as high and all the same hand-crafted production methods were to be adhered to. (We'll leave aside the question of where the added numbers of skilled craftsmen would be found.)

With the same methods and the same expenditure of labor, but with greatly augmented production, then, could the price remain the same?

While theoretically the value of the cars should remain the same, it is difficult to see where all the extra buyers could be found who could afford a Rolls-Royce. At the current, actual level of production, or supply, the "natural price" as Smith called it is approximately met; demand just about equals supply. But if production were capriciously increased, such conditions could not be maintained. Regardless of what an item "should" be worth, there are only so many people who can afford to pay the full "natural" price of such things as Rolls-Royces. That is the nature of demand/supply curves: demand may be sufficient to maintain a certain price at one level of production (supply), but not at another.

Such real-world economic considerations are not found in Marx's theory. His theory is essentially an effort to write about economics without regard to the fact that people are conscious, or to the fact that economics is a realm of human, social behavior. He seeks to set up economics as a quasi-physics, as an impersonal automaton driven by natural law, not human behavior. He rarely stoops to the prosaic, "un-scientific" level of saying, "People do this or that."

His automatistic formula, then, attributes a value to Rollses equal to the embodied labor. Even if as many Rollses were produced as there are now Fords, each should have its prescribed value. But this is an absurdity. This example demonstrates that an abstracted formula, an impersonal law of value, cannot be made sufficiently subtle, complex and variegated to approximate the workings of the real-world human economy. Marx's specious pseudo-physics of economics comes close, but it can never exactly mimic real economic complexities.

(Again, it should be said that later in his text Marx addresses such situations as this example, his arguments turning around "socially necessary" labor, "socially necessary" amounts of production, and so on. Those arguments will be dealt with in due time.)

Non-agricultural examples

We proceed now to Marx's non-agricultural examples. He says, "The same labor extracts from rich mines more metal than from poor mines. Diamonds are of very rare occurrence on the earth's surface, and hence their discovery costs, on an average, a great deal of labor-time. Consequently, much labor is represented in a small compass."

The classical view

To begin with, we must remember that Marx is attempting to show how his labor theory exerts itself in the real world. Scarce minerals, which typically are taken from poor mines, have as a result more labor invested in them than more abundant minerals, which are taken from richer mines. Similarly, diamonds and gold, we are to understand, are valuable because it requires a lot of labor to produce them — both the labor of searching for deposits of them and the labor of mining them and separating the actual valuable substance from large quantities of ore.

Again in these examples we are faced with the problem of how closely

Marx's labor theory approximates classical theory, and how hard it is to separate the supposed effects of labor theory from the workings of supply and demand. In the present examples the supply-and-demand explanation could be expressed this way: the high price of such things as rare minerals, gold, and diamonds, is due to the mere fact that they are rare, rather than to the large amount of labor required to produce them. However, the fact of their rarity does mean that the labor required to produce them will be large; this intertwining of factors is what makes it so hard to distinguish Marx's explanation from the classical one.

Marx's labor theory in this instance is a sort of reverse of the truth, attributing high value solely to the labor. It is not quite accurate to say that the high price of gold and diamonds is due to the high amount of labor embodied in them; rather, it is the high *demand* for such materials, and the high price that can be obtained for them, that makes it worthwhile to exert all that labor. The mere fact of their rarity, as Marx indicates, means that the amount of labor needed to obtain such articles will be large; but it is the rarity relative to demand, not the fact of the exertion of the labor itself, that makes gold and diamonds valuable.

(It is however common even today for commentators, even those writing from a classical-economics perspective, to write as if the amount of labor required, in and of itself, could account for a product's high value.)

One economist, R. Whately, author of *Introductory Lectures on Political Economy*, expressed the situation well. The following passage quotes not him but another author, summarizing his views:

> Whately. . . rejected, however, the idea that labour was essential to create value; and in a passage which has been quoted many times he expressed what he thought to be the real relation between cost and price. "It is not," he said, "that pearls fetch a high price because men have dived for them; but on the contrary, men dive for them because they fetch a high price." [13]

To elaborate on this point: returning to our basic Smithian analysis of price, we can say it is true that a high amount of labor tends to require a high price. The producer – in this case the mining company – must recover labor costs, including exploration costs, mining costs themselves, costs of separating precious material from ore, and so on. Thus the asking price, or the needed price, will be at a level sufficient to cover all this labor cost (as well as any rents and profits).

But the fact of a high requirement of labor, i.e. high labor costs, in and of itself cannot fatalistically predetermine that the price will be at the required level; labor does not automatically give a product a high market value, in other words. (And of course, contrary to Marx's underlying picture, there can be no question of labor's physically embodying or crystallizing itself into value, and thus directly constituting value by a process of metamorphosis.)

The process of establishing value does not work mechanistically and deterministically, in other words. Entrepreneurs can't simply put whatever effort is required into producing gold and diamonds, and know that the exertion of the effort itself will create enough value to recompense them. Rather, some consideration must be made of "what the market price will bear"; there must be consideration of a market that functions according to rules of its own.

A mine may contain gold or silver in some quantity, but not in sufficient concentration to make it worthwhile to mine it. If a mine will yield six dollars' worth of silver per ton, and if it costs forty dollars per ton to mine the ore, the market price of silver isn't automatically going to rise to forty dollars just because that is the "value" of the silver as determined by the invested labor, or by Marx's theory. The market itself (to use a pathetic fallacy) has a voice in things, in other words; it acts, as well as being acted upon – it is "dialectical," rather than being governed by fatalistic, predetermined categories.

To sum up, a high amount of labor necessitates, for the entrepreneur's sake, a high price; but it is not sufficient in itself to guarantee a high price.

It should be noted that when Marx says, "The same labor extracts from rich mines more metal than from poor mines," he probably means to compare mines of an abundant metal to mines of a rare metal. That is, he is not comparing the values of the same metal when produced from a poor or a rich mine – the value of either metal would be the same, being a "homogeneous" or average price (a uniform market price). So we must conclude, he is comparing different metals – comparing the amount of labor needed to mine a metal that is rare, in content of which mines are generally poor, to a metal that is abundant and of which rich mines can be found.

That is, for a rich mine, one containing an abundant mineral, a certain amount of labor produces a large amount of output; the ratio of embodied labor per unit of output is small. For a poor mine, one of a rare substance, the ratio of labor to output is large. This, Marx asserts, explains their respective values.

One indication that the market-oriented view is the correct one is that mining companies have to take some account of market prices in determining what deposits of minerals to mine. They don't mine every known source of a particular substance, in other words. Some deposits of gold ore, for example, don't have enough gold in them to make them commercially profitable to mine. The labor and expense of separating the gold from the ore is greater than the current market price of gold.

Such a situation may exist at one time, and at another time the price of gold may have gone up so high that it becomes profitable to work previously unprofitable mines, or even to refine the "tailings" or waste material from previously-worked ore, for unrecovered gold.

But when prices are low, the simple fact of mining a poor deposit, exerting a lot of labor, cannot automatically create a high value for the gold. And when the price rises, this will generally be because of some other factors in the economy – because market conditions have raised the price. This price rise for the metal can then result in the poorer mines' being brought into production. That is, other conditions help determine price, not just labor costs alone; value is market-determined and not an automatic reflection of embodied labor.

Of course, Marx's theory doesn't state that for an individual mine, the labor determines the value of its output. There must be an averaging, a determination of "homogeneous" value. However, in his view, if a mine poor in gold (and thus high in labor expenditure) were brought into production, there would be an overall rise in the value of gold, because the average amount of labor invested in producing a given amount of gold would be raised. (In reality, the price would be more likely to decline a little, because the supply would be somewhat increased.)

It might be objected that a very poor mine should be excluded from consideration, because, as Marx stipulates, the labor that constitutes value is the labor "under the normal conditions of production" and with the productivity "prevalent at the time." Thus you couldn't bring into production a mine much poorer in gold than the average mine and expect the labor exerted to be reflected in the price of the gold produced.

The short answer to this is that when you begin working a new mine, that mine becomes *part* of what goes into determining "prevalent" or "normal" conditions. There is no good reason to exclude a new mine. That is, with mines there are not just a small number of discrete, widely-separated rates of productivity (as in the case of hand-weavers of cloth and machine-weavers, for example). Rather, there are more likely to be numerous mines possessing ores of various richnesses; there is more of a continuum in the richness of mines. What has to be done is to draw a line somewhere on this continuum beyond which it is not profitable to mine the ore, or beyond which the mine cannot be considered to constitute "normal conditions of production." That is hard to do.

For example, suppose there are a certain number of deposits of gold ore being actively mined. Then suppose someone has a mine, just a little bit poorer than the poorest mine already being worked, and he decides to bring it into production.

Under these circumstances you couldn't categorically disqualify his mine as being too far removed from "normal conditions of production." There are differences of richness among all the mines – there is no more reason for disqualifying this new mine, because it is not quite as rich as the next-poorest mine, than there is for disqualifying the next-poorest mine because it is not as rich as the third-poorest. There is a continuum in the richness of ore and no objective basis for drawing an arbitrary demarcation point.

To put it another way, the figure of what is the "normal" or "prevalent" condition of production changes as you change other conditions; it is a moving target. Trying to exclude some mines because they don't meet the current average richness is illogical; any demarcation point is purely arbitrary.

At any rate, according to Marx's labor theory, the average or "homogeneous" amount of labor required to produce the gold should determine its value. Thus if our hypothetical mine-owner decided to bring his mine into production, his mine would have to be figured in with all the other mines in finding the average. And since his mine would have a lower gold content in the ore than all the other mines already in production, it would require a higher amount of labor to produce a unit of gold than all the other mines. So when this gold is averaged in with the rest, the value or price of the gold would have to rise.

That is: according to Marx's theory, all that is necessary for raising the price of gold is to bring a mine of marginal-quality ore into production.

That is an unlikely prediction. The value of the gold, far from being determined in isolation from the marketplace solely by the total amount of labor exerted in mining it, is set by other, external conditions – market conditions.

Rather than the number and the richness of mines being worked determining, in themselves, the value of gold, it is the market value of gold which determines which mines can be profitably mined. Value is not magically or fatalistically determined *a priori*, at the time of production, by a statistic of production like the exerted labor. It is determined by the whole aggregate of economic considerations, all the factors that enter into the reaching of bargains among buyers and sellers. It is determined by the "dialectical" interplay of supply and demand, a synergism, a mutual interaction between the two ends of the equation.

Thus it is not quite accurate to say that the large amount of labor required to produce gold is what causes the gold to have a high value. Rather, it is the high value of gold – the high demand for it, the high estimation placed on its use-value – that makes it worthwhile to expend the labor.

To return to our hypothetical example, then: if a marginal mine is brought into production, this fact cannot by itself cause the price of gold to rise; buyers are in no way influenced by it to be willing to pay more. Rather, it is more likely that the price of gold will decline a very slight amount, because of the slightly larger supply of gold being brought to market. Marx's artificial set of rules cannot be stretched to cover all the varied situations that can arise in the complex real-world economic arena.

Labor alone no source of value

In short then, the exertion of labor does not in itself give a product value, and the amount of labor exerted does not automatically and by itself determine the magnitude of exchange value.

There are many things we could think of that would require a lot of labor to acquire, but which don't have a high value. Wild pandas are rare, and to acquire wild panda dung would require "on an average, a great deal of labor-time." (Let us suppose that for our purposes dung from zoo pandas is a distinguishable and less satisfactory product.)

Moreover, it cannot be said that panda dung has no use-value – it is useful for fertilizer, if nothing else.

Can it then be said that wild panda dung has a value corresponding to "the mass of congealed labor-time" (human, not panda) embodied in it? No, because first of all, there is not the high demand for panda dung that there is for gold and diamonds. Panda dung is not highly prized, as gold and diamonds are, and thus the price which can be received for it does not justify the exertion of the labor necessary to acquire it. A product such as gold (or panda dung) takes a lot of labor to produce, but the market price must be high enough to make that labor worthwhile. This fact in and of itself shows that labor-content alone doesn't determine exchange value.

To the non-existent price for panda dung we might contrast the price of ginseng. According to at least one newspaper article, ginseng has not been proven to have significant benefits for health:

> At best, it has been shown to be a tonic or a mild pain reliever, like aspirin.
>
> But in Asia, it's widely seen as an aphrodisiac that also boosts the body's immune system, calms nerves, aids digestion and slows the aging process.[15]

Thus while there may be little or no actual use-value to ginseng, there is a market in it. As the article goes on to say,

> In opening week of ginseng buying season last week, [a certain buyer] bought more than 500 pounds. At $185 a pound, that's almost $100,000 changing hands in a week. . .
>
> And the wild stuff carries a far higher price than its cultivated cousin, which Orientals think is coddled and thus less potent.

The moral is: in the case of ginseng, for good reasons or bad, there is a demand for the product. The labor required to produce it, in and of itself, does not create value; that is done by a pre-existing market demand. There is no such pre-existing demand for panda dung, and thus no market for it.

Another example might be this: as reported in *U.S. News and World Report*, March 28, 1994,

> Rhino horn, used in China and Taiwan in traditional medicines, fetches up to $30,000 a pound. Powdered tiger bone, also used in medicine, can sell for $500 a gram.[16]

On the other hand, platypus spurs, as far as we know, have no market value at all, even though they are probably just as rare and would take as much "labor-time" to acquire as rhino horn.

As a prominent textbook puts it,

> [I]f it would cost $50,000 to print the national anthem on the head of a pin, but there is no demand for such a commodity, it simply will not be produced and would not command $50,000 if it were produced.[17]

And while labor alone doesn't ensure the existence of value, sometimes value can be added with absolutely no increase of labor at all. The following incident, pertaining to Stalin's collectivization of agriculture, is recorded:

> The ruthless character of the accelerated collectivization and the disorders that it incited, which threatened as they spread to bring about the fall of the government, led Stalin to sound the retreat. On March 2, 1930, he published an article, "The Vertigo of Success," in which he denounced the excesses of the collectivization campaign. . .
>
> Stalin's step backward. . . allayed the peasants' anger. The issue of Pravda in which this article was printed, and which normally sold for five kopecks, brought as much as ten rubles in the villages.[18]

In other words, in the case of a sudden rise in demand, apart from any added labor costs, the price can rise.

The determining of value or market price is a two-sided, "dialectical" matter. The value which people place on an item, their *valuing* of it, produces demand, which must reach some kind of balance or accommodation with the producer's or supplier's need to recoup the cost of producing the item. Value is not unilaterally created by the exertion of a certain amount of labor.

It might be objected that while panda dung has use-value, it does not have *enough* use-value to support a high price. This however would be to admit that use-value has a quantitative side and is not a monistic entity. That is, there are degrees of use-value; thus we can say that the value of gold is due to the fact that it is rare and is highly prized, i.e., it has high use-value. That is what gives it a high value and makes it worth the labor to produce gold. Panda dung may be rare, but it is not of high use-value; demand for it is low or nil, and the labor required to produce it would not be warranted by its price.

(And there are substitutes for panda dung; there are other sources of fertilizer. This is another issue that must be entered into the equation for figuring value. If one product requires a high expenditure of labor, while another product can be used for the same purpose but requires less labor, can the full "value" of the first product be consistently realized for it? Or will the price have to be lowered somewhat to meet the competition presented by the other product? Or for that matter, perhaps "manure" is a commodity classification and cannot be broken down into subgroups like "panda manure" – we don't know.)

Another example: labor no source of value

To give another example: elephant tusks are rare, and they require (presumably) a lot of labor to acquire. Thus, their price is high. On the other hand, elephant ears are also rare, but they do not command a very high price. They have use-value, insofar as elephant hide can be used for various products; but elephant hide is not as highly prized as elephant ivory.

Again, in this case it appears to be the existence of competing products which makes part of the difference. Elephant hide presumably is not very different from other types of leather, whereas ivory is a more nearly unique substance. Ivory's value as a decorative item comes from this uniqueness which, together with its rarity, gives it high value. By contrast, elephant ears are rare but not unique, and not uniquely prized. In a strictly utilitarian sense elephant ears have use-value, but they do not have enough use-value, they do not have unique use-value, and they are not sufficiently prized and desired to make it worth the expenditure of labor to acquire them. Insofar as they require a high amount of labor to produce, they would serve as a good example of Marx's theory; but they wouldn't repay the labor, and so the labor isn't done (at least not for the sake of the ears). This again shows that labor alone can't create market value.

Actually, in the case of ivory, it is likely that the value comes almost exclusively from its scarcity; the actual labor required may not really be very great. Elephants are rare, but it may not be true that "their discovery costs, on an average, a great deal of labor-time." Most elephants exist on wildlife reserves, and they are not extremely hard to locate; the labor involved may come more from evading law-enforcement officials than from finding the elephants. The total labor may be relatively small, and it may be that the factor of risk is the main consideration on the "production" side, rather than the labor.

Even tradition may play a part in the value of some natural products. A newspaper article on a clothing manufacturer includes this bit of information: "Hickey-Freeman suits still feature buttons made from water-buffalo horns, a century-old custom, even though most customers can't tell them from plastic." [19]

There may be a certain edge of superiority of buttons made from the natural product as opposed to plastic; but this is probably a situation where, if it weren't for the positive decision of one manufacturer, the market in the particular natural product involved would be non-existent or at least much-diminished. The use-value, or the superiority of use-value above that of synthetic products, may be slight or non-existent; but the manufacturer has chosen to use the product on his suits, passing the added cost along to his customers, who pay it. Thus between the two of them, demand is created, primarily by the conscious decision of the manufacturer for aesthetic and traditional reasons. If not for that conscious choice, the amount of labor required to secure the product would probably not be justified, for then there would be no demand at all for an expensive product. That is, to repeat: labor alone doesn't create the value.

For the most part, scarcity alone is sufficient to explain the high price, without considerations of labor costs. There are few elephants, and perhaps few people irresponsible enough to poach them (though there is a legal market to a certain extent), and the supply of ivory is small. Demand is relatively high, and these considerations, rather than "embodied labor," make the exchange value of elephant tusks high. Even if the labor costs were low, in other words, the price would still be high; the profit factor would just be larger.

In sum, the cost of ivory is high, while the value of elephant hide or ears is relatively small, rather than their both being quite valuable, as Marx's theory would predict. (We cannot however ignore the fact that there is more hide on an elephant, measured by weight, than there is ivory; the gross value of the entire hide may come close to that of the ivory.)

More about the classical view

As always, while we reject Marx's mechanistic picture of the way in which labor constitutes value, we cannot discount labor itself as a factor in determining price. Indeed, Smith makes remarks quite similar to Marx's about the relation of value to the labor required to produce gold and silver (*Wealth of*

Nations, Book I, Chapter V):

> The discovery of the abundant mines of America reduced, in the sixteenth century, the value of gold and silver in Europe to about a third of what it had been before. As it cost less labour to bring those metals from the mine to the market, so when they were brought thither they could purchase or command less labour. . .

Smith himself is not always consistent in his labor theory. But it is doubtful that he envisions by the above a "pure labor" viewpoint like Marx's. It is said not from a viewpoint of labor as the sole factor in determining price, or of labor as automatically and directly transmuting itself into value, but rather from within a context of Smith's view that the labor which a thing tends to command or be exchanged for on the market (the truest measure of its value) tends to correspond to the original "cost" of producing it in the sense of the labor exerted to do so. "Labour was the first price, the original purchase-money that was paid for all things," he tells us. And as labor was the first cost of everything, this cost tends to be reflected in exchange value, so that things produced by equal amounts of labor tend to be of equal exchange value on the market.

Labor is the predominant factor in mining ventures, but profits and rents also are pertinent. Smith points to these factors in other remarks about the market prices of metals (*Wealth of Nations*, Book I, Chapter XI, Part III):

> A commodity may be said to be dear or cheap, not only according to the absolute greatness or smallness of its usual price, but according as that price is more or less above the lowest for which it is possible to bring it to market for any considerable time together. This lowest price is that which barely replaces, with a moderate profit, the stock which must be employed in bringing the commodity thither. It is the price which affords nothing to the landlord, of which rent makes not any component part, but which resolves itself altogether into wages and profits.

Here too we see that Smith does not consider labor and other factors as automatically creating a fixed value; rather, market value is determined by market considerations, and the entrepreneur cannot be fatalistically certain that whatever labor costs he incurs in producing a commodity will be recompensed in the market price.

We can see too that for Smith the role of the labor required to produce gold and silver is that of a cost of production, which must be recouped in the market price. Labor is not a substance which metamorphoses directly into value. Thus Smith says,

That the silver mines of Spanish America, like all other mines, become gradually more expensive in the working, on account of the greater depths at which it is necessary to carry on the works, and of the greater expense of drawing out the water and of supplying them with fresh air at those depths, is acknowledged by every body who has enquired into the state of those mines.

The mechanism whereby labor contributes to value is via *cost*, not by metamorphosis of labor into value; higher amounts of labor mean higher production costs, and where there are higher production costs, the entrepreneur must receive a higher market price if his venture is to continue to function. (However, the market is not obligated to allow it to function; value is not fatalistically determined by labor.)

Thus if the discovery of gold and silver in the Americas lowered the cost of those metals, because the labor required to produce them decreased, this decrease in labor lowered the production cost (and supply was higher). "As it cost less labour to bring those metals from the mine to the market," the producers were under less severe constraints in regard to what price they could profitably accept. And while they might have liked to keep the price the same, someone was sure to undercut the others; as always, under these circumstances the price had to fall to more nearly the new natural price. Competition and market considerations of supply and demand assured that.

Thus when Smith says, "The occasional fluctuations in the market price of gold and silver bullion arise from the same causes as the like fluctuations in that of all other commodities," we come again ultimately to supply and demand. Market forces determine the value of gold and silver.

Overall, we can say that when there are more abundant mines, the amount of labor required is smaller, as Marx's theory says. The producer can afford to sell gold cheaper, because his costs are lower. But Smith's is ultimately a supply-and-demand theory, rather than a labor theory. The increased amount of gold, rather than the smaller labor required to mine it, is what ultimately determines the lower cost (as we see in the following remarks):

When more abundant mines are discovered, a greater quantity of the precious metals is brought to market, and the quantity of the necessaries and conveniences of life for which they must be exchanged being the same as before, equal quantities of the metals must be exchanged for smaller quantities of commodities. So far, therefore, as the increase of the quantity of the precious metals in any country arises from the increased abundance of the mines, it is necessarily connected with some diminution of their value.

Notice: the "increased abundance" is what lowers the value. In the same vein, with regard to the discovery of the American mines, Smith says, "[T]he increase of the supply had, it seems, so far exceeded that of the demand, that the value of that metal sunk considerably."

Smith, in short, sometimes writes as if in agreement with Marx, as if believing the high price of precious metals, gems, etc., is due to the large amount of labor it takes to find and mine such materials. Overall, however, as noted before, Smith has a different perspective from Marx; his "labor theory" does not proceed from the same assumptions as Marx's. It is safe to say that, if for Smith high amounts of labor cause high prices, it is because labor *costs* are one large factor of exchange value: the more it costs the producer to bring an item to market, the more he must charge for it. In this there is a rational, economic reason why labor costs effect price; there is not the mystical assumption of Marx's, that labor transmutes directly into value. And labor for Smith is not the whole story, the be-all and end-all behind exchange value. His view seems clearly the more realistic and evidence-based of the two.

For Smith, or for classical theory, the final answer or broadest picture is given by the workings of market forces, or supply and demand. As Smith says (concerning precious metals), "Their highest price, however, seems not to be necessarily determined by any thing but the actual scarcity or plenty of those metals themselves."

Marx would have us believe that the high price of precious metals is the result of the large amount of labor required to mine them. That is superstitious: the exertion of labor in and of itself cannot command a certain market price, or create economic value. It is reductionist – labor is not the only factor of value. It is a sort of confusion of cause and effect – it would be more accurate to say that the high value of the metals is what makes it worthwhile to exert the labor.

The high value of gold, diamonds, etc. is a result of their utility, their usefulness, the degree to which they are desired and prized: high demand in relation to the small supply. The high amount of labor makes it necessary to get a high price for them, but is not in itself sufficient to assure that result; other economic factors must also be at work to do this.

Jacob and gold

As for the comment, "Jacob doubts whether gold has ever been paid for at its full value": value by what standards? One standard of value is market price, or market value. By this standard, whatever is paid for gold and diamonds, that *is* their value; there is no other value but market value, at least in practical terms. You can get no more for a thing than the selling price, by definition.

However, there is a somewhat more fundamental standard, "natural price." In some sense this tells what the price of a thing "should" be; it should recompense the labor, rents and profits at a "normal" or usual rate. But it is not to be maintained that Marx means to appeal to this standard in saying that gold and diamonds were not paid for at their full value. Marx means to appeal to some other standard in saying so – either his self-defined "embodied labor," or some standard of Jacobs'. But his standard is specious. The gold, the diamonds, were paid for at a certain market price; that *is* the value of the gold or diamonds. Value, in economic terms, is market price – what a thing sells for – or else natural price, a slightly different concept, but in any event surely not the one Marx is using.

The word "value," as market value, *means* what a thing will bring on the market. Marx is giving examples to show how it is his labor theory which governs value; but then he says, gold and diamonds don't bring their full "value," meaning value in terms of his labor theory, value equal to their embodied labor. In saying that they don't bring a price commensurate with their embodied labor, he is showing that market price isn't governed by embodied labor. That is a disproof or counter-example to his labor theory, not an example of it.

Richer mines

"With richer mines. . . their value would fall." This is so because the supply would be larger, not simply because the embodied labor would be less. As stated above, the lower requirement of labor, meaning the lower production cost, would allow mine operators to lower prices; but only competition and market forces would force them to do so. The decline in the amount of labor required for producing the diamonds would mean lower production costs, and so the mine-owners could afford to sell at the lower attainable price and still make a profit. They might want to keep prices high, but the presence of competition would in most cases prevent it. Demand would not be sufficient at the old price to "clear the market" of all the diamonds. But this is a classical-economics explanation, attempting to find a line of cause and effect. Marx's version by contrast is simple-minded and reductionist; it is based on philosophical abstractions and argumentation, not economics.

Carbon into diamonds

"If we could succeed at a small expenditure of labor, in converting carbon into diamonds, their value might fall below that of bricks." Marx's prediction is correct – the price would fall, for synthetic diamonds at least. In terms of Marx's theory, this is because the expended labor is lower, and expended labor is by transmutation value.

The real reason can be seen in terms of two factors: the supply would rise, while the costs of production would fall. This latter factor is indeed a result of the smaller amount of labor required, as well as the smaller investment in such capital expenses as mineral rights to the land, mining equipment, shipping costs, and so on – all this, assuming diamonds were produced in a laboratory instead of being dug from mines.

Thus it appears once again that Marx is right – lower labor causes lower value. But how and why? These differ, as before. The "natural price," the price a capitalist "normally" wants and must have in order to produce profitably, is composed of labor, rents and profit; that is to say, the capitalist normally prices goods at a sum representing his costs of production, plus a profit. If production costs go down, the required price goes down. To put it another way, there can now be a supply offered at a lower price than was possible before; the supply curve has been redrawn, and competition is likely to assure that the price drops to reflect the new reality. The decline in production costs would tend to produce price competition – producers could *afford* to cut their prices, because production costs would be less; and they would tend to do so rather than to lose business to their competitors. To that extent the amount of "embodied labor" does control price, but not in the simple-minded manner Marx envisions.

Thus the lower labor costs result in a lower value (price), not because labor is "embodied" in the form of value or congealed labor, but because of the interaction of market forces.

(There is some reason to think, too, that real diamonds would always retain their original value, or at least a price premium over manufactured diamonds; this, despite the fact that the two would be functionally, or compositionally, identical. There is a certain cachet about that which is genuine – a certain consumer preference for it, an attribution of added worth due to its genuine origins. Consider the case of cultured pearls – they are in every sense real pearls; yet chance or accidental "wild" pearls still command the highest prices. The economic world is a complicated realm; too complicated for Marx's simple-minded formulas.)

Marx's labor theory is not a theory of market value; it is a system of abstract categories to which he adheres in spite of market value, a theory that exists in the realm of philosophical speculation. Thus when he says that gold and diamonds are not paid for at their full value, he means their full value as defined by his fantasy theory. The real world obviously pays their market value, based on standards of its own; and that is literally their full value. Marx's attitude is that his theory is definitive, and if market value doesn't align with it, its workings must be defective in some way: "My theory is correct; it is the facts that are mistaken."

Summation

Having cited his examples, Marx sums up his labor theory this way:

> In general, the greater the productiveness of labor, the less is the labor-time required for the production of an article, the less is the amount of labor crystallised in that article, and the less is its value; and *vise versa*, the less the productiveness of labor, the greater is the labor-time required for the production of an article, and the greater is its value.

In general, that is true; the more labor required to produce an article, the greater are the costs of production. And the higher the costs of production, the greater must be the final selling price.

Marx's examples, being non-quantitative, cannot show any exact mathematical relationship or equation; they can only show that, the higher the labor, the higher the price. This is an acknowledged fact, accepted also by classical economic theory. (That is, it is accepted that the higher the labor *costs*, the higher must be the selling price. It is not the raw hours of labor that make the connection, but the cost to the producer of those hours. Thus we have the phenomenon of differences in wage rates among various countries, and the transfer of jobs and manufacturing capacity to places of lower labor costs.)

What Marx really is trying to show, however, is not that market prices vary in proportion to the embodied labor, but that labor is the only determining factor. He wants to rule out rents and profits, the entrepreneurial elements if you will, and admit the validity of labor alone. By mere assumption he rejects the right of the capitalist to be compensated in the form of profit, accepting only the laborer's right to be paid his wages. This is arbitrary favoritism, not the reasoned arguments of a scientist.

Marx has set out to prove, define into existence, or merely assume his preconceived thesis. His examples attempt to superimpose his theoretical framework over events and to show his theory to be at work in producing real-world results.

Marx blandly presents the examples as if they verify his theory. Actually, where the facts as he cites them are accurate, the explanation for those facts is supplied not by his theory but by normal economics. His text in this instance is mostly an effort at indoctrinating the reader into viewing events through his conceptual framework, and of supposing his theory to be the explanation for various surface facts. In this as in most instances with Marx's theory, the facts are otherwise.

Marx proceeds to a muddled conclusion: "The value of a commodity, therefore, varies directly as the quantity, and inversely as the productiveness, of the labor incorporated in it."

It doesn't vary directly as the quantity *and* inversely as the productiveness; it varies directly as the quantity, *or* inversely as the productiveness, of the labor. Productivity itself is the reciprocal of the amount of labor embodied in each item, so that value can be expressed as directly proportional to the one, or inversely proportional to the other, but not both at once. Perhaps that was just a momentary lapse in terminology on Marx's part, however.

A final example

> *"I have a theory about television."*
> *"What's that?"*
> *"I don't believe it is possible!"*
>   – "The Return of Edwin Carp," an episode of "The Dick Van
>   Dyke Show"

Marx has one more example, or an elaboration on his labor theory, to present. He says:

> A thing can be a use-value, without having value. This is the case whenever its utility to man is not due to labor. Such are air, virgin soil, natural meadows, &c.

This comes as a revelation and a shock. It offends either one's knowledge of real estate or one's knowledge of scientific methodology. The statement is not an example of the workings of Marx's theory in the real world; rather, it asserts the validity of his theory in the face of the real world, in direct contradiction of all the facts which are self-evident in the workings of market economics every day. Let us examine some of those facts.

We are informed by Marx that a natural meadow, or in modern parlance, unimproved land, has no value. Yet someone who owns such land can sell it; there is a market for such land, and there are economic dealings in such land every day. The buying and selling of land, both improved and unimproved, proceeds as a matter of course, without paying any heed to Marx's stricture or decree that such dealings are illegitimate, contradictory, or impossible. There is no mechanism preventing the buying and selling of unimproved land – lightning bolts don't strike people attempting to make such transactions, and no bureaucratic committee looks up the subject in a book (Marx's book) and says, "Sorry – Marx says such deals are inconceivable." That is, such land does have market value.

There is a market for unimproved land, and people desiring to buy or sell such land usually have a fairly good idea of what the price should be. There are, in other words, certain more-or-less determinable factors that determine a given piece of land's market worth – location, general conditions in the market for farmland, surrounding conditions of development, and (to quote the well-known saying), again location.

In sum, the market in land, whether improved or unimproved, proceeds under rules of its own; these are the "capitalist" rules, the general workings of market economies. And they are not Marx's rules.

The facts in the case are so obvious that it seems superfluous to try to disprove Marx's statements; universal experience shows he is wrong. One (unknown) author puts it this way:

> Still more obviously false from the standpoint of economic reality was the assertion [by Marx] that objects in which no work-hours have been invested have therefore no value. An oil-field, a vein of coal, a forest, on which no human hand has as yet expended one hour of labor, may nevertheless be extremely valuable. . . [Marx's] result was in direct contradiction to the most palpable facts of everyday experience.

Marx does address such objections. Another such author describes his method of doing so, in these words:

> Have objects, in which no work-hours are embodied, really no value or price? Do not virgin forests, mines, oil-fields frequently have considerable value, and fetch a very handsome price? Here is a new decree [added by Marx]: "The price in that case is imaginary."

Marx's response, in other words, is an example of "Schumpeter's Observation of Scientific and Non-scientific Theories," which states, "Any theory can be made to fit any facts by means of appropriate additional assumptions."[20] That is, if enough sophistries and newly-invented provisos are allowed, any theory can be preserved. The result, however, is not science.

Marx's theoretical system implies as a logically-derived consequence the assertion that natural meadows have no value; no labor has been performed on them, and by the terms of his theory they have no value. This is what he asserts in his text as reality. He will continue this method throughout his text, in opposition to the facts of the real-world market.

Marx's theory is not a description of the reality of capitalist economies; he is giving us logical deductions, telling us where his axioms and theorems lead us. He is saying, "By logical deduction from my theory, it follows that unimproved land has no value." It is a statement of theory, not of fact. His system is deductive rather than inductive, and prescriptive rather than descriptive; it is not science.

As always, Marx insists on the validity of his deduced system, in preference over the merely "phenomenal" real world. In the present instance Marx sounds like a fictional character who said, "I have a theory about television. . . I don't believe it is possible!" Likewise, Marx has a theory about the market in natural meadows — it is impossible. Yet whatever occurs must *ipso facto* be possible; no amount of willful logic or intransigent dogma can override that fact. The scientist's duty is to adhere to the facts, to illuminate everyday occurrences by seeking the deeper meaning within the facts — not to overrule the facts.

More specifically, the problem with Marx's analysis is that he is working with a fictitious, contrived definition of the word "value." Rather than market value in the normal sense of the term, meaning the price receivable for an item, Marx is dealing with "value" as "the amount of embodied, crystallized, homogeneous labor socially necessary"; natural meadows have none of that. It is this mythological entity, or non-entity, that Marx is exploring for us.

And the problem is in what kind of statements Marx is making — the source of their authority. Throughout the rest of his text, Marx will make statements like the one above, which seem to apply to the workings of one or another element in capitalist economies. But they are not really descriptions of objective reality; they are deductions within Marx's closed formal system, telling what his preceding theorems predict or imply about future cases. His statements refer to his theoretical system and what can be deduced within it, not to objective capitalist economics as such. This should always be kept in mind.

If value is defined as "embodied labor," it may indeed be reasonable to conclude that natural meadows have no value. Likewise, Humpty-Dumpty's exclamation, "There's glory for you!" may make sense, if "glory" is defined as "a nice, knock-down argument."

In fact, natural meadows do have value; they are bought and sold every day. That is a good indication that Marx's definition of value is somehow ill-conceived and inadequate to the task of shedding light on the actual world of capitalistic, i.e., normal, economics.

Probably the original purpose of Marx's definition of value was purely and simply to define the capitalist's contribution to value out of existence, proving him to have no legitimate claim to profits or rents because he does not contribute labor, that is, value, to the economy. Thus Marx's capricious fiddling with words was intended from the outset to adjudge the capitalist an "exploiter" by pre-determined force of logic.

Related to this issue, it bears stating that natural meadows not only have value, they have value *by rights*. That is, it is not an aberration or an immoral or socially condemnable fact that they have value. Rather, it is entirely normal and proper that they do so. There has been a considerable amount of criticism, from various progressive or right-thinking social arbiters, to the effect that no one should have a right to own land, that "property is theft," and so on.

Apart from the merely fashionable condemnation of capitalists and "the rich," there is another stream to this criticism which might for short be called the primitivist view. Modern industrial society has for instance been frequently compared unfavorably to the manner of life of American Indians. Indeed, the use of land which results from its private ownership, with the opportunity for profit from its development or "exploitation," is far more conducive to the abuse and ruining of the natural environment than the use of land as practiced by tribal or hunter-gatherer types of societies.

Certain objections could be made to such idyllic pictures. Non-ownership of land is characteristic of hunter-gatherer societies; that is to say, it pertains to "primitive," in the sense of non-economic or pre-economic, subsistence societies. On the other hand, capitalistic societies, or societies on a level of a higher order of complexity, are probably impossible without ownership of land. Moreover, a return to a hunter-gatherer society is probably impossible, or would be disastrous for the size of populations there are in the world today. Such societies can probably serve as no model for us today, however much we might like certain features of them.

Final comments

In sum, the value which is attached to natural meadows is not impossible and not aberrational. With regard to Marx's examples, he manages to make his theory mimic the workings of supply and demand fairly closely, but in the end the two are distinguishable. He is fairly successful at fitting real-world events into the conceptual framework of his own theory, and making that theory seem to be the active agent behind those events. But his theory is distinguishable from reality, and the fallacies within his examples can be discerned.

Marx is not describing the real world, not telling what happens on the market with regard to value – with regard to the value of "natural meadows," for instance. Rather, he is expanding on the logical consequences of his theory – he is giving us deductions from his axioms. Marx is not really telling his readers how value is determined, in a cause-and-effect sense; he is telling how it is *derived*, i.e., deduced by abstract logic from chosen axioms.

Thus his method is not descriptive science; it is deductive, being based on logical deductions from chosen premises. And it is prescriptive, in that Marx declares his logical inferences, by fiat, to be reality and to overrule mere events in the "phenomenal" world.

Hence it is important to realize that when Marx avers that natural meadows have no value, he does not mean they have no value in the real world of capitalist economies (which he professed to describe). Rather, he means they have no value in the world of his axioms and theorems, as a matter of logical deduction in his theoretical world. This theoretical world, however, he does represent to be reality, or more real than mere "phenomenal" reality.

The phenomena and laws and assumptions which make up Marx's labor theory constitute a separate, fantasy world completely divergent from the real one. But where his theory meets actual reality, in real-world events concerning market value, Marx is finally unable to make the two merge seamlessly into one coherent whole.

NOTES – Chapter 4

1 Schwarzschild, Leopold, *The Red Prussian; the Life and Legend of Karl Marx,* London, H. Hamilton 1948.

2 Hindus, Maurice Gerschon, *Red Bread: Collectivization in a Russian Village,* 1st Midland Book ed., Bloomington, Indiana University Press, 1988, p.115.

3 Dolot, Miron, *Execution by Hunger: the Hidden Holocaust,* New York, W. W. Norton, 1985, p. 138.

4 Hindus, Maurice Gerschon, op cit., p.72.

5 Conquest, Robert, *The Harvest of Sorrow: Soviet Collectivization and the Terror-Famine,* London, Hutchinson, 1986, p. 237-8.

6 Gaucher, Roland., *Opposition in the U.S.S.R.,* New York, Funk & Wagnalls, 1969, p.214.

7 ibid., p.28-9.

8 Kravchenko, Victor, *I Chose Freedom: The Personal and Political Life of a Soviet official,* New Brunswick, N.J., Transaction, 1989, p.381.

9 ibid., p.381.

10 *Russia Speaks*, p.268.

11 "Wanted: An Enterprising Person With a Whole Lot of Corned Beef," *Wall Street Journal,* Nov. 15, 1989.

12 "The New Soviet Man," *National Review,* August 20, 1990, p.31.

13 Whately, R., *Introductory Lectures on Political Economy*, 1832, p.253.

14 Garagiola, Joe, *It's Anybody's Ballgame,* Boston, G.K. Hall, 1988, p.66.

15 "Ginseng is a backwoods big business," Indianapolis *Star,* Sept. 24, 1990.

16 *"An Issue For The White House: Tigers And Rhinos,"* U.S. *News and World Report*, March 28, 1994.

17 Samuelson, Paul Anthony, *Economics,* 2d ed., New York, McGraw-Hill, 1951.

18 Gaucher, Roland, op. cit., p.180.

19 "On the Rack: Hartmarx Squirms As U.S. Men Eye Foreign Suits,"
Wall Street Journal, Aug. 27, 1990.

20 Dickson, Paul, *The Official Rules,* New York, Delacorte Press, 1978.

5. LABOR-POWER

We have considered at some length Marx's "labor theory of value"; now we turn to what is in effect his theory of the value of labor (though that is not the terminology he uses).

The value of labor is a subject which, like the value of goods, must be considered in any broad-scale economic discussion; and like that topic, it has two sides.

There is first the question of what a given amount of labor ought to be worth, or we might call it the "fair" or "proper" value of labor. This side of the value of labor might be termed the moral issue, or perhaps the issue of justice as regards wages. We all have an idea or a general sense of how much the laborer should receive for his efforts, what it takes to live on, and such matters. We may have an inchoate rather than an articulated sense of what makes a fair wage, and different people may have different standards, whether they are based on a "fair, living wage" or whatever. It is doubtful whether it is within the capacity of economics as such to address this issue. The methods of economics, and of science in general, are inadequate for dealing with such matters. That is not to say the issue is inconsequential; but the arguments and reasonings for addressing the issue are shall we say more humanistic – derived from a human sense of justice, fairness, and moral behavior towards one's fellow men. In other words, they are not objective and measurable, and they don't derive from purely descriptive treatments of human economic behavior in the aggregate which may serve as one definition of economics.

This again relates to the nature of economics, and indeed all social "sciences" – they cannot be divorced from transcendent human and moral considerations. They are not descriptions of the mere mechanical workings of the inanimate universe; and unlike the natural sciences they cannot be reduced to purely mechanistic rules. Treatments of human phenomena that attempt to do so are only parodies of science.

The other side of the value of labor, the more strictly economic aspect, is the question of what factors, objectively speaking, determine the value of labor – meaning the magnitude of the wage which is received. This is more objectively determinable, and it admits of a more definitive and quantifiable treatment.

(There is a third side in addition to these two, namely, the question of what is the best standard for *measuring* wages, or measuring the value of what is received for labor. A dollar figure, for instance, doesn't tell the whole story; the value of a dollar is not fixed over a period of time. Moreover, not everyone is paid in dollars; different countries use different denominations of money, and the conversion of wage amounts from one type of currency to another is not without complications. Then too, various complicating issues enter the question. For instance, in some societies wages are not the most important element in determining how well off workers are; it is not so much a low wage as the absence of anything worth buying that presents a problem. This is an anomaly mainly of communist countries.)

First, we may look at what classical theory says about the above issues. In his discussion of what determines the value of labor, Adam Smith gives an answer from both viewpoints. His "natural price" can be extended from commodities to labor. "Natural price," meaning the value goods tend to have in the absence of any deformation of market conditions, probably comes closest to being a definitive statement of what is the proper or just price for goods: when a price received is sufficient to pay production costs plus a "normal" increment of profit, it is the market-clearing price and it is the "natural price." At this price the labor, rents, and profit encompassed by a commodity are paid at a normal or usual rate of return. Our ideas of what is the "normal" profit may vary, but it is possible to get some sense of what this rate is and should be, from observation of general conditions of the market. This concept of "natural price," as applied to labor, probably corresponds as closely as possible to the intuitive concept of a just or fair wage.

Then, as to the other aspect of value, Smith discusses the factors which determine the exchange value of goods in a cause-and-effect sense; and he analyzes the factors that determine this value, a value which may be higher or lower than natural price, depending on supply and demand.

This approach of Smith's probably comes as close as any to giving answers in concrete, objective terms to these elusive questions. At any rate, it must be admitted that the subject of the value of labor is as essential to an economic discussion as the value of commodities; one is the natural inverse of the other, the flip side as it were. The proper and actual remuneration due to the entrepreneur, the wages paid to the laborer, the cost of goods to the consumer —these are all essential factors which must be addressed when discussing and evaluating any economy.

Marx's problem

We have said that the value of labor is an essential topic in any economic treatise. Marx however would have faced barriers in discussing it. For him labor is the standard of value for all things; in fact, by the terms of his theory, value is by definition labor. Thus it would have made no sense, in the context of his treatise, to speak of the value of labor; labor is *itself* value, and the issue of value can be taken no further, reduced to no more elementary terms, than the quantity of labor embodied in a thing. To speak of the value of labor, within Marx's system, would be as fruitless as to speak of the value of value.

To put it another way, if we base our reasoning on what we have seen of Marx's theory so far, we might deduce the following: for Marx the value of anything, by definition and identically, is the amount of labor embodied in it. So if we ask the value of a day's labor, the answer immediately comes, Value is the amount of labor contained in the day: that is, it equals the duration of the working day. The value of a twelve-hour working day is twelve hours of labor.

This labor is not "contained" in the day in the same sense as labor is contained in a product; it is not "crystallized" or embodied in a day, presumably, because a day is not a physical thing like a commodity. But it is contained in a day in *some* sense; if we had to ask how much labor there is "in" a working day, or how much labor a day "contains," the above answer would no doubt be the most sensible one.

This may be seen to be appropriate from the capitalist's viewpoint as well as from the laborer's. The situation is this: the laborer invests twelve hours of labor in producing a commodity; that is, from the laborer's viewpoint, what he gives the capitalist is twelve hours of labor. That is to him the true measure of his effort or sacrifice.

By the same token, these twelve hours of labor end up deposited within the commodity, which the capitalist possesses and can sell; that is, the laborer has created a "value added" of twelve hours for the capitalist. So from the capitalists' standpoint, the "value added" by the laborer, or the market value of what the laborer has done, is those identical twelve hours of labor, which now endow the commodity with twelve hours of value. (This somewhat hair-splitting exercise is an attempt to distinguish between the two roles of that labor, or its role at different points in its existence – its two "forms," those being its initial form as active labor, and its "embodied" form as value.)

On one side of the ledger then, the laborer sacrifices twelve hours of labor; similarly, the capitalist receives a benefit of twelve hours of embodied labor. For there to be an equal exchange, we would say that the laborer should receive in return wages equal in value to his own gift or contribution to the capitalist; that is, the appropriate wage would be twelve hours of labor. The value of the raw labor would appear to be equal to the value deposited by the labor within the commodity; this "value" is identical with the labor itself. Thus the value received by the capitalist should equal the value paid to the laborer.

(A side issue: Marx equates the value of a commodity with its cost of production, but restricts that cost to the embodied labor alone, denying that the capitalist in his role as producer adds any value to the commodity. By this means he effectively proves that the capitalist is entitled to no return for his role in production. That is, he proves the capitalist cannot make a profit – at least profit as that entity is classically conceived of, as opposed to the Marxian concept, "surplus value". The capitalist must pay the laborer the proper wage for twelve hours of labor, and he must sell the finished product for no more than the money equivalent of the embodied twelve hours of labor. In his words, the capitalist "must buy his commodities at their value, must sell them at their value, and yet at the end of the process must withdraw more money from circulation that he threw into it at starting." And that is an impossible task. For Marx, the entire value of the commodity is the sum total of the labor hours of all workers involved which is embodied in it, and no more. Since profit is impossible, the capitalist is forced to "exploit" unpaid labor in order to make money – but more about this later.

One cautionary note: as we will see when we look at Marx's complete argument later on, he doesn't say the laborer receives the direct money equivalent of twelve hours of labor for a twelve-hour day, as we might simple-mindedly imagine; he only states that the laborer receives the full value for his day's efforts.)

Alternative answers

At any rate, for Marx the value of anything is its embodied labor; and the labor embodied in a working day of a certain number of hours' duration (we deduce) would have to be that same number of hours of labor.

If we did not restrain ourselves to reasoning from Marx's premises, it might be possible to devise a way around this impasse, by inventing a different standard for the value of labor. We might propose, for instance, that while on the one hand the value of a commodity is the amount of labor embodied in it, on the other hand the value of a day's labor is measured by the quantity of commodities produced by it. There is a certain appealing symmetry in this solution, which could conceivably make it a reasonable standard. After all, the worth of a laborer's efforts *to the capitalist* might best be measured by the amount of goods (measured in some universal standard units) the labor produces for him. That is, after all, the value-containing product which the capitalist secures. Conversely, the value of a particular commodity on the market has been equated to the amount of labor invested in that one item.

As noted above, there is intuitive force in the symmetry of this hypothetical solution. Analogies to it can be found in physics. For instance, we might look at the relationship among mass, force, and acceleration. The pertinent equation is $F=mg$, where g is the acceleration due to earth's gravity, the force F is an object's weight. (Weight is thus sort of the everyday guise of an object's mass.)

So if we begin with an object's weight, we can determine its mass; or conversely, if we begin with the mass, we can determine how much (at a given altitude above sea level) it would weigh. Given one quantity, we can find the other; it is just a matter of which side of the equation we start with, or, which quantity we know. We calculate a force by starting with a mass; or we calculate mass starting with the force; we don't try to find either mass of force in terms of itself.

This method might be compared to our hypothetical solution of measuring the value of commodities in terms of labor, and the value of labor in terms of commodities. There is precedent and credibility in this type of symmetrical interrelationship of two quantities. That is not to say definitely that this is the correct analysis at this point, but only to assert that it is a scientifically respectable one.

Marx's problem

This might be reasonable, and Smith for one makes at least some intimations toward this approach in his work. Marx however does not leave us this option. His analysis is much too rigid and concretized in its definition of value to allow for alternative senses or connotations of the word "value." His approach is Procrustean: value is, identically and always, labor. Value cannot be defined as labor for one entity (commodities) and goods for another (labor). His rigid, scientistic system decrees that value must be only labor.

To repeat: Marx's treatise rules out this possibility as a solution for him. Marx's method deals with one elementary or irreducible unit, which cannot be analyzed in terms of anything but itself, and which is not related to any other quantity. Value is labor, and only labor; thus one cannot ask the value of labor; it is like attempting to ask, What is the mass of one gram? The mass of a gram is a gram. The duration of one second is a second; and so on.

Thus, if Marx were to consider the question of the value of labor– and again, it would seem essential to his work that he consider the topic – he would be faced with great difficulties. He could only reason in a circle, and the result would be, The value of a twelve-hour working day is twelve hours of labor.

This is not to say that Marx discusses the value of a laborer's efforts in terms of "the value of labor"; we are just extrapolating from his theory as presented so far, using his premises to derive our own results. The foregoing is not an analysis of what he actually says, but an explanation of what he does not say, why it was impossible for him even to discuss "the value of labor," and perhaps why he analyzed the value of the laborer's contributions to production in the terms he did. It may be said in passing, however, that an economic theory in which it is impossible to discuss the value of labor, *in those terms*, must be seriously flawed.

Terms of the discussion

Labor-power appears in Marx's text at a point where he has just outlined a basic dilemma in the functioning of capitalism. It is not the dilemma of the impossibility of determining a value for labor; he does not acknowledge the existence of that dilemma. Rather, it is the dilemma of determining how the capitalist makes his money. (This dilemma, however, like the other one, arises because of Marx's reductionist equating of value to labor.)

We have seen Marx's exposition of the dilemma, which he refers to under the rubric of "contradictions in the formula of capital." With value equated to labor, the role of the capitalist in production is shown to be valueless, since he supposedly performs no labor; and the capitalist's compensation in the form of profit (as classically conceived) is proven out of existence. "If equivalents are exchanged, no surplus-value results, and if non-equivalents are exchanged, still no surplus-value," he states. Thus, "merchants' capital is an impossibility," and the same goes for producers' capital, rentiers' capital and money-lenders' capital. (Marx uses the term "surplus value" in preference to "profit," because profit, as an excess of selling price over production costs, is an impossibility.)

At any rate, by dogmatically equating value to labor, Marx has proven that the capitalist cannot make a profit, since he does no labor and thus creates no value and hence is owed none. As a result, then, the capitalist faces the dilemma that he "must buy his commodities at their value, must sell them at their value, and yet at the end of the process must withdraw more value from circulation than he threw into it at starting." To do this is impossible; that is, profit as classically conceived is impossible. "Surplus value," which has an entirely different meaning from profit, is the real basis for the capitalist's making of money.

Marx addresses the dilemma and introduces labor-power in the following words (Part II, Chapter VI):

> The change of value that occurs in the case of money intended to be converted into capital, cannot take place in the money itself, since in its function of means of purchase and of payment, it does no more than realise the price of the commodity it buys or pays for; and, as hard cash, it is value petrified, never varying. Just as little can it

originate in the second act of circulation, the re-sale of the commodity, which does no more than transform the article from its bodily form back again into its money-form. The change must, therefore, take place in the commodity bought by the first act, M-C, but not in its value, for equivalents are exchanged, and the commodity is paid for at its full value. We are, therefore, forced to the conclusion that the change originates in the use-value, as such, of the commodity, *i.e.*, in its consumption. In order to be able to extract value from the consumption of a commodity, our friend, Money-bags, must be so lucky as to find, within the sphere of circulation, in the market, a commodity, whose use-value possesses the peculiar property of being a source of value, whose actual consumption, therefore, is itself an embodiment of labor, and, consequently, a creation of value. The possessor of money does find on the market such a special commodity in capacity for labor or labor-power.

Here Marx establishes an artificial, factitious framework in terms of which to discuss the issue. First of all, we see the phrase "change of value"; that is what Marx conceives of as being the capitalist's source of income, the root of his ability to convert money into capital – Marx's substitute for profit.

At any rate, Marx casually identifies the search for the source of the capitalist's monetary gain with the search for a "change of value" in the commodity. Marx should not be permitted to insinuate this assumption into his theory without challenge; it is a theoretical stance adopted on the basis of no evidence, and at variance with commonplace, traditional economic understanding. Profit as classically conceived of is not considered to be a "change of value." Profit means that the value of the finished product is greater than the cost of production; or (if one includes profit as a cost of production) it means that the value of the finished product covers the costs of labor, rents, profit, capital expenditures – all the factors of production. There is no implied metamorphosis or "change of value."

Marx's term "change of value" is another example of his metaphysical philosophizing. That helps explain why he considered it necessary that there be a "change of value" in order for there to be profit or surplus value: value is fixed by his rigidly-defined categories, and is a pre-determined, *a priori* quantity once the commodity has been produced. Also, within the terms of his analysis this "value" is not only internalized labor, it is also what things sell for.

Marx has previously shown there can be no profit in selling at value. So there must be a *change* of value, a mutation or growth of the physical property, value, within the physical object. To simply say that entrepreneurs add on a percentage to the selling price for their profit, would be to admit too much free will and human choice into what is for him a closed, mechanistic system of physical entities.

That is, there cannot be profit to the capitalist on a normal or classically-conceived basis. There cannot be profit simply because the capitalist adds his desired increment of profit to the selling price, and because people acquiesce in paying it. In Marx's system all quantities and categories are bound by the internal logic and definitions of his analysis, which bind economics into rigidly constricted channels; the laws of his pseudo-physics of value must be obeyed, and those laws rule out profit.

Thus in the absence of profit, Marx conceives of surplus value as a "change of value," as some kind of additive metamorphosis in the quasi-physical entity called value; the congealed labor somehow expands.

He will proceed to describe how this metamorphosis occurs; and again it is instructive to note that it is something we could never have deduced ourselves. Only he knows the laws governing "change of value," only he knows where his argument is headed, and only he is able to derive the further steps in the argument for finding the source of the required "change of value." Standard methods of deduction applied to his starting premises would be of no help in predicting the course of his argument, for all his results are capricious and unfounded. He has converted economics into a "closed shop" which only he can work in. No one who is not in on the secrets of his mind, no one acquainted only with the real world of normal economics, could duplicate his results.

We will see that, as usual, the bizarre framework within which Marx conducts his investigation leads to bizarre arguments and conclusions, uniquely his own; or as the saying has it, "Ask a foolish question and you'll get a foolish answer."

Finding the change of value

Marx's investigation, then, takes the form of a search for a "change of value." As the first step in his search for this particular snark, Marx tells us the change of value "cannot take place in the money itself," since money only serves as money, is petrified and has no magical powers, and so on.

As regards that: no one ever suspected that there could be a change of value in the money, a metamorphosis undergone as it changes hands; so we can safely pass over this part. Money doesn't spontaneously grow or multiply with each cycle of buying and selling– we can accept that. (We're not talking about monetary exchange rates, in which there could be discerned a "change of value.")

Marx is reverting to his usual method: he has constructed a ludicrously implausible framework for the terms of discussion; now he will propose a couple of fatuous and patently absurd suggested solutions to the question at hand; and then having dismissed these straw men, he will produce his own solution, which will thus be presented as the result of reasoned "dialectical" argumentation.

At any rate, we go along with Marx in dismissing hard cash, petrified value, as the source of a "change of value." For the sake of argument we will also go along with him on his next step: "Just as little can it [the change of value] originate in the second act of circulation, the re-sale of the commodity, which does no more than transform the article from its bodily form back again into its money-form."

We can accept the gist of his point, while rejecting the bizarre conceptual framework.

Marx's description of the "second act of circulation" as doing "no more than transform the article from its bodily form back again into its money-form," is typical of his metaphysics. The merchant sells his goods, and Marx sees that act as one of exchanging the commodity's "bodily form" for money or "its money-form." As is typical for him, Marx somehow sees this exchange of two separate things as a transmutation of one thing from one "form" to another. We won't go once again into the sources of his metaphysical notions about "forms" and metamorphoses of entities; it can only be said that a confusion on such a fundamental level about simple, commonplace facts, renders Marx's treatise almost hallucinatory.

What is especially unfortunate about Marx's specious search for the "change of value" which occurs during the exchange of money for goods, however, is that it is precisely at this point that the "change of value" does occur. It is not a change of value as he conceives of it, but nevertheless there is a change. The capitalist has incurred certain production costs, and he wants to make a profit; he adds a mark-up for profit to his selling price; the buyer pays it. Thus value (or price) has increased because the capitalist adds a mark-up for profit. It's as simple as that. Profit occurs because economic exigency demands it. No one feels bound by the set of rules and prohibitions set up by Marx's hypothetical system. The real world blithely ignores his theory and its decrees. Thus there is profit at this stage, but not "change of value" as Marx construes it.

But let us continue to discuss the argumentation in Marx's own terms. He now comes to his rather glib conclusion (glib, but incomprehensible). He tells us, "The change must, therefore, take place in the commodity bought by the first act, M-C, but not in its value... We are, therefore, forced to the conclusion that the change originates in the use-value, as such, of the commodity, *i.e.*, in its consumption."

Well, if we're forced to that conclusion, we're forced to it, but it's not a very charming result. If we're offered an idiotic framework of analysis, with a contrived set of options, and all the options are ruled out except this one, then we're stuck with it. That is presumably what Marx desired, but not quite what we might wish.

"The change must, therefore, take place" in the first commodity or the first act of exchange. All right, if it doesn't take place in the other commodity, it must take place in this one. If it doesn't take place at the back end or in the middle, it must take place at the front end – that is, if we first assume it takes place at all.

Marx says the change doesn't take place "in its value" – again, we'll agree with that. There is no spontaneous swelling or augmentation or multiplication in the physical property called value.

"We are, therefore, forced to the conclusion that the change originates in [its] use-value, . . . *i.e.*, in its consumption." That conclusion may be totally bizarre and senseless, but if Marx says we're forced to it, then presumably we are. We will accept for now that this is the only alternative left to us, all others having been eliminated; therefore it stands proven to be the correct explanation.

The question then is, what can it possibly mean to say that a "change of value" occurs in the "use-value" or consumption of a commodity? (We note in passing that here Marx introduces yet another meaning for the term use-value; now it means not an item's usefulness in a general sense, nor the particular use or purpose to which it is put, but rather the active *use* of a commodity – that is, its consumption.)

The question becomes, how do you increase an object's value by using it up? What kind of apple becomes more valuable as you consume it? For that is now the character of the process of "change of value" as Marx envisions it. He says, "In order to be able to extract value from the consumption of a commodity, our friend, Moneybags [and there's a nice, dispassionate scientific term for you!], must be so lucky as to find, within the sphere of circulation, in the market, a commodity, whose use-value possesses the peculiar property of being a source of value, whose actual consumption, therefore, is itself an embodiment of labor, and consequently a creation of value."

It would seem that Marx has a formidable task ahead of him in finding this apple which grows more valuable by the eating – Marx no less so than the capitalist. We can only say in anticipation, that this commodity, or that is, its use-value, is a unique entity: it has started out as a property or characteristic of an object, and now it is an entity with characteristics of its own. This "use-value possesses the peculiar property of being a source of value," so that we have a property with properties – that is, second-generation properties. We cease discussing the commodity, the *object* that ties the properties to reality, and discuss the properties of its properties, much as we would discuss the specter of a ghost. Surely Marx should have had too great a philosophical background to allow himself to descend to such illusory metaphysics.

Labor-power, the special commodity

Having identified the problem, Marx moves quickly to the solution. The capitalist, he has told us, needs a commodity whose use-value is a source of value, whose consumption is "an embodiment of labor," or more simply, whose consumption is labor, and thus represents a creation of value. Now he says that, "The possessor of money does find on the market such a special commodity in capacity for labor or labor-power."

Labor-power, having been so glibly identified as the mystery component, is easily defined; Marx does so (somewhat belaboring the obvious) thus:

"By labor-power or capacity for labor is to be understood the aggregate of those mental and physical capabilities existing in a human being, which he exercises whenever he produces a use-value of any description." Labor-power is the ability to labor – simple enough.

And to complete the picture (skipping ahead in Marx's text), we see that: "The capitalist buys labor-power in order to use it; and labor-power in use is labor itself. The purchaser of labor-power consumes it by setting the seller of it to work. By working, the latter becomes actually, what before he only was potentially, labor-power in action, a laborer." The consumption of labor-power is therefore labor, or in Marx's terms "an embodiment of labor."

We have not yet seen how the purchase, or more exactly the "consumption," of labor-power enables the capitalist to extract "surplus value"; the explanation of that comes later. At this point we can only examine the concept of labor-power and the notion of its being what the capitalist pays for. (That is, Marx asserts that the capitalist doesn't pay for labor, but for labor-power – the capitalist buys labor-power first, he says, and the consumption of this labor-power, which is identical with labor, comes later.)

The first objection to be made to the theory of labor-power is that Marx advances it upon no evidence or objective justification. He simply makes a bald assertion that labor-power is what the laborer sells and what the capitalist buys, and this assertion is all the proof he offers. In general, we can characterize Marx's discussion of labor-value as the creation of (to use modern jargon) an "alternate scenario" of hired labor. Marx presents one interpretation of the facts, which he opposes to the normal or traditional interpretation. The original scenario, the one to which Marx opposes his own, is of course that the capitalist buys labor. He doesn't buy a commodity called "labor-power" and then consume it to make labor; he employs laborers for their labor, and pays them for their labor. He may pay for their labor by the hour – for labor is, as Marx has explained, measured by its duration in time. Or the capitalist may pay piece rates, so much for each unit of output. But even in the latter case it is a matter of the capitalist's paying for the *labor* required to produce a certain output; in that case it is labor measured in the amount of goods produced by that labor, not time. Either way, we would have to say that the traditional and common understanding is that the employee is hired for, and the capitalist pays for, the employee's efforts; his contribution to the production process; in short, his labor.

To this Marx opposes his alternate scenario: the capitalist purchases an abstract entity, a commodity called "labor-power"; this is defined as the *ability* to work, the *capacity* to perform labor. We might say this is "potential labor" – the potential or possibility of doing active labor (much as "potential energy" may be described as the capacity for yielding "kinetic energy"). Actual labor only appears later, in the consumption of the prior entity, labor-power.

Since Marx advances no arguments or evidence for portraying labor-power as what the capitalist buys, there are none to counter. We will therefore just investigate his bald assertion in the light of common knowledge and experience of what goes on in the production process.

First of all, the universal understanding of everyone, capitalists and laborers alike, is that labor is what is being purchased. The capitalist is interested in the production of his commodities, which is achieved by labor; the proximal, most immediate "commodity," if we may term it such, which he desires, is labor. Moreover, the capitalist and the laborer come to a wage agreement on the assumption and understanding that what is being paid for is labor. The terms of employment are so much money per hour of *labor*. That is the common understanding on everyone involved in the production process; so what grounds can there be for Marx to say that all these people are mistaken, that they are acting under a misapprehension of the real meaning of their contract, and that what is being paid for is not labor but labor-power?

There are no grounds at all; there is no outside authority to appeal to as proof. The realities of the employment of labor, of the contract for labor, are entirely determined in the human context, that is, by the contractual agreement between the various parties involved. There are no ultimate or superior laws of physics related to it, in other words; the laws governing material phenomena say nothing on the subject. The nature of the contract or agreement is entirely determined by the parties to it; their understanding of it defines it. If I offer you $200 to jump off the Brooklyn Bridge, that is an offer of money for an action; it's not a purchase of your "capacity for jumping off bridges," which is "consumed" by my setting you to the task of jumping. And if the employer and the laborer both proceed under the assumption that what is being purchased is a certain number of hours of labor each day, there are no grounds anywhere by which Marx can presume to overrule them or tell them they're wrong. To do so is simply arrogance and the belief that when he issues a decree or dogmatic pronouncement, the whole world should accept that at face value. As science that's not quite good enough.

Everyone directly involved in situations of the employment of labor, every laborer and employer, is of the opinion that labor is being paid for.

Marx, in asserting that they are all wrong, is like the lone soldier in a battalion who complains, "Everyone's out of step but me." There is ignorance and arrogance in this, but not science.

Marx's implication is that no one involved in the situation really knows what's going on – the capitalist only thinks he's buying labor, because he deals in conventional economic theories and accepted notions of reality. Marx, on the other hand, reveals hidden, inner truths unknown to less enlightened mortals and hidden from direct observation. This type of argument reduces eventually to a system of gnostic mysticism, a method of explaining away all objective reality by the invention of hidden, "inner" truths.

Marx of course specializes in revealing the inner reality which underlies overt, superficial reality. He finds the true essence behind deceitful "phenomenal" facts. Thus in the present case it might be argued that the capitalist thinks he is buying labor, but is confused by the surface, "phenomenal" data – that what he is actually paying for is the exercise of labor-power.

This kind of underlying essence is always easy to assert and difficult to disprove, because it lies in an unseen realm; it makes no real-world or "phenomenal" appearance and leaves no visible traces in the real world. Thus there is nothing to examine or refute. The entire argument lies only in Marx's mind and argumentation, and only he can tell what rules govern it.

However, for that very reason we must be suspicious of it. In every instance where the situation Marx discusses impinges on the observable world, it looks like the purchase of labor. Even Marx reveals that the pertinent factor is the "consumption" of labor-power, which occurs "by setting the seller of it to work." It is the consumption of labor-power which is "an embodiment of labor," or, which is plain old labor; and it is this consumption of labor-power, this *labor*, which is "a creation of value." And it is the creation of value, or the production of goods, which the capitalist desires. Thus the significant entity is labor; and to invent an intangible or abstract entity prior to labor, and to assert that, contrary to the capitalist's and the laborer's understanding of things, that is what they are trading in, is to complicate the issue with unseen and irrelevant entities. The picture can be explained much more easily and straightforwardly, without reference to nebulous, unobservable entities, by saying that labor is what is sold. Marx's "labor-power" adds nothing to the understanding of the situation; it is an unnecessary complication, a multiplication of entities, whose validity is supported only by his dogmatic proclamations. By the principle of Occam's Razor (not an infallible law, but a good rule of thumb), it is suspect.

Without "labor-power" the situation being discussed is just the same as with it; nothing goes unexplained, no observable phenomena must be left out. That's a pretty good sign that the concept of labor-power as what is being purchased is specious. Other than Marx's mere assertion of it, the only justification for the concept of labor-power is that Marx needs it to salvage his theory – to show how the capitalist can make money if Marx's assertions about the impossibility of profit are true. That is, the only reason for it is this dialectical "necessity."

This is not to say that labor-power doesn't exist. Certainly if someone works, we may deduce *a posteriori* that he has the capacity to work. (Whether in the absence of the work itself we could ever verify the existence of "capacity for labor" as an independent entity is another question.)

In fact if a person does *anything*, whether it be working or skiing or whistling, there can be deduced the existence of the capacity to work, or ski, or whistle. That doesn't make such things as "the capacity to ski" substantive entities in themselves. The multiplication of such entities could go on endlessly– we could go further and say that the capitalist trades the laborer the capacity to pay wages, which capacity the laborer consumes by actually drawing his wages. This could proceed in an infinite regress, level upon level, serving only to obfuscate and idiotize the discussion.

But if capacity to labor is logically necessary for the existence (i.e., performance) of labor, it is not sufficient to it. That is to say, labor-power is necessary but not sufficient for the production process; labor-power can (putatively) exist without being exercised. Surely the capitalist doesn't pay for a speculative entity which is necessary but in itself not sufficient – labor-power alone; he doesn't go down the street handing out money to everyone who looks capable of doing a day's work, thus buying *only* the capacity to labor. As even Marx admits, "The capitalist buys labor-power in order to use it." In other words, it is only the use of "labor-power" that aids his cause – only labor itself. That is what he pays for.

Obviously, the capitalist doesn't just go down the street passing out money to the "labor-capable," rewarding them simply for possessing the capacity to labor; for that would not constitute an agreement or contract to *supply* that labor-power. But, it could be argued, he does contract for the sole right to the laborer's labor-power during certain time periods of certain days; and this contract he exercises then by consuming the purchased labor-power.

The fact remains, however, that only the *exercise* of labor-power is paid for. It might be asked, if an employee who has sold his labor-power doesn't show up on a certain day, does he get paid? No he doesn't; the capitalist may have purchased his labor-power, but only on those days when he *exercises* that labor-power does the laborer get paid. If he leaves at noon he will be paid for half a day's *labor* – not labor-power.

(There are, though, salaried employees – people who can be absent from work on a given day and still be paid the same as usual. Are these then paid for their labor-power? It can only be said that these people have contracts calling for them to be paid so much a week, or month, or year; they are not hourly employees. This doesn't imply that only their *capacity* to labor is being paid for. If a certain employee doesn't have to punch a time clock, or doesn't have to be on the premises a certain number of hours in order to be paid, that is a result of freely arrived-at agreements. It doesn't mean that it is not the labor of the employee which the capitalist is interested in. If the employee who has sold his "labor-power" did no work at all, the fallacy of that assertion would soon be demonstrated.)

Fundamental difficulties

Let us proceed to an even more basic level in discussing labor-power as a commodity, and the buying and selling of labor-power. Can labor-power be conveyed? Can the laborer turn over his capacity for labor to the capitalist, so that the capitalist can consume it at his pleasure? That is how commodities are normally sold— if someone sells me an apple, I take it home with me. I don't need the seller to come over at a set hour and consume it for me. Marx's labor-power is a commodity that cannot be conveyed; and it is the only commodity that must be consumed by the seller – indeed, it must be "consumed into existence"; for labor, the creation of value, doesn't occur until this unique commodity is "consumed." And labor-power cannot even be shown to exist, if no labor is done.

If labor-power is a commodity, it should be "an object outside us," salable, actually conveyable. For instance, if I actually buy a violinist's labor-power, I should find myself endued with the capacity to play the violin; that is the only way I could be said to have purchased the labor-*power* itself. (If not, I can only contract for him to play – I can only buy his labor.)

Since that is not what happens, it becomes evident that what we have in Marx's "labor-power" is an elaborate sophistry; it is an exercise in Orwellian or Aesopian language. Marx is inventing a series of new and specious entities and definitions of words; and using this code language he portrays the purchase of labor as the consumption of labor-power. Insofar as labor-power, or the ability to perform labor, is a significant entity at all, it is not a commodity; it is not a substance, and not what is meant by normal use of the word "commodity." The "consumption" of this commodity could more properly be called the exercise of the laborer's abilities; it is not the consumption of a commodity in the normal sense of the word, and in any case it is done by the laborer, not the capitalist.

To all appearances, the "consumption of labor-power" most nearly resembles the performance of labor. It is not the consuming, that is, the using up, of a commodity by the employer, but rather the performance of a service by the laborer. This is another fundamental distinction Marx seems unable to grasp – the distinction between an action and an object, between matter and energy, between goods and services. (It is easy to fall into the use of such terminology as the "purchase of labor," as if labor already existed in a material form and the capitalist merely picked out a certain quantity of it and paid for it. But in normal economic discussions it can be assumed that all parties understand that what is meant is the contracting of a service. Such terminology is a convenient shorthand, that's all.)

The main point is that the laborer doesn't sell a commodity; he provides a service, namely his labor. The capitalist pays for that service; he doesn't buy a commodity and then "consume" it by setting the seller of it to work.

Quantizing labor-power

Another difference between labor-power and other commodities is that in the purchase of genuine commodities what is purchased is usually a certain fixed amount. It is doubtful that the laborer can be said to possess a fixed amount of labor-power, or if so, that this amount can be known.

Of course, what we are dealing with in Marx's text is usually the purchase, on a day-to-day basis, of labor-power; that is, the capitalist pays a certain amount for a day's labor-power. But how much labor-power is that? Capacity to work itself is not a quantitative property; it is more qualitative – one worker may be said to do good work, another poor work. When we try to measure the amount of labor-power, we usually end up thinking in terms of labor: the laborer can work twelve-hour days of hard physical labor; or the laborer can turn out a large number of units each day. Moreover, labor-power is probably the only commodity which is not sold permanently, but only for a day at a time – that is a situation more like rental of labor-power, not its purchase.

When we attempt to put a number on labor-power, we always come back to amounts of labor. It is doubtful whether there is a fixed amount of labor-power in a day's-worth of labor-power. The laborer may be required to exercise his labor-power for a fixed time period; that is, the capitalist may "consume" a certain amount of labor-power for each day's worth of it he buys. What that means is, the laborer works for a certain length of time each day. The quantity of labor-power reduces simply to an amount of labor; a day's labor-power, when the laborer exercises his labor-power for twelve hours, equals twelve hours of labor. The insertion of labor-power into the discussion does nothing but complicate it with meaningless irrelevancies. The result is the same as if we had just said, The capitalist buys labor, a certain amount of it each day.

Philosophical nature of labor-power

Marx's theory of labor-power is basically a reification of a concept, that is, an artificial concretization of an abstract entity. He attributes "thing-like" properties to a merely conceptual phenomenon.

Labor-power exists, of course; it can't be labeled a pure abstraction. But it doesn't exist as an independent entity. It could perhaps be considered a property either of the laborer or of his labor. It is, as Marx states, a capacity of the laborer; it tells how well he works, how much output he can produce, or some such measure of the degree of skill the laborer has acquired. As such, as a property of the laborer, it is inseparable from him; it is not a separate entity subject to trade.

Moreover, labor-power can only be observed in and verified by the labor actually performed. The proof of labor-power is in the labor. Labor both develops labor-power, as "practice makes perfect," and is the sole reliable demonstration of the existence of labor-power.

Marx seeks to take an entity with this secondary or abstract nature and elevate it to independent-object status; it is another example of his artificial concretization of entities. At the same time he implicitly demotes the status of labor. Heretofore labor had been presented as an independent, fundamental factor in production – something that stands alone as one of the basic factors in the economy, not reducible to anything else. Now it is portrayed as secondary or derivative: labor is the consumption of labor-power, which by that fact is shown to be a more fundamental entity. This is an internal self-contradiction within his theory.

If labor is not an independent entity, perhaps we had better go back to the start and rework Marx's definition of the value of commodities. That definition, one would think, should be stated in terms of the most fundamental entities; so we should have value defined in terms of the "homogeneous, socially-necessary consumption of capacity to labor," etc. We should have dealt with *capacity* to labor from the start, in other words.

Another problem with Marx's theory is this: if Marx had wished to point to an intangible entity as being what the capitalist buys, labor-power was not the only choice. The capacity to labor is not the only requirement for there to be labor. The laborer must not only be able to work; we may say he must be "ready, willing and able" to work. It is a well-known fact that there are other characteristics of workers, besides their inherent ability to do the work itself, which distinguish good workers from bad. Basic work habits, conscientious interest in the work, determination to work, steady attendance – all these things matter too. So in addition to "capacity to labor," the capitalist must look for "willingness to work" and "dependability for work." These elements and all others which can be imagined must also be factored into Marx's equations, if we are to accept such intangible entities as being what the capitalist buys.

Ancillary topics in labor-power

Marx now moves on to the topic of what might be called the historical conditions necessary for the sale of labor-power, or perhaps, characteristics of societies in which labor-power is sold.

> But in order that our owner of money may be able to find labor-power offered for sale as a commodity, various conditions must first be fulfilled. The exchange of commodities of itself implies no other relations of dependence than those which result form its own nature. On this assumption, labor-power can appear upon the market as a commodity only if, and so far as, its possessor, the individual whose labor-power it is, offers it for sale, or sells it, as a commodity. In order that he may be able to do this, he must have it at his disposal, must be the untrammeled owner of his capacity for labor, *i.e.*, of his person. He and the owner of money meet in the market, and deal with each other as on the basis of equal rights, with this difference alone, that one is buyer, the other seller; both, therefore, equal in the eyes of the law.

Marx takes a strange tack here; the passage takes the form of an analysis of the conditions logically necessary for the sale of labor-power. That is, he offers us an argument composed of deductions from abstract principles. It is sort of a universalistic approach – "these are the conditions logically necessary in any society whatsoever for the sale of labor-power." One would think it would have been more to the point to show what societies labor-power has actually been sold in, and what conditions led to this situation as a matter of historical fact (not as a result of deduced logical necessity).

Marx prefers a universalistic, deduced approach which covers all conceivable societies, including not only the real world but all possible worlds. It is as if he believes that nothing really exists until he deduces it; mere "phenomenal" existence is insufficient justification for accepting facts until they gain the support of systematic deductions.

Thus the language Marx uses here is not that of a report of facts, as "These are the conditions in capitalist societies that conduce to the buying and selling of labor." Rather, his is the language of deduction: "These are the conditions logically necessary." It adds a curious overtone to his discussion.

Marx begins: "But in order that our owner of money may be able to find labor-power offered for sale as a commodity, various conditions must first be fulfilled." A legitimate question could be raised here, incidentally. An argument could be made that in *any* society where there can be an "owner of money" there can be "labor-power offered for sale"; and thus to refer to the "owner of money" is already sufficient to indicate the existence of "labor-power offered for sale." Of course, Marx apparently thought the phenomenon of hired labor was unique to capitalist societies, not found in feudal society on the one hand or socialist society on the other. But regardless of his belief, it may be that in any complex society, any civilization with an economy at all (i.e., non-primitive societies), there can be and has been hired labor. Certainly it exists even in communist countries today. Of course, the state is by far the largest employer, and communist theorists might argue that that is a special case. But private employment of labor for odd jobs, repair work, tailoring, and indeed a host of tasks, also exists. As Solzhenitsyn ironically puts it, "The hiring of labor at a fair wage is permitted in the Soviet Union even today." So to phrase the problem as Marx does is somewhat to beg the question; if there is an "owner of money" there is inevitably also buying and selling of labor-power.

It can be said, in keeping with this, that Marx completely misses the point in his account of the conditions for the sale of labor-power. The sale of labor probably occurs naturally and spontaneously whenever grass-roots economics has sway, that is, wherever people are left alone and not stifled in arriving at their own economic arrangements.

Let us qualify this; first, we must understand that we are dealing with society of some complexity, so that economic arrangements and institutions exist. In tribal or hunter-gatherer societies there is little or no hired labor, nor any money, division of labor, rents, trade as a means of livelihood, or such elements of society on a higher level of complexity.

But where such complicated mechanisms do come into play, as long as there is not stifling control by some central power, there is probably hired labor. It is a part of "normal" economics, of natural human economic arrangements in societies where the economic milieu has not been deformed by an inordinate exercise of political power over economic affairs. (The existence of slavery or serfdom, sanctioned and enforced by political powers, may be considered one type of such deformation. It deforms the normal economic environment, making the holding of slaves more advantageous than free economic exchange, which latter may be regarded as the essential defining characteristic of capitalism.)

In fact, sometimes even when there *is* stifling control of the economy by central political power, there still is hired labor. Modern communist theorists have produced an abundance of arguments, theories and sophistries proving that the workers in communist countries are not hired laborers; yet they remain hired laborers, hourly-paid laborers, with the only distinction being that their employer is the state, or the Communist Party. A flood or Orwellian or Aesopian terminology has been invented to show that communism as it exists today is not "state capitalism"; but the communist state remains the sole employer and capital-holder.

But to continue with his discussion: "The exchange of commodities of itself implies no other relations of dependence than those which result from its own nature." This is a rather opaque statement; a meaning can only be tenuously gleaned from it. It might be given a reading, "The exchange of commodities implies nothing beyond what is needed for the exchange of commodities." That is unexceptionable, if uninformative.

Or Marx may be saying, "The exchange of commodities implies nothing about a society, including about the status of laborers, except those conditions favorable for an exchange of commodities." Again, we won't argue.

Marx may be saying that the exchange of commodities, per se, doesn't always imply there is sale of labor-power; it doesn't imply that labor-power is one of the commodities exchanged. The issue is muddied somewhat by Marx's vacuous phrase, "relations of dependence," a part of his pseudo-precise, pseudo-scientific jargon. It may refer here to hired labor, i.e. to the status of being an employee, or to the status of laborers and their relationship to their superiors in general.

Basically, though, what Marx appears to be saying is that the exchange of commodities, the existence of a market economy, does not imply non-market conditions of labor – indeed that it actually rules them out; that is, the sale of labor-power means we're not dealing with a slave society, but one characterized by hired labor. He proceeds, "On this assumption," – he is as usual relying on deductions from assumptions, not the description of facts – "labor-power can appear upon the market as a commodity only if, and so far as, its possessor, the individual whose labor-power it is, offers it for sale, or sells it, as a commodity." Labor-power can appear on the market only if someone offers it on the market – again, we can't argue with that. The real point he's making comes next, though: "In order that he may be able to do this, he must have it at his disposal, must be the untrammeled owner of his capacity for labor, *i.e.*, of his person." After much effort Marx has thus deduced that capitalist societies are not slave societies, but rather societies in which the laborer offers his efforts in return for wages. We knew that all along as a matter of observed fact; it seems superfluous to deduce it by abstract logic.

He amplifies on his point somewhat: "He and the owner of money meet in the market, and deal with each other as on the basis of equal rights, with this difference alone, that one is buyer, the other seller [the usual difference in a sale]; both, therefore, equal in the eyes of the law." With minor qualifications this is presumably true. At various times the law or economic conditions may seem to give more of a position of strength to one side or the other; but in theory and in principle, the sale of labor is a free exchange between equal agents. We agree with Marx on this point, and perhaps can even go so far as to suggest that it is a good thing for buyer and seller to be free agents. The fact that capitalist or democratic societies are not slave societies, and that people are left free, uncoerced by government, to make their own economic decisions, might be considered a strong point in favor of such societies. This characteristic contrasts not only with slave societies but also with communist societies, which are a glorified form of serfdom, with the state in the role of feudal lord and the laborer bound, in many cases, to whatever workplace the state designates for him. That has been the practical result in societies attempting to implement Marx's ideology: a one-party state in control of all resources, directing economic and all other activity from on high in the name of the people.

Marx himself had scant respect for such bourgeois prejudices as freedom; the most he could say in its favor was that, for a certain period in history in which the "historically inevitable" development of society produced democratic, "capitalist" nations, personal freedom was appropriate and "necessary." But with the arrival of a new historical age consisting of dictatorships of the proletariat, the passing of democratic freedoms was not to be mourned. It is perhaps the most serious indictment of Marx that he placed no value on freedom. The replacement of democracies with "socialist democracies," or one-party dictatorships (the party being nominally that of the people or the proletariat), dedicated to realizing his specious and convoluted theory, was a thing to be desired as long as it brought about the downfall of Marx's hated enemy, the capitalist.

A digression

The issue of freedom brings to our attention another possible method of organizing history, different from Marx's system of dialectical epochs. It would probably be more sensible to classify various historical eras or types of society by the degree of freedom, economic and otherwise, found in them, rather than by their position in a revolving series of historically-inevitable eras. A classification based on the degree of freedom doesn't have to put all societies existing at one time into one inflexible category; it does not fictionalize history as Marx does, and moreover it can serve as a basis not only of classification but also of evaluation. That is, to the degree that the Greek city-states allowed economic and political freedom, we might say, they were desirable; to the extent that there was slavery, they were bad. This is a somewhat simplistic manner of expression; but it emphasizes the point that human choice is an element in history and society's development, and that there are standards for judging societies, and values deserving to be advanced. This is in contrast to a "dialectical" theory in which human beings can only bow to the next historically-inevitable form of society, and in which no judgment can be made about what is good and bad among social developments.

To put it another way, we could classify economies by the degree of control exercised over them by central governments; and we could classify political systems by the degree of freedom (and on the other hand, order) they allow. Such things as slavery have only existed when sanctioned and enforced by the political powers. Likewise, feudalism was characterized by a breakdown of order, that is, of strong central authority on any wide extent; at the same time there was a granting of the legitimacy of serfdom by what powers of authority remained.

Some societies leave the economy relatively free from interference by government. Capitalism exists in democracies because of a freedom of grass-roots economic efforts from stifling interference on the part of government; and communism proposes to tyrannize over the economy, bringing everything back into totalitarian central control (and in this sense it is both reactionary and "imperialistic" in the economic realm of society).

Thus a strong case could be made against Marx's system of dialectical-historical eras, and in favor of classification in more humanistic terms, with the degree of freedom serving as a main discriminating factor. Marx's entire bizarre ideology and convoluted theory may be seen as an attempt to evade the issue of greater and lesser freedom in society, and to make tyranny acceptable by rephrasing the issue in terms such as "historic inevitability."

Slavery

Marx proceeds to distinguish, generously, between employee status and slavery: "The continuation of this relation demands that the owner of the labor-power should sell it only for a definite period, for if he were to sell it rump and stump, once for all, he would be selling himself, converting himself from a free man into a slave, from an owner of a commodity into a commodity. He must constantly look upon his labor-power as his own property, his own commodity, and this he can only do by placing it at the disposal of the buyer temporarily, for a definite period of time. By this means alone can he avoid renouncing his rights of ownership over it."

This is as feckless a description of slavery as one could desire; Marx reduces the distinction between employment and slavery to a razor-thin margin, either because of his inordinate antipathy toward the capitalist or because he really couldn't tell the difference between holding a job and slavery. It can only be said that a slave is not someone who has sold his *labor* "once for all," but someone who himself has been sold, someone who, as Marx truly points out, has himself become property, "a commodity." The condition and experience of servitude must be acknowledged as of an entirely different order from hiring out one's labor. It is not a mere quantitative difference or difference in the time period.

(The condition of being an indentured servant is more like what Marx describes here as slavery, but even indentured servants were indentured for a definite time; that is, they sold their labor – or someone else sold it for them – for a definite period, long as it may have been. They weren't sold once and for all.)

So slavery is not just the extension or elongation of employed status into an indefinite time period; and likewise, historically speaking, most slaves have not become so by their own actions, by selling themselves "rump and stump." Slaves have been war booty, or they have been hunted and captured expressly for the purpose of making them slaves; sometimes they have been sold to pay off their debts. In any event, slavery may be seen to have arisen from violence, from the exercise of naked power, more than from simple economic interactions. It seems deliberately mischievous of Marx to gloss over this distinction.

(A digression: in regard to the issue of slavery, of workers' selling their labor "rump and stump," a somewhat new phenomenon has arisen with communist societies. This is the phenomenon of "guest workers," laborers whose efforts have been sold by their country. A recent newspaper account describes the situation like this:

> They [some workers observed by the reporter in East Germany] are a small group of Vietnamese 'guest workers,' as the communists choose to call them. The perversion of socialist humanism lies in the fact that these are not 'guest workers.' They are slave laborers. They were rounded up by the Hanoi government and shipped off to the Soviet Union and other states of the comecon economic bloc. Hanoi earns trade credits with their labor. It can't produce enough goods to sell, so it sells people. [1]

Since these guest workers generally are committed to a fixed period of servitude, it would be technically more correct to refer to them as involuntarily indentured servants, not slaves. At any rate, since Communism is arguably a form of state capitalism, it correspondingly has invented the phenomenon of guest workers, a form of state slavery or state indentured-status.)

More on conditions for labor-power

Marx continues on the topic of the conditions for the sale of labor-power, or we might call it, the characteristics of societies where there is a market in labor-power: "The second essential condition to the owner of money finding labor-power in the market as a commodity is this – that the laborer instead of being in the position to sell commodities in which his labor is incorporated, must be obliged to offer for sale as a commodity that very labor-power, which exists only in his living self."

That is, labor-power is a commodity only if there are people in the society who have no other source of income except their labor-power. It will be recognized that this condition has historically been the lot of the great bulk of the human race, so there is no danger of the condition's not being met. It would probably be easier to find situations where there is no owner of money or possessor of independent wealth than one where no one is obliged to sell his labor-power. It takes an economic history, an accumulation of wealth, for there to be possessors of wealth; but we all come into the world with economic needs and usually with no pre-established way to meet them. Marx seeks to invest this situation, and the capitalist's employment of labor, with a sinister tone, implying that it is a great injustice that the capitalist is in a position to sell commodities while the laborer is not. But to repeat: it is not an unnatural condition not to own a productive enterprise; it is the norm. What is in a sense exceptional is for some people to have accumulated capital or productive enterprises and thus to be in a position to produce goods and to offer employment to others. The capitalist's position may be used well or abused; but the fact of its existence cannot be considered sinister in itself.

At any rate, we could restate the condition Marx is outlining by saying, labor-power becomes a commodity only if not everyone inherits wealth or has a source of income which allow him to avoid becoming a hired laborer. His proviso is somewhat superfluous, therefore. There are always those not born independently wealthy (where there is wealth at all; in non-economic forms of society, such as tribal or hunter-gatherer societies, there is arguably no such thing as money or wealth at all). And where there are owners of money and the sale of commodities, i.e. in societies where such things exist, the non-wealthy are obliged to sell their labor.

So whenever there are owners of money and commodities, there are wage laborers. Even in feudal societies, where serfdom was the usual status of the great mass of laboring poor, wage labor existed on a small scale. Even in "slave" societies, not all the poor were slaves; some small degree of wage labor, and other "capitalist," or uncoerced economic, arrangements have always existed in the interstices. For there have always been some small fragments of society not bound by the constrictions of power sanctioned by the state, whether that be in the form of serfdom, slavery, or whatever. Some small proportion of free exchange has always existed; and in regard to labor this has meant paid, wage labor. Thus an arrangement between the owner of money and the laborer, who is not in a position to sell commodities but must sell labor, is neither an unusual nor a sinister condition.

To recapitulate: this prerequisite for the existence of a market in labor-power amounts to saying little more than, There must be people and an economy. There are always those with no source of income other than the exertions of their own physical bodies, no economic resource except what resides in their own bodily powers. That is, there are always those who have to work for a living; that has been the condition of the great "mass" of humanity (to use a favorite Marxist term) throughout human history. To paraphrase a famous quip, "God must love those who are obliged to offer for sale as a commodity their own labor-power – He made so many of them."

To speak more abstractly, there are always the "unencumbered," lacking wealth or independent sources of income; there are always those not born with a silver spoon or a shoe factory in their mouths. And whatever is the predominant "entry-level" role in the economy of the moment, they must lend their efforts to it. In societies where there are money, commodities, and owners of money, this means the unencumbered must get a job. Marx is not exactly eliminating any conceivable situation by saying that there must exist those with nothing to sell but their labor.

We might point out also the other side of this coin; while the capitalist must find laborers, the laborer or would-be laborer must find a job. That is, he must find a way to meet his bodily needs; in capitalistic, or normal, societies, this means finding a job. For him, the issue is one-sided: how the capitalist finds labor-power for sale; and the capitalist's role is, for Marx, unnecessary and exploitative. The question of how the laborer finds a job, finds someone who is in the market for labor (which is all he has to sell) is of trivial concern to Marx.

Marx deplored this situation, of course; he thought it scandalous and oppressive that people, especially himself, should have to be beholden to anyone, should have to be subject to someone's will and keep in an employer's good graces in order to survive. Anyone who has ever held a job can sympathize with that sentiment. But it is childish to enlarge it into an indictment of society and a call for revolution, upheaval and bloodshed, and to convert one's personal grievances into a universal rule.

In any civilization, i.e., any non-primitive society, there will be such relatively complex institutions or human interactions as the employer-employee "relationships"; a complex society by its very nature will have such more or less formalized structural mechanisms which an individual must fit himself into – jobs to get, guilds to join, manors to be attached to. At least in capitalist society there is a certain diversity and a certain offering of alternatives – if you can't get along with one boss, you may find another who is more congenial. But *some* such relationship must exist and must be entered into. Communist countries have not eliminated that necessity; they have only imposed on the laborer the necessity of pleasing the state and the Party, and they have removed alternative employers.

When Marx rails against the very necessity of finding a job, a result of the complexity of any society even having an economy, then we must respond that the only alternatives are either a return to primitivism, or perhaps an advance to even more restrictive and repressive forms of organization of society than now exist.

It is interesting to wonder what type of society it would be where one didn't need to find a job; that is, where there was no need to establish a "relation of production" with an employer or some such figure, but where one could just get up in the morning and go to work. One could be a forager, that is, a Robinson Crusoe type in a wilderness, living off the land. Tribal society fits this picture, too – a person is more or less born into the working (hunting) group, and when old enough to join the hunt or perform other duties, he simply does so. No one has to enter a formalized relationship in order to work; members of the tribe just wake up in the morning and go hunting for food.

And other types of economic relationship that a person might be born into, or bound to, might qualify – serfdom, slavery, and perhaps certain traditional forms of "communal" peasant farming (where one large workable area is held in common and divided among all the families making up the community, being divided anew as more children are born). But slavery and serfdom are conditions of greater repression; they are examples of sanction of unwarranted power by the state. The only alternatives to a society with complex relationships and the need to find a job, are primitive and repressive forms of society. (Some have pointed out that communism is both.)

Looking at all such possibilities, then, we might say in general that these are the two alternatives to capitalism, i.e. to a society of openly-entered economic arrangement: the primitive and the repressive. Then there is a less-seen third alternative, the chaotic; an example of this would be the breakdown of society after the fall of Rome, leading to the Dark Ages. Travel was not safe, state power was fragmented, and the institutions of economics as well as government broke down. This tended toward a proliferation of self-sufficient estates and a decline into feudalism and serfdom, however; it is sort of a mixture of the "repressive" model and the self-sufficient foraging model.

Requirements for selling commodities

Marx next discusses briefly the issue of why not everyone has commodities to sell:

> In order that a man may be able to sell commodities other than labor-power, he must of course have the means of production, as raw material, implements, &c. No boots can be made without leather. He requires also the means of subsistence. Nobody – not even 'a musician of the future' can live upon future products, or upon use-

values in an unfinished state; and ever since the first moment of his appearance on the world's stage, man always has been, and must still be a consumer, both before and while he is producing. In a society where all products assume the form of commodities, these commodities must be sold after they have been produced; it is only after their sale that they can serve in satisfying the requirements of their producer. The time necessary for their sale is superadded to that necessary for their production.

The facts Marx relates here are to a large degree true, even commonplace; anyone who has ever desired to "go into business for himself" or to find a means of livelihood other than as a wage laborer, has run into and had to consider these difficulties. In order to sell a product, one must first have the wherewithal to produce the product and to subsist until money from sales begins to come in. As the saying goes, "It takes money to make money."

That is a problem for aspiring entrepreneurs, but it is perhaps not the sinister and lurid situation as which Marx portrays it (by his vocabulary, his rather sneering phrases such as "a musician of the future," and by the whole one-sided viewpoint from which he investigates the problem).

The issue of "capital formation," or of where the aspiring capitalist gets the funds to proceed, is a variegated one; there are perhaps almost as many answers as there have been entrepreneurs. But probably the main one has always been the very situation Marx so deplores – working for wages until such a time as the laborer has saved enough money to start a business.

Marx's rhetorical stance, however, is somewhat skewed; his question is why the employer of labor finds labor for hire, or that is, why not everyone is a capitalist. That is to assume that everyone wants to be a capitalist, or should be a capitalist, and (implicitly) that for some to be capitalists and others to be laborers is a mark of a fundamental injustice within society.

In a certain sense the capitalist of course does have a dominant position over those laborers he employs; and most laborers would agree that it would be more pleasant and lucrative to be a boss than to be a worker. But at the same time it is doubtful that all laborers are actively seeking ways to become entrepreneurs. And it is doubtful that it is theoretically possible for everyone in a society to "be in the position to sell commodities." Surely it would have to be a case of business on a very small scale if all were entrepreneurs and there were no employed laborers. But factually speaking such a situation probably could never exist, any more than everyone in a society could be a doctor or a lawyer (though it sometimes seems we are rapidly approaching the latter condition in the United States). Someone has spoken of the impossibility of "a village whose inhabitants lived by taking in each other's laundry"; and a society composed entirely of capitalists is just as impossible.

Thus Marx's analysis of why there is hired labor on the market, as if that were a strange or unnatural situation, seems to be coming at the problem from the wrong angle. A more appropriate line of investigation might be suggested by some of his other remarks. As he points out, "man always has been, and must still be a consumer, both before and while he is producing." That is, we all have to make a living; we all, individually and collectively, wake up in the morning faced with the problem of how to feed and clothe ourselves and supply our other needs. The issue seen in a broad framework is how the common, "unendowed" individual, with only himself to support himself, is to go about doing so, and what social organizations and arrangements further that aim. On a societal level, the question may be (as it was in the Great Depression), How do we get the economy off dead center? On a more elementary level the question may be phrased, How do we form a self-sustaining and self-perpetuating economy so that there will be economic endeavors ongoing, to which the unendowed worker can attach himself in order to make a living? How do we create a situation in which business creativity and initiative can find expression in the startup of new endeavors?

That is, to approach the issue from the standpoint of asking why there are people who must offer their labor for sale, is to take a narrow-minded and wrong-headed view of the question. Its only merit (from Marx's viewpoint) is that it does allow for Marx's biased and implicitly accusatory tone.

Marx has said that the producer of commodities for sale "requires also the means of subsistence"; for no one "can live upon future products." Marx states this point in order to show the difficulties posed by a "commodity" economy for a laborer aspiring to be a capitalist; it is actually true of *everyone*. The laborer requires his means of subsistence whether he desires to be able to sell commodities or not; he must find a way of making a living whether his eventual goal is to become a capitalist or not.

So it is faintly ridiculous for Marx to pose his central question as one of why there are those not in a position to sell commodities. Why are there poor people, or people with no built-in, ready-made sources of wealth? Because that's the human condition, that's why; we all come into the world naked and defenseless. No society to date has ever eliminated the existence of people with nothing but their own labor to sell; in fact, communist countries have greatly increased the numbers of those thus unendowed, by appropriating for the Party alone the role of capitalist.

Marx manages to deplore implicitly not only the fact that some people have commodities to sell and others do not, but the existence of commodities (as he defines them) as such. He has said, the laborer aspiring to produce commodities for sale must have the capital for the raw materials, and resources to subsist on while he produces the goods. What is more, "In a society where all products assume the form of commodities, these commodities must be sold after they have been produced; it is only after their sale that they can serve in satisfying the requirements of their producer."

By all products' assuming the form of commodities, Marx means (in his own lexicon), they are produced for sale, not for the producer's subsistence. Those societies wherein things are produced for sale (not "for use") are market economies – as opposed to fictitious forms of society where nothing is sold because everybody owns everything and goods are produced "for use." It is somewhat redundant to bring this stipulation into the discussion – we have been talking from the beginning only about societies characterized by a market in commodities, because we are talking about societies where "a man may be able to sell commodities other than labor-power." We are talking about producing goods for sale; so naturally we must include the time necessary for selling the goods after they are produced. Or in more prosaic terms, a new business or new capitalist must be able to support himself until he has built up a steady clientele and regular sales.

We might quibble with Marx's statement that the commodities must be sold, and that only then can they fulfill their producers needs. Presumably even in a capitalist or market economy, one could still produce goods for one's own subsistence – many farms in the previous century in the United States were largely subsistence endeavors, with only a small participation in the cash economy. It was not uncommon even in the first half of this century to find, say, a farm which produced hogs and other livestock and garden vegetables solely for subsistence, with perhaps a crop of tobacco as the only source of cash. Yet even in such a situation, the farm family had to first have the farm, and have the means to exist until the livestock and crops came to fruition.

But Marx's main point is well taken; if someone intends to produce goods for sale, he and his enterprise must be able to sustain themselves until the sales "get rolling." That much has always been true for the capitalist.

We must again quibble, however, with Marx's use of the glib phrase, "society where all products assume the form of commodities," as if that were one arbitrarily-chosen type of economy, set off against many other possible forms. Societies where products are "commodities," or market goods, are either "normal economies," or "market economies" or just plain economies (take your choice). Market economies are, it may be argued, the normal state of affairs and the only economies which actually merit the name. Centrally-controlled "command economies" function mainly to stifle normal, grass-roots economic activity, and thus they are more accurately called anti-economies. As a Czech journalist once expressed it, "Sometimes I have the impression that our government exists *only* to make our lives difficult." [2]

The fact is, wherever people are free to come to their own economic arrangements based on freely-entered-into agreements, and where there is not some artificial, exterior influence preventing such free grass-roots arrangements, there is exchange, including the sale of commodities. Where there is not some dislocative force, like an overbearing exercise of the power of the state in economic matters, or on the other hand like the breakdown of all safety and order required for travel and trade (as in the Middle Ages), there is trade and the production of "commodities."

In this sense a society where products "assume the form of commodities," where they are produced for the market economy, are those societies with an economy at all. They are the societies where economic rules and laws are allowed to govern in economic matters, rather than those where the state has arrogated to itself the role of strong-arming and attempting to thwart the workings of the economic realm of life. Marx seeks to contrast market economies with both primitive and authoritarian societies of the past (in which he nevertheless understates the extent of the production and sale of commodities); or else with some fictitious future society where nothing is sold, because everyone owns everything. Such comparisons are specious.

Summing up

Marx now begins to sum up the points he has just made: "For the conversion of his money into capital, therefore, the owner of money must meet in the market with the free laborer..." But hold it! Not so fast! The subject has been how the owner of money finds labor-power on the market, not how he converts his money into capital. Marx assumes here that the two are identical – that the capitalist only makes money by "exploiting" labor. (Later on he proves the point – a typical Marxian approach; he first defines or assumes a thing is true, and later proves it to be true, with his assumption and his proof bearing no relation to each other.)

At any rate, there are two particulars of this statement which must be challenged. First is Marx's usage of the word "capital" as meaning, roughly, profit – the *results* of the application of money to the entrepreneurial process. In fact, the commonly-used meaning of the term is the initial investment: the money, land, etc. invested at the front end of the entrepreneurial process in order to make money, rather than the resulting profit which is made. Capital is "the money it takes to make money," not the money so made.

Second, it is at least theoretically possible to acquire a profit, or capital return, without employing labor. A man may own a small piece of rental property, on which he does all repairs and maintenance, and collects the rent and performs other duties, all by himself. He may thus gain a capital return, in the form of rents, without using hired labor. Presumably, one could even produce a product and gain profit on it, all alone or as a family enterprise; it would be difficult to separate the element of simple payment for labor from that of profit, but nevertheless the element of profit would be there. The assumption and postulate that profit or capital return comes only from the "exploitation" of hired labor, is a central theme of Marx's and one that should not be granted as a foregone conclusion.

The free laborer

Marx continues:

> For the conversion of his money into capital, therefore, the owner of money must meet in the market with the free laborer, free in the double sense, that as a free man he can dispose of his labor-power as his own commodity, and that on the other hand he has no other commodity for sale, is short of everything necessary for the realisation of his labor-power.
>
> The question why this free laborer confronts him in the market, has no interest for the owner of money, who regards the labor market as a branch of the general market for commodities. And for the present it interests us just as little. We cling to the fact theoretically, as he does practically. One thing, however, is clear – nature does not produce on the one side owners of money or commodities, and on the other men possessing nothing but their own labor-power. This relation has no natural basis, neither is its social basis one that is common to all historical periods. It is clearly the result of a past historical development, the product of many economical revolutions, of the extinction of a whole series of older forms of social production.

As already discussed, the capitalist does indeed look to hire laborers (unless his enterprise is a very small-scale one); and likewise the laborer must find in the market a capitalist with work to do and money which he is "free" to dispose of as he wishes. In short, both parties engage in the normal, everyday activities of economic life as their needs require. It is not a one-sided arrangement and it is difficult to see (as yet, anyway) what there is about it to justify Marx's sinister portrayal of it.

As to "the question why this free laborer confronts" the capitalist and so on, this part of Marx's text seems to be little except a verbal sneer. Certainly we couldn't say for sure whether the "owner of money" thinks about "the question why this free labor confronts him in the market" or not. (It is however a commonplace fact of life, one that is part of everyday economic reality; thus there is a natural tendency to take it for granted as part of the natural order of things – perhaps that is the point Marx is making.)

But (to continue) whereas it may be accepted as a natural thing, Marx points out, "nature does not produce on the one side owners of money or commodities, and on the other men possessing nothing but their own labor-power."

Of course not – nature produces only the latter; we all come into the world naked, possessing nothing. And for the laborer looking to feed himself, it is perhaps fortunate that there are enterprises that have been built up over a course of years of work, that can offer him a job. No one, let us say, is endowed by nature *per se* – by biological or geological nature – with wealth; but it may be termed a natural result in a free-market economy that some will build businesses and acquire wealth and others will be hired workers. Not all can belong to either category – there must be some of both. There is no sinister, oppressive force "stacking the deck" to produce the result; in that sense the result *is* natural.

Marx's comments reveal something of a dog-in-a-manger attitude. He seems to be grumbling about why the laborer's lot is not as easy as the capitalist's, and perhaps thinking laborers like himself deserve wealth as much as the capitalist. That may very well be the case; economic reward is not strictly tied to moral virtue. Some people are simply better at economic affairs than others. But another person's wealth generally does not increase our own poverty–generally the contrary (for to repeat, the owner of a factory gives work to the "unendowed"). We all have to function in the economic world, and not simply rail at those in more fortunate circumstances.

Where Marx condemns the existence of the wealthy and the poor as unnatural, he could just as easily say, "Nature does not produce on the one side people who are able to play the piano, and on the other side people possessing nothing but the ability to play the radio." Such a comment is no criticism. And to extend the analogy, it cannot be used to condemn either the individual who likes music and learns to play the piano, or the person who is not interested in music and does not learn to play. Each follows his own tastes and inclinations. This is not to say that the laborer's lot is not in general harder than the boss's. Nor is it to deny the fact that the way should be kept as clear as possible of unwarranted obstacles to any individual's attempts to better his economic status.

Marx continues, "This relation has no natural basis, neither is its social basis one that is common to all historical periods. It is clearly the result of a past historical development, the product of many economical revolutions, of the extinction of a whole series of older forms of social production."

First of all, as to the matter of fact: the "social basis" of this "relation" has been common, in some form and degree, to very nearly all historical periods. To belabor a point: in any society that has been sufficiently advanced even to have an economy, if the central ruling power has not held an absolute stranglehold on all economic endeavors, free-market interactions have always sprung up. They may not have been predominant, but they have existed. A discussion of this issue, however, is best left to historians, who are better equipped to deal with it than this author (or Marx).

It might at first seem a very faint criticism on Marx's part to accuse hired labor of being "the result of a past historical development," since he was the great apostle and expounder of historical development. In fact, nearly every aspect of human civilization could be labeled a product of historical development; that is no criticism.

What Marx is doing, however, is placing hired labor again within the context of his dialectical theory of history, with its cyclical epochs replacing one another in succession. That is, he is putting hired labor "in its place" as pertinent or valid for one historical period only. There is nothing intrinsically valid about it for all time, in other words; there is nothing about it which makes it "correct" or useful as a matter of basic principles; and especially, there is nothing within the nature of mankind, society, or civilization which makes it a perennial economic institution. Hired labor is a product of the evolving cycles of history, a feature of one cycle only (the current one), and thus can be displaced. Its appearance on the scene was not "natural," intrinsic, or fundamental, but rather incidental. Thus it could (as Marx desired) pass away.

Marx's dialectical history thus serves him as a standard by which to pass judgment on various economic elements – a standard different from more natural or intuitive standards. Rather than asking whether the hiring of labor is good or useful for an economy, or equitable in its basic essentials, or deeply rooted in human nature, he asks whether it is eternal, natural, or logically necessary. He puts the question within a perspective of the inexorable, pre-determined cycles which he claims to perceive in history. His theory replaces all humanistic or human-values-oriented judgments with an artificial, pseudo-scientific, and ineluctable one. As so often happens in Marx, the result makes no intuitive sense from a human or common-sense perspective but is supposedly "proven" from his pseudo-scientific perspective.

The essence of capitalism

Marx now goes on to show what is the central, defining feature of capitalism, distinguishing that feature from various others, within a historical perspective:

> So, too, the economical categories already discussed by us, bear the stamp of history. Definite historical conditions are necessary that a product may become a commodity. It must not be produced as the immediate means of subsistence of the producer himself. Had we gone further, and inquired under what circumstances all, or even the majority of products take the form of commodities, we should have found that this can only happen with production of a very specific kind, capitalist production. Such an inquiry, however, would have been foreign to the analysis of commodities. Production and circulation of commodities can take place, although the great mass of the

objects produced are intended for the immediate requirements of their producers, are not turned into commodities, and consequently social production is not yet by a long way dominated in its length and breadth by exchange-value. The appearance of products as commodities presupposed such a development of the social division of labor, that the separation of use-value from exchange-value, a separation which first begins with barter, must already have been completed. But such a degree of development is common to many forms of society, which in other respects present the most varying historical features.

We might paraphrase the beginning of this passage as, "Like hired labor, other aspects of economics already discussed are also the result of past historical development." Unlike those others, however (Marx will show), hired labor is the defining characteristic of capitalism, and its appearance marks the advent of true capital.

As to commodities themselves, they arise through a process of historical development, giving rise to certain historical conditions: the product "must not be produced as the immediate means of subsistence of the producer himself." Actually, this is nothing but Marx's definition of a commodity – an item produced for sale, not for use by the producer. But presumably it was a matter of some time and thus a certain process of historical development before market goods appeared human history, Marx does not list any specific conditions for the appearance of the phenomenon (conditions like a certain amount of complexity in society, a certain degree of advances in productive methods so that division of labor could appear, and so on). But we may assume there were "definite historical conditions." Like just about every other phenomenon in human society, market goods "bear the stamp of history." (Whether they bear the stamp of his neatly-divided, predetermined epochs is another question.)

Marx continues with an even less informative, or more tautological statement: the possibility that for "all, or even the majority" of products to be commodities, or market goods, "can only happen with. . . capitalist production," or a market economy. That is almost by definition – if all or most goods are produced by capitalists for the market, then that is *ipso facto* a market economy. We might quibble with Marx's characterization of this as "a very specific kind" of economy or production, however. Again and again, Marx seeks to set capitalism off against various other supposed types of economies, as one choice among many, and as an arbitrary set of arrangements as opposed to many alternatives. But on the contrary, capitalism might be called not a specific type of economy, but a universal type, or a general type, or perhaps even the only truly *economic* type. Capitalism is "grass-roots" economics, or democratic economics, wherein people are free to come to their own economic arrangements by free will and mutual consent. It is economics of a different order from state-controlled economics on the one hand and primitive, economy-less societies on the other.

(We note in passing Marx's weird, "object-oriented" style of writing. He focuses the terms of his discussion minutely on things, and removes people from the picture as the active agent. For example, certain conditions are necessary "that a product may become a commodity"; society is not yet "dominated. . .by exchange-value"; use-value "becomes separated" from exchange-value. The human intermediary disappears in such expressions, where objects are what perform actions, develop, affect society, etc. It would be more reasonable to speak of the above matters in terms of trade; that is, rather than saying a product spontaneously "becomes" a commodity, we can say that economic agents (entrepreneurs) produce goods for the market; rather than being dominated by exchange value (a thing), we can say society is characterized by trade or market economics (a human activity); and rather than speaking of use-value becoming separated from exchange value (two things that spontaneously drift apart), we can speak in terms of the rise of exchange or trade. (And in any event, exchange value doesn't become *separated* from use value, it is added to it.)

But the use of impersonal terminology and the passive voice gives a distorted picture of economics; it presents it as a complex of economic objects, taking actions and entering into relationships spontaneously. It eliminates the role of people, along with their economic nature and motivations. Marx's framework of statements like "products take the form of commodities" and "use-value becomes separated from exchange value" is hopelessly inadequate for presenting a realistic picture of economic realities. It is however appropriate that Marx, the great materialist, writes in such an object-oriented manner; his focus is always on things.)

Marx continues, showing that unlike the sale of labor, commodities can exist in other than fully capitalistic societies. "Production and circulation of commodities can take place" on a small scale within societies not otherwise capitalistic. That is, "such a degree of development is common to many forms of society, which in other respects present the most varying historical features." That is no doubt true, and the production of goods for sale has occurred in the interstices and odd corners of the most varied societies, from ancient patriarchal empires through feudal society and on up.

He continues:

> On the other hand, if we consider money, its existence implies a definite stage in the exchange of commodities. The particular functions of money which it performs, either as the mere equivalent of commodities, or as means of circulation, or means of payment, as hoard or as universal money, point, according to the extent and rela-

tive preponderance of the one function or the other, to very different stages in the process of social production. Yet we know by experience that a circulation of commodities relatively primitive, suffices for the production of all these forms.

The gist of this passage seems to be that money, like commodities, "bears the stamp of history" but yet is not the defining element of capitalism.

At any rate the existence of money, like that of commodities, "implies a definite stage in the exchange of commodities." As to "the particular functions of money" which Marx enumerates, it would take Marx himself to explain the meaning of all of them and to elucidate how they differ from one another; though some of them, like "universal money," are more obscure than others. Marx evidently considers each of them as distinctly identifiable and separable from the others, and he evidently thinks it possible to distinguish the functioning of one from the others in actual practice. By such dissection it is possible to determine "the relative preponderance of the one function or the other," that is, the preponderance of each corresponding to a different stage.

A discussion of these various functions would be out of place here (or perhaps better, it would be "foreign to the analysis" at this point). But it appears that Marx's ideas about money are a microcosm of his entire thought, a scientism in miniature; there are the neatly divided, artificially distinct categories for the functions of money, definitely related to facets of another phenomenon (in this case the various stages in economic development). It is all too orderly, precise, well-defined and regular to correspond to reality.

We need not consider now the extent and relative preponderance of the various functions. Suffice it to say that "we know by experience that a circulation of commodities relatively primitive, suffices for the production of all these forms" – "forms" being Marx's all-purpose occlusive term. To paraphrase, we might say that money was developed a long time ago, and has been a common feature of economies for eons; so that all the functions of money have in some degree or other been fulfilled for centuries, even in relatively primitive societies.

This is indeed true of money, and commodities, and despite what Marx says, labor also. Whenever there has been a degree of freedom in any civilization for free economic interaction, all the elements of free exchange have been present; and there is no reason to suppose the hiring of labor to have been a special case any different from the above-named elements.

Of course, later in his text Marx will identify the exploiting of labor-power as the sole source of the capitalist's wealth; it is the key to his ability to exist and the crux of the injustice he inflicts on the exploited worker. Thus Marx seeks to identify hired labor as the defining characteristic of capitalism and as unique to it; in this way capitalism can be shown to be evil at its core, and uniquely evil. But it is doubtful whether economic historians could discern in the bare facts of history the marked distinction between hired labor and other elements of free enterprise that Marx describes.

Marx has shown that the "circulation of commodities" and the use of money can exist in various degrees in "many forms of society," even where they are not dominant and the society could not be called capitalist. But, he continues,

> Otherwise with capital. The historical conditions of its existence are by no means given with the mere circulation of money and commodities. It can spring into life, only when the owner of the means of production and subsistence meets in the market with the free labourer selling his labour-power. And this one historical condition comprises a world's history. Capital therefore, announces from its first appearance a new epoch in the process of social production.

Marx's reasoning here is basically a process of deducing the "historical conditions necessary" for this or that economic element, constructing philosophical arguments from thin air. It might have been more appropriate if he had instead examined history and told us whether the various elements had arrived together.

As it is, he in effect tells us first that the existence of money and commodities is not logically equivalent to or logically sufficient for the existence of hired labor. That may or may not be true, but it is not really the point. It may be that the general conditions that allow money and commodities to develop, also allow the hiring of labor to occur. That is, though the particulars he compares may not be equivalent (hired labor is not identical to money and commodities), the underlying "generalities," or general conditions, may be the same.

For a start, we could say that if "the mere circulation of money and commodities" doesn't obviously or logically satisfy the necessary conditions for hired labor, it is certainly a good start. If there is money and there are privately-owned commodities (which means privately-*produced* commodities), chances are good that there will be privately-employed laborers. Certainly there are people who could hire them, and money to pay them with.

Actually, it might be helpful to restate the question we're investigating here. The more interesting question would be, whether hired labor has existed in societies which could not be considered capitalist – Egypt of the Pharaohs, the Roman empire, and other societies; that is, whether hired labor could exist in societies "not yet by a long way dominated" by hired labor.

Marx however seems to phrase the question in much narrower terms; he is apparently asking whether "a circulation of commodities [by means of money] relatively primitive, suffices" for the existence of hired labor.

His answer is no; and it is indeed possible to imagine situations where money and commodities exist, but not hired labor. Feudal conditions might be envisioned where feudal lords engaged in trade with the commodities produced on their estates, but where there were no wage laborers, only serfs. That is not to say there actually were no wage laborers during feudal times, simultaneously with money and commodities; it is only saying that, logically speaking, money and commodities don't automatically imply hired labor.

Yet historically speaking (and addressing the broader question), hired labor has existed in some degree in "many forms of society," from the dawn of history – not just in modern industrial capitalism. But again, that is a matter of historical inquiry, too complicated for consideration here.

A different paradigm

Actually, an analysis other than Marx's has already explained the phenomena under consideration quite insightfully, in terms of two categories different from Marx's own.

Hired labor could be categorized quite perceptively in the terms introduced by historian Sir Henry Maine: as part of the change from status to contract. Both in ancient patriarchal societies and during feudal times, the great mass of participants in production process such as a matter of status: they were born into slavery or serfdom, and their function as well as their position in society was fixed from birth. On the other hand, the proletarian of today isn't born into a particular job, or to a particular master. He must find an employer as a matter of mutual agreement and is not bound by law to a given role.

Thus the phenomenon of hired labor is indeed not only distinct from the phenomena of money and market commodities, it can also be seen to be of a distinct *category* or class of phenomena. However, it is not hard to see that the two categories may be closely aligned, and have been so in history, and that events leading to the rise of one might be conducive to the rise of the other.

After all, Marx says capital, which he presumes is identical with hired labor, "can spring into life, only when the owner of the means of production and subsistence meets in the market with the free labourer selling his labour-power." This is pretty much tautological, stating just that hired labor can exist only when someone free to sell his labor meets with someone in a position to buy it. Thus the requirements for the existence of hired labor include the existence of money for paying the laborer, and commodities produced by someone who has need of laborers. And if there are free entrepreneurs, not bound to any birth-determined social status, there are likely also to be free laborers. The two are not as disparate as Marx seems to think.

As to the rise of capital and/or hired labor, Marx concludes, "And this one historical condition comprises a world's history. Capital, therefore, announces from its first appearance a new epoch in the process of social production."

It may be a new epoch, but its seeds have been discernible in previous epochs. That is to say, capitalism cannot be considered another epoch just like preceding epochs; it is in some sense more valid or more natural than the others. It can be termed "normal economics," economics as permitted to function by its own internal rules, on a grassroots or individual level. It is economics functioning in its own sphere, with its role not appropriated by central authority.

In this sense capitalism could arguably be compared to democracy; the rise of democratic rule could be termed a new epoch, replacing hereditary rule based on "divine right." And yet in some sense democratic rule could be considered not just another epoch like preceding ones, but a more intrinsically valid system, more in keeping with the internal principles of the realm of human existence involved. And like capitalism, it was foreshadowed in societies centuries before it achieved complete development. And in these terms too modern-day communism can be seen not as a new epoch but as a return to previous social mechanisms: as in patriarchal societies, the communist state owns all property, and the communist subject is born into a status of servitude at the state's pleasure.

So rather than a pre-determined series of disparate social epochs, history shows various social arrangements, subject to human control, occurring in various degrees simultaneously with one another and recurring in different eras under different names and theoretical rationales.

Recapitulation

To recapitulate, then: Marx is attempting to portray wage labor as a unique phenomenon, different from all other features of capitalist economies. Unlike such elements as money and market commodities, wage labor only appeared in modern times. For him this is a logically necessary assertion; for capitalism is to him almost identical with wage labor, since capitalism can only exist by the exploitation of unpaid "surplus value" from the laborers. Thus capitalism logically requires wage labor, and when wage labor appeared historically it necessarily meant the appearance of capitalism.

However, this attempt to reduce capitalism to wage labor and to isolate wage labor to the modern era fails. Wage labor, like all other aspects of free economic interaction, has found room to function in societies throughout history.

Just to give a few sketchy examples: in the Roman Empire, slavery "reached substantial proportions" at about 150 BC, but afterwards "we find slaves being commonly replaced by free wage-earners on the imperial estates. . . Free workmen included artisans operating on their own, and also wage-earners employed by city firms, by owners of large estates, and by mining undertakings." In the ancient Greek world "even a slave could often have an existence very similar to that of the free workman, paying a rent to his patron and living. . . on the proceeds of his work." And, "as far as we can tell the story was much the same in the Etruscan and Carthaginian worlds. . ." (all quotes are from *The Ancient World*).

Going even further back, we learn that "Tiumenev cites data according to which hired workers constituted from 5 to 20 percent of the work force" of ancient Sumeria. Temple employees were paid by one of two methods, "allowances in kind and the granting of land plots for 'sustenance'." [3]

Wage labor also existed during the Middle Ages, after the great retrograde step that occurred with the breaking up of society at the fall of the Roman Empire. The author of *The Wheels of Commerce* addresses the subject, in words reminiscent of Marx's:

It is perfectly clear however that the labour market. . . was not a creation of the industrial era. The labour market was the market upon which a man offered himself, without any of his traditional means of production, if he had ever had any: a piece of land, a loom, a horse or cart. All he had to offer was his arm or hand, his "labour" in other words. . . The phenomenon can be seen with unusual clarity in the case of the miners of Central Europe. Having long been independent artisans, working in small groups, they were obliged in the fifteenth and sixteenth century to put themselves under the control of the merchants who alone could provide the considerable investment required. . . and they became wage-earners. . . In the West, the transition to wage-earning, an irreversible phenomenon here, often happened quite early and, above all, more frequently than is usually supposed. [4]

The author gives various examples:

From the thirteenth century, the Place de Greve in Paris and the nearby Place "Juree" by Saint-Paul-des-Champs. . . were the usual places for hiring labour. . .

Between 1253 and 1379, documents prove that there were wage-earners in the Portuguese countryside. . .

[In the late 1300's, at Auxerre in Burgundy] every day in summer, day-labourers and employers would meet on one of the town's squares at sunrise – the employers often being represented by a sort of foreman, the *closier*. This is one of the earliest labour markets of which we have *concrete* evidence.[5]

That last example sounds much like the daily labor "shape-up" once practiced among such day-laborers as dock workers, or construction laborers gathering in store parking lots in the morning to be hired for the day. The practice was known as long ago as Biblical times – a similar labor market is spoken of in the parable in Matthew 20.

Thus wage labor does not appear as unique to modern industrial capitalism. It has appeared, along with other elements of market economics, wherever arrangements based on free mutual agreement have been allowed any sway.

In fact the dominance of capitalistic phenomena like money, market commodities, and wage labor, along with capitalism itself, probably should not be considered as primary elements. They are secondary; the "historical conditions" necessary for them were such things as the separation of the economic from the political, and social arrangements based on contract rather than on status. It is arguable that the rise of nation-states and democratic rule are the primary factors, which freed up and gave reign to the underlying desire of people to engage in free economic interaction. It is in terms of these political developments and the consequent expression of a latent economic nature that the history of capitalism could best be analyzed.

NOTES – Chapter 5

1 Melloan, George, "Will East Germans Really Say Goodbye To All That?" *Wall Street Journal*, March 12, 1990.

2 Quoted in Tyrmand, Leopold, *The Rosa Luxemburg Contraceptives Cooperative; a Primer on Communist Civilization,* New York, Macmillan, 1972, p. 157.

3 Shafarevich, I. R., *The Socialist Phenomenon,* New York, Harper & Row, 1980, p.158.

4 Braudel, Fernand. *Civilization and Capitalism, 15th-18th century,* Berkeley, University of California Press, 1992, *vol. 2,* p.52.

5 ibid., p.52.

6. THE VALUE OF LABOR-POWER

Moving on to the topic of the value of labor-power, Marx says (Part II, Chapter VI),

> We must now examine more closely this peculiar commodity, labour-power. Like all others it has a value. How is that value determined?

Let's stop there and anticipate Marx in a couple of ways. We might try to extrapolate from what he has said so far, in order to deduce for ourselves what determines the value of labor-power before we look at his answer. Since he is constructing a syllogistic system, we should be able to apply logic to his theory and carry it forward ourselves to the correct conclusions.

We can go further, still without peeking at the answer, by including Marx's next statement: "The value of labour-power is determined, as in the case of every other commodity, by the labour-time necessary for the production. . . of this special article."

Extrapolating Marx's concept of what "determines" value

Marx's now addresses the task of telling us what determines value. As he has previously stated, the value of anything is determined by "the quantity of. . . the labour, contained in the article." Starting from the theorems and definitions which constitute his theory so far, he will extend the logic by deducing what determines value.

But first, using our own powers of reasoning, can we figure out how much labor is contained in a day's labor-power? Can we deduce how much labor it takes to produce a day's labor-power?

Well, we know that labor-power is the ability to perform labor, and in the most direct sense of this term, labor doesn't create labor-power at all; rather, labor drains or exhausts one's labor-power. If labor-power means physical strength, stamina and "energy," then the longer and harder we work, the more tired we become and the less current capacity to labor we have left.

Labor thus diminishes one's present ability to labor, rather than increasing it. To suggest a parallel from physics, we can say that kinetic energy is the consumption or use of potential energy; that is, potential energy is the capacity to perform work, and kinetic energy is work itself. If we consume potential energy, say the energy stored in a battery, by setting that energy to work, we gain kinetic energy. But as we do so, our reserve of potential energy, our "the capacity to do work," becomes smaller – the battery runs down. That is, labor, in the sense of the exercise or use of potential energy, doesn't produce "labor-power" – it consumes it. For our answer, we need to know what produced that stored ability to labor.

Likewise, labor is our present, economic sense doesn't produce the ability to labor; it consumes it. What we need, after a session of hard work, is such things as rest, nourishment, and relaxation, to restore our stamina and ability to work. These things produce, or restore or "reproduce," the ability to labor – labor itself doesn't.

As Marx himself expresses it, "Labour-power, however, becomes a reality only by its exercise; it sets itself in action only by working. But thereby a definite quantity of human muscle, nerve, brain, &c., is wasted, and these require to be restored. . . If the owner of labour-power works to-day, to-morrow he must again be able to repeat the same process in the same conditions as regards health and strength." Labor saps one's ability to labor further; it doesn't increase it.

So if we use this sense of the term labor-power, meaning strength, stamina, etc., there is no answer to the question of how much labor is required for producing labor-power. No amount of labor produces labor-power, but just the reverse; it drains it. Rest, nourishment, and all the various elements necessary for health and vigor, are what produce labor-power.

Thus again, when we use this sense of the term labor-power, we see that Marx's analysis, wherein the capitalist buys and consumes labor-power rather than employing labor, is hopelessly muddled, even by the terms of his own analysis. His analysis, his paradigm, is that of material goods, commodities, being produced by the application of a definite amount of labor, which labor is embodied or deposited within the commodities as their value. "[The] bodies of commodities, are combinations of two elements – matter and labour." If something is not material, i.e. doesn't *have* a body, this paradigm doesn't apply. An immaterial or intangible "labor-power" cannot have value, that is to say its value cannot be determined using Marx's theory or his paradigm as originally expressed. The idea that the capitalist employs labor, rather than buying labor-power, fits both the facts and Marx's paradigm better in this instance.

There are other possible viewpoints on the question, however, depending on which formulation of the definition of value we use. If we consider value as the "amount of labor contained" by the commodity, we might proceed by asking: How much labor is "contained" (in some sense) in a day's labor-power? The obvious response to that would be, twelve hours (the length of the working day) – because that is the only amount of labor that we can readily imagine as being "contained" in a working day. However, that is an incorrect deduction; that is, it is a wrong guess as to Marx's answer. For we must remember, what is meant by the labor "contained" by an item is the labor necessary for its production. We would be looking for a certain amount of labor deposited in "a day's labor-power" prior to its existence, while the labor-power is in the process of being created – not while it is being used. Thus when we try to decide how much labor is contained in a day's labor-power, we should look for something other than the labor resulting from the exercise of the day's labor-power. It would seem logical that the two amounts should be the same, however, sort of on the analogy of potential and kinetic energy: what we put into an object as potential "ability to do work" should be what we get back in the form of kinetic work. This is only rough, intuitive logic however (and Marx stood for nothing if not the principle that intuitive understandings are generally wrong).

The real difficulty is that Marx's whole concept of labor-power, of the capitalist buying a day's labor-power which is an object or commodity in its own right, and of labor as the consumption of that already-purchased item, is metaphysically and philosophically incoherent and bears no resemblance to the real world. When we reason in terms of our knowledge of real-world economics, we diverge from Marx's theory.

Extrapolating (again)

If we don't consider the value of a day's labor-power to be simply the length of the working day, we can arrive at a different analysis of the labor required to produce labor-power. That is, we can think of labor-power, not in the sense of the stamina and strength required to do labor in a purely physical sense, but as the skill, knowledge and experience required to do a job in a technical or economic sense. In this sense labor-power is a result of practice and experience, and thus in a sense a result of labor. As Marx puts it:

> In order to modify the human organism, so that it may acquire skill and handiness in a given branch of industry, and become labour-power of a special kind, a special education or training is requisite, and this, on its part, costs an equivalent in commodities of a greater or less amount. This amount varies according to the more or less complicated character of the labour-power.

In this sense the labor required for producing labor-power basically includes everything the worker does up to a certain point in his life. We might envision a certain level of proficiency or skill, and consider the labor required to produce "capacity to labor" to be all the labor necessary to bring the worker up to that pitch of proficiency. For instance, if we take journeyman abilities as the standard or acceptable level of skill, as the level yielding work of a 100%-acceptable quality (and journeyman is a good approximation, being halfway between apprentice and master), then we would want to find out how much work, or practice or experience, is needed in sum total to bring the worker to a journeyman's level of skill.

In other words, we should note these points: the labor necessary for producing "capacity to labor" is necessary as practice or the development of a degree of skill; it is in that sense that the labor produces the ability to do work, and not in the "normal" sense of labor producing a product on an assembly line.

Moreover, the development of a skill is a cumulative process. For instance, a violinist doesn't play the most demanding works from the first moment he picks up a bow. It's not a matter of the beginner playing something slowly and badly, while a master plays it quickly and well. For practical purposes and for purposes of employment, the beginner can't play it at all. In the same way, a beginning stone mason perhaps wouldn't be trusted to carve gargoyles on ornamental embellishments. The point is, in some cases it's an all-or-nothing matter: a certain level of skill has to be present, or the worker can't do the job at all. Before an apprentice brain surgeon performs his first operation, there has to be present a level of skill sufficient to assure the patient survives. Thus all the work necessary to develop the required level of skill, must somehow be pro-rated over the productive life of such a worker, to find out how much of the preliminary practice is attributable or accountable to each day's actual "labor-power."

The situation is complicated by the fact that some of the "practice" labor is also productive, so that certain days of labor early in the worker's life are not only labor embodied in producing future capacity to labor (more skillfully), they are productive in their own right. Thus some of the labor must be pro-rated at a lesser degree to producing "capacity to labor" at the lower degree of skill. The situation becomes very complicated, or would if anybody ever actually tried to base any real-world calculations on it.

In any event, our paradigm might be something like this: add up all the actual work, job training and experience up to the point where our laborer has the standard acceptable level of skill. (We'll include only actual labor for now, not education, to simplify things.) Divide this total by the number of days in the worker's entire working life beyond the point where he has attained that degree of skill. This figure is then the pro-rated amount of labor previously embodied in creating the ability to labor in a journeyman laborer.

To this quantity add, say, two hours of each day's labor by a journeyman or master laborer, on a continuing basis, as necessary to maintain or "reproduce" the ability to labor – for some continuing practice is necessary for perpetuating the laborer's skill, and we must put that amount of each day's labor in the account books under "maintaining of labor-power." (This gives us some basis for determining the value of labor done at a master's degree of skill.)

This entire "scenario" or conceptual picture is hypothetical, merely an extrapolation from Marx's text but possibly a reasonable approach to interpreting Marx's theory in concrete, numerical terms. Of course, it would be an accounting nightmare to try to determine what youthful activities contributed to future "capacity to labor" and at what rates. Nevertheless, the above is one answer we might arrive at, extrapolating from what we have read of his theory so far. It is an answer in terms of "how much labor is embodied in producing a day's capacity to labor." And one of its notable features is that it measures labor; it avoids a tendency of Marx's analysis to define value by adding up the *commodities* necessary to produce some entity, whether it be the capacity to labor or the laborers themselves.

The preceding might be a reasonable answer to the value of labor-power, in the light of what we've been given so far. That value would be impossible to calculate numerically; but in any event it is not the answer Marx gives, so again we may look at other possibilities. (Nor is it the real-world answer, we might add.) So while consistent with Marx's analysis so far, it is unsatisfactory, practically speaking. We will therefore discard it, much as Marx dismisses or omits it, and will go on to consider other possibilities. But we can keep it in mind, and see if the answer Marx actually gives is as much in accord with previous portions of his theory as our exposition is.

Labor and commodities, commodities and labor

Suppose we loosen our requirements in looking for the value of labor-power. If we drop Marx's stipulation that value is only labor – that is, if we don't try to extend Marx's definition of the value of ordinary commodities to labor-power – we can arrive at a fairly reasonable theory of the value of labor-power, or at least of the laborer's contribution to the production process.

As we have noted, attempting to express the value of labor, or labor-power, or (to use a neutral term) the laborer's efforts, as an amount of "embodied labor," leads to "absurd tautologies." We can avoid that pitfall by taking a sort of reciprocal or complementary approach, defining the value of commodities as an amount of labor, and the value of labor as an amount of commodities. (What amount, we will investigate later.)

That is, whereas the value of commodities is defined as an amount of labor, the value of labor (or labor-power) may be defined as an amount of commodities. Although this is also in a sense circular reasoning, it is at least a circle with two distinct halves – it avoids the self-defeating logic or "absurd tautology" of trying to find the amount of labor required to produce labor.

To be more specific about this approach, the value of a day's labor (-power) could have been defined with some plausibility as the amount of goods produced by a day's labor (an amount measured in some manner, whether by the money price, or the number of units produced, or whatever). Thus while the value of one produced item is the amount of labor embodied in it, the value (to the capitalist) of a laborer's daily efforts could be said to equal the number of items produced, which items the entrepreneur thus has available to sell as a result of that labor.

To repeat, when we apply this method to value, we say the value of commodities is an amount of labor, and the value of labor (-power) is an amount of commodities. We already have the value of commodities defined as the amount of labor required to produce them. For labor, or labor-power, we could define the value as the amount of commodities produced by the day's labor.

This has a couple of immediate advantages to recommend it. For one, it has a certain amount of intuitive credibility. It seems sensible that the value of a laborer's efforts, to the employer, could roughly be judged by the amount of commodities those efforts produce for the employer. That is, at the end of the day, how much "product" (measured by money value or in some other terms) does the capitalist have to sell as a result of the laborer's work? This is a good gauge of how much the capitalist can afford to pay the laborer – that is, a good gauge of the value of the laborer's efforts.

Another merit is that, using this standard of value, a rough equality is enforced between the theoretical value of the laborer's work and the value of the goods produced; and that rough equality is actually present in real life. For example, if one laborer produces commodities with a "value added" of $100 a day – by producing goods the capitalist can sell for $100 profit – then $100 is a good base figure which can serve as a standard for the wages that can be paid. The laborer may not get it all – the capitalist has to get his profit out of the "value added"; but the $100 serves as a starting point for judging what the wage could be and how fair the actual wage is.

Similarly, on a more fundamental level, there is an equality between the labor performed in a working day and the value of the commodities produced in a working day. For instance, if the working day is twelve hours long, then typically the commodities produced in a working day will have a "value" or embodied labor of twelve hours of labor; and the laborer's wages in money should be such as to enable him to purchase a high proportion of the produced goods (i.e., of their "value added").

Of course, using this dual definition there would be problems in establishing money values for both wages and commodities. We know the money amount of the wages should nearly equal the value-added, in money, of the commodities; but starting from a blank slate the actual figures could be chosen arbitrarily; it is sort of a "chicken-or-the-egg" problem. Thus it is hard to know how the particular levels of money wages and money prices of goods came about. Using only the dual definitions, we cannot determine how wage and price levels were established; but we can tell if they are nearly in accord. And then too, the real world doesn't begin with a blank slate – prices evolve and arise over time, through the continuing course of history and the normal process of "higgling and bargaining," applied to wages this time.

As Smith says (*Wealth of Nations*, Book I, Chapter VII):

> There is in every society or neighborhood an ordinary or average rate both of wages and profit in every different employment of labour and stock. This rate is naturally regulated. . .partly by the general circumstances of the society, their riches or poverty, their advancing, stationary, or declining condition; and partly by the particular nature of each employment.

> Wages being highest when this expence is lowest, it seems evident that they are not regulated by what is necessary for this expence; but by the quantity and supposed value of the work.

> The price of labour, it must be observed, cannot be ascertained very accurately anywhere, different prices being often paid at the same place and for the same sort of labour. . .Where wages are not regulated by law, all that we can pretend to determine is, what are the most usual; and experience seems to show that law can never regulate them properly, though it has often pretended to do so.

Evidence for the dual definition

One strong point in favor of this reciprocal-definition system can be drawn from its logical implications, namely: the more advanced the production methods are – that is the greater the productivity of the methods of production – then the greater should be the wages. This theoretical result may be deduced from the dual definitions of value, and it is indeed valid – indeed it is the fundamental determiner of "standard of living."

The reciprocal approach has intuitive appeal from several standpoints; a case could be made for its validity in the real world. But it is not the ultimate answer or best answer for what (in the real world) determines the value of a day's labor. It is not, moreover, the answer Marx gives; though, as we will see, his answer to what determines the value of labor-power uses the basic "reciprocal" approach, defining the value of labor-power as an amount of commodities. The specific amount he arrives at, however, is completely different from the one we have outlined above, and in addition Marx does not acknowledge his use of the reciprocal approach or its logic – he pretends he is still using his "embodied labor" standard, while actually deriving the answer by a roundabout approach which boils down to reciprocal definitions.

Evaluating the two systems

The two described approaches to determining the value of labor-power – measuring the amount of training, practice and experience required, or using the reciprocal-definition system – are the only two alternatives that come readily to mind when trying to derive "the amount of labor required to produce labor-power." Neither of these is adequate; neither is what Marx eventually resolves upon. But both answers are derived by applying logic to Marx's text in order to apply his definition of value to the particular phenomenon of labor-power (something Marx himself did not do).

Marx's answer

Let us now pick up Marx's analysis where we left it:

> We must now examine more closely this particular commodity, labour-power. Like all others it has a value. How is that value determined?
>
> The value of labour-power is determined, as in the case of every other commodity, by the labour-time necessary for the production, and consequently also the reproduction, of this special article. So far as it has value, it represents no more than a definite quantity of the average labour* of society incorporated in it. Labour-power exists only as a capacity, or power of the living individual. Its production consequently presupposes his existence. Given the individual, the production of labour-power consists in his reproduction of himself or his maintenance. For his maintenance he requires a given quantity of the means of subsistence. Therefore the labour-time requisite for the production of labour-power reduces itself to that necessary for the production of those means of subsistence; in other words, the value of labour-power is the value of the means of subsistence necessary for the maintenance of the labourer.

---

* I.e., it is the amount of average labor or "homogeneous labor."

Notice that Marx has not explicitly abandoned his theory of value with its requirement that value must be an amount of embodied labor. He purports to still adhere to it, yet for the value of labor-power he advances as his most immediate or proximate answer, an amount of commodities. The particular amount is, "the means of subsistence necessary for the maintenance of the labourer." Of course, as we move further away from labor-power – further down Marx's chain of "necessities" or deductions – we go from the "means of subsistence" to the value (or labor invested in producing) the means of subsistence. But the most proximate answer, the quantity closest to what Marx is trying to evaluate, is the "means of subsistence" – the typical "market basket" of goods which the laborer may be deemed to consume each day. We can with some justification regard that as his actual answer: it is what, he says, is necessary for the production of labor-power.

It will be remembered that Marx's labor theory has accustomed us to consider the value of a commodity as being equal somehow to the labor directly embodied in that commodity. So in the present case Marx has had to do some maneuvering to justify using the labor invested in the market basket of commodities, rather than the labor embodied in labor-power. Marx is not going to tell us how much labor is embodied in producing labor-power, but rather how much labor is embodied in producing the laborer's "means of subsistence." Since that subsistence is in turn necessary for labor-power, he thus feels justified in calling his answer the value of labor-power.

At any rate, we now have the premise that value equals the labor embodied in the laborer's "means of subsistence." Marx will proceed along those lines, seeking to identify the various categories of goods that fall under that heading. But we will first backtrack to examine in more detail the methods by which he succeeded in equating the value of "means of subsistence" to the value of labor-power.

Value of the means of subsistence

Value, we understand, is the labor necessary for producing a particular commodity. That is, the model or paradigm of value is one of a physical product being produced by "average" or homogeneous human labor; this labor is applied to the physical object in question and therefore literally embodies itself within that produced commodity.

(This labor may also be applied to the commodity indirectly. If you're raising beans, you hoe away the weeds from your beans; or you loosen the soil by chopping at it. You don't chop the beans. But the labor can be deemed to be performed "on" the beans, and as a result it is embodied in the beans, not the soil.)

At any rate, to discover the value of labor-power, we have to learn how much labor is embodied in labor-power during the course of its production. However, labor-power doesn't really fit Marx's paradigm, not being a physical entity produced by human labor. There is a physical entity nearby, however. Marx reduces value to, not the labor embodied in producing labor-power, but the labor embodied in producing that innocent by-stander, the "means of subsistence" or typical day's market basket of goods. This switch was necessary, because labor-power is an inappropriate subject for application of Marx's definition of value. And it is unjustified under the terms of Marx's theory and its internal logic so far.

"Consequently the reproduction"

The first issue we have to confront is the logic in that peculiar verbal tic of Marx's, "and consequently also the reproduction" of this special commodity. That is the first time we have seen Marx refer to a commodity as being not merely produced, but "reproduced"; and we would like to have some basis for deciding whether, if value is the labor necessary for production, it indeed follows that it is "consequently" also the labor necessary for "reproduction."

As is so often the case, Marx makes that logical link without giving any justification for it; he insinuates the principle into his text as if it were an obvious conclusion. But in fact we have no justification for it other than Marx's decree. In investigating the concept of the "reproduction" of commodities, we can assume that the term means their "production again" – their production a second time, in some sense. We might think of an apartment or house, which can be renovated or refurbished; or an automobile engine, which can be rebuilt or remanufactured. These might be valid senses in which commodities are "reproduced." In such cases, "reproduction" occurs some time after the initial production, and is done in an effort to restore the commodity, that is to reverse the process of consumption (or wearing-out). For example, a commodity, say an engine, is produced; under normal circumstances it has a certain useful life-expectancy, say 100,000 miles of driving. We could stipulate that the original value (the embodied labor, or the selling price) is consumed or dissipated at a steady, linear rate, so that with 25,000 miles on the engine, it has 75% of its initial value left. We try to restore part of that value by investing or embodying more labor in it – by reboring and relining the cylinders, etc.

Marx's paradigm applies basically unchanged in such cases. More labor is embodied in the commodity, replacing some of the embodied value previously used up. The creation (or "recreation") of value occurs in the same manner as with the originally-exerted labor; it embodies itself in the commodity as value, and the value of the used item increases by the amount of the "reproducing" labor. The process of "reproduction" of commodities, in this sense, is quite similar to the process of mere production; remaking an article is in its essence like making it in the first place. Perhaps for this reason, Marx has not found it necessary to discuss the "reproduction" of pedestrian physical objects in such cases as the repairing of vehicles, mending of clothing, repairing and refurbishing of homes, and so on. No special category has had to be invented for them.

Alternative meanings of "reproduction"

To "reproduce" a commodity could mean one of two or three things, therefore. The first thing that comes to mind, when we speak of the "reproduction" of commodities, is: we produce one, and then we produce another one. This is the most obvious sense of the term, and corresponds most closely with something happening in the real world.

Alternatively, we might think that "reproduction of commodities" is an esoteric term for the refurbishing, rebuilding, reconditioning and so on of commodities. In this sense of the word, reproduction means we produce a commodity, and then at some point in its lifetime we put more work into it, reproducing what we have already produced to partially reverse the wearing-out process.

What we most likely do *not* mean by the term, is that we produce a commodity (labor-power); then *use it up* ("The purchaser of labour-power consumes it by setting the seller of it to work"); and then *reproduce* the self-same labor-power, that is, produce it again from scratch the next day, but so it is the very same labor-power, the same commodity, not a new one or a copy of the original. That is the picture that emerges from Marx's description, and it is bizarre.

Reality check

The reason it is bizarre, of course, is that labor-power, the capacity to do labor, is an attribute of a person; that is, it is a property of an object, not an object or entity in its own right. Marx's definition of the value of commodities originally applied to physical goods and the labor required to produce them — not to disembodied attributes of things or people. That is why Marx introduces his sophistical usage of the word "reproduction" — in order to drag labor-power under the aegis of the category of commodities, so he can apply his definition of the value of commodities to it.

His usage of "reproduction" is just a beginning sophistry, the first in a series of specious logical inferences which Marx applies to labor-power. It legitimizes his categorization of labor-power as a commodity, i.e., it further preserves the appearance that labor-power is a commodity like others, whose value is fixed by the labor required to produce or reproduce them. Of course, labor-power (an attribute) is consumed or depleted every day and must be restored or "reproduced." So Marx will supply a special explanation of how the value of this special commodity is determined, revolving around this special method of production, or daily depletion and renewal, called "reproduction."

"So far as it has value, it represents no more than a definite quantity of the average [i.e., homogenous] labour of society incorporated in it." This is just a restatement of his definition of value; we recognize in "the average labour of society" that same homogeneous, social labor which is value. It has nothing to do with market value – it is helpful to remember how far we have diverged from reality.

Deductions and redefinitions

> *If all people were eliminated from the earth, $.76 of every dollar could be saved.*
> – Cully Abrell and John Thompson, *Moses May Have Been An Apache* [2]

Now we will examine a series of deductions or redefinitions which Marx uses to arrive at his desired conclusion about the value of labor-power.

"Labour-power exists only as a capacity, or power of the living individual. Its production consequently presupposes his existence." That's true – you can't have an attribute of an object without having the object itself. You can't have a disembodied characteristic, whether mass or weight or volume, without an object which possesses those properties. This again points up the fact that Marx's labor-power is not a normal commodity.

Naturally labor-power does logically require the existence of the laborer or "living individual"; that individual has to exist as the repository of labor-value. And looking at it from another aspect, the laborer also has to exist in order to produce that "special article," labor – for labor "exists" or is performed only by the laborer or "living individual." Thus from two viewpoints the laborer must exist if labor-power is to exist. If we need a proof of the necessity of the laborer, Marx's reasoning is conclusive.

Of course, it may strike the reader a little odd that Marx has to prove the existence of the laborer. Not only does the production of labor-power presuppose the existence of the laborer; almost everything in Marx's discussion presupposes that. The subject is economics, a human realm; the entire field presupposes the existence of human labor, human society, human economic activity. Such basics don't really have to be restated or proven at this point. The effect is something like one author's facetious pseudo-news item: "If all people were eliminated from the earth, \$.76 of every dollar could be saved."

We all know that if there were no people, there would be no dollars, no economic activity; some things can be taken for granted, without proving them.

At any rate, we can take the existence of the laborer as given. Marx probably only emphasizes this point because it serves as a starting point for a chain of logical necessity: he has anchored this chain at the near end with the logical presupposition that the laborer exists. He now advances the argument:

> Given the individual, the production of labour-power consists in his reproduction of himself or his maintenance. For his maintenance, he requires a given quantity of the means of subsistence. Therefore the labour-time requisite for the production of labour-power reduces itself to that necessary for the production of those means of subsistence; in other words, the value of labour-power is the value of the means of subsistence necessary for the maintenance of the labourer.

Reality check: Marx has managed to prove in just a few paragraphs – to compel by logic, as it were – the value of labor-power to be of a certain magnitude. Again, this is an instance of the principle, Logic can compel the facts. Marx has advanced no factual data to establish a chain of causation or to show what "determines" value in a cause-and-effect sense. He has shown "by a purely deductive argument" what this real-life quantity must equal; he has not shown what real-life factors determine, in a cause-and-effect manner, the market value of labor (-power). This is a superstitious, anti-scientific method.

By a purely formal, logical argument, by words on a page, Marx presumes to authoritatively establish the value of labor-power. Something has to be specious about such a process; for value is a real-world quantity, determined by certain real-world factors. Arguments and logical maneuvers can't authoritatively determine what that real-world magnitude must be. It is a matter of varying factors and considerations and their interaction. Marx's approach is like devising a logical argument proving what a batter will do on any given trip to the plate; pat formulae for such "adventitious" events must be specious.

Thus, Marx's argument, judged purely as a method, is specious. We can say so even before we examine very closely the content of the argument; we know by its form and its overall characteristics that it is fallacious. To put it another way, by "what determines value" Marx means something different from what science means. Marx means what he can *logically equate* to value, based on his theory so far. Science means what *determines* value in actual fact, in a cause-and-effect sense.

Content of the argument

So, Marx has proven that the value of labor-power equals the value of the means of subsistence. Let's look at the path of his argument once again.

First of all, the existence of the laborer is a logical prerequisite of the existence of labor-power. That is, the laborer is necessary for labor-power. This is the first item in Marx's chain of things necessary for the production of labor-power – not labor, or even a commodity, but the laborer himself.

As concerns the laborer, the production of labor-power is equivalent to the upkeep of the laborer and his reproducing himself. That is, the maintenance and reproduction of laborers is necessary for the existence of laborers. This is the second link in the chain.

Maintenance implies "means of subsistence," or the commodities necessary for maintaining human life; a certain quantity of the means of subsistence is necessary for the laborer's maintenance or upkeep or simply, "living." And a certain quantity of labor was necessary for producing those "means of subsistence" – that is, they have a value. This is the third link in the chain.

So let us examine that chain of "necessity," that sequence of things, each necessary for the next, leading ultimately to labor-power. We have a certain amount of means of subsistence being necessary for the laborer's maintenance and reproduction; the laborer's maintenance and reproduction being necessary for a continuing supply (i.e. existence) of laborers; and a continuing supply of laborers being necessary for the production, of labor-power. Expressed graphically, we have:

CHAIN OF NECESSITY

Means of subsistence ➜	Laborer's maintenance ➜	Laborer's existence ➜	Labor-power

A direct line of "necessity" connects the first item in the chain to the last; thus, Marx asserts, because "means of subsistence" is indirectly necessary for the existence of labor-power, the means of subsistence can safely be *equated* to labor-power. Or perhaps more precisely, we can put his argument like this: value is the labor "necessary" for producing an item; and the labor necessary for producing the "means of subsistence" is also necessary (though twice removed logically) for producing labor-power. Therefore by the terms of his definition, the labor necessary for "means of subsistence" is the value of labor-power.

To consider Marx's definition thus is however to forget the entire framework of his definition. Value is the labor actually performed on a commodity, being thus embodied in it during the course of its production. It is the "necessary" amount of labor in that it is the actual amount of labor performed in order to produce the item. It is not the labor connected by a chain of logical inferences or "necessities"; it is the actual labor invested in producing the commodity in question. In our case the commodity is labor-power, not some market basket of "means of subsistence." We need to know *how much labor is invested in producing labor-power*, not "how much labor is invested in producing means of subsistence, which is necessary for the laborer's maintenance, which is necessary for there to be laborers, who are necessary in order for there to be labor-power."

Thus the "labour-time requisite for the production of labour-power" doesn't so much "reduce" itself to the labor necessary for producing the means of subsistence, as *extend* itself to it. It is a stretching of the definition, an added step in the chain of logic — not a reduction or elimination of anything. His phrase "reduces itself" implies logical equivalency — that he is justified in collapsing his three-link chain of necessities into one, removing the middle terms and equating the value of "means of subsistence" to the value of labor-power. He is by no means justified in doing so.

The fact is, Marx's argument is mere hand-waving; it's just rhetorical flourishes and double-talk. He may show that one thing is necessary for another; he may adduce a chain of necessities for the existence of labor-power; but that doesn't justify his declaring one end of the chain equivalent to the other. Many things are necessary in order for labor-power to exist, but that doesn't mean that those things are the value of labor-power.

In other words, it may be said of the laborer that "for his maintenance he requires" many things; and thus many things are necessary in order that labor-power exist. (The existence of the earth itself is necessary in order for there to be labor-power; Marx himself brings up this point later on. Perhaps we should say that the value of labor-power, the labor "necessary" for labor-power includes all the labor exerted in creating the world?)

But when Marx says, "Therefore the labour-time requisite for the production of labour-power reduces itself" to such and such, he is flouting his own definition. His logic is specious; there's no "therefore" to it.

For one thing, there's no reason to stop the chain of necessity where Marx does. If value includes whatever is necessary for a product, we can keep working backwards past the "means of subsistence." A certain amount of labor was necessary for those means of subsistence; labor-power was necessary for that labor; the laborer was necessary for that labor-power; and so on in an infinite regress. If our only standard is what is "necessary" in any sense of the word, and if we seek to establish a chain of necessity, there is no basis for cutting the chain short at any point; we should keep going as long as we see one more thing "necessary" for what we already have. This is the kind of nonsense that results from forgetting what our definition really meant in terms of a paradigm of value; in fact, it is what results from forgetting reality entirely and dealing only in invented categories and logical manipulations.

Marx's whole chain of necessity, with the "this is the house that Jack built" quality of its reasoning, proves nothing about the value of labor-power. The real moral of the whole exercise is that labor-power doesn't readily adapt to being treated the same way as physical commodities, produced by human labor in a normal production process; and likewise that the value of labor-power is not readily adaptable to analysis in terms of Marx's definition and theory of value. Labor-power is not a commodity in the sense of being a physical entity, a material object bought and sold. Marx has introduced it into the discussion to evade the necessity of determining a value of labor; but it brings with it the complications and the added sophistries of Marx's theory of the value of labor power.

The fact is, the capitalist buys (contracts for) labor; labor is what produces the commodities he wants, and labor is what he pays for. Labor-power is strictly a red herring, brought in to distract the reader from the real issue; and the *value* of labor-power is even more so.

By the same token, we could stop the chain of necessity short of where Marx does. Perhaps the subsistence itself could be considered the value of labor-power, rather than going all the way to the value of the subsistence. This of course is the previously-mentioned "reciprocal" view, and we now see that it is more or less the essence of Marx's reasoning, though it is not his rendered conclusion. It is at least as respectable as his view. Since labor-power is not produced by labor, but by food, rest, and all that is included in "means of subsistence," we might just as well call those things themselves the value, and forget about trying to find a quantity of labor to call the value of labor-power.)

Necessary means of subsistence

So far then, we know that the value of labor-power is "the value of the means of subsistence necessary for the maintenance of the labourer." As we set out to look at Marx's exposition of what constitutes these necessary means of subsistence, there are a few questions which we might want to keep in mind.

First, an observation: it is the means of subsistence *necessary* for the laborer which we are concerned with, not the means he actually receives; we can't assume at this point that the two are identical. Roughly speaking, the necessary amount of means of subsistence is the amount required to "keep body and soul together," or at least keep the workman strong enough to work. The question arises, then, of who determines what means of subsistence are necessary for the laborer, as opposed to the means actually received (which may be higher or lower than the necessary means)? By what standard is the amount "necessary" determined?

Furthermore, if the means of subsistence necessary are different from the means actually received, can we assume that only the necessary portion is the value of labor-power? If the amount received is greater than the necessary amount, i.e., greater than the *value*, how does the excess come about? Then again, if the amount received is different from the value, isn't that a contradiction – for doesn't value mean essentially "what is given in exchange for something"?

These complications of the subject mean there are two separate issues: first, what determines the value of labor power, and what determines the necessary amount of means of subsistence; and second, if the two are different, why that is so, and what role the means of subsistence plays in the analysis if it isn't equal to the value of labor-power.

On the other hand, if it turns out that the necessary amount of means of subsistence equals the amount actually received, then we need to know how the two turn out to be equal, or by what standard a certain amount of "means of subsistence" is declared the necessary amount. In such a case, it will become apparent that Marx will have just deferred the essential question one step; he will have declared the value of labor-power to be logically equivalent to the value of the means of subsistence which the laborer receives, but we will still need to know what determines, in a cause-and-effect sense, that amount.

(Note too some contradiction in Marx's aims and assumptions. In the present case, we tend to revert to a real-world viewpoint, where value is defined as "what is given in exchange for a thing." Marx is proceeding based on a different definition, revolving around the necessary embodied homogeneous labor.)

What constitutes the "necessary means"

Marx now sets about elaborating on what is included in the necessary means of subsistence; this exercise will be seen to be nearly synonymous with categorizing the expenditures made by the laborers, i.e., determining what they buy with their pay. We know that:

> . . .the value of the labour-power is the value of the means of
> subsistence necessary for the maintenance of the labourer. Labour-

power however, becomes a reality only by its exercise; it sets itself in action only by working. But thereby a definite quantity of human muscle, nerve, brain, etc., is wasted and these require to be restored. This increased expenditure demands a larger income. If the owner of labour-power works to-day, to-morrow he must again be able to repeat the same process in the same conditions as regards health and strength. His means of subsistence must therefore be sufficient to maintain him in his normal state as a labouring individual.

That is indeed true: to be able to work one requires sustenance and rest. After a period of work there must be a period of rest or recuperation; that is the nature of the expenditure of muscular energy. But the essential failing of Marx's analysis is this: our subject is the value of labor-power, i.e., the amount of labor (value) required to produce labor-power. But what is necessary for the maintaining of "labor-power," i.e., for maintaining a fit and rested, work-ready condition, is not labor but "subsistence" – things like food and rest. Thus although Marx is addressing the topic of the value of labor-power – i.e. the amount of labor necessary for producing labor-power – we are not being shown an amount of labor directly necessary for the production of labor-power, but rather an amount necessary for producing something else, the commodities constituting "subsistence." He equates this by sophistries to the desired answer. Here we can see clearly the shortcomings of Marx's analysis of the value of labor-power.

Another point of interest is this: Marx may claim to tell us what determines the value of labor-power, but he is not telling us what determines the wage level – and isn't that what we really meant by the question? It is one thing for Marx to analyze what things are necessary for the laborer's continued health and fitness to work; we may even agree with his analysis. But the question once again is, How is the wage determined, i.e. what is the mechanism? How does the wage level spontaneously attain a magnitude in accord with Marx's analysis? For presumably, the market spontaneously acting on its own, via the interaction of economic forces, somehow has set the wage level which Marx now analyzes. The market did not wait for his analysis before deciding to function; presumably there must be some spontaneous, market-driven mechanism which causes wage levels to be set, independent of Marx's analysis. We would like to know what this mechanism is.

In other words, Marx may analyze what is necessary for the laborer's "means of subsistence." But that is a *post facto* analysis. Unless he has some theory of a mechanism, telling us how the market wage reached a certain level, he is not really telling us what *determines* the value of labor-power, i.e., what determines wages. We want to know what factors caused wages to be what they are, and the mechanism by which these factors exerted their influence. Absent that explanation, Marx is only dividing the laborers' expenditures into categories; he is telling us what they spend their money for. He is not telling us what determines how much means of subsistence they can buy, i.e., the real amount of their wages.

Note too that the real subject of interest to us is labor, and the value of labor. Marx has to work his way around to that topic by means of an elaborate transition: "Labour-power, however, becomes a reality only by its exercise; it sets itself in action only by working." By this and other means he will make some sort of logical connection between labor-power, his ostensible subject, and labor, the real subject. Labor-power implies labor, he seems to say: thus when we speak of one we can just as easily speak of the other. What he really had to do, however, was to speak of labor-power while meaning labor, because of the impossibility of analyzing the "value of labor." By such means appearances are preserved.

Smithian viewpoint

Of course, in classical economics too the subject of "means of subsistence" is not neglected. It comes into view in *Wealth of Nations*, but again, in a different role and with different emphasis. While addressing a somewhat different issue, Smith adverts to the subject of the need for rest and recuperation after bodily exertion (Book I, Chapter VIII):

> Great labour, either of mind or body, continued for several days together, is in most men naturally followed by a great desire of relaxation, which, if not restrained by force or by some strong necessity, is almost irresistible. It is the call of nature, which requires to be relieved by some indulgence, sometimes of ease only, but sometimes too of dissipation and diversion. If it is not complied with, the consequences are often dangerous, and sometimes fatal. . .

That is, sometimes the laborer needs only rest, and sometimes recreation and amusement (the word "dissipation" having taken on a disreputable connotation since Smith's day). In this respect Smith shows one advantage over Marx, that he recognizes that it is not muscular exertion alone that necessitates recuperation; mental and emotional fatigue also take a toll. In this sense Smith recognizes that human beings are not like work horses, or indeed machines; that there is an element beyond the physical which must be attended to. This is a somewhat different approach from Marx's, though the topic is superficially the same.

Smith refers to another side of the issue by saying, "a man must always live by his work, and his wages must at least be sufficient to maintain him."

Here again the subject is the "maintenance" of the laborer, or his means of subsistence. Smith is describing a sort of lower limit or "bottom line" as regards the laborer's maintenance. Both Smith and Marx address the issue of the absolute rock-bottom price a laborer can afford to take for his wages; we will compare their comments later on.

In fact Smith refers to the subject of the laborer's subsistence even more directly, making a statement almost like Marx's:

> The real recompense of labour, the real quantity of the necessaries and conveniencies of life which it can procure to the labourer, has, during the course of the present century, increased. . .

Smith's approach comes from the opposite tack from Marx's (as usual). His subject is, What determines the real wage? The quantity of "necessaries and conveniencies" doesn't determine what the wage will be; but rather, once the laborer is paid, the amount of "subsistence" his wage will buy is the real measure of the value of the wage (though not, as in Marx, the determiner of that value). Smith is saying, the real standard for determining if a laborer is well-paid or badly paid is not a money figure, but how much goods he can buy with his wage – i.e., the laborer's standard of living. This is the reverse of saying the laborer's standard of living determines how much he will be paid.

That Smith's is a different and much more complicated analyses than Marx's is indicated in some degree by such comments of Smith's as this:

> What are the common wages of labour, depends every where
> upon the contract usually made between those two parties [*the*
> *"master" and the workmen*], whose interests are by no means to same.

That is, Smith begins with a recognition of the contractual element in the determination of wages – the fact that they are fixed as a result of the interaction of people, that they are determined by events, namely the interactions in the bargaining process or the "clash of contradictory interests" of bosses and workers. Wages are not, in other words, determined by definitions or the *a priori*, intrinsic logic of a theoretical system, as Marx would have it.

Again we see a clue to an alternative definition for the value of labor-power which Marx could have chosen, in Smith's reference to the quantity of goods the wage will buy. In Smith's analysis the quantity of "means of subsistence" purchasable with the wage serves as a measure of the true value of the wage. Starting from a knowledge of the money amount of the wage, we can calculate how much "means of subsistence" a wage will buy, or what a typical "market basket" might be. The money wage, and the general price level, together determine how much goods the wage will buy. (Marx's approach, saying that how much goods the wage will buy determines, rather than measures, the value of labor, is circular reasoning. *)

In any event, Marx too could have modeled his theory along those lines; he could have (as, tacitly, he did) defined the value of goods as their embodied labor, and the value of labor as some quantity of goods — not the labor invested in those goods, but the goods themselves. He could have used the goods producible by a day's labor, or the goods purchasable with a day's wage, or some other quantity of goods as the value of a day's labor (-power). That he purported to stay within his original definition, whereby value is always determined by embodied labor, admitted many contradictions and complications into his text.

Goods Making Up the "Means of Subsistence"

Marx now proceeds to enumerate various categories of goods making up the "means of subsistence," and then makes another point:

> His natural wants, such as food, clothing, fuel and housing, vary according to the climatic and other physical conditions of his country. On the other hand, the number and extent of his so-called necessary wants, as also the modes of satisfying them, are themselves the product of historical development and depend therefore to a great extent on the degree of civilization of a country, more particularly on the conditions under which, and consequently on the habits and degree of comfort in which, the class of free labourers has been formed. In contradistinction therefore to the case of other commodities, there enters into the determination of the value of labour-power a historical and moral element. Nevertheless, in a given country, at a given period, the average quantity of the means of subsistence necessary for the labourer is practically known.

Marx is still categorizing the immediate physical necessities or "means of subsistence" of the laborer, among these being clothing, fuel and housing. The laborer's natural wants vary "according to the climatic and other physical conditions of his country." Marx is now drawing closer to the subject of what determines the amount of means of subsistence which is deemed necessary.

------

* There might be a certain basis for it however, and a certain amount of synergy and mutual influence between the two. A worker in bargaining for a wage probably is influenced by the "cost of living" and thus has a figure in mind to shoot at.

That is, he makes an approach toward the topic but not a very convincing one. The value of labor-power, he tells us, is determined by the necessary amount of "means of subsistence." But this "necessary" amount is not judged or evaluated in the straightforward sense of the word; it doesn't mean the minimum amount necessary to actually maintain health, strength and thus the ability to labor, or labor-power. It doesn't mean the minimum required standard of living, or even the "poverty level." Rather, for him, the necessary means of subsistence is whatever amount is actually received – the prevailing wage level, if you will. He says there is a historical and moral element "entering into the determination" of this amount; it is "the product of historical development." That is, the standard is not the amount absolutely "necessary," the amount required at a minimum, the amount literally necessary. Rather, it is the current amount, whatever that is; and the standard or the factors that determined the amount are "historical," "moral," and so on.

In a way, this sense of the word "necessary" is appropriate, in that it is consistent with Marx's usage elsewhere. The amount of "necessary labor," which is the value of a commodity, is the actual amount embodied in it; and that is probably an appropriate definition (if not an appropriate use of the word "necessary"). This is true in the case of actual commodities, because people tend to use the most efficient, least labor-intensive means generally available for producing a commodity, and so the actual labor is probably close to the minimum amount realistically "necessary" for producing it. But as for the standard of living, which tends to rise with more efficient production methods – and which workers try to maximize – its *actual* magnitude can't be considered equivalent to the minimum necessary means of subsistence.

The drawback is that it is not an absolute standard. If we were using the "necessary amount" in the literal sense of the minimum necessary, we could probably formulate some method for putting a numerical figure on it, apart from mere custom and usage. But in the sense Marx uses it, the "necessary amount" is no standard at all; it simply means whatever amount currently prevails – i.e., whatever is, is right. To simply take the current amount of means of subsistence as the definition of the value of labor-power is not an independent standard; it simply endorses the status quo.

But to continue with Marx's analysis: he tells us that one thing that influences "his natural wants," and by inference the amount of necessary means of subsistence, is climatic and other conditions. There may be some validity in that – in tropical climates a grass hut may be an adequate and accepted type of home, whereas in less balmy regions a more substantial house is necessary. But more remarkable than what Marx says in this regard is what he omits: if we are addressing the issue of what determines the amount of means of subsistence which the typical laborer actually obtains with his pay, i.e., the amount "necessary" in the sense that it is the actual wage rate (the entire wage being thus automatically deemed "necessary"), then the foremost and obvious factor is the state of technology. That is, if in nineteenth-century Great Britain the standard of living was advanced beyond that of the fourteenth century, or indeed beyond that of the ancient Romans, it is mainly because of the Industrial Revolution, i.e., because the tools and methods of mass production had greatly advanced over previous eras. The state of productivity, the amount of goods one typical laborer can produce, is acknowledged to be the single greatest factor determining the standard of living; and the single greatest determiner of the level of productivity is the overall state of technology.

Marx manages to skirt that well-known economic truth, however. His explanation of variations in the "necessary" amount of means of subsistence – meaning the amount actually received – is in part the following:

> His natural wants, such as food, . . . vary according to the climatic and other physical conditions of his country. On the other hand, the number and extent of his so-called necessary wants, as also the modes of satisfying them, are themselves the product of historical development, and depend therefore to a great extent on the degree of civilization of a country, more particularly on the conditions under which, and consequently on the habits and degree of comfort in which, the class of free labourers has been formed.

This too is sort of a non-explanation, mere hand-waving. Marx gives a lot of reasons why the standard of living of workers is what it is – that is, why the amount of goods they can buy with their wages is what it is – but manages to avoid mentioning the crucial one. The state of technology, which determines the degree of productivity, should have been a natural subject for Marx, because the state of "forces of production" is a central element in his dialectical theory. But in the present instance the topic would not serve his purposes, and thus he skirts it. We are told coyly that the laborer's wants "are themselves the product of historical development," without being told what factors, changing over a period of time, caused the standard of living to change.

Of course, as previously stated it is hard to separate cause from effect in examining wages and price levels. The necessary or required money wage is partly determined by the general price level of goods; and price levels are themselves influenced by the labor costs (in money) of production; that is, the two are mutually dependent. Probably, just as Marx indicates, the most that can be said is that over the course of time, first one factor or the other changes; and the two factors, mutually interacting, attain the levels they do as a result of the inchoate course of "historical development."

Another example of that interaction, on an elementary level, might be this: the wage level and working conditions that the members of a labor union will accept are at least partially determined by what is usual and normal. If a proposed contract does not substantially meet prevailing conditions or even exceed them, workers may be inclined to strike. But then again, what is usual or normal has partly been determined by previous contracts or "historical development." The entire set of interacting factors is perhaps too complicated to set forth in a single well-defined line of cause and effect; and thus the best answer may be just to identify the pertinent factors and say that they interact in a course of "historical development."

The problem with Marx is that he invokes minor factors without mentioning the main one. He mentions "climatic and other physical conditions"; and also the "degree of civilization of a country," which apparently refers to the standard of living – how many amenities people have become accustomed to, the state of luxury they are used to in their daily lives. (Marx is presumably referring to the same thing when he mentions another factor, "the habits and degree of comfort in which, the class of free labourers have been formed.") That is, it is the degree of "civilization" or development they have attained in their consumer goods that determines the "means of subsistence" people are accustomed to receive. But in invoking this, Marx leaves out the more fundamental causative factor, that makes that degree of "civilization" possible – namely, the state of productivity.

In any event, Marx tells us that, "In contradistinction therefore to the case of other commodities, there enters into the determination of the value of labour-power a historical and moral element." We might quibble with that first phrase; we could probably discern a similar course of historical development for the price of commodities; but we must remember that for Marx, the value of commodities is cut and dried – it equals the embodied labor.

We might also quibble with his discerning of a "moral element" as relates to the value of labor-power. He hasn't specifically identified one; but perhaps he is alluding to the idea of value as whatever is the normal or usual wage – that each laborer ought by rights to receive the wage others receive – what is normal, usual and necessary. Perhaps that is the moral imperative referred to.

At any rate, we can probably agree with Marx's main point, that an element of historical development is significant in determining the value of labor-power or the wage level. At a given time the basic standard of living and required wage are pretty well known, and laborers and capitalists alike generally hew to that line.

Theorizing about the value of labor-power

> *"I have no data yet. It is a capital mistake to theorize before one has data. Insensibly one begins to twist facts to suit theories, instead of theories to suit facts."*
> – Arthur Conan Doyle, "A Scandal in Bohemia"

We can now continue with Marx's listing of the various categories of goods included in the laborer's "means of subsistence," that is, the various categories of things which the wage goes to buy. He seems to write from a curious viewpoint (although it is a common one for him). Once again, he seems to be building a logical category *a priori*, rather than describing existing facts *a posteriori*. He seems to be devising a logical case telling why each itemized category of goods is logically "necessary"; and once having proven it to be necessary, he then is justified in including it in the "necessary means of subsistence."

In other words, Marx writes as if he were inventing a world from scratch, building reality from purely hypothetical logical exercises; we are to believe that whatever he finds to be logically "necessary" will *ipso facto* be deemed part of the value of labor-power. Again it is a case of assuming that logic can determine the facts.

By contrast, a real-world economy cannot work like that. It doesn't await Marx's judgment as to what is logically "necessary." It functions according to rules of its own, and laborers in fact attain a certain level of means of subsistence apart from Marx's logical arguments; it is this actual means of subsistence which Marx needs to describe.

In fact, he is generally accurate in describing what kinds of things are included in the means of subsistence. But he writes as if he were establishing these categories himself, by pure force of logic. This is a strange viewpoint.

As even Sherlock Holmes said, the facts must be discovered first, with no preconceptions – otherwise one finds oneself adapting the facts to the theory instead of vice versa.

That is the flaw in Marx's method. The flaw in his logic is that it is reversed. More precisely, it doesn't really identify any factor which, in a cause-and-effect manner, actually determines the value of labor-power. It purports to rule certain things in or out of the necessary means of subsistence, but actually it just accepts whatever is the current standard of living, without identifying any factors which served to establish that standard at its actual magnitude. His analysis of the determiner of the value of labor-power is just an endorsement of the current value, however that value was reached.

The only causative factor he identifies is "a historical and moral element"; that means, wage levels evolved *somehow*. Whatever is the present wage level or standard of living, it constitutes the "necessary means of subsistence" which determines the value of labor-power. There is no element of causation in such an analysis, and thus the use of the term, what "determines" the value, is misleading.

On the other hand, there is a sense in which the real value of a wage is the amount of goods which can be purchased with it. In this sense the value of labor-power can be judged or "determined" by the purchasable means of subsistence. If this seems self-contradictory, the point can perhaps be clarified by once again considering the difference between the measure of the determiner of value. Let us state again the essence of Marx's definition or analysis: the value of labor-power is determined by the amount of means of subsistence required for the laborer. Since whatever the laborer is able to buy is by definition "necessary," this means that the value of labor-power is determined by what the laborer buys with his wage. That sounds backwards. Rather than saying the value of labor is determined by the wage, we would intuitively believe it should somehow be the reverse —the value of labor should in some sense determine the wage. That is, there should be some intrinsic or independent standard for judging what a day's labor is worth, and in some manner the wage should be seen to conform to that value. To say that the value of labor (-power) is "determined" by the wage is simply an endorsement of the status quo.

It can be seen to make sense, however, if we think in terms of the *measure* of value, rather than its determination: "The value of one's labor, or the value of the wage, is the entire ensemble of goods and services which can be purchased with it" – what would be wrong with that?

Nothing, as a description or measure of value; it only loses its pertinence if taken as an explanation of what determines value in a causative sense. As regards the measure or indeed definition of value, we have seen that exchange value means, what a thing is exchangeable for on the open market. Labor, or labor-power, is manifestly exchanged for the wage; and it is arguable that the best measure of what it is exchanged for is the amount of goods which can be purchased with that wage. So as a description of what is exchanged, or as a statement of the best measure of the value of labor, Marx's analysis makes sense. It tells what is exchanged for labor (-power) – the wage; and what is the best measure of the value of the wage – the goods it will buy. But it doesn't purport to tell why or how the wage attained its particular magnitude; in that sense it doesn't tell what determined the value of labor-power in a cause-and-effect sense. It only tells us how to measure (or "determine," in that sense) the already-established value. It is a description of the exchange after the fact; it does not prescribe or tell what prescribes that value in a cause-and-effect sense.

The value of labor-power is best measured by the amount of goods or "means of subsistence" the wage will buy. That is how we measure or "determine" the value of labor-power. But as to how that value was initially fixed, established, set, or "determined," i.e., as to what factors caused it to obtain the magnitude it achieved, Marx's analysis can tell us nothing. For that purpose it is merely a truism.

The overall effect of Marx's analysis is much like a report on the costs of raising and keeping workers – much as a dairy farmer might compute the costs of keeping dairy cows. Marx writes as if the "means of subsistence" were subject to his will, and that he could allow or disallow given items, depending on the results of his logic concerning whether or not they are "necessary," much as a farmer can decide what kind of feed to give his cattle, how big a barn to build, etc. There is no sense, in other word, that he is describing a situation and a standard of living that already exists, independent of him and his analysis. This is mainly the result of his habit of writing as if it were up to him to prove what things are necessary for the maintenance of the labor and labor-power; if unproven, he implies, the particular item cannot be included in the necessary means of subsistence. Thus he comes across as someone "keeping workers," who makes a list of supplies to purchase in order to keep them in good health.

Of course, there are passages in *Wealth of Nation* with a similar-sounding viewpoint, so perhaps it could be considered a common failing. For instance there is this passage (Book I, Chapter VIII):

> But though in disputes with their workmen, masters must generally have the advantage, there is however a certain rate below which it seems impossible to reduce, for any considerable time, the ordinary wages even of the lowest species of labour.
>
> A man must always live by his work, and his wages must at least be sufficient to maintain him. They must even upon most occasions be somewhat more; otherwise it would be impossible for him to bring up a family, and the race of such workmen could not last beyond the first generation.

Smith too seems to be describing the cost of labor in terms of the cost of raising and keeping workmen, and the minimum required to keep them from dying off. But for one thing, it is not a central theme of Smith's analysis; rather it is a sort of aside, with the value of labor being analyzed predominantly in other terms. Smith is mentioning one practical consideration, that being something like a floor on the wages that can, for purely physical or biological reasons, be paid. It is a description of extraordinary or limiting conditions, apart from the more normal economic analysis.

Smith also says,

> The wages paid to journeymen and servants of every kind must be such as may enable them, one with another, to continue the race of journeymen and servants. . . The fund destined for replacing or repairing [or "reproducing"], if I may say so, the wear and tear of the slave, is commonly managed by a negligent master or careless overseer. That destined for performing the same office with regard to the free man, is managed by the free man himself.

And indeed, the one special circumstance is almost never met. As Smith says,

> There are many plain symptoms that the wages of labour are no where in this country regulated by this lowest rate which is consistent with common humanity
>
> First, in almost every part of Great Britain there is a distinction. . . between summer and winter wages. Summer wages are always highest. But. . . the maintenance of a family is most expensive in winter. Wages, therefore, being highest when this expense is lowest, it seems evident that they are not regulated by what is necessary for this expence; but by the quantity and supposed value of the work.

And that latter phrase is the crux of the matter. We want to know how to judge the value of the work; or more precisely, we want to know how the economy "judges" the value of the work, meaning, what factors determine the work's value and determine what wage will be given in exchange for it. We are not satisfied in this inquiry by being told how to judge the value of the necessary means of subsistence. We want to know, in ordinary, direct terms, the value of *labor*.

Smith continues with some comments that show where Marx's analysis might be pertinent:

> . . .a slave, however, or one absolutely dependent on us for immed-iate subsistence, would not be treated in this manner. His daily sub-sistence would be proportioned to his daily necessities.

A slave would not be treated like a free laborer, and paid market wages. In a situation such as a slave's, not governed by market economics, the type of analysis Marx writes would be pertinent. For cattle or slaves, the owner decides at his own discretion what will be included in the necessary means of subsistence. But market economics for wages cannot be reduced to such simple calculations.

Smith echoes Marx's analysis (or rather vice versa) to an extent by agreeing that the value of the wage can be measured in terms of its purchasing power:

> The real recompense of labour, the real quantity of the necessaries
> and conveniencies of life which it can procure to the labourer, has,
> during the course of the present century, increased perhaps in a still
> greater proportion than its monetary price.

But Smith doesn't indulge in Marx's reverse logic, wherein the value of labor-power is determined by the wage paid for it. He is only indicating that the value of the wage – not of the labor itself – is best measured in terms of the amount of goods it will buy, not by a money figure.

Ultimately, Smith returns to a familiar theme in analyzing what governs the exchange value of labor:

> The money price of labour is necessarily regulated by two circum-
> stances; the demand for labour, and the price of the necessaries and
> conveniencies of life. The demand for labour, according as it happens
> to be increasing, stationary, or declining, or to require an increasing,
> stationary, or declining population, determines the quantity of the
> necessaries and conveniencies of life which must be given to the
> labourer; and the money price of labour is determined by what is
> requisite for purchasing this quantity.

That is, the exchange value of labor is governed first and foremost by demand, in the form of a quantity of goods. (This quantity probably is related to or limited by the general level of productivity.) And then secondarily the value of labor translates into a money wage.

By contrast, in Marx there is not the interplay of market forces in determining what amount of goods must be given in return for labor; rather he views the quantity as more or less fixed in a given historical period. And then too, he translates this quantity of goods into its embodied labor, rather than to a money wage:

> The value of labour-power resolves itself into the value of a
> definite quantity of the means of subsistence. It therefore varies with
> the value of these means or with the quantity of labour requisite for
> their production.

Consequences

Marx identifies the value of the means of subsistence which can be purchased with the wage, not as merely the value of the wage but as the value of the labor-power itself. This leads to some quirks of logic and to some serious implications later on. First, as noted, there is the fact that it is reverse reasoning, whereby the magnitude of value of labor-power is determined by what is given for it – a non-explanation or infinite regress – for then one must ask, What determines what is given for it?

There are other implications too. In taking the value of labor-power as determined by a "necessary" amount of means of subsistence, a particular market basket of goods, Marx assumes that that quantity is pretty much fixed for a given historical era. He assumes the amount of "means of subsistence" is a fixed constant. (If that is not obvious at this point in his text, he makes it plain later, and in other works of his. It becomes a settled assumption that workers receive a "subsistence wage," fixed always at a bare subsistence level.)

The "means of subsistence" then is the fixed, unvarying point from which his analysis can proceed; it is the unchanging fulcrum around which other quantities can rotate. As a consequence, there is this fact: if technological advances improve the productivity of labor, so that the labor required to produce a fixed set of goods – their embodied labor – declines; and if the value of labor-power is a fixed set of goods; then the value of labor-power, in terms of labor, declines as the productivity increases. That is, in a situation like the Industrial Revolution, where productivity underwent a generalized upward leap, the result would be not an increase in the "necessary means of subsistence" (for that is fixed), but rather a decrease in the labor required to produce those means of subsistence; that is to say, a decrease in the value of labor-power.

This is in direct contradiction to all common sense and all our experience of increases in productivity. When productivity increases, the standard of living also increases; the ordinary laborer is able to buy more with his wage.

Suppose, instead of taking the amount of "means of subsistence" or purchasable goods as the fixed point, we took the money wage level as more or less fixed (at least short-term). This is undoubtedly more realistic. Then suppose a new, more productive type of equipment came into use. Let's use Marx's example, where the amount of labor required to produce cloth drops by half: a laborer formerly employed to weave cloth by hand, receives let us say the same wage to tend a power loom. But the amount of labor embodied in the cloth is much less, so presumably the money price of the cloth is much less. So now the laborer can buy more cloth with the wage. At least as concerns that one commodity, the amount of purchasable "means of subsistence" increases as the labor content of goods decreases. This "scenario" is no doubt more in accord with reality.

Means of subsistence

Let us continue with Marx's identification of the various factors of the "means of subsistence":

> The owner of labour-power is mortal. If then is appearance in the market is to be continuous, and the continuous conversion of money into capital assumes this, the seller of labour-power must perpetuate himself, "in the way that every living individual perpetuates himself, by procreation." The labour-power withdrawn from the market by wear and tear and death, must be continually replaced by, at the very least, an equal amount of fresh labour-power. Hence the sum of the means of subsistence necessary for the production of labour-power must include the means necessary for the labourer's substitutes, i.e., his children, in order that this race of peculiar commodity-owners may perpetuate its appearance in the market.
>
> In order to modify the human organism, so that it may acquire skill and handiness in a given branch of industry, and become labour-power of a special kind, a special education or training is requisite, and this, on its part, costs an equivalent in commodities of a greater or less amount. This amount varies according to the more or less complicated character of the labour-power. The expenses of this education (excessively small in the case of ordinary labour-power), enter *pro tanto* into the total value spent in its production.

Marx even gives a formula taking into account the various frequencies with which different commodities must be purchased:

> Some of the means of subsistence, such as food and fuel, are consumed daily, and a fresh supply must be provided daily. Others such as clothes and furniture last for longer periods and require to be replaced only at longer intervals. One article must be bought or paid for daily, another weekly, another quarterly, and so on. But in whatever way the sum total of these outlays may be spread over the year, they must be covered by the average income, taking one day with another. If the total of the commodities required daily for the production of labour-power = A, and those required weekly = B, and those required quarterly = C, and so on, the daily average of these commodities = 365A + 52B + 4C + etc.

Marx makes a big show out of actually analyzing the daily required means of subsistence of a laborer, but his childish mathematics is just for show. In the end, he picks a figure out of his hat:

> Suppose that in this mass of commodities requisite for the average day there are embodied 6 hours of social labour, then there is

incorporated daily in labour-power half a day's average social labour, in other words, half a day's labour is requisite for the daily production of labour-power.

How does Marx arrive at the figure, 6 hours of social labor? He picks it at random (or, more likely, he picks it because it will serve his purposes well in ensuing arguments). Thus Marx's hand-waving and folderol, his great show of mathematical precision, is just for laughs. It's like the old joke about how to weigh a hog when you don't have a scale: you find a big boulder and balance a heavy beam on it; you put the hog on one end of the beam and then look around until you find a large rock, just the right size to put on the other end of the beam to just balance the hog; then you guess the weight of the rock. Similarly, Marx makes a great show of being mathematically accurate about the various factors of the "means of subsistence," and then in the end he just guesses or randomly picks the value of labor-power.

But let's examine Marx's use of terms in the quoted passage. Suppose that in the mass of commodities "requisite" for the laborer's average day — that is, the commodities consumed in an average day — there are embodied 6 hours of "social labor," or to be more precise, six hours of "homogeneous, socially-necessary" labor. Then there is incorporated daily in labor-power half a day's average social labor — that is, there is incorporated in the laborer, or in the goods he consumes, half a day's labor (assuming the typical day's labor was 12 hours). This labor is incorporated in the commodities the laborer consumes; these commodities are necessary for the continued vitality of the laborer; that vitality is necessary for the existence of labor-power; and these six hours of labor are thus, via a chain of "necessities," equal to the value of a day's labor-power. Thus Marx can say, "in other words, half a day's labour is requisite for the daily production of labour-power. This quantity of labour forms the value of a day's labour-power...."

To belabor a point, the half a day's labor in question doesn't produce labor-power, it produces the means of subsistence; and only by extension does it lead to the production of labor-power.

The numeric value

Now Marx seeks to put a numerical figure on the value:

> If half a day's average social labour is incorporated in three shillings, then three shillings is the price corresponding to the value of a day's labour-power. If its owner therefore offers it for sale at three shillings a day, its selling price is equal to its value, and according to our supposition, our friend Moneybags, who is intent

upon converting his three shillings into capital, pays this value.

This passage foreshadows the essence of Marx's "case against capital." Notice that at this point in his text, Marx has already defined or deduced that the value of a day's labor-power is half a day's labor. In other words, by his supposition the value of goods the laborer receives each day (i.e., buys with his pay), which equals the value of his daily means of subsistence, is six hours of labor. Moreover, the usual working day in Marx's time was twelve hours; the laborer's full working day was that long. So by Marx's supposition, the laborer was receiving means of subsistence "worth" six hours of labor, in return for each twelve hours of performed labor. Thus the basis is already established for showing an "internal contradiction" in the capitalist system. We can see, even before Marx points it out, that the laborer is defrauded of six hours of labor or value every working day.

As to the particular figure Marx arrived at for the value, that was easily chosen. Three shillings was in Marx's time the standard day's wage, or so he tells us. Marx doesn't really tell us by what process of reasoning he arrived at the figure three shillings; but it is safe to assume it is not in blatant violation of the facts at the time, and also it allows his reasoning to work out to the conclusion he desires. It is safe to say that he chose three shillings because it was a fairly representative wage at the time. But Marx presents the line of causation backwards. He says, First, the value of labor-power is three shillings; and second, the capitalist pays that amount. In actual fact, the capitalist first pays that amount, and for that reason the value is three shillings.

That is the easy part of his analysis. There are other figures he chose, too. He assumed that half a day's labor was the amount embodied in a laborer's daily consumed commodities; and he assumed that half a day's labor also equated (somehow) to three shillings. (That is, crudely speaking, he assumed that twelve hours of labor was worth 6s.)

Note that the only one of these figures actually known, as opposed to assumed, was 3s., a typical day's wage. Therefore when the figure, three shillings, enters the discussion, it seems to verify Marx's entire line of reasoning; for lo and behold, at the tail end of his argument a figure appears which everyone can see is the actual valid one: a day's wage is typically three shillings. But Marx is like an archer who first fires his arrows against a wall and then paints the bull's-eyes around them. The figure was chosen first, and Marx's argument was drawn around it, so as to make it seem to turn out correct.

What the reader is presented with is this: three shillings is represented as the value of the laborer's daily subsistence, meaning it is the laborer's daily wage; and that turns out to be valid. This figure is also equated to six hours of labor, but Marx chose those numbers to suit himself. (We don't really have a standard yet for determining how much labor is "incorporated" in a quantity of money.) This gives his argument an air of validity, but it is really based on arbitrary assumptions.

One error the reader should guard against is thinking six shillings was the wage for a typical day's labor. That is an easy conclusion to jump to. Marx says "half a day's average social labour is embodied in three shillings," and it is natural to assume that therefore a day's labor must equal six shillings. But Marx is not reasoning from what is paid for a certain amount of work; he is not saying "the typical pay given for half a day's labor is three shillings." He is not reasoning from what is paid for something (like labor), but always from the standpoint of how much labor is required for producing a given item. Six hours of labor produces the day's means of subsistence; likewise six hours produces three coined shillings (though it is not really clear, so far, how he knew that). The value of a day's labor-power is therefore six hours, or three shillings, and because Marx assumes that commodities are always paid for at their value, and because he assumes what is being purchased is a day's labor-power, the price – i.e., the day's wage – should be three shillings. There is nothing so straightforward and obvious in the analysis as saying, If six hours of labor are worth three shillings, then twelve hours should be worth six shillings. There is an entire convoluted line of logic diverting Marx's theory away from the simple facts of the hiring of labor by the hour.

But in any event, the thing to remember is that when Marx says, "half a day's average social labour is embodied in three shillings," he is not referring to the wage for half a day's labor. His reasoning comes from the other direction, from a day's means of subsistence, the labor embodied in it, and the labor embodied in three shillings. And from the argument so far, it won't be hard for Marx to show that the laborer is cheated.

It might be thought that Marx's approach is not too far different from classical theory; for Smith too takes a somewhat similar approach. At least, he says that the value of the wage can be determined most truly in terms of goods and services it can procure, and only secondarily in terms of the money figure. In his words,

> The money price of labour is necessarily regulated by two circumstances: the demand for labour, and the price of the necessaries and conveniencies of life. The demand for labour. . . determines the quantity of the necessaries and conveniencies of life which must be given to the labourer; and the money price of labour is determined by what is requisite for purchasing this quantity.

Thus Smith too expresses the wage primarily in terms of a quantity of commodities, and secondarily in terms of the money price of the commodities. This is quite similar to Marx's analysis. But to repeat, Smith is not picking a quantity of goods or means of subsistence at random, nor is he giving a hand-waving explanation such as "historical development." He is saying supply and demand determine the value of labor, or the wage that must be paid. There is a line of cause and effect established; he is not, like Marx, taking the rate of pay (in commodities) as a given or fixed point, and picking out the rest of his figures arbitrarily to support his reasoning.

Real-world analysis

At any rate, the owner of a day's labor-power (that is, presumably the laborer who has a day's labor-power all packaged up and ready to sell) sells it for three shillings a day, which we are relieved to hear is its value. We would be more inclined to say, the value of a day's labor is three shillings *by virtue of* the very fact that he sells it for three shillings. The value is determined by supply and demand, by the bargains struck or the price mutually agreed on by buyers and sellers. It doesn't exist somewhere else, independently, apart from the economic interactions that determine it. The wage mutually agreed on (in the aggregate number of instances) by employer and laborer, is the value. It is specious to say as Marx does, that three shillings is already the value of a day's labor-power and so ought to be the figure arrived at when capitalist and laborer agree on a wage.

If the selling price equals the value, Marx says, "our friend Moneybags" (that melodramatic villain), pays the full value. Value for him has a pre-established magnitude; he says the wage agreed on should equal it. By contrast, in classical theory, the selling price, the wage agreed on, is by definition the exchange value.

There is one more minor aspect of Marx's theory we take issue with. He speaks of Moneybags, "who is intent upon converting his three shillings into capital." That is a misuse of the word. His money is already capital, i.e., money spent in order to make more money. The problem is that Marx defines capital as surplus value, or profit, squeezed out of the exploitation of hired labor.

The minimum limit

We now proceed from the value of labor-power to the minimum limit of its value:

> The minimum limit of the value of labour-power is determined by the value of the commodities, without the daily supply of which the labourer cannot renew his vital energy, consequently by the value of

those means of subsistence that are physically indispensable.

Marx now defines the value of labor-power as a subsistence wage. But we thought the value of labor-power itself was in all cases determined by the value of those commodities – not the "minimum limit." After all, value is the "labor necessary to produce" something, and in this case it is the labor necessary to produce the commodities necessary to maintain or "reproduce" labor-power. But as regards what is the necessary amount, we have learned that a "historical and moral" element, or factors of historical development, shape this – that a certain level of means of subsistence becomes accepted and thus is the "necessary" amount. Therefore we believed, value is not determined by any minimum amount physically necessary; it is determined by the general prevailing wage level, or the means of subsistence which it is necessary to pay laborers, in general.

That is, Marx says, "at a given period, the average quantity of the means of subsistence necessary" is known; that quantity is simply the prevailing standard of living, and that is the value of labor-power – not a bare physical minimum. So the bare minimum, by Marx's previous definition, is not the value of labor-power. It would seem Marx is introducing a new standard here.

There is a certain amount of reason to what he says, however. He is not really saying (yet) that value is determined by the minimum amount of means of subsistence. (He does gravitate to that viewpoint later on.) He is saying value is determined by the means of subsistence purchasable with the wage, but only so long as that amount is at least sufficient to preserve life and health. If the actual wage falls below that, it can no longer be considered the true value of the labor-power. In Marx's words,

> If the price of labour-power falls to [or, below?] this minimum, it falls below its value, since under such circumstances it can be maintained and developed only in a crippled state. But the value of every commodity is determined by the labour-time requisite to turn it out so as to be of normal quality.

Marx's reasoning is rather contrived; we must remember, his standard of value is, the amount of "homogeneous, socially necessary labor." Within this standard we include the requirement that the produced commodity be of normal quality. We might consider this a qualification of his original theory– that the commodity must be of normal quality or else the labor doesn't "count" as labor, or the value doesn't "count" as value. It pretty much goes without saying, however; we always expect goods to be of "normal" quality. We wouldn't accept substandard goods as defining the value of goods. (This however evades the issue of the various degrees of quality. Sometimes there are various price ranges and levels of quality of goods; it is not so much a matter of either being of "normal" quality or not; rather there are various ranges depending on what people want to pay and how much quality they are willing to pay for. A professional baseball player's glove and a little leaguer's glove may both be of "normal" quality for what they are; each will have its own appropriate value.)

But Marx is fitting his paradigm and his definition of value somewhat clumsily to labor-power. His line of reasoning is that if the price of labor-power falls to the minimum he has just described – presumably he means if it falls *below* the minimum – then the "product," labor-power, can no longer be successfully produced of "normal" quality. The laborer's strength and vitality, i.e., his capacity to work, would no longer be at a "normal" level. The "product" would no longer be of normal quality.

The reason the price is then below the value, or below the minimum limit of value, is that value in this exceptional case no longer fits the definition. Value is defined as "social labor," or the amount of labor socially necessary under normal, state-of-the-art conditions of production. Now in addition he stipulates that the product must be of normal condition and quality, however that is defined and whatever standard is used for it. If the "product" is not up to par, the labor invested in producing it cannot be considered the "socially necessary" amount. Under these circumstances labor-power "can be maintained and developed only in a crippled state," i.e., not in a normal state. Only normal socially-necessary homogeneous labor determines value – not sub-normal quantities of labor. In short, "the value of every commodity is determined by the labour-time requisite turn it out so as to be of normal quality."

This part of Marx's analysis is quite similar to a previously-quoted passage from *Wealth of Nations*, indicating that there is a practical bottom limit to the wage that can be paid to laborers. To repeat, Smith says a laborer's wages must support him and his family, "otherwise it would be impossible for him to bring up a family, and the race of such workmen could not last beyond the first generation." In other words, there are practical considerations mandating that wages cannot be that low for long. But again, this is a situation that doesn't occur very frequently; and it is not the central point of Smith's analysis.

It would have to be said that Smith's explanation has more bearing on the real world. Marx is still continuing his fiction of labor-power as a physical commodity, and introduces another convoluted line of logic, designed to fit it into his definition and to relate normal quality of the "commodity" to the setting of a minimum practical wage. Later on, the real pertinence of this part of Marx's text will become apparent, when he begins to assume that the actual wage received is always this minimum amount – that the value of labor-power is always this "minimum limit," or in modern parlance, a "subsistence" wage.

The point to notice is that Marx speaks of the "minimum limit of the value of labour-power," saying that if the wage falls below this minimum, it falls below its value. That is, he applies the term "value" also to the minimum limit of value. The minimum limit of the value is also the value (in another sense) of labor-power. This contradiction soon disappears from Marx's text, however, because he gradually assumes that the laborer always is paid the minimum value, the minimum means of subsistence, a "subsistence" wage.

We should bear in mind, as this transformation of meaning occurs, that the value of labor-power originally was the amount of means of subsistence (or, the labor invested therein) actually paid – the wage level actually arrived at by a historical process of development, by a historical and moral element," or however. But by accretion and attrition, Marx brings the meaning around to the bare minimum means of subsistence necessary for physical survival. This latter definition is unjustified by the original terms of Marx's analysis – that is the essential point.

Marx's analysis of the value of labor-power actually ends up being quite similar to Smith's analysis of the "real recompense of labour," the actual value of the wage. In each case the wage is equated to the quantity of means of subsistence, or goods of various kinds, that can be purchased with the wage. (However, Marx takes it one step further and resolves on the labor required to produce those goods.)

It might seem then that Marx and Smith are in agreement, and the two analyses are at root the same. The exchange value of the labor should by definition equal the wage, or price given in return for the labor; and value of labor, or of labor-power, should then best be measurable by the wage.

But what we really want to find out is what determines the magnitude of the wage; not simply how to measure it, but what determines, what factors govern, the price of labor. Smith's analysis of the real value of the wage, "the real quantity of the necessaries and conveniencies" it can purchase, is essentially a static one. It takes the wage level as a given, not asking how it came to be what it is, but only seeking the best way to measure what it is. It only asks, What is the best measure of the value of the wage? It doesn't ask how that value was affixed. Its subject is the measure of value, not the determiner of value.

Marx's analysis should have given us an explanation of what determines the magnitude of the value of labor-power. That is his announced topic, the question he initially set out to answer. But, as we have seen, by a series of "necessities" and a chain of logic, he equates the task of finding the labor required to produce labor-power, to the task of finding the quantity of goods required to maintain or "reproduce" the laborer, and then to the task of finding the amount of labor required to produce that quantity of goods. The goods necessary to maintain labor are ultimately reduced to whatever can be purchased with the wage. In short, by convoluted logic he declares an analysis of the value of the wage to be the answer to the question of what determines the value of labor-power.

So Marx sets out to find what determines the value of labor-power and ends up declaring that it is identical with the value of the wage – that it equals the labor embodied in producing what is purchasable with the wage. For that latter quantity, he picks a number at random (or rather, at will), and the net result is this: the value of a day's labor-power is half a day's labor (six hours of labor, at least as conditions were when he wrote).

Marx really gives us a non-explanation of the value of labor-power. We would expect the value of labor-power to determine, in some sense, what is paid for it. (Or to put it more accurately, we would expect an analysis of what determines that value to tell us what factors determine the wage that is paid.) However, for Marx, the reasoning goes the other way: what is paid for the labor-power determines its value. If that is his answer – if the value of labor-power is determined by what is paid for it – then our question becomes, What then determines what is paid for it? The discussion becomes an infinite regress, or rather, the original question remains despite Marx's redefinition of it. It is all very well for Marx to declare the value of labor-power to be identical to the value of the means of subsistence, or wage paid. But the question still remains, What determines the wage paid? Where does the number come from? How is it established? There are substantive issues involved, which cannot be removed by mere sophistry.

A Possible Objection

Marx now rebuts a possible objection to his analysis, in a portion of his text that has probably lost most of its meaning for us today. He quotes a certain Rossi, who seems to be objecting to Marx's spinning off of the capacity for labor (labor-power) as an independent entity separate from labor. Marx says,

> It is a very cheap sort of sentimentality which declares this method of determining the value of labour-power, a method prescribed by the very nature of the case, to be a brutal method, and which wails with Rossi that, "To comprehend capacity for labour (puissance de travail) at the same time that we make abstraction from the means of subsistence of the labourers during the process of production, is to comprehend a phantom (être de raison). When we speak of labour, or capacity for labour, we speak at the same time of the labourer and his means of subsistence, of labourers and wages." When we speak of capacity for labour, we do not speak of labour, any more than when we speak of capacity of digestion. The latter process requires something more than a good stomach. When we

speak of capacity for labour we do not abstract from the necessary means of subsistence. On the contrary, their value is expressed in its value. If his capacity for labour remains unsold, the labourer derives no benefit from it, but rather he will feel it to be a cruel nature-imposed necessity that this capacity has cost for its production a definite amount of the means of subsistence and that it will continue to do so for its reproduction. He will then agree with Sismondi: "that capacity for labour … is nothing unless it is sold."

It is difficult to understand the points being made here, or how Marx's comments are a rebuttal of Rossi's. The latter seems to be saying that when considering labor-power, we can't "abstract from" or leave to the side the laborer's means of subsistence – the two go hand in hand and must be considered together. And similarly for labor and the capacity to labor; for Marx objects, "When we speak of capacity for labour, we do not speak of labour. . ." That is, in some sense Rossi opposed Marx's setting forth of labor and capacity for labor as two independent entities, to be considered separately; or else he opposed "means of subsistence" as the answer to the value of labor. The language is too obscure to admit of much certainty.

At the same time, Marx seems to consider that Rossi's criticism also involves the issue of whether "means of subsistence" is related to the value of labor-power; for he says, "When we speak of capacity for labour we do not abstract from the necessary means of subsistence" – that is, we do not eliminate means of subsistence from the argument, we do not chip it away. "On the contrary, their value is expressed in its value." Marx simply reasserts that the value of the means of subsistence determines the value of the labor-power.

There are a couple of incidental observations that can be made about the passage. The fact that human beings must have a means of subsistence, that they have certain basic necessities such as food, shelter and clothing, Marx labels as the fact "that this capacity has cost for its production a definite amount of the means of subsistence and that it will continue to do so for its reproduction." We would do well to consider that the various necessities are simply requirements for life; all of human existence cannot be put into one category or one accounting column as "maintenance of the capacity to labor." People are more than mere tools of production, and life and health are important for reasons other than "the production and consequently also the reproduction" of labor-power. Marx's tendency towards reductionism has again led him astray.

We might also note that Marx mentions human needs as a "nature-imposed necessity." Marx often writes as if the requirements of life were imposed by the capitalist as a means of making sure people would have to work for him. Actually, it is a fact of life, a "nature-imposed necessity," and not an aspect of any one type of society. Furthermore, the capitalist also is subject to it; if he cannot sell his product at a profit, he too suffers the pangs of "a cruel nature-imposed necessity." Like labor-power, the finished product of the capitalist "is nothing unless it is sold" (at a profit).

Value and use-value

Marx now passes to another aspect of the sale and "consumption" of labor-power:

> One consequence of the peculiar nature of labour-power as a commodity is, that its use-value does not on the conclusion of this contract between the buyer and the seller, immediately pass into the hands of the former.

Marx is still maintaining his picture of labor-power as a commodity which is sold and, later, consumed during the actual exertion of labor. Thus rather than saying "The labor is paid for only after it is performed," he employs the terminology of physical commodities. The point he misses is that there is a difference between labor and commodities, between goods and services. In ordinary circumstances it would make no sense to say that someone buys a commodity, and receives it, but does not receive the use-value of it – as if use-value could be spun off into a separate entity on its own. It would be impossible to separate an apple from its use-value, for instance – anyone in possession of an apple possesses its physical properties along with it, as well as the use or "use-value" of it. Possession may not be "nine points of the law," as the saying goes, but it is certainly the entire key to having not only a physical commodity, but its properties and its use-value along with it.

Marx does use one accurate term in the above passage, however. He says, "on the conclusion of this contract between the buyer and the seller. . .." The employment of labor does not fit the paradigm of the sale of a commodity. Rather, it is the contracting of a service, and as Marx goes on to say, the service is only paid for upon completion or performance of the contract.

Marx continues his theme:

> Its value, like that of every other commodity, is already fixed before it goes into circulation, since a definite quantity of social labour has been spent upon it, but its use-value consists in the subsequent exercise of its force.

Marx distinguishes further between the value and the use-value of this supposed commodity, adding further absurdities to his portrayal of labor-power as a commodity. Its value is one thing, he tells us, which is fixed and known beforehand even before the "commodity" is sold. Its use-value only manifests itself later, when the "commodity" is "consumed," that is, when the labor is performed. The use of the commodity is the exercise of labor-power, meaning actual labor itself. And labor occurs at some time after the sale of the commodity, i.e., after the hiring of the laborer. Thus, since there is a time interval between the conveying of the commodity (labor-power) and the conveying of its use-value (labor), the commodity is only paid for later. Thus unlike all other commodities, it is not paid for at the time of its purchase, in a straightforward exchange of money for the commodity, of cash "on the barrel head" in exchange for a commodity physically handed over. Rather, labor-power is paid for at the time of its consumption, or upon the "exercise of its force," which occurs "by setting the seller of it to work." (For as Marx says later in his text, "[L]abour-power in use is labour itself. The purchaser of labour-power consumes it by setting the seller of it to work.") Only labor-power has this characteristic, that its use-value is separable from itself; that its sale does not immediately convey its use-value along with all other properties. In this sole case, payment is not immediate, but occurs only after the instantiation of its use-value.

This ridiculous picture could better be replaced by saying that labor is sold, i.e. contracted for, first, then performed, then paid for.

It may be noted in passing that the quoted passage reinforces Marx's static, pre-determined picture of the value of commodities: value is already fixed and built into the commodity before it goes to market, "since a definite quantity of social labour has been spent upon it." It contains that amount of embodied labor even before it is offered for sale, as a sort of invisible price sticker. Value is contained inside the commodity, as congealed "social labour" (meaning the labor "socially necessary" using up-to-date equipment). Value is not determined dynamically by supply and demand or market conditions. It is self-contained in the commodity, once it has been produced, and mysteriously "manifests itself" in selling price (even though no one may even know what the hidden inner "Value" is). Value is not an aspect of social interactions but a physical property of certain objects. Goods sell for a certain price because that is their internally-contained value – it is not that they have a certain value by virtue of selling for a certain price. Thus value in Marx's lexicon is a "metaphysical" rather than dialectic property.

Marx continues,

> The alienation of labour-power and its actual appropriation by the buyer, its employment as a use-value, are separated by an interval of time.

This is a good specimen of Marx's jargon. Consider his use of the term "alienation." Great significance has been attached to Marx's theory of alienation; much has been written about it, and "social alienation" has been deemed to be highly pertinent to capitalist societies today. But in passages like the above, we see that "alienation" is just an inflated term for "sale." The owner of labor-power "alienates" it by selling it; that is, he owned it, but now he no longer owns it, having sold it: it has been "alienated" or separated from him. There's nothing more to the term than that.

On the other hand there is the term "appropriation." This is ordinarily a disparaging Marxist term for "taking possession of," but in the current instance the meaning is slightly different. Here it means consumption of the commodity, or of its use-value, or "exercise of its [the labor's] force." Alienation, or sale, by the seller, and appropriation or "its employment as a use-value" by the buyer, "are separated by an interval of time." Thus Marx's overblown terminology is advanced in support of his overblown theory, of labor as consumption of the use-value of labor-power, which is the commodity sold by the laborer but not consumed until later, when the buyer sets the seller to work. Labor-power is sold first ("alienated"), and the use-value of it is squeezed out of it later in the form of labor ("its actual appropriation by the buyer"). This picture could be greatly simplified, Occam's-razor-wise, by saying labor is contracted for and "sold," then paid for after its performance.

> But in those cases in which the formal alienation by sale of the use-value of a commodity, is not simultaneous with its actual delivery to the buyer, the money of the latter usually functions as means of payment.

It is no great mystery that money is the means of payment, or that the buyer pays it. And in the case of labor-power, alienation or sale is always "not simultaneous with its actual delivery." But Marx continues with his comments on this phenomenon:

> In every country in which the capitalist mode of production reigns, it is the custom not to pay for labour-power before it has been exercised for the period fixed by the contract, as for example, the end of each week. In all cases, therefore, the use-value of the labour-power is advanced to the capitalist: the labourer allows the buyer to consume it before he receives payment of the price; he everywhere gives credit to the capitalist. That this credit is no mere fiction, is shown not only by the occasional loss of wages on the bankruptcy of the capitalist, but also by a series of more enduring consequences. Nevertheless, whether money serves as a means of purchase or as a

means of payment, this makes no alteration in the nature of the exchange of commodities. The price of the labour-power is fixed by the contract, although it is not realised till later, like the rent of a house. The labour-power is sold, although it is only paid for at a later period. It will, therefore, be useful, for a clear comprehension of the relation of the parties, to assume provisionally, that the possession of labour-power, on the occasion of each sale, immediately receives the price stipulated to be paid for it.

Marx discerns exploitation in this situation too, that the worker is not paid upon the sale of the commodity, but only after it is "consumed." That is, because labor is paid for only after it is performed, the laborer is said to advance credit to the capitalist. There is a certain amount of truth to this; the labor is generally performed before it is paid for. Sometimes though it is the other way around. People sometimes contract for the construction of a house or for household repairs, paying in advance. In these situations too the party that is advanced money or "credit" sometimes defaults.

We can ignore such statements as that "the use-value of the labour-power is advanced to the capitalist," that the buyer of "labour-power" is allowed "to consume it" before paying for it, and so on. These are descriptions of a fantasy world. But the fact remains that labor is usually first performed, and then paid for.

Marx then proceeds to stipulate that for purposes of his analysis, it will be permissible to assume that labor-power is paid for on delivery, or actually, upon purchase (for how labor-power can be delivered prior to the actual performance of the work eludes us). That is, Marx says it will be acceptable, or "useful. . . to assume provisionally, that the possessor of labour-power, on the occasion of each sale, immediately receives the price stipulated to be paid for it." Indeed it is hard to see what difference it could make to the analysis, so we can accept that assumption as well.

Marx now turns from the value or price paid for labor-power, to its obverse, the value or amount of benefit gained from the labor-power by the purchaser, the capitalist:

> We now know how the value paid by the purchaser to the posses-
> sor of this particular commodity, labour-power, is determined. The
> use-value which the former gets in exchange, manifests itself only in
> the actual usufruct in the consumption of the labour-power. The
> money owner buys everything necessary for this purpose, such as raw
> material, in the market, and pays for it at its full value. The consump-
> tion of labour-power is at one and the same time the production of
> commodities and of surplus value. The consumption of labour-
> power is completed, as in the case of every other commodity, outside

the limits of the market or of the sphere of circulation. Accompanied by Mr. Moneybags and by the possessor of labour-power, we therefore take leave for a time of this noisy sphere, where everything takes place on the surface and in view of all men, and follow them both into the hidden abode of production, on whose threshold there stares us in the face "No admittance except on business." Here we shall see, not only how capital produces, but how capital is produced. We shall at last force the secret of profit making.

In other words, Marx is about to reach the payoff of his argument, the denouement of the proof, showing that profit as conventionally conceived of is impossible, but that the capitalist makes money by extracting "surplus value" from the efforts of exploited workers.

First a look backward, however: "We now know how the value paid by the purchaser to the possessor of . . . labour-power, is determined." To recap: the value of labor-power is determined by the "value of the means of subsistence necessary for the maintenance of the labourer."

Moreover, "The use-value which the former," i.e., the capitalist, "gets in exchange, manifests itself only . . . in the consumption of the labour-power." That is, for the value of what the capitalist receives out of the exchange, we have to look at the actual labor performed. This was true first, last and always; and Marx's bizarre picture of the purchasing of labor-power, whose value is determined by its "usufruct," its consumption, its performance; and with labor being not simply labor but the use-value of the consumption of labor-power; shows a complete loss of contact with reality. "The consumption of labour-power," which Marx states is both "the production of commodities and of surplus value," is a fantasy concept. While Marx announces that before us lies the secret of surplus value, it is likely that only his multiplication of nonexistent entities to infest the concept of "labor" will allow him to uncover that scandalous secret.

Fairness for the capitalist

> *"We pretend to work and they pretend to pay us."*
> *"They couldn't possibly pay us as little as we work."*
> – Soviet folk sayings

Marx does make one accurate, almost generous remark about the capitalist. He says, "The money owner buys everything necessary for this purpose, such as raw material, in the market, and pays for it at its full value."

What is semi-generous about that remark is that it might lead the reader to conclude that the finished product belongs to the capitalist rightfully; that having paid for all the raw materials, the labor (-power), and in fact every element of the production process, the capitalist of rights owns the produced goods. Such a conclusion would be more generous than the actual Marxian viewpoint on the matter, expressed elsewhere: that the laborers, because their labor produced the commodities, actually own them and the capitalist's possession of them is an act of "appropriation," "expropriation," or exploitation. Moreover the fact that the laborers produced the product but do not own it, that they see, as it were, their children whom they have raised being torn from them and sold on the market, is classified as the "alienation" of the product from the laborers or vice versa, and is portrayed as a social malady. In the light of that type of perverse, obstinate, malicious argumentation, the above merely factual remark offers a refreshing contrast.

Marx continues much in the same vein:

> This sphere that we are deserting, within whose boundaries the sale and purchase of labour-power goes on, is in fact a very Eden of the innate rights of man. There alone rule Freedom, Equality, Property and Bentham. Freedom, because both buyer and seller of a commodity, say of labour-power, are constrained only by their own free will. They contract as free agents, and the agreement they come to, is but the form in which they give legal expression to their common will. Equality, because each enters into relation with the other, as with a simple owner of commodities, and they exchange equivalent for equivalent. Property, because each disposes only of what is his own. And Bentham, because each looks only to himself. The only force that brings them together and puts them in relation with each other, is the selfishness, the gain and the private interests of each. Each looks to himself only, an no one troubles himself about the rest. And just because they do so, do they all, in accordance with the pre-established harmony of things, or under the auspices of an all-shrewd providence, work together to their mutual advantage, for the common weal and in the interest of all.

(That is, the normal desire to make a living is characterized as selfishness or greed. That is opposed to the prevailing motivation in communistic societies, which is force itself — the regime decides on the aims and how to reach them, and the people are driven like workhorses to achieve those aims.)

The latter comments are an excellent statement of the principle of the "invisible hand," meaning that each person tends to his own business or looks after his own interests, as people naturally do, and yet the net result is support for the "common weal," or the prosperity of society as a whole and a furthering of the interests of all. That is, people primarily intent on pursuing their own interests end up, in the aggregate, serving the common interest.

Someone who opens a grocery, a fast-food restaurant or a convenience market hopes to make a living from it. But it is in the interests of consumers to be able to find a place to buy a Coke quickly and easily. It is in the interests of potential laborers to have places to apply for work. And in general, economic activity is essential; a milieu wherein people can find a ground for economic activity based on the expectation of monetary return, is conducive to the workings of an economy as such. As shown by such periods as the Great Depression, what is needed above all, the *sine qua non*, is economic activity – to move the ball off dead center, get the economy rolling (since it is so much easier to sustain a functioning economy than to get one moving from a dead stop). Economic activity, motivated as it is by the "selfish" desire to make a living, furthers this end.

A robust economy, then, favors everyone, and "a rising tide lifts all boats." This end is achieved not necessarily by conscious altruism or serving of the common weal, but by normal economic motivations as they result in economic activity and economic interactions freely entered into.

By contrast, in Communist countries with their "command-driven" economies, the leaders or issuers of those commands try to replace normal human economic motivation, ostensibly by the desire to serve the people and the common good, but actually by the orders of the regime, backed up by force and the threat of punishment. The principle is much like the facetious mock notice, "The floggings will continue until morale improves." Ironically, although such regimes set out to serve the common good, the results are dismal, because they have replaced genuine economic motivation and behavior with specious theories, and have tried to make society conform to those theories by force. They are eternally trying to "square the circle," and as it turns out, they don't relent in that hopeless quest until events overtake them and the economy deteriorates to such an extent that it collapses in on itself and forces change on the regime.

What Marx has been unable to do, in his accusations against capitalism, is to separate economic behavior from other behavior; i.e., to separate people when they are acting upon economic motivations only, from people as such and per se.

That is, to say that "no one troubles himself about the rest" is to assume that people are merely economic automata, acting mindlessly in accordance with economic drives. But people aren't mere economic engines; they act on a variety of motivations. If, strictly speaking, "no one troubles himself about the rest" when acting solely on economic motivations, yet people act from a mixture of motivations. The question is, what kind of society furthers and gives latitude to these other motivations as well? The answer is at least as likely to be, societies with freedom and prosperity, where people at least have a little something left over to share, as one where people are little better than rabbits in a cage, with rations doled out by their keepers.

If everyone acted always from motivations of economic theory, there would be no charities, no fund-raising drives to find cures for diseases, no charitable giving at all. But more than that, the workings of varied human motivations cannot be separated from everyday economic activities. A capitalist who hires someone may be partly motivated by the consideration that that person really needs a job. A customer may frequent one shop rather than another, not because the prices are lower or the merchandise better, but because the workers there are friendlier and more pleasant to deal with. Anyone who can portray people as economic engines, driven by economic motivations only, has never frequented a small-town coffee shop or a neighborhood restaurant or even a McDonald's – otherwise that illusion would have been quickly dispelled.

Summary

To recapitulate: Marx derives the value of labor-power by a series of deductions, to wit: value is the labor needed to produce a commodity; in the case of labor-power, it is therefore also the labor necessary to produce the laborer, which means it is the labor necessary to produce the means of subsistence which sustains the laborer. This is the value of labor-power.

There is circular logic in this, in that the "necessary means of subsistence" supposedly determines the value of labor-power, but it is the wage paid for the labor which determines the amount of means of subsistence which can be purchased. Moreover, some of the links in Marx's chain of deductions are questionable; the laborer must indeed exist in order for there to be labor-power, but that does not mean the labor necessary to produce labor-power can be equated to the labor necessary to produce the laborer. But it would have been difficult in any case to discover the amount of necessary to produce labor-power, because it is not a commodity produced or manufactured by labor, and the entire picture Marx tries to fit it into is inappropriate. On a broader perspective, the entire concept of labor-power as what is purchased, of its consumption as equaling labor, and all the rest of Marx's picture, is utterly specious. Labor-power is an empty concept, a non-entity, devised to make up for the fact that Marx's theory cannot give us the value of labor, since labor *is* value. Labor-power is yet another "fudge factor" tacked on to patch up his theory.

NOTES – Chapter 6

1 "The Heart of Romp 'N' Roll," Louisville *Courier-Journal*, Nov. 2, 1992.

2 Cully, Abrell and Thompson, John, *Moses May Have Been an Apache! and Other Actual Facts!*, Pittstown, N.J., Main Street Press, 1988.

7. DENOUEMENT

We are now about to "force the secret of profit making," that is, show how the capitalist actually gains wealth. As we will see, Marx will first show that profit as conventionally considered is impossible. That is because the value of the finished product is not greater than the sum of the constituent values, i.e., the constituent "labors" which went into it; and thus there is no added increment above costs which would give the capitalist a profit. After showing that the capitalist cannot make a profit through an "increase of value" (his notion of profit) he will show how the capitalist does acquire gain: through "surplus value," or in his terminology, "the production of absolute surplus-value."

In place of profit

Marx begins his discussion of "the Process of Producing Surplus-Value" (Part III, Chapter VII), by returning to his concept of labor-power. He says:

> The capitalist buys labour-power in order to use it; and labour-power in use is labour itself.

This is in line with his doctrine that labor-power is the commodity the capitalist buys, and that labor-power is converted into labor after its purchase: "The purchaser of labour-power consumes it by setting the seller of it to work. By working, the latter becomes actually what before he only was potentially, labour-power in action, a labourer."

Again, it seems irrefutable that the exercise of the ability to labor is labor itself. However, the "ability to labor" is not something one can buy or sell. One can't put it in boxes and hand it over to the buyer, as one can do with other commodities; and in itself it is not a performable service, i.e. not labor. It is an abstract notion. Moreover, it would seem that it is the laborer, not the capitalist, who exercises that ability, or who "consumes" labor-power; so this would be a case, contrary to the norm, where the seller and not the buyer consumes the commodity.

Marx's notion of labor-power seems questionable in the light of such considerations. However, the introduction of this abstract entity into his analysis is what eventually gives Marx the tools he needs in order to show the capitalist to be an exploiter of surplus value. This will become more apparent as we continue.

Looking at Marx's argument, we see that he first applies his own peculiar brand of cracked analysis to various incidental aspects of the "labour-process," that being his term for the production process. (It is a revealing bit of jargon. He imputes validity only to labor, denying the value of the contributions of all other agents involved in production, especially those of the capitalist, who organized and initiated the whole endeavor.) In the present instance, Marx departs from his two usual writing modes – the mystification of simple topics and the over-simplification of complicated ones – and adopts a third mode, the tedious belaboring of obvious topics. He struggles mightily to explain the obvious in passages like the following:

> An instrument of labour is a thing, or a complex of things, which the labourer interposes between himself and the subject of his labour, and which serves as the conduction of his activity. In a wider sense we may include among the instruments of labour, in addition to those that are used for directly transferring labour to its subject, and which therefore, in one way or another, serve as conductors of activity, all such objects as are necessary for carrying on the labour-process. These do not enter directly into the process, but without them it is either impossible for it to take place at all, or possible only to a partial extent.

Probably nothing needs to be added to that passage as an explanation of tools. It is worth pointing out that much or what Marx says could be said of the capitalist and his role in the production process; without his efforts, including the tasks of organizing the entire endeavor, supervising and coordinating it, and financing it through his capital, production would scarcely be possible. If the capitalist and his capital are necessary for the production process, just as labor is, then perhaps his contributions should have been accorded value in Marx's analysis.

Marx continues:

> Once more we find the earth to be a universal instrument of this sort, for it furnishes a locus standi to the labourer and a field of employment for his activity.

It furnishes not only a field of employment, but a field of gravity. No doubt it would be very difficult to produce commodities if there were no planet Earth and if we were all floating through space without a locus standi to stand on; but in such circumstances, producing commodities would probably be the least of our worries.

Marx's remarks about the necessity of the earth are as incongruous as the facetious pseudo-news item quoted previously, to the effect that if all life on Earth disappeared, we could save 76 cents of every dollar.

Marx continues the theme:

> In the labour-process, therefore, man's activity, with the help of the instruments of labour effect an alteration, designed from the commencement, in the material worked upon.

That much is commonplace. The phrase "designed from the commencement" speaks of planning, an aspect of human endeavor. People first have an object in mind; then they work, using tools and machines, to produce the conceived-of item. Marx adds his own peculiar metaphysical slant on this, however:

> The process disappears in the product; the latter is a use-value, Nature's material adapted by a change of form to the wants of man. Labour has incorporated itself with its subject: the former is materialised, the latter transformed. That which in the labourer appeared as movement, now appears in the product as a fixed quality without motion. The blacksmith forges and the product is the forging.

The deep, metaphysical point Marx is making here is not easy to grasp. His remark, "The process disappears in the product," for instance, is difficult to see as anything but fanciful rhetoric, vaporous metaphysics. We might say the process shapes the product; that, at least, would have some objective meaning. We can see labor – work, or energy – being exerted to shape or construct a product. But the process doesn't take up residence in the product; energy doesn't become matter, or transmute into matter, or congeal into a property of the finished product. Marx cannot seem to conceive that labor can shape, mold or transform the material object without the merging of their two identities. (As for the process disappearing, it does so whenever the work stops – that is, when the process stops.)

But this is well-trodden ground by now; suffice it to say that the fanciful expressions and metaphysics in the quoted passage reflect once again Marx's Hegelian influences and his theories of processes as entities in themselves, and of labor as an internally-contained "process-turned-property" of the physical commodity. The reader need not puzzle over all the deeper meanings and ramifications of a statement like, "The blacksmith forges and the product is a forging." There is much less there than meets the eye; a more prosaic statement of the reality of the thing is, "The blacksmith forges, and the result is a horseshoe." Then again, Marx is a good example of the principle that sometimes an author writes, and the result is a forgery.

We come at last to a sort of summing up of Marx's view of "the labour-process" (or we could say more simply, labor: for labor is a process and Marx's term is therefore redundant).

> The labour process, resolved as above into its simple elementary factors, is human action with a view to the production of use-values, appropriation of natural substances to human requirements; it is the necessary condition for effecting exchange of matter between man and Nature; it is the ever-lasting nature-imposed condition of human existence and therefore is independent of every social phase of that existence or rather, is common to every such phase.

That may be a description of labor, or the productive process, "resolved into its simple elementary factors," but then labor was a pretty simple concept to begin with. Marx is belaboring the obvious – for we already knew that "labor" implies "human labor" or action; and it's generally understood that labor applies to producing things, or to doing things of an economic nature, as opposed perhaps to doing things for fun or doing things that don't produce tangible results.

He does make one pertinent point, however – that the need to labor is a "necessary condition," an "ever-lasting nature-imposed condition of human existence." It is indeed true that under any conditions with which we are familiar in known human history (at least since Adam and Eve), mankind has been faced with the necessity of working. The necessities of life don't fall into our hands; they have to be wrested from nature by our unremitting effort. This is a reality of human existence, a fact of life common, as Marx points out, to every phase of human history. The point is, it is indeed a "nature-imposed" necessity, imposed by the very nature of the world, and not by any individual, group, social class or type of organization of society.

This is significant, because at times Marx seems to write as if the blame for that fact of life belongs to the capitalist class. If they didn't create the situation, he implies, they at least profit from it.

For example, he says, "If his [the laborer's] capacity for labour remains unsold, the labourer derives no benefit from it. Moreover, 'capacity for labour'. . . is nothing unless it is sold." That is probably true, under capitalist societies. But it is not a unique flaw of such societies, and it is not the capitalist's fault. Similarly, under hunter-gatherer or agrarian societies, if someone has the capacity to hunt but there is no game to hunt, his capacity does him no good. If one has the capacity to farm, yet a drought prevents him from farming, that capacity does no good. Capitalists did not invent the necessity for laboring, and they did not invent the condition that the capacity to labor must find an outlet in order to do any good. What is different about capitalist societies – or let us call them, societies complex enough to have real economies – is that exercising the capacity for labor means finding a job. Only the form of that necessity changes.

Marx ignores this truth when, in the *Communist Manifesto*, he and Engels write, "[The bourgeoisie] has resolved personal worth into exchange value," as if capitalists had decreed the necessity of finding a job, and as if their decree had reduced laborers to the level of beings functioning only in the economic sphere. Marx can seem to impute blame by calling the working class "a class of labourers, who live only so long as they find work, and who find work only so long as their labour increases capital. These labourers, who must sell themselves piecemeal, are a commodity, like every other article of commerce, and are consequently exposed to all the vicissitudes of competition. . ."

It may be a feature of capitalist societies that laborers must find employment; but the basic necessity of finding work is an age-old fact. It is only the form of finding work which is different in different types of society. Modern man must work, must occupy a role appropriate to the type of economy extant – and this usually means finding a job. One can't simply go out in the morning hunting game or looking for wild roots and berries. Not only is game too scarce and the population too great; society itself is different. Now there is civilization and an economy; society is more complicated, intricate and "advanced," the degree of complexity and organization is greater, than in a hunter-gatherer society. When Marx condemns the capitalist for the laborer's need to find a job (while admitting the age-old necessity of laboring), he is, in a disguised manner, criticizing complexity in society as such. It is important to recognize that in railing against such things as the selling of labor, the market in commodities, the "cash nexus," and the existence of capitalists, merchants, renters and so on as elements of an economy, Marx condemned civilization itself, or complexity in society as such. When he condemns the need "to sell one's labour-power," he refuses to admit that there is only one real alternative to it, namely, to live in a society which has not advanced in complexity to the point of having an economy, that is, a hunter-gatherer society – not a realistic option today. Even so-called socialistic societies don't eliminate the necessity of finding employment; they only make the state the all-powerful, sole employer, and call the situation by other names, disguising the reality with Marxist jargon.

Further comments on the justice of capitalism

Marx now makes some comments bearing on the justice of capitalist economies, though that perhaps was not his intention. This is one of the semi-honest passages one occasionally comes across in his work. He begins:

> Let us now return to our would-be capitalist. We left him just
> after he had purchased, in the open market, all the necessary factors
> of the labour-process; its objective factors, the means of production,
> as well as its subjective factor, labour-power.

One might be inclined to see in Marx's term "subjective factor," an admission that labor-power, the ability to do labor, is an intangible entity, a capacity of the human being and thus not objectively observable — unlike labor itself, for instance. If that is assuming too much, it might be best to consider that "subjective factor" is Marx's synonym for "human factor," and that he is distinguishing purely material or mechanical factors like raw materials, productive machinery and so on, from human factors such as labor, or as Marx would have it, labor-power.

He continues:

> The labour-process, turned into the process by which the
> capitalist consumes labour-power, exhibits two characteristic
> phenomena. First, the labourer works under the control of the
> capitalist to whom his labour belongs; the capitalist taking good care
> that the work is done in a proper manner, and that there is no
> unnecessary waste of raw material, and no wear and tear of the
> implements beyond what is necessarily caused by the work.
>
> Secondly, the product is the property of the capitalist and not that
> of the labourer, its immediate producer. Suppose that a capitalist pays
> for a day's labour-power at its value; then the right to use that power
> for a day belongs to him, just as much as the right to use any other
> commodity, such as a horse that he hired for the day. . . The labour-
> process is a process between things that the capitalist has purchased,
> things that have become his property. The product of this process
> also belongs, therefore, to him, just as much as does the wine which
> is the product of a process of fermentation completed in his cellar.

All in all, the above is a fair and accurate statement of the situation. The capitalist pays for the various factors of production, such as the labor, raw materials, rental or purchase costs of a physical plant, costs of productive machinery, and so on. Then he produces the product "at a venture," i.e., taking a chance that he can sell the finished product at a profit. The capitalist pays all the costs incurred in producing the commodity, and thus as Marx admits, owns the finished product; no one else has any claim on it.

(However, even while giving a certain amount of credit where it is due, Marx is able to inject a sneering tone into his text. Here he compares laborers to horses and subtly implies that to the capitalist, his laborers are no more than cogs in the wheel, mere elements of production with no more identity than horses or wine.)

We can make certain observations about the productive process as described in the quoted passage. For one thing, we do not see any obvious standard for determining whether the capitalist is paying his laborers a "correct" wage; nor do we see any absolute standard for saying only a fraction of the day is paid for by the wage and thus is "necessary," the rest being unpaid or "unnecessary." No evidence or support for such *a priori* standards can be discerned; the capitalist pays the labor costs, so much per day, and that becomes a factor in determining the price he must receive. No evidence in the bare facts themselves can be seen for Marx's theory of the "proper" or necessary length of the working day.

Another issue is this: though Marx admits here that the capitalist of rights owns the finished product, he implies elsewhere in his oeuvre that such a result amounts to exploitation, that the capitalist wrongfully "expropriates" or "appropriates" the commodity which the laborers have produced. They produce it socially, and the capitalist expropriates it individually – a "contradiction." For example, in the Communist Manifesto he says,

> Capital is a collective product, and only by the united action of many members. . . can it be set in motion.
> Capital is therefore, not a personal, it is a social power.

But Marx shows that although capital is a "social" phenomenon, and although the labor of the workers produces the finished commodity, the capitalist "appropriates" a social entity for personal gain, an unjust or exploitative outcome. In Marx's perverse view, the capitalist should bear all the expense of the production process, should bear the risk of being able to sell the product, and should exercise the initiative of organizing the whole process; and yet the finished product should belong to the workers or to "society." That is Marx's idea of justice. It should be said here that the capitalist doesn't appropriate the product; he produces it, and of rights owns it. As with all ideologies, hatred was at the root of Marxism; and Marx's hatred for capitalists caused him to grasp at any excuse to lodge an accusation against them, blinding him to the patent illogic of his accusation.

Indeed, in the very next paragraph of the text we are considering, Marx will speak of "the product appropriated by the capitalist." Now, to "appropriate" means to grasp or seize something already existing; it is not the same as producing or even buying it. The invidious notion Marx is trying to convey is that the capitalist seizes the commodity away from its rightful owners. Thus as he often does, Marx is talking out of both sides of his mouth. He grudgingly acknowledges the capitalist's right to the product, but only in a specific context and for Marx's own limited purposes (hard as they may be to discern at this point). Later he will revert to his more usual position, that the capitalist is always wrong and always an exploiter in every instance and circumstance. Marx often expressed such diametrically opposed views, his opinion at a given point in his writings depending on the context or the purposes to be served. His truth was dependent on "necessity," i.e., on the rhetorical needs of the moment; that's dialectics.

It is interesting that Marx compares the capitalist's ownership of the worker's day's labor-power to "the right to use" commodities "such as a horse that he has hired for the day. . ." We might wonder why Marx uses the term "a horse that he has hired for the day," rather than "a horse whose day's labor-power he has purchased." Is there a difference between the two? Why is the horse rented (or "hired"), rather than its labor-power being purchased? Perhaps Marx himself could not always keep up the pretense – could not always use his convoluted circumlocutions, but occasionally slipped into writing in normal terms.

That is probably one reason Marx speaks of a horse "that he has hired [i.e., rented] for the day." Another reason is that it is a normal usage and something within the average person's frame of reference, whereas to speak of "a horse whose day's-worth of labor-power he has purchased" would be to go beyond the bounds of any normal person's cognizance. It is a concept foreign to the intuitive economic viewpoint of almost everyone, and should be so, largely because it is a fallacious concept or a "nominalist fallacy" – a name for something which does not exist. That is, it is a nonsense phrase.

One hires labor either by the individual job – for instance, hiring someone to do a certain repair at an arranged price; or at "piece rates," for instance certain jobs like assembly jobs in the garment industry; or by the day or hour, where the wage paid depends on the duration of the labor. Marx's rigid system and his bizarre categorization of labor-power as a commodity cannot be made to adequately reflect reality in these areas.

The production of surplus-value

We are now ready to address directly the topic of how the capitalist makes money. As Marx would have it, this is not by profit as classically conceived, but by exploitation of the workers via "the production of surplus value." He approaches the topic as follows:

> The product appropriated by the capitalist is a use-value, as yarn,
> for example, or boots. But, although boots are in one sense, the basis
> of all social progress, and our capitalist is a decided "progressist," yet
> he does not manufacture boots for their own sake. Use-value is, by

no means, the thing "qu'on aime pour lui-même" in the production of commodities. Use-values are only produced by capitalists, because, and in so far as, they are the material substratum, the depositories of exchange-value.

Again, Marx resorts to sarcasm in his phase, "our capitalist is a decided 'progressist'," but such ad hominem remarks add nothing of substance to his argument. It reveals a bias against the capitalist, a bigotry and even hatred at work – not reason.

Marx displays in this area of his theory an almost "Victorian" * prudishness toward economic matters. He was revolted by, and revolting against, economics per se – it is important to observe that fact.

As Hayek said about people like Marx, "What they resent is, in truth, that there is an economic problem."[1]

Marx wasn't railing only about who made the money; he was revolted by the "cash nexus" as such. It is a shame that someone with such an infantile prudery toward grown-up realities came to be accepted as an authority.

As for the false dichotomy between use-value and exchange value: the two cannot be separated. (This is indicated among other things by the modern theory that market value is related to "marginal utility.") Boots only have exchange value because they have use-value; and if they are made for reasons of their exchange value, still they are sold to be used. The fact that the motives of the capitalist do not meet Marx's high and noble standards has no bearing on the justice of capitalism.

If the capitalist produces for exchange value, so does the laborer – he is there primarily for the wage, not because boots are "the thing which he loves for itself." How then are the workers' motives any nobler than the capitalists'? Only Marx's bias made him find a distinction. For, continually short of money and subject to the pain and humiliations of such a condition, Marx concluded that the fault was not in him but in the "system." Every time he went into a shop to buy something, they asked him for money; this was a horrible affront to him, which he blamed on the capitalists' greed. He made a universal theory out of his own personal setbacks, and like one who "would kill every rose in the universe because his own sense of smell is gone,"[2] he strove to bring ruin and destruction on all those shopkeepers, manufacturers, capitalist economies, and an entire normal way of life, because his own perspective of it was bleak and his experiences of it humiliating.

It should not be forgotten, either, that, contrary to Marx's criticisms, there is very often an element of love, or appreciation, in a productive, successful business.

----

* We will call it "Victorian," though much of the Victorian reputation for prudishness was unearned.

A love for and understanding of making a fine product may be forgotten from time to time, but it is not nonexistent, as Marx claimed. It is not unusual to find architects who love architecture, carpenters and construction contractors who love building, and in fact workers, craftsmen, professionals and capitalists of all types who get satisfaction from a job well done and from an excellent "product," even if that product is something as intangible as a case well argued in court.

The desire to realize a vision, to make a reality of something previously conceived of in the mind, is found in entrepreneurs perhaps as often and strongly as a mere desire to earn money. Marx could never understand this, having no trade or craft himself other than agitating.

To Marx, everything was limited to a very minimal set of rigid alternatives. One was either a villain, like the capitalist, or a heroic victim, like the proletarian. Marx could not contemplate subtlety, variety, shades of gray, or multiple categories. A capitalist could not be motivated both by a need for money (or love of money, or greed) and by an appreciation of the product itself. Mixed motives and shades of gradation could never be accommodated by Marx's either-or, black-white, crudely Procrustean and "metaphysical" thought processes.

Ultimately, the capitalist, like the worker and everyone else, is driven by economic necessity – the need to make a living. It is strange that Marx, for whom "necessity" was the magic byword justifying and legitimizing anything and everything, would discriminate against just this one response to necessity. For the capitalist responds to necessity in his own way, just as the laborer does in his. It is a matter of inclination, personal preference, and opportunity as to which method is chosen – not inherent moral worth.

To continue with Marx's exposition:

> Our capitalist has two objects in view: in the first place, he wants to produce a use-value that has a value in exchange, that is to say, an article destined to be sold, a commodity.

(Come what may, from time to time an actual fact intrudes into Marx's analysis.)

> . . . and secondly, he desires to produce a commodity whose value shall be greater than the sum of the values of the commodities used in its production, that is, of the means of production and labour-power, that he purchased with good money in the open market.

The above is an accurate description of the concept of profit, if it were not for the deterministic connotations of Marx's notion of value. It is accurate enough to say that the capitalist wants to produce a commodity which he can sell for more than it cost to produce. He wants to produce a product with a higher exchange value, a higher market price, than what he paid to produce it. And stated thus, it is a goal often achieved: thousands of products are sold every day at a profit.

When we consider Marx's viewpoint, however, we can see how he can "prove" profit is impossible. For Marx, value is a deterministic quantity, almost a physical property; it is an amount of labor contained or congealed in a commodity, fixed from the moment when the commodity has been produced, and thus its magnitude is pre-determined entirely by the labor that was exerted in producing the goods. Value is not, for Marx, determined dynamically, by the haggling and striking of bargains under market conditions; it is a property as fixed and pre-ordained as the weight, volume, and shape of the finished commodity. Once the item is produced, the capitalist cannot add on a percentage to that fixed value or price for his profit.

In such circumstances, the capitalist's task takes on a different aspect. He wants to produce a commodity "whose value shall be greater than the sum of the values" of the constituent commodities. When value is seen as a static property of the commodity, that stated task becomes as difficult as producing a commodity whose weight is greater than the sum of the weights of its parts. But remember, the situation takes on that aspect only because Marx reduces value to the level of a thing, rather than a dynamically-determined result of events, i.e. a process. The master dialectician here takes a reductionist, doltish, "metaphysical" view of value; and thus he can appear to apply to value, a social phenomenon, the laws governing material things.

As we look at Marx's examination of the capitalist's process of trying to make money, it will be useful to keep in mind these two separate views of value and the deterministic assumptions under which he is laboring.

Putting numbers to the theory

Marx now proceeds with his analysis of the value of the finished product, demonstrating that the whole equals the sum of its parts, and not more. He gives a quantitative example:

> For spinning the yarn, raw material is required; suppose in this case 10 lbs. of cotton. We have no need at present to investigate the value of this cotton, for our capitalist has, we will assume, bought it at its full value, say of ten shillings. In this price the labour required for the production of the cotton is already expressed in terms of the average labour of society [i.e., "homogeneous, socially-necessary labour"]. We will further assume that the wear and tear of the spindle, which, for our present purpose, may represent all other instruments of labour employed, amounts to the value of 2s. If, then,

twenty-four hours' labour, or two working days, are required to produce the quantity of gold represented by twelve shillings, we have
here, to begin with, two days' labour already incorporated in the yarn.

Very well, we can assume that 10 pounds of cotton are used, and that
the capitalist bought it at its full value. But what exactly does it mean to say
that he paid full value?

It is easier to know what we mean by paying full price. For any particular
item there is a prevailing market price, or a range of values within which most
stores' prices will fall. Some "shopping around" or a general familiarity with
the merchandise will tell us what the prevailing price, or list price, or normal
price, should be. This prevailing price is what we consider to be the full price,
or the full value.

This market price is the value in a market sense, value in the real world
where price is determined by the interaction of buyers and sellers. Marx's
world is much more deterministic, and value is a pre-determined entity. What
does it mean for him to say the capitalist pays full value of the cotton? It
means: once the cotton has been produced, it has a certain fixed value
contained in it, its magnitude determined (supposedly) by Marx's logical
categories. He assumes this value is 10 shillings, saying, "In this price the
labour required for the production of the cotton is already expressed." That
is, the value of the cotton is already determined by the labor it "contains,"
before we or the capitalist find out what anyone pays for the cotton on the
open market. To say that the capitalist buys the cotton at its full value is to say
he pays the money equivalent of this inwardly-contained value.

By contrast, in classical theory, what the capitalist pays (under "normal"
market conditions) is by definition the actual value of the cotton. Value
means, what one normally has to pay for something on the open market – it
is not an *a priori* category of which market price is only a "phenomenal" form,
as in Marx's theory.

We will accept Marx's assumption about wear and tear on the spindle,
and his use of that to represent depreciation of all the productive equipment.
Capital equipment of course is not a separate category of production costs –
it can in its turn be resolved into a certain amount of congealed labor (much
as in *Wealth of Nations* all factors are resolved into rents, labor, and profit).

One difficulty we might foresee with Marx's theory is that while values
are always calculated in terms of labour, prices as we know them are most
often expressed in terms of money. The problem is how to make the
connection or conversion between the two.

In classical theory – that is, in the real world – it is not difficult to
determine the money equivalent of value. For value practically is money; it is
the prevailing market price, and there's nothing derived or secondary about it.
It doesn't express some logical category or inner property like congealed

labor. (This is not to say that it is not determined or governed by a variety of factors and market considerations.) On the other hand, in Marx's theory value is entirely determined as a theoretical category completely separate from money. It equals the contained labor. The problem then is discovering how that attains a corresponding money price; in what terms can the price be said to "correspond" to the labor?

One possibility for establishing a correspondence or correlation, for one schooled in market economics, would be to say that the market price of a commodity equals the market price of the labor. That is, we begin with the fact that, in the cotton under consideration, a certain amount of labor is incorporated. If we know that twenty-four hours of labor have been incorporated in the cotton and in wear and tear on the spindle, then we would might think it logical to calculate thus: The wage for twenty-four hours (two working days) of labour is twelve shillings; therefore the money equivalent of the value of cotton and spindle is twelve shillings.

Or to put it another way – we know that the cost of these factors, the cotton and the representative fraction of the spindle, is 12 shillings. And we know 12 shillings is two days' wage. Thus we can deduce that two days, or twenty-four hours, of labor have been embodied in the cotton and spindle.

That is, we begin with the amount of labor embodied in a unit quantity of a product, which we know by some unspecified method; we take the prevailing wage, and thus the price, for that amount of labor; and thus we attain a money equivalent of the value of the commodity, which is then its "proper" market price.

Of course, Marx does not use this method. For one thing, it is too market-oriented; it is not deterministic, not based on *a priori* categories. It is based on the happenstance of whatever is the market price of labor. (And besides, for Marx there is no market price of labor – labor-power, not labor, is bought and sold.)

Moreover, that method is a variety of the "reciprocal" approach, where the value of commodities is labor, while the value of labor is an amount of commodities. Marx does not use such reciprocal definitions – for him labor is the value of everything, and a method must be found for reducing everything to labor and labor only: the goal is to express all values, prices, wages, etc. in terms of labor.

So Marx does not adopt that conversion method for equating amounts of labor to their appropriate money equivalents. Rather, he works via the intermediary of a hard commodity, gold; the labor required to produce a certain quantity of that metal is set equal to the amount of coined money which contains that quantity of gold. Thus he says, "If then, twenty-four hours labour, or two working days, are required to produce the quantity of gold represented by twelve shillings, we have here, to begin with, two days' labour already incorporated in the yarn." That is, if two working days produced the yarn, and also two working days produced the gold in twelve shillings, then the proper price of the yarn is twelve shillings, while its value is two days of labor.

Thus Marx finds a way to relate the value of a commodity directly to the labor incorporated in the commodity, and to assign it an equivalent money price, all without any reference to the price paid for the labor (the wage). The "value" of the commodity depends solely on the amount of labor required to produce it, and the market price (its value expressed as money) is independent of the wage rate.

It will help us understand "what depends on what" in Marx's analysis if we rearrange the order of his assumptions. Let's begin with this: we will assume that twenty-four hours of labor, two days' worth, produce twelve shillings worth of gold. That is, we assume that the conversion factor for labor to money is, twenty-four hours to twelve shillings. (The working day is twelve hours.) We can take this assumption first, because it is independent of the others.

Now, Marx has assumed that the cotton costs ten shillings (paid for at its full value). He could just as easily have assumed that the cotton required twenty hours of labor to produce: twelve shillings equals twenty-four hours of labor; so 10/12 of 24 hours is 20 hours. To say the cotton costs 10 shillings, using Marx's theory, is to say that first of all it required 20 hours to produce – that fact comes first, and the 20 hours of congealed labor then finds its expression as a money equivalent, or market price of 10 shillings.

Marx also assumes that the wear and tear on the spindle (and all productive equipment) is an expense to the capitalist of two shillings; that is, he assumes that four hours' worth of labor, or value, out of the full complement that produced the productive machinery, is worn away.

(That is the way the chain of events would proceed, within the terms of Marx's theory. But in actual fact, in writing his text Marx no doubt worked backwards. That is: the first observable fact is that the cotton costs 10 shillings; Marx undoubtedly worked backwards from that fact to make the example work out correctly in terms of hours of labor – for he had no way of knowing the facts about the labor, and made no effort to actually measure the embodied labor of the cotton and the fraction of spindle.)

It is possible that he had somehow measured the complete amount of labor required to produce a typical production plant, and determined the usual working life for such machinery, so as to pro-rate the labor in the given amount of yarn. More likely, though, he began with the final price of the yarn – an easily determinable figure – and retro-fitted all his other figures to work out correctly to that total. What is almost certain, at any rate, is that Marx did not directly measure the labor embodied in the cotton, the spindle, or any other factor of the yarn's final value. He no doubt started with the money figure which had to be represented by each factor and used his conversion factor, one shilling to two hours of labor, to derive the corresponding quantity of labor. In other words, his whole example could have been constructed without making any reference to the quantity of embodied labor in any factor; those quantities were derived by inference, based on the assumptions of his theory, and are entirely extraneous and exiguous to any observed facts. They don't lend support to the validity of his theory, but were deduced based on his theory, thus begging the question of whether the facts support his "labor theory of value."

At this point it might be useful to refer once again to the question of the mechanism used to convert labor to money prices. Marx uses a conversion factor of one shilling per two hours of labor; it might be pertinent to ask, Do the capitalists also use that same conversion factor? That is, do they consciously calculate the hours of labor embodied in a unit of their product, use the "statutory" conversion factor, and thus put the appropriate price on their finished goods? If they do not do it consciously (which of course they don't – people didn't know and didn't use Marx's theory in all the centuries before he wrote), then by what mechanism do goods automatically come to acquire a price in accord with Marx's theoretical stipulations? No self-acting market mechanism is brought forth in Marx's work. He supplies a system of logical categories which states that value must equal a certain magnitude; he then assumes the real world has no choice but to fall into accord; but he never supplies a reasonable explanation of how his system could function in the real world.

Additional factors

We see, then, that the cotton plus wear and tear amount to two days' labor, "because" two days' labor can be equated to the quantity of gold in twelve shillings. (That line of causation exists only in Marx's mind, however.)

To this labor is added the labor of the production of yarn:

> We now know what portion of the value of the yarn is owing to the cotton and the spindle. It amounts to twelve shillings or the value of two days' work. The next point for our consideration is, what portion of the value of the yarn is added to the cotton by the labour of the spinner. . .
>
> We proceed upon the assumption that spinning is simple, unskilled labour, the average labour of a given state of society.

He may as well assume that spinning is simple unskilled labor, because he never gives an objective standard for determining just what "degree of difficulty" should be assigned to any given type of labor. Of course, it might be possible to form a general idea of how a certain type of labor should be recompensed, using such standards as the amount of education required, the degree of physical exertion or manual dexterity required, and so on. But when it comes to calculating an exact proportion over and above base wage or base level which a certain type of labor represents, we are given no objective basis of calculation by Marx. Any appearance of presenting such a basis results mostly from starting with the observable wages (market value) and working backwards from that to present a pseudo-analytic reason for evaluating the labor. Marx is attempting to show that his theory explains the wage rates actually set by supply and demand. But Marx's theoretical explanation is just detritus, extraneous verbiage added on to make his theory seem to be what is at work in the real world. The real explanation is given by classical market economies. Marx's theoretic picture tries to mimic the results of supply and demand, but that picture adds nothing to the understanding of those events; it is an extraneous fudge factor.

At any rate, Marx is now calculating the "value added" of the actual manufacturer of the yarn. Since only labor counts as value (and only the hired employee's labor – not the capitalist's), the value added is simply the labor invested by wage laborers at the current stage of production. Marx continues his analysis:

> If in one hour 1 2/3 lbs. of cotton can be spun into 1 2/3 lbs. of yarn, then 10 lbs. of yarn indicate the absorption of 6 hours' labour.

(Hence the term "absorbent cotton?" No, the labor is "absorbed" into the cotton in the same sense in which it is "congealed," "crystallised," "embodied," "materialised," "incorporated," transmogrified, incarnated, or otherwise deposited in the cotton.)

> We assumed, on the occasion of its sale, that the value of a day's labour-power is three shillings and that six hours' labour are incorporated in that sum, and consequently that this amount of labour is requisite to produce the necessaries of life daily required on an average by the labourer.

That is not exactly the order of Marx's logical deductions as he stated the case the first time. His argument was, Start with the known amount of "necessaries of life"; then assume that six hours of labor are incorporated in those daily "necessaries of life"; then, because that amount of labor is in some sense necessary for the (re-)production of a day's labor-power, deduce that six hours of labor is the value of a day's labor-power.

In other words, the line of deductions goes:

> a known quantity of necessaries {*implies*} → six hours of labor are
> embodied in the necessaries {*implies*}→ six hours = the value of
> a day's labor-power

not in the reverse order, as he alleges here.

Again, the figure three shillings comes from using Marx's conversion method: the same amount of labor is putatively invested in producing three shillings in minted coin as is invested in the "necessaries" of a day's labor-power – six hours.

This roundabout analysis of labor, labor-power, and money values, to repeat, accomplishes some crucial things for Marx. It eliminates the obvious and ordinary method of reasoning, wherein the cost of labor is a factor in the price of the finished product, and where the prices of goods and the cost of labor are mutually dependent. In Marx's theory, the wage rate has nothing to do with the value (price) of goods. His theory also separates the value of a day's labor (-power) from the length of the working day – a key factor in his analysis later on. For Marx, the value of labor is not, "so much per hour of labor," as in normal economic analysis. Rather, the value of labor-power is determined in reverse fashion, by the value of the goods a typical laborer can buy with a day's wage. (That is, Marx represents it as so, but actually the value of labor-power is a number Marx picks out of a hat.)

Likewise, Marx's analysis separates the price of goods from the cost per hour of labor; they are unrelated because, for one thing, the value of labor is not determined on a per-hour basis. Value equals so much for a day's labor-power (with the length of the day unspecified). If this separation could not be made, Marx would have had a hard time maintaining that the value of labor-power, as determined by the amount of goods which can be purchased with the day's wage, is grossly out of proportion to the value of goods produced for the capitalist by the labor. For the two would otherwise have been interrelated (as they are in fact), and could not ever get too far out of proportion. But Marx's roundabout analysis manages to decouple them, thus clearing the path for Marx's indictment relating to the exploitation of the working class via unpaid "surplus value" or extra work.

To continue with his argument about the impossibility of profit:

> If now our spinner, by working for one hour, can convert 1 2/3
> lbs. of cotton in 1 2/3 lbs. of yarn, it follows that in six hours he will
> convert 10 lbs. of cotton into 10 lbs. of yarn. * Hence, during the
> spinning process, the cotton absorbs six hours' labour.

———————————

* minus a certain percentage for "wastage."

There are six hours of labor invested or embodies in the cotton. Furthermore,

> The same quantity of labour is also embodied in a piece of gold of the value of three shillings. Consequently by the mere labour of spinning, a value of three shillings is added to the cotton.

Notice once again the difference between Marx's theory and classical theory. Marx says that "the mere labour" adds a certain value to the cotton — apart from market considerations, apart from determining whether anyone will pay the newly-determined price. That is the nature of Marx's deterministic system. It is a system of theoretical categories, not a description of the real world.

Marx continues:

> Let us now consider the total value of the product, the 10 lbs. of yarn. Two and a half days' labour have been embodied in it, of which two days were contained in the cotton and in the substance of the spindle worn away, and half a day was absorbed during the process of spinning. This two and a half days' labour is also represented by a piece of gold of the value of fifteen shillings. Hence, fifteen shillings is an adequate price for the 10 lbs. of yarn, or the price of one pound is eighteen-pence.

Marx gleefully envisions the effect of his inexorable logic on the capitalist:

> Our capitalist stares in astonishment. The value of the product is exactly equal to the value of the capital advanced. The value so advanced has not expanded, no surplus-value has been created. . .

The impossibility of profit

The capitalist stares in astonishment, but of course we are discussing a fictional, hypothetical capitalist. It's easy to flummox a hypothetical capitalist to any degree desired. In the present instance the capitalist is astonished because Marx has proved that it is impossible to do what the capitalist does every day, namely make a profit.

That is, Marx has shown that profit in the classical sense is impossible; for as he says, "The value of the product is exactly equal to the value of the capital advanced. The value so advanced has not expanded, no surplus-value has been created. . ." Of course, under the heading "capital" Marx includes only labor costs (including the labor costs of the raw materials used – labor costs at every stage of production). If value is restricted to labor costs only, of course there will be no margin left over for a profit, no "expansion of value" – Marx's notion of profit. If value is restricted to labor only, then the value of the finished product will not increase; the whole value will just equal the sum of its parts, or the sum of the labor invested at the various stages of production. That's no great mystery, and it's no great surprise that Marx's total value or "adequate" price equals only the sum of all the labor expended.

The problem is, that is not how the real world works; it's not how the actual price is arrived at. Marx says, "fifteen shillings is an adequate price" for the yarn; but that means "adequate" by his definitions and standards. The point is, his standards are not the operative ones. To call something an "adequate price" by his standards means that it is the end result of a series of deductive exercises aimed at establishing what the value must be; it is "adequate" in terms of Marx's axioms and theorems. That is an entirely separate thing from real world economics.

We can therefore make a slight semantic objection to what Marx says, that "fifteen shillings is an adequate price for the 10 lbs. of yarn, or the price of one pound is eighteen-pence." When he says "an adequate price," it is clear he is speaking of his analysis or mathematical exercise: the final answer derived from his equations is fifteen shillings. But when he says "the price of one pound is eighteen-pence," he equates his theory to reality. He means the theoretical result is eighteen pence, and hence the real-world price is eighteen-pence; but that is an unwarranted assumption. While Marx may believe his abstract analysis of the real world to be correct, it is not scientifically legitimate to make that bland assumption, and to equate the two without proof, as if everyone were as convinced by his logic as he himself was.

(Note – the term labor "costs" has been used above. Of course Marx does not speak in those terms but rather of labor as itself directly constituting value, once it has congealed within the commodity. The money equivalent, or phenomenal form, or cost of labor is only an indirect measure of value. However, Marx could have achieved the same result without resorting to his theories of congealed value and such esoterica of his labor theory. If he had defined labor costs, the money price of labor, as the only factor of value and the only element worthy of remuneration, the result would have been the same – the final value would be just the sum of the various labor costs. The key element is that he eliminates profit from the outset, finessing the point by defining it out of existence, and allowing labor alone to count as value. The details may be important to his analysis, adding an air of credence or at least abstruseness, but they don't affect the final result.)

Reality check

We might compare reality to theory by asking this: Though 15s. is the cost of production and 15s. is also the "value" of the finished product, what would prevent the capitalist from charging more than the prescribed "value," if necessary to make a profit?

In other words, Marx's theoretical deductions don't have the force of law; they can't reach out and physically restrain the capitalist from charging such a price as he deems necessary to make a profit. Nor can they restrain the customer from paying that price, if he so desires and it is the best price available. So what's to stop the capitalist from making a profit?

For while Marx has proved to his own satisfaction that profit, identified as "an increase in value," is impossible, if we ignore his analysis for a moment and just think of the unembellished facts of the matter, it is hard to see how profit can be impossible. That is, if we think about the capitalist and his likely actions, it is difficult to see how profit can be prevented. After all, the capitalist has certain costs of production; he presumably knows approximately what his per-unit costs are; he wants to make a profit; and he would naturally price his product accordingly. Given these facts, it is hard to say what prevents his making a profit.

The question then, setting aside Marx's convoluted theory, is much like the story of the Irishman who visited Niagara Falls. The tour guide, in the course of his spiel, announced that, "Over six million gallons of water go over these falls every minute." Unimpressed, the Irishman burst out, "Sure now, and what's to stop it?"

Similarly, as to how the capitalist can make a profit, the question must be: "Sure and what's to stop it?" If the capitalist prices his good as such a level as to make a profit, what is to prevent customers from paying that price? (Of course, Marx assumes things are bought and sold at their "correct" value as defined by his theory, but what if people in the real world perversely refuse to play by his rules?)

Assuming the capitalist is manufacturing as efficiently (i.e., cheaply) as possible – using the "normal" state-of-the-art equipment and the minimum amount of labor "socially necessary" – what is to prevent buyers from paying his price? Under our assumptions, no one else can substantially undersell him; people can't get the goods any cheaper elsewhere; so what prevents them from paying the capitalist's price?

Marx has shown that profit, as classically conceived, is impossible. But anything that actually exists cannot be impossible. In this instance, Marx is somewhat like the fictional character, previously quoted, who considers television impossible; Marx too denies the existence of a phenomenon we all witness every day.

Of course, his argument is not that the capitalist can't make money; rather it is that the mechanism by which he does so is misunderstood – that it is not "an increase of value," or in common parlance profit, but a much more sinister and exploitative mechanism called "surplus value." But before we accept his alternative theory of surplus value, we have to see normal profit definitely eliminated; and Marx has failed in that endeavor.

There is one more point we can look at as a foreshadowing before we move on. Marx gives the "capital advanced" for 10 pounds of yarn as being 15 shillings; this includes the price of a day's "labour-power," which is three shillings.

That is, the actual spinning – the labor performed at our capitalist's stage of production – requires six hours of labor, or "indicate(s) the absorption of 6 hours" labour." This amount of labor also equals the "value" of a day's labor-power; six hours of labor, three shillings, a day's labor-power, or a days' worth of the "necessaries of life" – all are equivalent.

We note, however, that at the time Marx wrote, the length of the working day was twelve hours. Thus six hours may be the value of a whole day's labor-power for Marx, but it is only half a day's labor – that is, it is only half the length of the day actually worked. Here we see how a day's labor-power can equal half a day's labor; for Marx himself refers to the six hours as half a day: he says, "half a day was absorbed during the process of spinning," and he gives the total labor as 2 1/2 days. Thus the groundwork has been laid for showing that a day's labor does not equal a day's labor-power, or that the capitalist exploits unpaid labor and gains wealth from the sweat of the toiling masses.

Six hours is a complete day's labor-power, because Marx worked backward from the supposed value of the "means of subsistence." Basically, he purports to have measured the value of the wage received, or the "necessaries" it will buy, and worked backwards from that to compute the correct day's labor-power as six hours. (This is really a figure he picked arbitrarily.)

On the other hand, six hours is half a day's labor simply because twelve hours was the normal duration of the working day at that time. Thus he derives the point that half a day's labor equals the value of a day's labor-power. That becomes the key to his case for "exploitation" of unpaid labor.

Further reality check

If we can ignore Marx's convoluted theory for a moment, we would be tempted to say that if three shillings is paid for a day's labor, and the day's labor is twelve hours long, then three shillings is the price of twelve hours of labor, not of six hours. Certainly that would be the understanding of the capitalist and the laborers; "twelve hours for three shillings" was no doubt the basis of their contracts, and some due consideration must always be given to the reasonings of people actually engaged in an activity, as opposed to the theories of dilettantes looking on from the outside.

Marx's sleight-of-hand has equated a day's labor-power to half a day's labor, and the value of a day's wage to half a day's labor, by working backwards, supposedly from the "means of subsistence" received, and by simply picking a number out of his hat for that value. Thus he has managed to completely divorce his theory of the value of a day's labor-power from what is actually done for the wage and the economic value of what is done. From that kind of stacked deck he can pull out any results he wants.

What if we ignored Marx's theory of a value of labor-power, and simply proceeded on the assumption that the capitalist pays so much money for so many hours of labor? One of two things could result. If three shillings is indeed the wage for a day's labor, then three shillings becomes the price of twelve hours of labor, not six. Thus the expenditure of the capitalist for 2 1/2 days of labor – 30 hours – is 7 1/2 shillings, not 15.

On the other hand, if 3 shillings is really the price of six hours of labor, then the capital expenditure for the yarn is indeed 15 shillings. But in this case, since six hours of labor costs three shillings, the day's wage, for a full 12-hour day, must be six shillings, not three.

In either of these cases (both of which remove Marx's gimmick by which a day's labor-power equals half a day's labor) it becomes actually impossible for the capitalist to make money by any means, either through profit as conventionally conceived or through exploited surplus value. The outlay always equals the final value, as indeed it should within Marx's theory, for the total amount of labor equals the sum of its parts. The capitalist makes no profit, but neither does he make surplus value. In fact, capitalists can gain no wealth and capitalism cannot exist at all. The fact that we know the capitalist does make money, shows that Marx's theory can be reduced to absurdity. He can destroy the concept of profit as classically conceived, but he brings down the whole edifice with it; with his escape hatch removed, the result becomes a mere absurdity, and the capitalist is proved theoretically to be incapable of doing more than breaking even. Capitalism is proven to be impossible. That shows the importance of Marx's theory of labor-power, and of his assertion that the value of a working day doesn't depend on its length.

Profit is impossible

Marx sums up the situation as follows:

> The value so advanced has not expanded, no surplus-value has been created, and consequently money has not been converted into capital. The price of the yarn is fifteen shillings, and fifteen shillings

were spent in the open market upon the constituent elements of the product, or, what amounts to the same thing, upon the factors of the labour-process; ten shillings were paid for the cotton, two shillings for the substance of the spindle worn away, and three shillings for the labour-power. . .

There is in reality nothing very strange in this result. The value of one pound of yarn being eighteen pence, if our capitalist buys 10 lbs. of yarn in the market, he must pay fifteen shillings for them. It is clear that, whether a man buys his house ready built, or gets it built for him, in neither case will the mode of acquisition increase the amount of money laid out on the house.

There is something at first glance compelling about Marx's comment that "value. . .has not expanded, no surplus-value has been created," simply because of the viewpoint from which he writes. The value of the commodity is the sum of the "labors" embodied in it, just as its weight is the sum of the weights of its parts. In such a case you would not expect value to expand, any more than you would expect an object's weight to suddenly begin increasing of its own accord.

But that is a flaw of Marx's scientism, a part of his attempt to treat economics as quasi-physics. Marx misrepresents the matter both by limiting value to labor alone and by the scientistic manner in which he depicts value, making it appear a mere physical property. He thus eliminates real economic and human considerations from his analysis – making sure that the need to make a profit, and human freedom in arriving at an asking price, cannot enter into the discussion.

All of this leads to the current point in Marx's text: profit, or an increase in value as he considers it, is impossible. That is, profit as an excess of selling price over production costs (the capitalist's costs – not including his own profit) is impossible. For on Marx's assumption all things are sold at their actual value – which assumption we will also accept. And since value is just the sum of the embodied labor – for simplicity's sake let's just say the sum of labor costs – value is equal to the capitalist's expenses, and there's nothing left over for product.

Thus profit is impossible; and more to the point, any method for the capitalist to legitimately make money, is impossible. Of course Marx recognized that capitalists made money, and he will go on to show how they did it – by exploiting unpaid toil of the working classes. But he has shown that the money – the supposed "profit" – is not made by the method normally assumed, and thus that the capitalist has no legitimate right to make money.

Summing up

We would have to say, first, that Marx has shown nothing new by his whole example; he has merely given a numerical illustration of what he has already "proved" in his text: value equals embodied labor, and the ultimate value of a finished product equals the sum of all the constituent "labors" that went into producing it.

The component "labors" are these:

```
cotton (raw material) . . . . . . 10s. = 20 hours
wear and tear on equipment. . . .  2s. =  4 hours
direct labor. . . . . . . . . . .  3s. =  6 hours
-----------------------------------------------------
totals . . . . . . . . . . . . .  15s. = 30 hours
```

The value of the finished goods is 15s. or 30 hours of labor – it equals the sum of the constituent "values," with no expansion of value, or profit.

We might note in passing that Marx has an idiosyncratic definition of the word "capital." He uses it to mean profit, or rather surplus value: when value is "expanded," surplus-value is created, and "consequently money [is] converted into capital." That is, the making of a profit means money is "converted into capital."

Capital actually means, in normal usage, the money that is invested in production. It is the money invested at the front end of the process, regardless of its source – not the money gained as profit at the back end. Money becomes capital when it is invested. It is the use to which the money is put, not its source, that determines whether or not it is capital, as the word is normally defined. Why Marx invents a special definition for the word is a matter open to conjecture, but it may simply have been a case of (to quote Samuel Johnson) "Ignorance, Madam, pure ignorance."

Indeed, Marx himself at times uses the normal definition. He speaks of the value of the product as being "equal to the value of the capital advanced," i.e., equal to the money invested in production of the product. It is not uncommon for Marx to alternate between two or more conflicting definitions of a word as it pleases him at various points in his work.

Profit as classically conceived is an excess of the price received over and above the cost of producing the item; it is not an "expansion of value." Profit is as simple and common a phenomenon as "A is greater than B." Just as there is in general no physical or mathematical law that prevents one quantity from being greater than another, so there is no economic law that prevents a selling price from being greater than the cost of production; yet Marx pronounces profit impossible.

Debate

The impossibility of profit is the whole subtext behind an argument which now follows between Marx and his imaginary capitalist. The ensuing debate is not over whether capitalists do in fact make money somehow – Marx would be the first to admit that they enrich themselves from the sweat of the working classes. The debate is over what Marx has putatively shown, that they do not make this money as "profit," as an increase in value for the item. In this sense the debate is over whether they legitimately make money and have a legitimate right to it.

The last part of the above-quoted passage, about buying a house ready-built as opposed to building it, is a sort of proof of the thesis that the capitalist can't make a profit. Marx says "there is nothing strange" in that result; for the capitalist could buy a product like his own on the open market for the same value as has been calculated. Thus if he could buy it for that price – if that is its going market price – plainly he can sell his own product for no more than that; for there's nothing special about his version of the product. He can't get more than the going price for his merchandise. This again reinforces the conclusion that the value of his product is exactly equal to the value of the constituent "labors," or roughly speaking, equal to what he paid to produce it. No "increase of value" occurred, and no profit is possible.

There is a certain amount of circular reasoning in this; if we accept Marx's original proof of the value of the product, then we also accept that "if our capitalist buys 10 lbs. of yarn in the market," he also pays 15 shillings. (For Marx, producing the product is merely another "mode of acquisition," and as such it cannot result in an "increase of value" above that of the constituent "labors.") Thus the corroborating example also depends on a prior acceptance of Marx's proof. Our rebuttal (speaking as classical, or bourgeois, or normal economists) would be that yes, he can buy the product on the open market for the same price as he himself sells at, but in both cases that price will include an increment, added to the price on purpose, for the capitalist's profit. If he buys on the market, he pays the other capitalist's profit. If he produces it, his production cost is less than the market price, and his selling price includes his profit. That is the crux of the difference between bourgeois economics and Marx's deterministic version: in market economics there is room for human action, and human decisions affect things.

Marx now engages in an extended colloquy, a sort of mini-debate with the imagined capitalist, who as we remember is astonished at Marx's demonstration that he cannot make a profit – that is, profit as Marx defines it, not necessarily profit in normal parlance, as an excess of selling price over production costs.

The importance of the issue is this: we may say that in the classical view, profit is a normal, necessary part of the process, and furthermore that it is not per se evil or injurious to the hired laborers. On the other hand, Marx will later advance his theory of how money is made, and his answer will be, by exploitation of unpaid labor from the employees – a deceitful and oppressive practice.

So the coming debate between Marx and his imaginary or straw capitalist has all the more pertinence in that it is not about the mere details of Marx's analysis, but also about the capitalist's right to make money and the legitimacy of his role as capitalist in society.

The fact that Marx is supplying both sides of the argument lends an element of unreality to the proceedings; there are more direct, obvious responses which we might imagine the capitalist making. These would probably involve rejecting Marx's entire argument root and branch, however, and that is beyond the scope of Marx's argumentation.

The argument

The argument begins:

> Our capitalist, who is at home in his vulgar economy, exclaims: "Oh! but I advanced my money for the express purpose of making more money." The way to Hell is paved with good intentions, and he might just as easily have intended to make money, without producing at all.

Marx's response to the hypothetical capitalist's objection is irrelevant as well as insolent. It doesn't address the capitalist's objections at all, but merely flippantly dismisses them. The fact is, the capitalist didn't try to make money without producing at all. In fact, the capitalist is the initiator of the whole production process (in the case of his particular enterprise), and he bears the financial risk of the endeavor. His recompense, the profit from the enterprise, has classically been considered his by rights, as payment for his role in production.

Of course, Marx considers the capitalist a mere parasite who contributes nothing to the production process because he (putatively) doesn't labor and thus adds nothing of value. In this sense the capitalist's role, for Marx, is the same as intending to make money "without producing at all," and without working at all – purely parasitically.

The capitalist, however, is not reasoning from the premises of Marx's system, but from real life and from a practical, common-sense basis of experience. Thus he is affronted by the idea that he either can make no profit, logically speaking, or is entitled to no profit, morally speaking. When told he can expect no (legitimate) income from his enterprise, he naturally tends to ask, Why would I bother with it if there were no chance of making money from it?

That is a legitimate question, and one that Marx doesn't answer. (His ultimate answer would have to be that the capitalist does indeed make money from the enterprise, but only via exploited, unpaid "surplus value"; that is, he makes illegitimate income.)

The ultimate question however is how Marx can single out labor alone as worthy of recompense for its role in production. The capitalist initiates the enterprise, keeps it moving, takes the risk, and thus provides jobs for workers and products for the market. The question is how Marx can arbitrarily rule out profit, the capitalist's return, from being a legitimate factor of production. The capitalist plays a pivotal role; and as the hypothetical capitalist states, he does so only because he expects a return. His function is needed, and his profit is fair recompense for fulfilling that function.

That is the normal viewpoint and the normal state of things, accepted as legitimate by those involved. If, as Marx says, profit were impossible and the capitalist undeserving of payment, the whole enterprise would grind to a halt. Thus the capitalist not only deserves to make a profit, he must have the possibility of making a profit if he is to function at all. Marx's "labor theory of value" doesn't address this dilemma.

Further debate

Marx's theory is that profit is impossible. Since this theory goes against the weight of centuries of experience, as well as common sense and the evidence of our own eyes, he surely owes more explanation than such flippant responses as the present one.

To continue with Marx's debate with the capitalist:

> He threatens all sorts of things. He won't be caught napping again. In future he will buy the commodities in the market, instead of manufacturing them himself. But if all his brother capitalists were to do the same, where would he find his commodities in the market? And his money he cannot eat.

Marx asks, "Where would he find his commodities in the market?" More to the point, where would Marx? Where would anybody? The profit is the price all consumers pay for the ability to find goods on the market. Something must be paid to everyone involved in the production process, and in the capitalist's case, this takes the form of profit. If profit were impossible, there would be no capitalists, nor any market economies. That is more a disproof of, than a support for, Marx's theories.

The capitalist switches from arguing against Marx's proof to trying to find some way around it (that is, around the predicament of being unable to make a profit). Marx delights in informing him that there is no way around it.

Of course, the supposed capitalist actually knows he doesn't have to find a way around it; he knows he's making money. But we can presume he is responding only to the purely theoretical analysis presented by Marx so far, and we can view his response in that light.

At this point, the capitalist makes a rather feeble attempt to get around Marx's strictures. He says that, if there is no possibility of profit, he will cease producing a commodity – a logical response. He will "buy the commodities in the market"; this most likely means he will buy the commodities he formerly produced, and then resell them – he will become a merchant rather than a manufacturer. (It could also mean that he will buy only the commodities he needs for his own personal consumption, rather than producing them.)

This is a feeble escape attempt, because if there is no profit to be made in producing, neither is there any to be made by buying and selling. (Nor can a living be made by merely consuming.) By the terms of Marx's analysis, only productive labor creates value; not buying and reselling, and not profit. Marx's theory rules them both out equally.

Marx makes a different response to the capitalist, however. He says that if all capitalists had the same idea, if they all quit producing because there was no possibility of profit, there wouldn't be any commodities for sale on the market. Thus there would be no chance that the capitalist could switch to buying and selling for a living, nor to buying for his own consumption.

Isn't that actually an argument against Marx's thesis, however? If there were no possibility of profit, there would be no commodities produced by capitalists. Thus profit is necessary for the whole process to function, and it is paid by the consumers as the capitalist's due recompense. Moreover, the very fact that commodities do appear on the market indicates that the capitalist is being recompensed in some manner – though again, Marx would claim it is by unpaid labor or "surplus labor."

But Marx's response seems to indicate that there's no way around the dilemma for the capitalist – he cannot make a legitimate profit, and he can't quit. First of all, what would he do with his money, if he couldn't invest it in making more? And second, where would he get goods for his own personal consumption, if capitalist production ceased? Thus Marx's comment, "His money he cannot eat."

So Marx apparently believes the capitalist should continue to produce, and in fact must continue to produce, even without the possibility of making a profit – surely a perverse point of view. (That is, it's Marx's viewpoint so far; he seems to imply that it is the capitalist's social responsibility to produce goods, even at a loss. But of course, later in his text he will show that the capitalist doesn't suffer a loss, because he really makes obscene sums of money off the toiling proletariat. We haven't yet come to his explanation of the real source of the capitalist's money.)

It is apparent, at any rate, that Marx's policy is never to give the capitalist a break of any kind. Marx just has a determination to curse the capitalist under all circumstances. He won't let him make a profit, and he won't let him quit. The capitalist is damned if he does and damned if he doesn't.

So we actually have two visions or "alternate scenarios" of an economy ruled by Marx's theory. Either the capitalists all continue producing, even without the possibility of profit, just because they have no choice; or all capitalist activity ceases and there is no capitalist production, no buying and selling, and no commodities for sale. With only labor counting as value, all will presumably have to labor – there can be no merchants, no capitalists, no bankers, or lenders; we are forced into a subsistence economy, perhaps on the model of feudal society. That would seem to be where we are driven by Marx's analysis, yet he purports to describe capitalist society. His picture must be severely flawed somewhere.

Debate, part three

The argument continues:

> He tries persuasion. "Consider my abstinence. I might have played ducks and drakes with the 15 shillings; but instead of that I consumed it productively, and made yarn with it." Very well, and by way of reward he is now in possession of good yarn instead of a bad conscience; and as for playing the part of a miser, it would never do for him to relapse into such bad ways as that; we have seen before to what results such asceticism leads. Besides, where nothing is, the king has lost his rights: whatever may be the merit of his abstinence, there is nothing wherewith specially to remunerate it, because the value of the product is merely the sum of the values of the commodities that were thrown into the process of production. Let him therefore console himself with the reflection that virtue is its own reward.

Here the capitalist returns to the subject of legitimacy, that is, his right to earn something from his investment of capital. Again Marx doesn't directly address the issue, opting rather for an impudent response.

The issue at hand has often been discussed under the heading of "deferred gratification," an aspect of capital formation: the owner of money chooses to invest it in productive enterprises, in hopes of a profit in the future, rather than buying goods to consume immediately. That fact in itself, that capital has been invested and consumption deferred, of course doesn't guarantee a profit, and it is not a complete proof of the legitimacy of profit. It is more an explanation of an aspect of capital formation than a proof of anything.

But all of this evades the central issue raised by the capitalist: it is a question of incentives. If people are going to invest their money as capital, rather than for gratifying their more immediate desire to consume goods, there must be a financial incentive. Profit supplies that incentive. The normal economic mentality understands this and reasons from it. If Marx is going to contend that there is really no such incentive, that profit as such is an illusion, then he must produce strong proof.

One thing is true, however: the capitalist's return on his investment is not a reward for his virtue. It is not bestowed by anyone to reward his deferred gratification; rather, it comes about because the capitalist has judged his product, people's wishes, and the market correctly, and has produced a product people are willing to buy at a price level sufficient to return a profit to him. He must defer gratification, it is true; but profit comes not as a reward for the virtue (if any) of that, but by the workings of the free market, i.e., by human economic behavior. The satisfaction of producing a product that he knows is good may add to his pleasure; but the entire matter is not a question of virtue and awards bestowed. Insofar as the capitalist's remarks may seem to imply the contrary, that is indeed a mistaken notion.

(It has been previously debunked sufficiently, too – Adam Smith dismissed the factor of benevolence in a famous passage about a customer's dealings with the butcher and other shopkeepers.)

The crux of Marx's response, and a concise statement of his theory of the impossibility of profit, is his statement that "there is nothing wherewith specially to remunerate [his investment], because the value of the product is merely the sum of the values of the commodities that were thrown into the process of production." This could be viewed as resembling classical economics – the price of the finished product goes to cover all the production costs at all stages from raw materials to finished product. That much is fairly unexceptionable. But there are a couple of salient differences in Marx's theory, as we have seen. First, for Marx value equates to labor alone, and the value of the product is merely the sum of the hours of labor embodied in the product; factors like profit, rents, and interest money are disallowed. Secondly, for Marx the whole thing is a mechanical process, or a logical equivalency, as automatic as saying that the weight of a box of rocks equals the total of the weight of individual rocks. There is no room for market forces, or the setting of prices by supply and demand, or the vagaries of human behavior.

Thus if we accept Marx's theory, there is indeed nothing wherewith to remunerate the capitalist, and profit is impossible.

(And again, Marx implies that the capitalist is expected to continue to produce without profit, just for the good of society. Because, "as for playing the part of a miser, it would never do for him to relapse into such bad ways as that." No, he must keep his money working, whether or not he makes a profit, because the system needs him. Presumably, even if he could not extract unpaid surplus value, if he continually broke even, he should still stay in business, just so capitalism could continue in existence long enough to dialectically evolve into communism.)

On the other hand, if we do not accept Marx's assumptions, then there is something wherewith specially to remunerate the capital expenditure. For a theoretically "pure" case, consider Marx's example of machine-woven cloth: when machines came into use, they cut by 50% the labor required to weave cloth. Now, such machines required a considerable capital expenditure; and to get factories going there was also labor to be hired and paid for. All this capital investment allowed entrepreneurs to produce cloth with 50% of the invested labor of hand-woven cloth. That means, if the capitalist received nothing, if he just charged enough to pay his laborers, the cloth could sell at half the price of hand-woven cloth (disregarding any labor invested at previous stages, in the yarn for instance). However, the capitalist wouldn't do that; he would charge, let us say, 60% of the cost of the hand-woven cloth. This would allow him to pay his labor costs and other operating expenses, pay off any loans he had taken out for the equipment, and receive a percentage of profit for himself. In addition, he could employ laborers who were previously unemployed, or less desirably employed. And over and above all else, he could lower the cost of a common necessity, thus making the money possessed by his employees and everyone else worth more in purchasing power. This whole picture is the process of the raising of the standard of living, and it has been going on at least since the Industrial revolution. (In other words, this is how "capitalist" economies really work.)

Thus, if one adheres to classical theory, there is indeed something wherewith to remunerate the capitalist: the money of consumers, who buy his product in preference to more expensive goods. Society's entire economic plane is raised by capital investment in such technological advances. To repeat, though, it is not a matter of some voice of authority rewarding the capitalist or designating some fund as remuneration for the capitalist's "abstinence." The process functions automatically, as a result of market exchanges. Marx's sophistry to the contrary, that the capitalist cannot make a profit, is really hard to believe if viewed in the light of common sense and experience.

But to return to the capitalist's objection: if he is to undertake capital investment, with the danger that the public may reject his product or that he may lose money because of competition or for other reasons, there must be the incentive of profit. If the owner of money is to be induced to do something other than play ducks and drakes, there must be the possibility of profit. This notion is generally understood and generally accepted; the capitalist's remarks express universal human nature and economic reality.

Marx has rebutted the capitalist's objections by reasserting that the capitalist cannot expect profit as a reward for his investment; rather, he should console himself with the fact that "by way of reward he is now in possession of good yarn. . ." But neither does this answer gratify the capitalist:

> But no, he becomes importunate. He says: "The yarn is of no use to me; I produced it for sale." In that case let him sell it. Better yet, let him in the future produce only things for satisfying his personal wants, a remedy that his physician M'Culloch has already prescribed as infallible against an epidemic of over-production.

Marx has theoretically, though not practically, snatched away from the capitalist the possibility of making a profit, and then attempted to pacify him by saying ownership of the product is the capitalist's reward. Of course that is not enough for the capitalist, who rightly objects that he produced it for sale – and by that is implied, for sale at a profit. People don't produce tons of yarn, or toothpaste, or anything else for their own personal use, but as a way of making a living via profit. That is the nature of commerce in an economy characterized by specialization, trade, division of labor, and a high degree of complexity. It is with the understanding of this complexity that capitalists undertake their enterprises. Marx denies the validity of that understanding, but it is mere willful blindness on his part.

Marx's rather insolent advice to the capitalist to "for the future produce only things for satisfying his personal wants," is thus a condemnation of complexity in society as such. He considered it shameful for anyone to make a profit, and endorsed production only for one's personal consumption; in other words, he prescribed a subsistence society with none of the institutions that mark highly-organized societies (profits, rents, wage labor, money, interest, etc.). As a matter of personal ideology or ethos, he preferred a society of subsistence workers, perhaps along the lines of the self-contained manors of the Middle Ages.

This peculiar viewpoint of Marx's is frequently expressed today in the witless phrase, "Production for use," or sometimes, "For people, not for profit," a sort of shorthand condemnation of profit, business, and capitalist society. It envisions perhaps a country where everything is run as a charity and there is no economy at all and hence no need for money. Or perhaps it touts, as Marx did, subsistence production, production for one's own use but never for sale for a profit. It is a puerile, reductionist notion. In a complex economy – in a civilization – you cannot separate "use-value" from "exchange-value," nor goods produced "for people" from goods produced "for profit."

At any rate, Marx disapproves of profit and claims it is impossible. (The capitalist makes money, but it's via a subterfuge, via stolen "surplus value," not by profit as such.) The capitalist has always proceeded upon the assumption that profit is possible, and that is why he produced the goods – for sale at a profit. But the capitalist is arguing at a disadvantage – he is not allowed to challenge the whole convoluted argument by which Marx "proved" profit to be impossible. Standing outside the argument, we can reject Marx's thesis root and branch, and not merely object to this or that minor point. That is what the hypothetical capitalist would have to do, in order to win the debate with Marx.

Provider of jobs

Marx now takes his hypothetical argument onto another tack:

> He now gets obstinate. "Can the labourer," he asks, "merely with his arms and legs, produce commodities out of nothing? Did I not supply him with the materials, by means of which, and in which alone, his labour would be embodied? And as the greater part of society consists of such ne'er-do-wells, have I not rendered society incalculable service by my instruments of production, my cotton and my spindle, and not only society, but the labourer also, whom in addition I have provided with the necessaries of life? And am I to be allowed nothing in return for all this service?"
>
> Well, but has not the labourer rendered him the equivalent service of changing his cotton and spindle into yarn? Moreover, there is here no question of service. A service is nothing more than the useful effect of a use-value, be it of a commodity, or be it of labour.

We first have to demur as to Marx's caricature of the capitalist. His playlet takes on some of the classical characteristics of propaganda here; he invents an obnoxious personality which he imputes to the capitalist, thus creating a caricature in a sort of morality play. To be specific: it is not strictly necessary for Marx's capitalist to call the laborers "ne'er-do-wells," nor to pride himself on doing society "incalculable" service; Marx just throws those remarks in to give his readers an emotional reaction against the capitalist, and to malign the capitalist's character.

Let us turn to more substantive issues, then. The capitalist and Marx are still arguing at cross-purposes. The capitalist is arguing on the topic of the legitimacy of profit, i.e., the elusive issue of whether he has done anything to deserve to make money. Marx has been responding mostly with arguments about the possibility of profit, that is, with a rehash of his theoretical arguments proving that profit is impossible. These two bases of argument don't meet on common ground. We should oppose arguments for the legitimacy of profit to arguments against its legitimacy, and arguments for its possibility to arguments against its possibility. (Arguments for the possibility, or reality, of profit would include references to the real world, as well as all the previous objections against Marx's thesis.)

As to legitimacy, similar arguments to the capitalist's are often made: the capitalist performs a useful function in society by not only producing goods but providing jobs; the responsibilities of capital formation and investment are assumed by the capitalist, at the risk of losing his investment. This is a needed function, and some incentive is necessary to induce people to perform it. The capitalist, like everyone else involved in the production process, deserves a return from the final product; those who share in the baking must have a share in the eating – that's a basic notion of legitimacy.

On the other hand, it's not as though anyone had been granted supreme powers to adjudicate such questions and to distribute economic "rewards." When the capitalist says, "am I to be allowed nothing in return?" it's not as if there were some bureaucrat or commissar who had power to allow or disallow it (although Marx tries to disallow it by sheer force of logic). Rather, it is an economic exigency which functions on an automatic level, under rules of its own; it requires no central direction, but is an organic function of human society. People undertake economic activity in response to incentives. Thus the real issue is the possibility or reality of profit – and Marx's supposed disproof of that possibility.

Marx's response in this case is that no return is due him because he has already received his return. The labourer has "rendered him the equivalent service of" doing the work – making the yarn.

That much is true; the capitalist and the laborer exchange equal values, labor for wages. The capitalist has possession of the resulting product, the yarn. (And notice –Marx implicitly grants the legitimacy of the capitalist's possession of those goods.) And the capitalist will mark those goods up a certain percentage above their cost and charge that price, making a profit. It is from the customers, not from his laborers, that he receives a profit, a payment in return for the "incalculable service" he has rendered.

The last part of Marx's response is of interest only as a good example of Marxian jargon, characterized by the invention of special definitions of words and a tendentious, dogmatic insistence on the use of these special definitions rather than the normal meanings of words accepted by the whole world other than Marx. Through the use of such jargon, Marx's prose becomes a dense, incomprehensible concatenation of nonsense phrases.

Is there really any reason why we need a specialized, ad hoc definition for the common, ordinary word "service"? Marx "proves" the capitalist doesn't render society or the laborer a service, by inventing a specialized definition of the word. A service, we are informed, is "the useful effect of a use-value," and only that. We are forbidden to impute any other sense to the word, or to give it its normal meaning, which is something like "a favor," "a deed which aids someone else," or something on that order. We may not be exactly certain what Marx means by "the useful effect of a use-value," and anyway that's not the point. Perhaps it means the useful effects of a commodity, as when someone lends you a tool or some other useful item –the use of the tool then constitutes "the useful effect of a use-value."

But the point is, Marx invents a special definition of the word, to allow him to prove his point by force of definition. By insisting on his definition and refusing to admit any other, he "proves" that no service has been rendered in the present case. Such proofs by force of (re-)definition are mere intellectual thuggery; they prove nothing and only reduce substantive issues to a matter of specious semantics and nonsense phrases.

In short, people who are willing to think of a service as "the useful effect of a use-value" will appreciate Marx's arguments here.

But to continue:

> Our friend, up to this time so purse-proud, suddenly assumes the modest demeanour of his own workman, and exclaims: "Have I myself not worked? Have I not performed the labour of superin-tendence and of overlooking the spinner? And does not this labour, too, create value?" His overlooker and his manager try to hide their smiles. Meanwhile, after a hearty laugh, he re-assumes his usual mien. Though he chanted to us the whole creed of the economists in reality, he says, he would not give a brass farthing for it. He leaves this and all such like subterfuges and juggling tricks to the professors of political economy, who are paid for it. He himself is a practical man; and though he does not always consider what he says outside his business, yet in his business he knows what he is about.

Turning from the creed of the economists, which Marx so disparaged, to that of the ideologues, such as himself, we can say first of all: one must ignore the propagandistic elements of Marx's little morality play – his depiction of the capitalist's character and facial expressions, from "purse-proud" to "modest demeanour" to a hearty laugh and his "usual mien." Those elements are just character assassination.

The capitalist's essential argument is that he also works and thus deserves a return – even though, as Marx would have it, the capitalist himself doesn't believe this argument. Again, the capitalist is arguing for the legitimacy of his monetary gain.

His argument is valid, but irrelevant. Insofar as he works (and initiating, managing and directing an enterprise is work), he deserves recompense for that work; but that recompense falls under the category of wages, not profit – i.e., that is not the capitalist's share.

Adam Smith warned of confounding these categories. Among his pertinent comments are these (*Wealth of Nations*, Part I, Chapter VI):

> When [wages, profits and rent] belong to different persons, they are readily distinguished; but when they belong to the same they are sometimes confounded with one another, at least in common language.
>
> A gentleman who farms a part of his own estate, after paying the expense of cultivation, should gain both the rent of the landlord and the profit of the farmer. He is apt to denominate, however, the whole gain, profit. . .
>
> Common farmers seldom employ any overseer to direct the general operations of the farm. They generally too work a good deal with their own hands, as ploughmen, harrowers, etc. What remains of the crop after paying the rent, therefore, should not only replace to them their stock employed in cultivation together with its ordinary profits, but pay them the wages which are due to them, both as labourers and overseers. Whatever remains, however. . . is called profit.

That is, as explained in classical economics, the capitalist who labors directly on the product would have recompense which could be divided up into portions attributable to different factors – wages and profits, in the capitalist's case. Thus his payment for day-to-day work would be considered the wage factor of his pay; the return for money risked and for the entrepreneur's role as such, as owner of the enterprise, would be the profit. If the capitalist hired a manager and took an entirely "hands-off" stance toward the business, the sum he would have to pay the manager would be the size of the labor factor; the capitalist's net return would tell us his profit. (And from the fact that he could hire a manager and would have to pay him wages, we can see the validity of the claim that the capitalist "also works" and deserves some return on that basis.)

Marx further impugns the capitalist's character by implication and innuendo. He scolds his imagined capitalist because he doesn't "give a brass farthing" for the "creed of the economists," i.e., for economic theory. The capitalist "is a practical man," who goes about his business regardless of the "subterfuges and juggling" of economists (especially Marx, no doubt).

There is nothing scandalous or unnatural about that. The rarefied upper reaches of theoretical economics are not accessible to the majority of people. Such theories are full of contending schools and contrary arguments, and even economists (especially economists) cannot agree on them. Furthermore, it takes years of study even to approach those lofty regions. How is a capitalist, a practical business-owner with a business to run and a living to make, supposed to become an egghead of that type?

Furthermore, Marx's comments are found in a treatise designed to prove that the capitalist cannot possibly do what he is in fact doing every day — make a profit. Marx's own theory is a good explanation of why entrepreneurs pay little attention to theory.

Marx apparently thought the whole capitalist world should come to a screeching halt because he had published his pronouncements that profit is impossible. He berated his straw capitalist for ignoring theory. But he didn't carry enough weight as a scientific economic theorist to make the whole world cease functioning because of his scribblings — at least, anywhere except in his own mind.

Surplus value

Having seen that profit as conventionally conceived is impossible, we are now ready to "force the secret of profit-making" — that is, to examine the process of "the production of absolute surplus-value."

Marx discusses this topic at some length, but the story is briefly told. We have established that the value of a working day is six hours of labor. That is, the "means of subsistence" which the laborer gets for each day's labor, is "worth" six hours of labor. This is because it took six hours to produce the "means of subsistence" which the laborer can buy with a day's pay. Thus, the value of a day's labor-power is six hours of value. (The money equivalent is 3s.)

Moreover, it is common knowledge that the length of the working day at the time Marx wrote was twelve hours. Thus we have two points: the laborer worked twelve hours and received the money equivalent of six. The laborer supplied the capitalist with twelve hours of value (twelve hours of labor), and received six hours of value in return. That discrepancy holds the "secret" of surplus value.

Note: the first six hours of the day, which the laborer works in return for the six hours of "means of subsistence," i.e., for pay, Marx called "the necessary part of the working day." The remaining six he called the unnecessary part, and they constitute the "surplus value" received by the capitalist.

Retracing the argument

This theoretical disparity can be crudely expressed (ignoring Marx's convoluted elaborations) as: the laborer works twelve hours and is only paid for six. There's not a lot of theoretical refinement in that. The reason Marx can make that assertion, to repeat, is that he has disconnected the pay laborers receive from the work they do. First of all, he denies that the laborer is paid for labor; the laborer doesn't receive a certain amount of pay per hour of labor, but rather a certain amount of pay for a whole day's labor-power. And the value of a day's labor-power is in no way determined by the length of the working day, i.e., by the amount of labor performed. Rather, it is so to speak determined in reverse fashion by the pay given for it (pay in the form of "means of subsistence"). Thus the value of a day's labor is disconnected from the amount of labor in the day, i.e., from the length of the working day. This allows Marx to state that the two aren't equal, and to invent any figure he wants to as the "necessary" part of the working day.

That is Marx's theory of "surplus value," reduced to its simplest elements – almost idiotically simple, one might say. He has laid the groundwork for that theory, and little needs to be added, though he will expand on the subject at some length. We now turn to his further comments on the subject:

> Let us examine the matter more closely. The value of a day's labour-power amounts to 3 shillings, because on our assumption half a day's labour is embodied in that quality of labour-power, i.e., because the means of subsistence that are daily required for the production of labour-power, cost half a day's labour.

Because "on our assumption. . ."? Someone should have explained to Marx that assumptions don't compel reality; that assertions of fact don't become true because "on our assumption" this or that is true. But such proceedings are typical of the half-baked stew of unfounded assertion, specious definitions, contorted logic and dogmatic pronouncements which makes up Marx's text. It is like the old joke about the two economists who fall in a pit; one says he knows how to get out: "First, assume a ladder."

But at any rate, we are familiar with the path of logic Marx is referring to. The "means of subsistence" is equal to what the laborer can buy with his pay; Marx has declared this to be the same as the value of a day's labor-power. (It is value of labor-power because what the capitalist buys is not labor, but labor-power – a day's-worth at a time.) And on his assumption, the "value" of that means of subsistence – the amount of labor embodied in producing them – is half a day's labor, six hours; in money terms that is 3 shillings.

By this method Marx has disconnected the amount of labor performed in a day from the value of the laborer's efforts. The length of the working day does not enter into the determining of the value of labor-power. Whether the laborer works ten hours a day or twelve is irrelevant to the value of the working day, because what determines his proper pay or the value of his services is not labor, but the value of labor-power; and by reverse logic Marx finds that the means of subsistence (essentially, the wage) determines the value of labor-power – not vice versa. Marx takes the level of means of subsistence as a given, as an axiomatic, unexplained fact.

Thus he is in a good position to claim that the amount of labor done in a day is different from the value of the wage; if the amount of labor does not even enter into the determination of the wage, naturally the two figures can turn out to be different; the laborer can work 12 hours and be paid 6 hours of "value."

At any rate, Marx has discovered and/or assumed that the value of a day's labor-power is half a day's labor; the laborer works a full day and is paid "means of subsistence" worth half a day.

(A side issue: what if Marx had assumed the "means of subsistence" to be worth 11 1/2 hours of labor? That the capitalist was only receiving an unpaid half-hour, equal to 1/23 of the amount of paid labor, or 1/24th of the whole working day – approximately 4% "profit" or surplus value? Would that have been as scandalous as assuming he gets 100% surplus value? That is, even apart from Marx's revisionist explanation of the source of the capitalist's gain, perhaps if that gain were in a normal range of profit it would have been no great scandal? We can't know now; but we can see that Marx's assumptions are always those that reflect worst on the capitalist.)

He continues:

> But the past labour that is embodied in the labour-power, and the living labour that it can call into action; the daily cost of maintaining it, and its daily expenditure in work, are two totally different things. The former determines the exchange-value of the labour-power, the latter is its use-value.
>
> The fact that half a day's labour is necessary to keep the labourer alive during 24 hours, does not in any way prevent him from working a whole day. Therefore, the value of labour-power, and the value which that labour-power creates in the labour process, are two entirely different magnitudes; and this difference of the two values was what the capitalist had in view, when he was purchasing the labour-power.

Reality check

Let us set aside Marx's convoluted reasonings once more and check in with the real world. What the capitalist had in view was the normal understanding of market economics: that he would pay so much per man-hour of labor; that his production costs per unit would add up to a certain amount; and that he would add a certain percentage to his unit costs for profit and charge that much per unit. Thus he would make profit from the buyer, by adding his own remuneration into the final price – not from his employees, by exploiting unpaid labor from the laborers.

But to return to Marx's text: he compares the "past labour" embodied in the labor-power and the "living labour" it produces. Let's just paraphrase his remarks: the amount of value (i.e., labor) paid for a day's labor-power ("past labour") is different from the amount of labor done in a day ("living labour"). The number of hours the laborer works in a day is different from the number of hours of value (labor) the capitalist pays him. The value of the laborer's contribution to the capitalist, is different from the value of the capitalist's contribution to the laborer. This is maintainable only because in Marx's theory, the one has nothing to do with determining the other.

Marx now goes on to put a theoretical gloss on his crude framework:

> What really influenced him was the specific use-value which this commodity possesses of being a source not only of value, but of more value than it has itself. This is the special service that the capitalist expects from labour-power, and in this transaction he acts in accordance with the "eternal laws" of the exchange of commodities. The seller of labour-power, like the seller of any other commodity, realises its exchange-value, and parts with its use-value. He cannot take the one without giving the other. The use-value of labour-power, or in other words, labour, belongs just as little to its seller, as the use-value of oil after it has been sold belongs to the dealer who has sold it.

(Note – here we see an example of a "service" that satisfies Marx's definition.)

This convoluted argument is Marx's explanation of how the capitalist can pay six hours of value for a working day of twelve hours of labor. As we have seen, the capitalist doesn't buy labor, but rather labor-power; he "consumes" labor-power by setting the laborers to work; and the use-value of labor-power, the juice that comes out when labor-power is squeezed, is labor itself. This entire preposterous scenario is Marx's version of the employing of labor; its root idiocy might be considered the definition of labor-power as a physical commodity, to be sold and then consumed later on, yielding labor. That is an explanation for scientific illiterates – or for people out of touch with basic reality.

To examine certain particulars: the specific "use-value" of labor-power is that it is "a source of not only value, but of more value than it has itself." Marx uses the term "use-value" here in one of his broader senses, as the use or usefulness of a product (not as meaning the product itself). Thus labor-power is a commodity like a vessel of oil from which you can pour more oil than is contained in it; it is an apple which becomes larger the more you eat from it.

What Marx really means is that less labor or value is paid for the working day than the length of the working day itself; the laborers work twelve hours and are paid six. His convoluted rationalizations about the capitalist's paying the exchange-value and receiving the use-value, etc., is just his method of fitting that simple fact into the theoretical framework he has established – telling, in terms of his theory, how twelve hours is given for six hours, or how the laborer works twelve hours and is paid six. The intricacies of his rationalization are of less interest than that main point.

He continues:

> The owner of the money has paid the value of the day's labour-power; his, therefore, is the use of it for a day; a day's labour belongs to him. [Doesn't he mean a day's labor-power?] The circumstance, that on the one hand the daily subsistence of labour-power costs only half a day's labour, while on the other hand the very same labour-power can work during a whole day, that consequently the labour which its use during one day creates, is double what he pays for that use, this circumstance is, without doubt, a piece of good luck for the buyer, but by no means an injury to the seller.

We should remember, Marx makes the assumption throughout his text that all things are paid for at their value; the capitalist pays the full value of a day's labor-power, and in that respect doesn't cheat the laborer. It is an odd thing however, that while the capitalist gives six hours of labor or value, in return for what develops into twelve hours of labor, those two quantities are not compared. For an equal exchange, we could expect the number of hours of value given and received to be equal or nearly so; that would seem to be an equal exchange. The beauty of Marx's system is that he compares the number of hours of labor in what the capitalist gives (the six hours of value in the 3s. which is the laborer's pay), to the hours of labor also in what the capitalist gives (the daily "means of subsistence," or rather the six hours of labor embodied in it). Because they are equal, the capitalist has paid the full or correct value of the labor-power. But those two quantities cannot help but be equal, and it is hard to see how they can serve as a basis for judging a commensurate exchange. Whatever the money rate of pay is, the value of the pay (in the form of commodities or "necessaries") will equal the value of the labor-power, which is equated to the means of subsistence.

Thus, to repeat tediously, the "daily sustenance," or value of labor-power is not causally connected to the length of the working day. The "daily sustenance" can cost "only half a day's labour," or six hours, while on the other hand the length of the working day can be twelve hours; and no hurt or injury is done, because the full value of the labor-power is paid. Or, "this circumstance is . . . a piece of good luck for the buyer, but by no means an injury to the seller," i.e., the laborer.

(Here we see that Marx makes no moral accusation. He will change his tune on this issue later, however; a great part of Marxist literature is devoted to excoriating the capitalist for the morally reprehensible act of squeezing unpaid "surplus value" out of the laborer.)

Numerical example

Marx continues:

> Our capitalist foresaw this state of things, and that was the cause of his laughter. The labourer therefore finds in the workshop, the means of production necessary for working, not only during six, but during twelve hours.
>
> Just as during the six hours' process our 10 lbs. of cotton absorbed six hours' labour, and became 10 lbs. of yarn, so now, 20 lbs. of cotton will absorb 12 hours' labour and be changed into 20 lbs. of yarn . . . There is now materialised in the 20 lbs. of yarn the labour of five days, of which four days are due to the cotton and the lost steel of the spindle, the remaining day having been absorbed by the cotton during the spinning process. Expressed in gold, the labour of five days is thirty shillings. This is therefore the price of the 20 lbs. of yarn, giving, as before, eighteen pence as the price of a pound.
>
> But the sum of the values of the commodities that entered into the process amounts to 27 shillings. The value of the yarn is 30 shillings. Therefore the value of the product is 1/9 greater than the value advanced for its production; 27 shillings have been transformed into 30 shillings; a surplus-value of 3 shillings has been created. The trick has at last succeeded; money has been converted into capital.

The "trick" is actually much simpler than that. The capitalist spends, let's suppose, 27 shillings to produce some product; he wants to make a profit, not being in business to break even; so he adds, let's say 3 shillings to the 27. He charges that amount, customers pay it, and everyone is happy. There is no more "secret" to profit than that, and no need to "unnecessarily multiply entities" to complicate the explanation.

Marx's main point in the text above is fairly straight-forward, but a few minor points are worth comment. First, "Our capitalist foresaw this state of things, and. . . [t]he labourer therefore finds in the workshop, the means of production necessary for working, not only during six, but during twelve hours." The reason the laborer finds materials and means for working twelve hours, is that the working day is twelve hours long. The labor is contracted for on the basis of twelve hours a day, and moreover the wage is based on a twelve-hour day. The capitalist couldn't foresee anything related to Marx's theory. Marx tries to show that it's his theory at work in all this, but that is both unbelievable and probably unknown to the capitalist.

As to the cotton's absorbing 12 hours of labor and so on, such terminology again reflects Marx's ridiculously concretized picture of value as a thing deposited within a commodity. In more rational terms, we would say that production costs are additive; that as more hours of labor are invested in producing the product, production costs increase and thus more must be charged as the selling price. There is a "value added" at each step of the production process, in other words; the final price or value is the sum of what is added at each step along the way.

Another point: Marx says "There is now materialised in this 20 lbs. of yarn the labour of five days. . . Expressed in gold, the labour of five days is thirty shillings. This is therefore the price of the 20 lbs. of yarn . . ."

We can't be quite so complacent about that. Yes, according to Marx's formulas the yarn "contains" five days of labor and "therefore" the price is thirty shillings. But it violates common sense and our notions of cause and effect to think that a market price can be compelled by force of logic, or can follow Marx's series of syllogisms on a page. No mechanism has been adduced to show how the price could conform itself to Marx's formulas, or what the forces producing such a result could be. Our sense of what is plausible or likely rebels and tells us the real world doesn't govern itself by Marx's theory and his formulae.

The rate of surplus value

Another significant point which isn't at first obvious: in the present sample situation, the ratio of "surplus value" to the cost of production is 1/9; that is, what we might call the profit margin is 1/9. This however will vary, depending on the amount of production costs incurred other than direct labor; it depends on how much the capitalist must pay for the raw materials he uses, in proportion to the labor he employs. To put it another way, the ratio of unpaid labor to paid labor for a particular capitalist, is 1 to 1; the laborer is paid a value of six hours, and in return works twelve hours – six hours paid and six hours unpaid. But the percentage of profit also depends on how much labor was invested at previous stages of production, because those production costs too are carried forward and contribute to the final selling price.

That is, labor is not the capitalist's only expense; in the present case the capitalist spends 24s. on the raw materials he uses, and 3s. on labor; and he gets 30s. for the yarn, including 3s.-worth of unpaid labor. The ratio of unpaid labor to expenses is thus 1/9. But the capitalist who produced the cotton may have had very minor expenses other than labor, and his ratio of paid to unpaid labor could have been more nearly 1:1. He could have paid 12s. for four days of labor, and sold the product for 24s. So if we "dissect" a product into its component labors at every step of the way, all the capitalists overall gain "surplus value" at a ratio (to paid labor) of 1:1. The ratio of surplus value to expenses will be 1:1 in the aggregate, meaning 100% profit or surplus value over the entire society. "Money is converted into capital" in that ratio. (Marx will adopt the terminology of calling the costs carried forward, for the raw materials, the "fixed capital," and labor costs the "variable capital.")

A couple of more issues that Marx addresses deserve comment. He says,

> Every condition of the problem is satisfied, while the laws that regulate the exchange of commodities, have been in no way violated. Equivalent has been exchanged for equivalent. For the capitalist as buyer paid for each commodity, for the cotton, the spindle and the labor-power, its full value. . . The consumption of the laborer-power, which was also the process of producing commodities, resulted in 20 lbs. of yarn, having a value of 30 shillings. The capitalist. . . sells his yarn at eighteen pence a pound, which is its exact value. Yet for all that he withdraws 3 shillings more from circulation than he originally threw into it.

This seems to be an impossibility. Everything is paid for at its full value in Marx's scenario (and that is a universal assumption in his work – that things are always bought at their proper, full value), and yet the laborer is cheated. The laborer receives full value for his efforts, because he gets the daily "means of subsistence" which is by definition the value of labor-power. The capitalist pays for his raw materials (cotton) and productive equipment (the spindle) at full value. And the only thing improper, or the only thing not fully determined, is the length of the working day. The capitalist works the laborers twelve hours instead of six, but that is apparently his prerogative – the length of the working day doesn't appear anywhere in Marx's equations. In fact, if the laborers work twelve hours a day, all things are paid for at their value; and if they only work six hours a day, all things are still paid for at their value. The only difference is, in the latter case no "surplus value" is created. This is a fractured version of economics.

Thus the capitalist can, by Marx's theory, gain six hours of unpaid, "surplus" value each day, while paying for everything at its proper value. The laborers aren't cheated, at least in the sense that they don't receive less than proper value for their efforts. They do however work longer than "necessary."

Turn the question around: are the laborers giving more than proper value in return for their pay? They seem to be, because they work twelve hours and are only paid six hours of "value." But what they are paid for is not labor, but labor-power; and a day's labor-power, we are to believe, has one fixed value regardless of how many hours are actually worked. So, to repeat: labor, as something bought and paid for, does not appear anywhere in Marx's equations. It is that strange fact that supports his conclusion that the laborers receive full value for their efforts; it allows Marx to derive his entire theory of "surplus value."

In one sense Marx is consistent. His concept of classical "profit" is that it is the result of selling the finished product for more than its value; thus traditional profit, he proved, must be impossible. His own theory, it must be said, at least avoids that pitfall.

Thus we can take this remark as a final summation by Marx:

> If we now compare the two processes of producing value and of creating surplus-value, we see that the latter is nothing but the continuation of the former beyond a definite point.

It is hard to say beyond exactly what point; it is not labor carried on beyond the point where equivalent is exchanged for equivalent — equal values are exchanged regardless of how long the work is carried on. We could say labor is carried on beyond the point where it is "necessary" — that is the terminology Marx adopts, calling the first six hours the "necessary" part of the working day. Perhaps the designated point is, beyond the point where the labor performed equals the value of the daily "necessaries." But at any rate it is a point not governed or regulated by anything in Marx's formulae, and that fact is at once a glaring indication of the lack of reality behind his theory and the linchpin that enabled him to develop it in the first place.

NOTES – Chapter 7

1 Hayek, Friedrich A. von, *The Road To Serfdom*, London, G. Routledge & Sons, 1944, p.98.

2 C. S. Lewis.

3 Seventh Army U.S. Interrogation, quoted in Wilmot, Chester, *The Struggle For Europe*, London, Collins, 1971, p.622.

4 Arendt, Hannah, *The Origins of Totalitarianism* (part III, *Totalitarianism*), New York, Harcourt Brace Jovanovich (a Harvest Book), 1973.

5 Crozier, Brian, *The Fundamentals of Conflict*, p.24.

6 ibid., p.24.

7 Arendt, Hannah, op. cit.

8 Arendt, Hannah, op. cit.

9 Arendt, Hannah, op. cit.

10 Minogue, Kenneth R., *Alien Powers: the Pure Theory of Ideology*, New York, St. Martin's Press, 1985.

11 Shirer, William L., *The Rise and Fall of the Third Reich; a History of Nazi Germany*, New York, Ballantine Publishing Group (a Fawcett Crest book), 1983, p.82.

About the author

The author, educated as a computer programmer and consultant, is now a free-lance writer, with articles published in *Chronicles – A Magazine of American Culture*; the British magazine *Quarterly Review*; and online at *New English Review*, NewsRealBlog, WorldNetDaily and EnterStageRight.